Cyberspace, Cybersecurity, and Cybercrime

Sara Miller McCune founded SAGE Publishing in 1965 to support the dissemination of usable knowledge and educate a global community. SAGE publishes more than 1000 journals and over 800 new books each year, spanning a wide range of subject areas. Our growing selection of library products includes archives, data, case studies and video. SAGE remains majority owned by our founder and after her lifetime will become owned by a charitable trust that secures the company's continued independence.

Los Angeles | London | New Delhi | Singapore | Washington DC | Melbourne

Cyberspace, Cybersecurity, and Cybercrime

Janine Kremling
California State University, San Bernardino

Amanda M. Sharp Parker
Campbell University

Los Angeles | London | New Delhi
Singapore | Washington DC | Melbourne

FOR INFORMATION:

SAGE Publications, Inc.
2455 Teller Road
Thousand Oaks, California 91320
E-mail: order@sagepub.com

SAGE Publications Ltd.
1 Oliver's Yard
55 City Road
London EC1Y 1SP
United Kingdom

SAGE Publications India Pvt. Ltd.
B 1/I 1 Mohan Cooperative Industrial Area
Mathura Road, New Delhi 110 044
India

SAGE Publications Asia-Pacific Pte. Ltd.
3 Church Street
#10-04 Samsung Hub
Singapore 049483

Acquisitions Editor: Jessica Miller
Editorial Assistant: Jennifer Rubio
Content Development Editor: Laura Kirkhuff
Production Editor: Tracy Buyan
Copy Editor: Diane Wainwright
Typesetter: C&M Digitals (P) Ltd.
Proofreader: Eleni-Maria Georgiou
Indexer: Robie Grant
Cover Designer: Michael Dubowe
Marketing Manager: Jillian Oelsen

Printed in the United States of America

Library of Congress Cataloging-in-Publication Data

Names: Kremling, Janine, 1977- author. | Parker, Amanda M. Sharp.

Title: Cyberspace, cybersecurity, and cybercrime / Janine Kremling, California State University, San Bernardino, Amanda M. Sharp Parker, Campbell University.

Description: First Edition. | Thousand Oaks : SAGE Publications, [2017] | Includes bibliographical references and index.

Identifiers: LCCN 2017018240 | ISBN 9781506347257 (pbk. : alk. paper)

Subjects: LCSH: Information society. | Information technology—Management. | Computer crimes. | Computer crimes—Prevention.

Classification: LCC HM851 .K74 2017 | DDC 303.48/33—dc23
LC record available at https://lccn.loc.gov/2017018240

This book is printed on acid-free paper.

17 18 19 20 21 10 9 8 7 6 5 4 3 2 1

• Brief Contents •

• Detailed Contents •

• Preface •

Hey Android, where is my car? Hey Siri, where is my boyfriend? Android and iPhones know: They know where you are, they know where you have been, they know who you talk to and for how long, they know who you sleep with, and they know when and where you go for lunch and dinner. They may know more about you than your family. And they keep it to themselves—that is, until a hacker plants a malware on your phone and then has access to all of that information. Your iPhone will also willingly give up all of your stored contacts to the hacker so that the fraudster can now send phishing e-mails infected with malware to your family and friends. And your friends and family will click on the link because it's coming from you—or so they thought.

Your phone also knows your banking information through your mobile banking app, your Facebook and Twitter login, your airline login, your e-mail password, and the list goes on. All of that information is worth real money on the darknet—the criminal marketplace. The same is true for your computer. Imagine you are working on your term paper, trying to access a web link, when your computer sends you a reminder that you need to update Adobe Flash if you want to access the file. What do you do? You hit "download." You immediately realize that your computer has just been hijacked by a malware because your computer locks up and you see a message on your screen saying, "Your data has been encrypted. You will not be able to access your data until you pay the ransom of $150." Would you pay? Well, it depends on how badly you want your computer files back. What if the attack was against a hospital? Would they pay? Of course—because the consequences of shutting down the hospital would be much worse. Cybercriminals are well aware of the predicament the hospital faces. The same is true for banks and other institutions. Ransomware has become one of the main threats to hospitals because they are highly vulnerable.

The emergence of computers and the Internet has changed our lives in ways that nobody could have imagined, and it will continue to change future lives. Many of these changes have greatly contributed to life conveniences, such as online shopping, banking, communicating, and working from our home office. It also includes going to your doctor's office and having all of your records stored and shared electronically. You can start and heat or cool your connected car from your iPhone. You can use your phone to change the thermostat in your house and turn your house alarm on and off. GPS always finds the right way for you—and so do stalkers who have access to your location data provided to them by your GPS. By now, you already know that the Internet and digital world not only greatly increase the convenience of our lives, they have also greatly increased the vulnerabilities we are exposed to.

The economy has also profited from the digital evolution. With the ability to collect data and monitor people's behaviors and habits, companies can now market their products much more specifically to certain population groups, and scientists can conduct studies that enhance and sometimes save people's lives. At the same time, criminals also quickly realized the advantages of the Internet for their purposes, and governments found great improvements in their ability to spy on people and other countries. The boundaries between what is public and what is private have become blurred, and some argue that true privacy has become a myth. For instance, Google Earth enables anyone to zoom into your house and backyard, the National Security Agency is listening in on millions of people around the globe, companies monitor e-mail correspondence of employees, and websites track consumer behaviors by planting cookies on personal computers. Many tasks can now only be completed online, thereby removing the possibility to stay completely private or to protect your personal information.

In this age where reliance on computers and the Internet has become inevitable, cybercriminals are developing fraudulent schemes at a rapid pace—attempting to avoid detection by law enforcement and cybersecurity companies. In the early 1990s, computer crimes began to rise due to the increase in the prevalence and use of electronics. Criminal organizations, especially drug traffickers, began to build their own communication network and quickly started to take advantage of the available technologies. They realized the potential benefits of computers and networks for their illegal activities much faster than the people who developed these technologies, and they were quick to use it for their purposes, outpacing law enforcement for the past decades.

When security companies such as McAfee are putting out their updates for virus detection software, cybercriminals have long moved on to a new type of virus not detectable by the software. The criminals are always one step ahead. Similarly, when law enforcement shuts down a child pornography website, the criminals can easily move the content to other websites. It's an elusive chase in which the criminals are the ones leading the way. Data and identity theft is rampant, and most people know very little about how to protect their private data, even if they are aware of the risks. In fact, data theft has become one of the most persistent threats because our data holds our lives—our mortgages, loans, retirement savings, health benefits, Social Security—and if that data gets into the criminals' hands, lives can be ruined. Few people think about this threat as they access their online banking account or submit their credit card number on a website. The convenience of online transactions is more important to many people than the security of their lives. Criminals know this and exploit it.

The U.S. government has made some strides toward increased cybersecurity. In March 2016, the Department of Homeland Security created an automated information-sharing system, thereby increasing the ability of agencies and organizations to share information in real time. This new system also includes private companies. The ability of the United States to defend cyberspace will depend on the successful cooperation between private and government organizations. In fact, it's the private corporations, such as Dell, Microsoft, and McAfee, who are leading the cybersecurity efforts. Much of the success of cybersecurity efforts will also depend on the preparedness of companies and the government for major cyberattacks. It is impossible to secure all devices and networks 100% from attacks. We must accept that certain vulnerabilities will always remain. One such vulnerability is the human factor, whether it be by accident or on purpose. The better prepared companies and government agencies are, the faster the recovery will be from an attack.

These are only a few examples of what this book discusses. This book is not only about the past and present of cybercrime and cybersecurity but also about the future, and how cybercrime and cybersecurity may impact people's everyday lives, and how criminal justice professionals must be prepared to confront the changing nature of cybercrime. Everyone is vulnerable. The way computers have been used to connect people, companies, governments, and criminals is a great threat that most individuals are unaware of. More frightening, many companies are unaware of the threat cybercriminals pose for critical infrastructures such as the electric grid. And even if the company is aware of the threat, they often do too little to safeguard infrastructures and products, whether it's because of the economic costs associated with such safeguards, the inconveniences safeguards may cause, or because they don't have effective safeguards.

This book introduces criminal justice and other social science students to the world of cybercrime and cybersecurity. It provides a basic overview of cybercrime, cyberthreats, and vulnerabilities of individuals, businesses, and governments. The book discusses strategies to reduce vulnerabilities through cybersecurity measures, and ends by looking into the future to see what may be ahead and how it may change our lives.

Overview

The book is designed to enhance student learning by providing case studies and examples, engaging students through exercises, and encouraging students to critically think about the various topics. The first part of the book provides a basic understanding of the Internet, vulnerabilities, and cybersecurity. Chapter 1 deals with how and why the Internet developed and the main vulnerabilities we currently face. Chapter 2 introduces students to the nature and origin of cybersecurity and cyberspace intrusions.

The second part goes into much detail on cyberthreats to computers, individuals, businesses, and governments. In Chapter 3, students learn about the cyberthreats to computers, such as worms and viruses. Chapter 4 details threat factors in which computers are used as a tool. These threat factors include fraud and financial crimes, pornography and exploitation, and cyberbullying. Chapter 5 discusses cyberthreats to local, national, and international organizations. Students also learn about the different types of hackers. Chapter 6 follows with an overview of cyberwarfare, specifically cyberespionage and cybersabotage.

The third part of this book provides insight into the threat of cyberterrorism and the dark web, which has become a much discussed topic in the media. Chapter 7 explains what cyberterrorism is, the technologies used by terrorists, the targets, and damage potential. Chapter 8 dives into the deep web and darknets, how criminals access and exploit it, and which products are available to "customers."

The final section discusses cybersecurity operations and policies in more detail. Chapter 9 focuses on cybersecurity operations and the role of law enforcement. Chapter 10 explains national and international cybersecurity policies and legal issues arising from the policies. The last chapter looks into the future of cybercrime and cybersecurity, focusing on evolving threats and perpetrators as well as evolving issues with regard to the collaboration and training between law enforcement and the private industry.

Digital Resources

study.sagepub.com/kremling

Calling all instructors!

It's easy to log on to SAGE's password-protected Instructor Teaching Site for complete and protected access to all text-specific Instructor Resources. Simply provide your institutional information for verification and within 72 hours you'll be able to use your login information for any SAGE title! Password-protected Instructor Resources include the following:

- Test banks provide a diverse range of prewritten options as well as the opportunity to edit any question and/or insert personalized questions to effectively assess students' progress and understanding.
- Editable, chapter-specific PowerPoint slides offer complete flexibility for creating a multimedia presentation for the course.

Use the Student Study Site to get the most out of your course! Our Student Study Site is completely open-access and offers a wide range of additional features. The open-access Student Study Site includes the following:

- Mobile-friendly eFlashcards strengthen understanding of key terms and concepts.
- Mobile-friendly practice quizzes allow for independent assessment by students of their mastery of course material.

• Acknowledgments •

JANINE KREMLING

First of all, I would like to thank Jerry Westby and Jessica Miller from SAGE Publishing for their consistent encouragement and help in getting this book finished within the established time frame. They have been amazing to work with, and I am very grateful for their efforts. I would like to give a huge thank you to my coauthor, Amanda M. Sharp Parker, for her dedication to the success of this book, and I would also like to thank the chair of my department, Dr. Larry Gaines, for his continued support and inspiration. I have learned much from him in the past 8 years. He is truly a role model, and I am very fortunate to have been able to work with him.

Finally, I have to express my gratitude to my parents, who have always been there for me, believed in me, and supported me throughout my life. Without their unconditional love, I would not have been able to accomplish all my goals. They have also taught me that a positive attitude, enthusiasm, and hard work will pay off. I wrote much of this book while I was in Germany during the summer, and I was able to focus solely on this project. I'm deeply appreciative of their efforts to inspire me and challenge me to do my very best.

AMANDA M. SHARP PARKER

First and foremost, I have to thank my coauthor, Janine Kremling, who has attempted to rope me into this project for the past 4 years. Two years ago when I agreed to coauthor the text, I had no idea what a whirlwind it would be. So thank you, Janine, for your guidance, patience, and mentorship.

Thank you to all at SAGE Publishing who helped us complete this project on time, especially Jerry Westby and Jessica Miller.

To the criminology department at the University of South Florida and the HCP department at Campbell University: Thank you for all your support in my research endeavors, especially the development of my cyber classes and subsequent projects that coincide with it.

Finally, to my kiddos, Tatiana and Jaxon, for their patience, love, and support. Thank you for putting up with mommy's long hours, early mornings, and countless afternoons of doing homework in my office while I was writing. You two are my inspiration, and everything I do is for you. I love you to the moon and back.

SAGE and the authors would like to thank the following reviewers, whose input helped shape this book:

Mark H. Beaudry

K. A. Beyoghlow, American University

Terry Campbell, Kaplan University Online

Craig P. Donovan, Kean University, College of Business & Public Management

Mary Beth Finn, New Charter University

Steven H. Klein

Eugene Matthews, Park University, Missouri

Dennis W. McLean, E-campus, Homeland Security, Keiser University

Brooke Miller, University of North Texas

Marcos L. Misis, Northern Kentucky University

Barbara L. Neuby, Kennesaw State University

Matthew E. Parsons, Erie Community College, Buffalo, New York

Irmak Renda-Tanali

Pietro Savo, Daniel Webster College, and College of Health and Human Services, Trident University

Holli Vah Seliskar, Kaplan University

Jake Wilson, University of Cincinnati

Cyberspace, the Internet, and the World Wide Web

Learning Objectives

1. Explain how the Internet developed.
2. Explain the purpose of the Internet.
3. Describe what "vulnerabilities" are.
4. Discuss how criminals are benefiting from the Internet.
5. Discuss the difference between cyberspace, the Internet, and the World Wide Web.

When Stanford University students Bill Hewlett and Dave Packard built one of the first computers weighing 40 pounds in 1968, they could not foresee that 1 year later a computer at Stanford University would receive the first message from another computer located some 350 miles away at the University of California, Los Angeles (UCLA). They certainly could not foresee that 50 years later the economic competitiveness of the United States would be closely tied to the digital economy created by the Internet, making trillions of dollars every year. Much of the critical infrastructures, including the financial industry, health industry, and power grid, are connected via the Internet.

Hewlett and Packard could not foresee that the Internet would become a normal and essential part of everyday life for most Americans and people across the globe. According to the U.S. Census Bureau, more than 74% of all American households were using the Internet in 2013, and overall, more than 3 billion people are virtually connected.[1] In 2017, there were 3 trillion Internet transactions every day processed by 220,000 servers across the globe. There are 80 million web application firewall (WAF) triggers per hour and 20 terabytes of attack data daily. About 30% of all login transactions, such as people logging into their e-mail account or

Amazon, are abuse attacks. With the increasing use of cyberspace by computers and connected devices, the amount of data processed will continue to increase—and so will the amount of cyberattacks.[2] Without the Internet, companies like Amazon, Facebook, and YouTube would not exist, and services we perceive as necessary and convenient would not be available. For instance, ordering goods and services online, downloading music, streaming audiobooks, reading textbooks on the computer, or "skyping" with friends overseas would not be possible. The Internet has created a great amount of job opportunities and has enhanced our lives in so many ways that it is hard to imagine what would happen if the Internet were to disappear.[3]

As much as we value the upside of our connected world, where everything seems to be available at our fingertips, the inventors of computers and the Internet also did not foresee that the users themselves would employ it to attack one another. One of the founders of the Internet, David H. Crocker, stated, "I believe that we don't know how to solve these problems today, so the idea that we could have solved them 30, 40 years ago is silly."[4]

The capabilities of the Internet have attracted criminals and criminal organizations who are taking advantage of the information and interaction infrastructure offered by the Internet and exploiting vulnerabilities inherent to the Internet. Organized criminal gangs such as drug traffickers, human traffickers, the Mafia,

IMAGE 1.1 ● What Happens in One Internet Minute

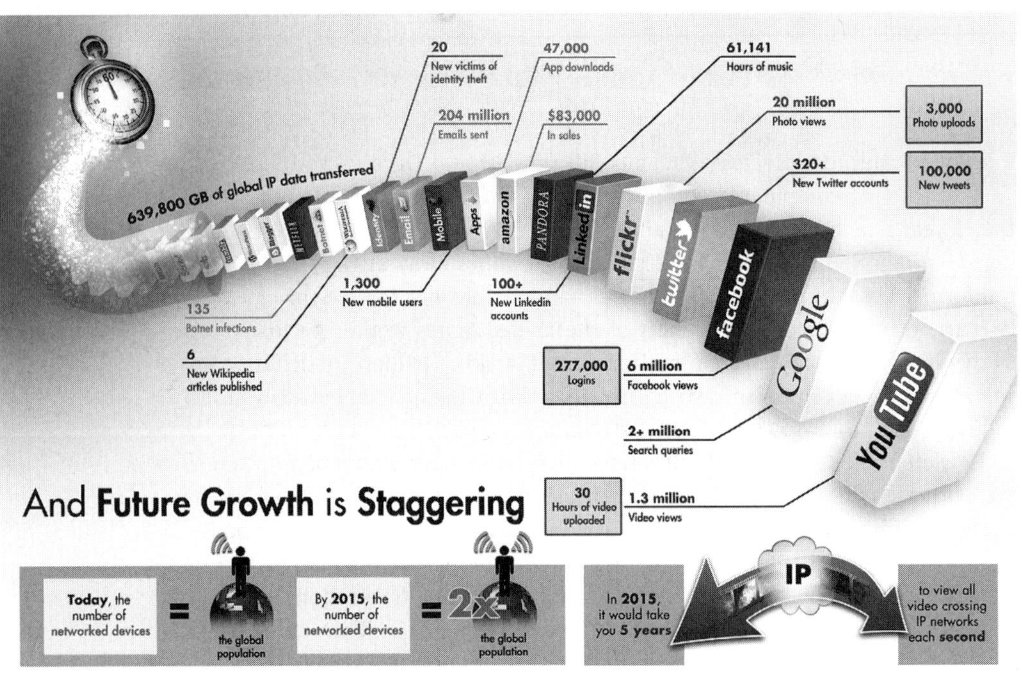

Internet Minute Infographic by Intel Free Press, https://www.flickr.com/photos/54450095@N05/6780720740. Licensed under CC BY 2.0, https://creativecommons.org/licenses/by/2.0/legalcode.

and many others very quickly discovered the opportunities a connected world offered. In addition to these traditional organized crime groups, a whole new world of cybercriminals has developed where hackers rob companies by using ransomware and taking virtual money as pay, or by stealing personal data and manipulating devices. More than 100 million Americans have experienced breaches to their personal data. President Obama called cybercrime "one of the most serious economic national security challenges that we face as a nation" and stated that we are in a "cyber arms race."[5]

Even though the development of cybersecurity measures has made great strides, it is still *people* who have to create, implement, and enforce cybersecurity policies. The best technology is worthless if it's not used or it is used inappropriately. The criminals who attack these companies are very sophisticated and motivated. But it's not only criminals who are accessing private data; the government also spies on individuals and companies. Revelations by Edward Snowden exposed what is likely the greatest eavesdropping in history by the National Security Agency (NSA).

This book goes into great detail on the different types of cybercrime, the motivations and mind-set of the criminals, and available cybersecurity measures. This first chapter lays the groundwork by giving you an understanding of the history of the Internet, why cybercrime has been able to flourish, and why cybersecurity still has a long way to go to catch up. President Obama said the Internet is the Wild West and cybersecurity is the sheriff. There is much work to do for the sheriff.[6]

CASE STUDY 1.1

The Dark Side of the Internet

The 2016 Data Breach Investigations Report[7] shows that more than 4.2 billion personal records were exposed in 2016. This constitutes an all-time high. The three biggest data breaches took place on Yahoo, MySpace, and FriendFinder networks with a total of 2.2 billion records exposed. With more than 1 billion compromised records, Yahoo currently holds the number-one spot in the history of data breaches. In September 2016, Yahoo announced that a "state-sponsored actor" stole the personal data of 500 million users in late 2014. Three months later, Yahoo announced another data breach of about 1 billion accounts dating back to August 2013. Yahoo has notified its users and urged them to create a new password and change security questions. The stolen data include names, account login credentials, e-mail addresses, telephone numbers, birth dates, and other information users entered into their accounts.[8]

What Do You Think?

1. What could criminals do with the private information obtained from Yahoo?
2. Should companies like Yahoo, who store personal data, be held accountable if victims experience negative consequences such as identity theft? If so, how would you hold them accountable?
3. If you were the CEO of Yahoo, what negative consequences would you expect in the aftermath of the data breach?
4. Do some research on Yahoo after the announcement. What were actual negative effects on the company?

The Beginning of the Internet and Cyberspace

The history of the Internet goes back to the first telegraph in 1836. The telegraph revolutionized the way people communicated by using a code (the Morse code, which consisted of dots and dashes), which is similar to the way computers communicate today using 0s and 1s. Between 1858 and 1866, the transatlantic cable was the first cable to allow instantaneous communication across the Atlantic Ocean. Today, cables connect people across the entire globe. Telephones were first used with computers in 1976 and later provided the basis for Internet connections via modems that have to be plugged into the computer, or more currently wireless connections.

The Internet was born during the Cold War era, at a time when America was bracing for a nuclear war. Donald Davies, a Welsh scientist, and Paul Baran, an American engineer, were working on communication technologies from two different perspectives: war and peace. Baran focused on technologies that would minimize the consequences of a nuclear attack by the Soviet Union by building a communication system with redundant links that would allow people to communicate even after an attack. Davies focused on technologies that would enable people to share data on computers continuously.[9]

In 1958, the Advanced Research Projects Agency (ARPA) was created by President Dwight D. Eisenhower with the intent to outpace the Soviet Union in the technology sector after the Soviet Union surprised the United States with two technological events. The Soviet Union had launched the first intercontinental ballistic missile and the first satellite (Sputnik 1), which provided the ability for global communication via satellites. The United States feared that the Soviet Union was technologically superior and could threaten America's national security. ARPA was created with the goal to turn the United States into a technology superpower. In 1972, ARPA was renamed to the Defense Advanced Research Projects Agency (DARPA).[10]

In 1962, J. C. R. Licklider of Massachusetts Institute of Technology (MIT) published a document describing the possibility of social interactions through networking—what he called the Galactic Network.[11] One year earlier, Leonard Kleinrock of MIT had published a paper on the feasibility of communication between computers via packet switching (as opposed to the then-used circuit switching).[12] Packet switching was imperative for social interaction via networking because it enabled data to be stored and moved as packets using a data path that many users could access. Packet switching set the stage for services such as Facebook and Twitter. In contrast, circuit switching only allowed for communication between predetermined persons, similar to a telephone call. Another crucial technological development with regard to social interactions via networking was enabling computers to talk together.[13]

Jack Ruina from DARPA took an interest in Licklider's paper and proposal. In October 1962, he asked Licklider to connect the computers from the U.S. Department of Defense at Cheyenne Mountain to the computers at the Pentagon and the Strategic Air Command. Licklider's vision of the Galactic Network inspired other researchers, including Larry G. Roberts.[14]

In 1967, Larry G. Roberts released his plans for the Advanced Research Projects Agency Network (ARPANET), which first connected computers across university campuses, starting with the first node in California at UCLA, and ultimately grew into the Internet. In 1972, Larry Roberts wrote the first e-mail utility program, and over the next decade, e-mail became the largest network application. In 1981, ARPANET was expanded with the help of the National Science Foundation (NSF) and the founding of the Computer Science Network. Through this collaboration between NSF and the inventors of the Internet, several technological developments took place that laid the groundwork for what we know today as the Internet with all of its services. One of the main developments was the introduction of the Internet protocol suite (IPS/IP) in 1982, which is still used today as the standard networking protocol. To further advance the Internet, it was necessary to build smaller computers with greater capabilities that could also be used by households. This happened quite rapidly and created issues in regard to operations and management of the Internet.[15]

CASE STUDY 1.2

The First-Ever Web Server

IMAGE 1.2 • First-Ever Web Server

First Web Server by Coolcaesar at the English Language Wikipedia, https://commons.wikimedia.org/wiki/File:First_Web_Server.jpg. Licensed under CC BY-SA 3.0, https://creative commons.org/licenses/by-sa/3.0/deed.en.

Cyberspace, the Internet, and the World Wide Web are fairly recent inventions. Tim Berners-Lee, who was working for European Organization for Nuclear Research (CERN), invented the first web server, the first web browser (World Wide Web) in 1989, and the first web page in 1991.[16] The intent was to create a service that would allow scientists to share information automatically rather than having to inquire about what other institutes were working on. The World Wide Web was supposed to enable scientists around the globe to access scientific knowledge instantaneously and freely, and contribute to the scientific knowledge by adding information. Hence, the first web browser was called World Wide Web because Berners-Lee used a global hypertext system that would allow anything on the web to link to anything else. It also allowed users to edit information, which served the goal of having as many people contribute to the knowledge sharing as possible. The first website ever—http://info.cern.ch/hypertext/WWW/TheProject.html—was created in August 1991 for the sole purpose of explaining Berners-Lee's website project. In 1993, CERN issued an official statement making the World Wide Web available to the general public. In its statement, CERN asserted, "CERN relinquishes all intellectual property rights to this code, both source and binary and permission is given to anyone to use, duplicate, modify and distribute it." This sentence effectively made the Internet an open-source environment where everyone could

(Continued)

(Continued)

post anything they wanted to, develop apps, and programs. This, of course, also created the vulnerabilities to cyberattacks as it opened the door for cybercriminals. Tim Berners-Lee left CERN in 1994 and founded the World Wide Web Consortium (W3C) at MIT.

IMAGE 1.3 ● First-Ever Website

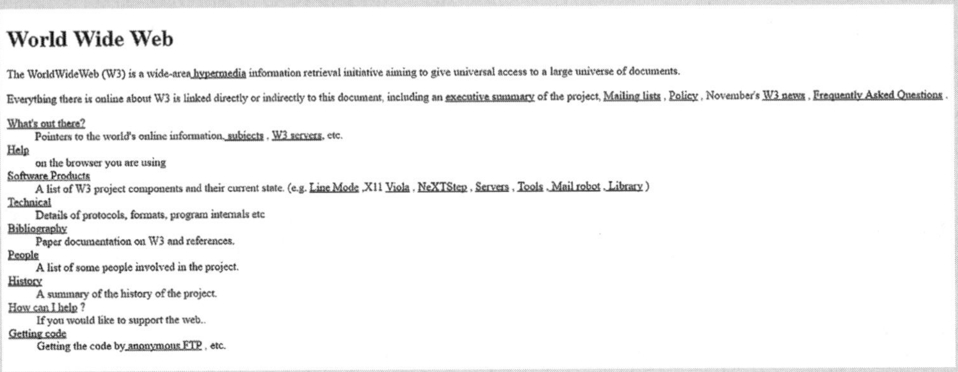

World Wide Web

The WorldWideWeb (W3) is a wide-area hypermedia information retrieval initiative aiming to give universal access to a large universe of documents.

Everything there is online about W3 is linked directly or indirectly to this document, including an executive summary of the project, Mailing lists , Policy , November's W3 news , Frequently Asked Questions .

What's out there?
Pointers to the world's online information, subjects , W3 servers, etc.
Help
on the browser you are using
Software Products
A list of W3 project components and their current state. (e.g. Line Mode ,X11 Viola , NeXTStep , Servers , Tools , Mail robot , Library)
Technical
Details of protocols, formats, program internals etc
Bibliography
Paper documentation on W3 and references.
People
A list of some people involved in the project.
History
A summary of the history of the project.
How can I help ?
If you would like to support the web..
Getting code
Getting the code by anonymous FTP , etc.

European Organization for Nuclear Research

The Purpose of the Internet

"The Internet is at once a world-wide broadcasting capability, a mechanism for information dissemination, and a medium for collaboration and interaction between individuals and their computers without regard for geographic location."[17] The Internet developed around three distinct aspects: (1) operations and management, (2) social, and (3) commercialization.

Operations and Management Aspect

With the spread of personal computers (PCs) and workstations to more people, and the growing number of people who utilized the Internet, researchers had to make it easier for people to use. Until then, host names were numeric addresses that users had to know and remember. This was not feasible for household users, so Paul Mockapetris of the University of Southern California developed the Domain Name System, which resolved hierarchical host names (e.g., www.fbi.gov) into an actual Internet address people could visit. Other major issues were increasing the capabilities of routers, operating systems, and software. Finally, as more households began using the Internet, it became necessary to separate the military network (MILNET) from the research network (ARPANET). MILNET became its own network and ARPANET became the Internet.[18]

Social Aspect

Several organizations, companies, and universities worked together to grow the Internet to become a major part of our everyday life. In 1988, the National Research Council (NRC) in collaboration with the NSF published the report "Toward a National Research Network." This report was the basis for the development of high-speed networks.[19] Five years later, NRC published the report "Realizing the Information Future: The Internet and Beyond," which laid the groundwork for the information superhighway.[20] The document also included anticipated issues that would need to be addressed, including copyright, ethics, pricing, education, and regulation of the Internet. The Internet was built to be a free and open-access tool, but the founders realized that without some type of regulations it would not be feasible. We return to the fact that the Internet was built as a free and open source in the next section when we discuss security vulnerabilities.

The social aspect of the Internet has become one of the most important purposes of the Internet. People go shopping online, meet in online cafes, share pictures and opinions, search for partners, download music, get a university degree, find a job, and participate in life-streaming events. The list of social events available to people through the Internet is endless. Facebook, Twitter, Instagram, and millions of apps enable people to engage with others in the virtual world. There is no need to meet someone in person because we can simply use FaceTime or any other app that allows us to telephone with a live picture. Letters have been replaced by e-mail, instant messages, and tweets. Real life has gone virtual in many ways. These technologies have brought great conveniences for people, connected people around the globe, and provided economic opportunities that were unthinkable when ARPANET was created. But because the Internet and these technologies were not developed with security in mind, the evolution of the Internet has also created substantial dangers for people's lives. For instance, bullying has always been a concern for school children, parents, and administrators, but cyberbullying has taken these concerns to a much higher level, even making it one of the top priorities of policy makers. Another example is child pornography. Before the invention of the Internet, criminals had to mail or exchange pictures. When police seized the pictures, they became inaccessible. Now there are millions of child pornography pictures available on the Internet, and even if law enforcement shuts down a pornography website, the pictures have already been shared with millions of people, and they remain on the Internet forever.

Commercialization Aspect

As the Internet began to grow, other groups and companies began to see the potential the Internet had with regard to commerce. The opportunity to create new businesses and markets was one of the strongest incentives to advance the technology quickly. Private companies developed private network services, which created competition and a push for working relationships between the inventors of the Internet and vendors who were interested in developing services for Internet users. In 1988, the first Interop trade show was held with 50 companies and 5,000 engineers. Today, there are seven Interop trade shows per year across the world with more than 250,000 attendees. In sum, commercialization has had a great impact on the development of the Internet since the 1980s and led to an increasing use of the Internet by people on a day-to-day basis.[21] Businesses and private citizens started online shopping, online banking, online education, etc.

LEGAL ISSUE 1.1

NAPSTER: THE FIRST FILE SHARING PROGRAM

The Internet provided a free and open access tool for information, data, and research, and also to music, films, and other copyrighted products. This has become a major issue for the music and film industry. Until 1999, CDs and DVDs were the main product used by the music and film industry to serve the customer market. As people around the globe started to realize the potential for sharing files via the Internet, the way in which music was shared also started to change. The first file sharing program was Napster, a program that provided free music as MP3 files to users.[22] In 1999, college student Shawn Fanning began his online music sharing program as a small project that quickly grew bigger and raised considerable concern in the music industry. As a response to the free file sharing, the music industry filed a lawsuit for copyright infringement, and in 2001 Napster was shut down. This was not the end of the file sharing business, however. To the contrary, it was the beginning. Since Napster, many other companies have started to offer music and films for free on the Internet, which is a persistent challenge to the music and film industry and their desire to protect their products and profit. But possibly even more important, companies such as Apple realized the business potential of these MP3 and similar files and began to build their products to facilitate file sharing, including iPods, iPhones, iPads, and so forth. Customers can now legally download music from iTunes with the ability to only buy the songs they really want or pay a low monthly fee to companies such as Pandora to listen to music all day. Consumers can download films for a few dollars or subscribe to Netflix, Hulu, Amazon Prime, and other subscription services.

What Do You Think?

The music and film industry believe that they cannot survive if people only buy music and films online because subscriptions and download fees don't generate as much money as CDs and DVDs. Customers argue that for too many years they paid too much money for a CD with only one song they liked, or bought DVDs with movies for too much money to then find out that the movie wasn't really that great. What do you think could be done to solve the problem of protecting musicians and film makers but also give consumers a fair deal?

Vulnerabilities of the Internet

The Internet was built to be a free and open source, with only a minimum of oversight. The original purpose was to freely exchange data and messages among a limited number of researchers. The inventors gave little thought to the possibility of criminals abusing the Internet. With the increased access and the evolution of the Internet from a research tool to a more consumerist and social tool, the door has also opened for criminals. The freedom and openness of the Internet provides many advantages for the users, such as ease of use, fast access, and low-cost software, but it also has its drawbacks—that is, it is vulnerable to a wide variety of cyberattacks that can create great damage for private users, companies, and governments. The next section of the chapter explains what vulnerabilities are and provides an overview of the five main vulnerabilities.

What Is a Vulnerability?

"A security vulnerability is a weakness in a product that could allow an attacker to compromise the integrity, availability, or confidentiality of that product."[23] For instance, computer administrators have the ability to change the permission on any file on the computer, install software, delete files, etc. If an unprivileged user were able to access the computer remotely and change permission on files, install software, delete files, etc., that would constitute a security vulnerability. Thus, in most companies, only the computer administrators have the ability to do so. There are five distinct gateways that create vulnerabilities for anyone who uses the Internet. These five gateways to vulnerability are (1) time and space, (2) lack of barriers to entry, (3) anonymity/identity, (4) asymmetries of cyberspace, and (5) 1s and 0s. The *Washington Post* series "The Net of Insecurity" discusses why the Internet is inherently vulnerable and why these vulnerabilities are inevitable.

Reference Article

Net of Insecurity

http://www.washingtonpost.com/sf/business/2015/05/30/net-of-insecurity-part-1/

Time and Space

In the past, personal interaction and criminal activity typically required physical proximity. For instance, thieves had to get close to the victim to steal a purse with the money and credit card information. Today, a thief can be on another continent and use the Internet to steal money or credit card information from someone. Wars used to be fought with swords, and later with bows and arrows, siege canons, and artillery. As technologies developed, airplanes now drop different types of bombs over countries. Furthermore, we can, and do, use drones in war zones rather than soldiers. This development, moving away from social interaction at close proximity to interaction from a far distance, is important for the understanding of cybercrime and cybersecurity. When users have instantaneous access at a distance to the Internet, it is then also easy for criminals to gain access to information users have on their computers or in a cloud. There are many opportunities for criminals to access computers and sensitive information. Why is that?

The main purpose of the Internet is to move information quickly and reliably, and thus it was designed to be open and frictionless. Users want instantaneous access to services from around the globe without any hassles that could be caused by security measures.

We also have to remember that the founders of the Internet were mainly concerned with the technical challenges of making the Internet available to as many people as possible; security simply was not their main concern. Since criminals have the same global access to the Internet as noncriminal users, they don't need to be anywhere near the victim to perpetrate their crime. Also, criminals may be able to commit a greater number of crimes because they don't have to physically go anywhere.[24]

Lack of Barriers to Entry

Whereas countries have physical borders that serve to keep criminals out of the country, the Internet has no such borders. For instance, when e-mails are sent from one country to another or even from one continent to another, there are no checkpoints to see if the e-mail contains a malware or if the e-mail was sent by a terrorist group who is planning a terrorist attack. This borderless Internet traffic threatens nation-states' ability to control their territory and the flow of information and goods.

Different countries have developed different strategies to deal with this problem. Some countries, such as the United States and Germany, have almost no restrictions on connectivity to the global network. This, of course, makes it near impossible to control the Internet traffic or limit what users say and send. Other countries, including New Zealand and Australia, try to maintain some control over the traffic by limiting Internet connectivity to the global network. This allows them to control some of the traffic to and from their residents. China has probably the most restrictive Internet strategy. Because China only has three undersea Internet cable arrival points, its government is able to control what type of traffic can be received and sent. This, of course, greatly limits what the Chinese citizens can do on the Internet and allows the government to suppress information sharing when it is against their interest. For instance, when opponents of the Chinese government try to share information about human rights violations, their posts never get sent and the senders are at high risk of being arrested. Restricting the connectivity reduces vulnerabilities but greatly diminishes the ability of people to use it freely.

Anonymity/Identity

Another problem is that users can remain completely anonymous if they choose to do so. The problem this creates is that users don't know with whom they are doing business, with whom they are talking, or whom they can trust. For instance, in online chat rooms, young girls may believe that they are chatting with a similarly aged boy, when in reality they may be chatting with a criminal who is trying to take advantage of them. You can never be quite certain to whom you are talking because all of the identifying information could be false, including pictures, names, age, profession, etc.

Since the initial purpose of the Internet was to transmit information quickly and without hurdles, requiring identification was not a concern of the developers. Also, as discussed earlier, at the beginning there were only a few users and they knew each other. Identification was not necessary. The game has changed, however. Specifically, in 1969 there were only four nodes or devices (i.e., computers), whereas today there are more than 2 billion nodes (devices including computers, cell phones, notepads, etc.), which is about one third of the population, and growing. The substantial growth of the Internet occurred very quickly, and the problems associated with the lack of identification did not become apparent until later, when more and more users were victimized by criminals who were quick to take advantage of the opportunities the free and open Internet provides.

The lack of identification also makes it easy for criminals, criminal organizations, and terrorist groups to hide—making it very difficult for law enforcement to figure out who the criminals are, what they are planning to do, and how to arrest them. This problem is compounded by the fact that the criminals often operate from outside the jurisdiction where the crime occurred, raising issues of who has the authority to pursue the criminals. For example, the United States has no jurisdiction in other countries if the criminal is operating from outside the United States. So even if the police can identify the criminal and his or her location, they would need the cooperation of the police in that country. Unfortunately, most of the time the police cannot determine who the criminal is and where he or she is because criminals use aliases, hide identifying information, use untraceable devices, or use the identities of innocent people.

Whereas criminals are very good at hiding their identifying information, many users are unaware of the risks of leaving identifying and secret information while surfing the Internet. Every time we access the Internet we leave traces of who we are, what we like, what we search for—and Internet websites use that information to send targeted advertisements. They collect the user's information for their purposes. This information, of course, is also out there waiting to get snatched by criminals. Most users do not take enough precautions, such as using encryption software, using programs to remove identifying information, using secure networks, and using secure passwords. This leaves many users vulnerable to cybercriminals who are looking for the information.

Asymmetries of Cyberspace

A small number of criminals can cause a great amount of damage because cybercrimes do not require a sophisticated industrial base or significant financial resources. Criminals also know that their efforts will likely lead to success because there are so many potential victims and so few barriers or oversight. For instance, you probably have received occasional e-mails from a person from Nigeria or some other country offering millions of dollars for help with a transaction using your bank account and the payment of a small transaction fee. Most people realize that these e-mails are fraudulent and simply delete them. That doesn't deter the senders from continuing their mass e-mails though. Why is that? The senders believe (and rightfully so) that if they send enough e-mails, some people will respond and send the transaction fee. Since the costs for sending the e-mails are so low, the sender will make a profit even if only very few respond every time he or she sends the mass e-mail. If the sender had to mail traditional letters (snail mail) they would likely lose money, but via the Internet it is free to send e-mails, multiple e-mails can be sent at one time, and it takes very little time as compared to traditional letters.

The asymmetries of cyberspace are disconcerting not only for individual Internet users but also for governments. It doesn't take an army to take down a country. For instance, a small group of terrorists who successfully block the electronic grid of the United States and therefore impair our daily life, which depends on electricity, could create an incredible amount of damage. Or worse, a terrorist group invades the computers of a nuclear power plant and blows up the power plant. Not much life would be left around the plant. To this day, the nuclear catastrophe of Chernobyl in the Ukraine and Fukushima in Japan shows the damage that could occur. The strength of a nation-state depends on its intellectual capabilities rather than its military capabilities. Thus, any country could potentially challenge the United States and Europe if the country has the intellectual capabilities—including North Korea, China, Russia, or Iran. This is also true for terrorists and organized crime groups who have such intellectual capabilities.

1s and 0s

The logical layer (or the computer code) of the Internet consists of 1s and 0s. From the code of 1s and 0s, it is not possible to determine what that specific code will do—that is, whether that code will execute the program we meant to download or whether it will plant malicious software on our computer. It is also possible that the downloaded program will do both—install the program we wanted and plant malicious software. Even though the malware does have a specific signature, users cannot typically distinguish the malware from the innocent Internet traffic. Rather, users find out after the incident that they have been attacked, their identity was stolen, or that their computer was used to commit a crime. At that point, it is very difficult for the innocent user to reverse the damage of the attack. It is also very difficult to prevent malicious software from invading a computer because a user would have to treat all Internet traffic as malicious, which would greatly interfere with the daily use of the Internet.

THINK ABOUT IT 1.1

Imagine you are the computer administrator at a large company. Several employees come to you complaining that they want to be able to install software on their work computers and change permission to files. They are upset because every time they need to install an update or new software for work purposes, they have to call you and wait for you to do the things they could do quickly by themselves.

What Would You Do?

1. How would you respond?
2. Would you give them administrator rights to their computers so they can make any changes they want? Why or why not?

What Distinguishes Cyberspace, the Internet, and the World Wide Web?

In order to understand cybercrime and cybersecurity, it is important to have a good grasp on the basic terminology that will be used throughout the book. These definitions are important insofar as they ensure that we have a common understanding when we discuss cybercrime and cybersecurity. *Cyberspace* is defined by the National Security Presidential Directive 54/Homeland Security Presidential Directive 23 as "the interdependent network of information technology infrastructures, and includes the Internet, telecommunications networks, computer systems, and embedded processors and controllers in critical industries."[25] In other words, cyberspace refers to the virtual environment in which people communicate and interact with others. Cyberspace consists of four different layers: (1) physical layer, (2) logic layer, (3) information layer, and (4) personal layer.[26]

The physical layer consists of the physical devices, such as PCs, networks, wires, grids, and routers. These physical devices are located within jurisdictions, which is important for law enforcement when they search for physical devices used to run criminal enterprises and other cybercrimes, which is discussed in detail in coming chapters. The logic layer is where the platform nature of the Internet is defined and created. Stated differently, cyberspace depends on the design of the Internet. It is built out of components that provide services for users, such as social media, content, shopping, etc. The information layer includes the creation and distribution of information and interaction between users. Users can create information by building a website, linking to other websites, and posting information on social media websites such as Twitter, Facebook, or Yelp. Users can also access information, including music, books, videos, and pictures. The top layer consists of people—people who create websites, tweet, blog, and buy goods online.

Attacks on cyberspace can occur at each of the four levels. Communication and interaction can be identified (known) or anonymous. The anonymity of cyberspace creates opportunities for cybercrime that would otherwise not exist and which are different and unique compared to other forms of crime. For instance, hackers would not be able to break into a computer and steal information without cyberspace. The term *cyberspace* is used because other terms used by the government, such as *cybercrime, cyberattack, cyberthreat,* or *cybersecurity,* are derived from the term cyberspace.

As you can tell from the definition above, the Internet is a part of cyberspace:

> The Internet is a global system of interconnected computer networks that are set up to exchange various types of data. This 'network of networks' connects millions of computers, including those in academic, business, and government networks, transcending geographic and national boundaries.[27]

Without this global data communication system, people would not be able to interact and exchange information. The term *Internet* is often used interchangeably with the term *web* or *World Wide Web.* The Internet and the web are distinctly different, however.

Whereas the Internet refers to hardware and software infrastructure that connects computers around the globe, the World Wide Web refers to a service that can be accessed via the Internet.[28] This service consists of interconnected documents and a variety of resources. The documents and resources are connected and accessible via hyperlinks and uniform resource locators (URLs). Several web browsers (i.e., Safari, Firefox, Explorer) allow users to access the information available on the web. A hyperlink is

> a reference or navigation element in a hypertext document that offers direct access to another section of the same document or to another hypertext document that is on or part of a (different) domain.[29]

For instance, the hyperlink https://www.fbi.gov/about-us/investigate/cyber takes you to the FBI's cybercrime website. A hyperlink could also be embedded in words, such as FBI cybercrime website, which is called hypertext. Users can simply click on the word(s) or the link and are directed to the FBI cybercrime website. These hyperlinks provide easy access to information relevant to the content the reader is interested in. Hyperlinks are unidirectional—that is, a user can link from their content to another website's content without asking for approval from the owner of the destination page or any action by the owner of the destination page. This unidirectional system allows anybody who has a website to link to other users' websites.

A hyperlink is one way to get to more content, but users also have other options. For instance, if you are searching for information on the web, you may often use URLs, which provide a reference to a resource on the Internet.[30] URLs have two main components: the protocol identifier and the resource name. For example, for the website https://www.fbi.gov, the protocol identifier is "https" and the resource name is "fbi.gov." In this sense, the URL is comparable to the address you would put on a letter to tell the postal service to whom to deliver your letter.

LEGAL ISSUE 1.2

IS IT A CRIME TO LINK TO INFRINGED/ILLEGAL CONTENT?

Under the Digital Millennium Copyright Act (DCMA), Universal City Studios, Inc. brought a lawsuit against three hackers who had provided software that could decrypt digitally encrypted movies on DVDs. The hackers also provided hyperlinks to other websites with decryption software. At the time, motion picture companies were using encrypted DVDs as the main method of distributing movies to consumers. The hackers argued that providing decryption information on their website was protected under the First Amendment, which guarantees the freedoms of speech and press, thus the hyperlinks to websites with infringed/illegal content is also protected by the First Amendment. The U.S. District Court disagreed and stated that by providing decryption software and hyperlinks to websites with decryption software, the hackers had violated copyright laws, specifically the DCMA.[31]

Imagine you are the judge on the U.S. District Court and you have to decide a case where the defendant is accused of violating the DCMA by providing hyperlinks from his legal website to a website that sells stolen goods. How would you rule in this case? What would be the mitigating or aggravating factors you would consider?

WHAT CAN YOU DO?

Preparing for the Job of the Future: Careers in Cybercrime and Cybersecurity

1. FBI Cyber Division

A job in the cyber division includes safeguarding classified information; examining forensic information related to computers, technology devices, and data storage media; and disrupting the actions of data thieves and saboteurs. The FBI also employs a Cyber Action Team (CAT) that is deployed to any place in the world where criminals attempt to compromise government security. The CAT team includes highly trained tactical personnel who monitor, pursue, and apprehend criminals. A BA or MA in criminology or criminal justice may be expected.[32]

2. Cyber Police Officer

Cyber police officers create, maintain, and protect law enforcement databases. They also protect the computer network and connected devices. Applicants may have a degree in forensics or information networking and telecommunications with a minor in justice studies.[33]

3. Computer Crime Investigator

The computer crime investigator is responsible for recovering file systems that have been hacked, gathering evidence and computer system information, testifying in court, and training law enforcement on computer-related issues. Corporations typically hire applicants with degrees in computer forensics and computer sciences.[34]

4. Department of Homeland Security (DHS) Cybersecurity

Cybersecurity professionals work on cyber incident response, cyber risk and strategic analysis, vulnerability assessment and detection, intelligence and investigation, and digital forensics and forensic analysis. The DHS also has a cyber student volunteer initiative where students work alongside cyber leaders in the DHS. The Department also offers scholarships for service to students who are interested in becoming cybersecurity experts and want to work for DHS.[35]

5. Department of Justice

Officers working for the Department of Justice work on threats to national security, economic prosperity, and public safety. The key priorities are currently cyberstalking, computer hacking, and intellectual property theft.[36]

6. The U.S. Secret Service

The Secret Service investigates and prevents counterfeiting, as well as securing critical infrastructures. The Secret Service also employs an Electronic Crime Task Force and a Financial Crime Task Force.[37]

7. Threat Intelligence Analyst

The Threat Intelligence Analyst collects, analyzes, identifies, and escalates security incidents for all business units, including employees and customers.

Summary

The purpose of this chapter is twofold: First, the chapter provides a basic overview of the origin and development of the Internet, cyberspace, and the World Wide Web. The authors discuss how the Internet has changed in the past 20 years and provide some examples of the dangers of the Internet. The chapter also explains the key terms students need to understand and be able to distinguish.

Second, the chapter aims to provide students with an overview of the five security vulnerabilities and the key causes of these vulnerabilities. Students should be able to explain what vulnerability means and how these five gateways create security vulnerabilities for anybody who accesses the Internet.

Key Terms

Cyberspace 1
Digital Millennium Copyright Act 14
Domain Name System 6
Hyperlink 13
Hypertext 13
Internet 1
Internet Protocol Suite 5
Malware 10
Personal Computer 6
Uniform Resource Locator 13
Vulnerability 9
World Wide Web 1

Discussion Questions

1. How does the Internet differ from cyberspace?
2. Describe the four different layers of cyberspace. How does each layer contribute to the function of the Internet?
3. Discuss how the Internet developed. What was its original purpose? How has that purpose changed in the past 20 years? How do you see the future of the Internet, or stated differently, what do you think will change in the next 20 years?
4. What are the main security vulnerabilities? Which of the vulnerabilities do you think is the most difficult to address for security experts? Explain your answer.
5. Imagine you are the manager of a nuclear power plant near New York. You have to do computer updates in your plant just like on your private computer. What are the risks/vulnerabilities you are facing with every computer update? What would be some possible consequences if your computer was infected with a malware? What precautions would you take to keep your computers safe?

Internet Resources

European Organization for Nuclear Research
http://home.cern/about/topics/birth-web/where-web-was-born

Massachusetts Institute for Technology, Computer Science and Artificial Intelligence Laboratory
https://www.csail.mit.edu/

Washington Post, Net of Insecurity: A Flaw in the Design.
http://www.washingtonpost.com/sf/business/2015/05/30/net-of-insecurity-part-1/

Defense Advanced Research Projects Agency
http://www.darpa.mil/about-us/about-darpa

Further Reading

Leiner, B. M., Cerf, V. G., Clark, D. D., Kahn, R. E., Kleinrock, L., Lynch, D. C., . . . Wolff, S. (2017). *Brief history of the Internet.* Retrieved from http://www.internetsociety.org/internet/what-internet/history-internet/brief-history-internet

Witt, S. (2015, April 27). The man who broke the music business. The dawn of online piracy. New Yorker. Retrieved from http://www.newyorker.com/magazine/2015/04/27/the-man-who-broke-the-music-business

Digital Resources

Want a better grade?

Get the tools you need to sharpen your study skills. Access practice quizzes and eFlashcards, at **study.sagepub.com/kremling**.

What Is Cybersecurity?

Ignorance is not bliss when it comes to cybersecurity.

—**Singer and Friedman**[1]

Learning Objectives

1. Understand the evolving nature of the term *cybersecurity* and the challenges presented with it.
2. Analyze the origin of cyberspace legislation and the direction it is headed in the future.
3. Differentiate between private and public-sector cybersecurity, and the pros and cons of each.
4. Discuss the role that wireless networks (Wi-Fi) have played in making the issue of cybersecurity even more complex.

Companies spend millions of dollars on firewalls, encryption, and secure access devices and it's money wasted because none of these measures address the weakest link in the security chain: the people who use, administer, operate and account for computer systems that contain protected information.

—**Kevin Mitnick**[2]

THINK ABOUT IT 2.1

What Is Cybersecurity and Why Is It Important?

Imagine a hacked planet. Our modes of communication are taken hostage. Nobody knows for sure where they are going when they get into their self-driving car or onto the self-driving bus or train because they have no control. Rather, it's hackers who control people's movements. There can be no trust in infrastructure. Without trust, there is no banking, trading, or economy. Nothing is predictable because reality is constantly changed by hackers who blend true with fake news. In such a hacked society, democracy fails and our medical system fails because doctors don't know whether medical records are correct or even accessible. The critical infrastructures are constantly under attack such that they fail. When the power grids fail, traffic lights don't work, alarm systems go out, store cash registers stop working, banks can't open, and people live in a world of chaos. When the water systems fail, people cannot drink the water that comes out of their faucet, or maybe no water will come out of the faucet anymore. When the power goes out, debit and credit cards are worthless, ATM and banking systems shut down, and individuals without cash are in big trouble.

In such a dystopian society, no one can be trusted, not our government, not our transportation system, not our power system—nothing in our "smart" world will work as we would expect. This is the world without cybersecurity. We need cybersecurity so that we can have trust that our connected cars drive where we want them to drive, to keep our water safe, to ensure that we have power and medical services, and so people can buy goods with their credit cards and withdraw money from the bank. The cybersecurity of the future will be highly integrated with business technology, and some professionals are already referring to it as *business security*.

There are many definitions of cybersecurity, but what is it exactly?

When you think of cybersecurity, think of a fire extinguisher. Even though most businesses have never had a fire, they still have fire extinguishers in case there is one. Schools and universities have fire extinguishers and perform fire drills to practice what to do in case of a fire. And because everyone is aware of the dangers of fire, many private citizens also have fire extinguishers in their homes. Most people share a common knowledge about fire. First, it is an opportunistic threat. If you leave a candle burning on the Christmas tree (which is likely very dry) and forget to blow it out, the tree may well catch on fire and the fire will spread very quickly. Second, a fire does not care what you did yesterday. Even if you blew out the candle on the tree yesterday, today is a new opportunity for the candle to set the tree on fire. Third, fire exploits the smallest vulnerabilities. If the candle is touching any few needles of the tree, the fire will catch onto those few needles and then spread to the entire tree. Finally, fire does not stop until it owns everything—that is, until the entire tree is on fire. The fire extinguisher is a security measure. If the house does not have a fire extinguisher, then it may not be possible to stop the fire from spreading from the tree to other parts of the house, and the house will likely be on fire long before the firefighters arrive. Had there been an immediate response to the fire using a fire extinguisher, the damage would have been much less. Cyberattacks are very similar to a fire.[3]

What Would You Do?

1. So how do you prevent such an attack?
2. What exactly is cybersecurity?
3. How does it affect our everyday lives?
4. What are the biggest threats associated with cybersecurity?

Origins and Nature of Cybersecurity

The origin of cybersecurity dates back to the 1970s. In 1977, the federal government recognized that open access to computer systems could create security breaches; however, the proposed Federal Computer Systems Protection Act did not pass congressional scrutiny. In the 1980s, specifically 1983, there was a rise in hacking attempts, which some credit to the release of the movie *WarGames* (see Think About It 2.2). The deputy assistant FBI director pushed for antihacking legislation, but it was not until 1987 when the Computer Security Act was signed into law that security measures for online systems were strengthened. Specifically, the Computer Security Act was one of the first legislations to establish minimum security practices in federal computer systems and advance protection of these systems.[4]

The following year, the U.S. Computer Emergency Readiness Team (CERT) Communication Center was founded by the Defense Advanced Research Projects Agency (DARPA). CERT, which now boasts the goal of striving "for a safer, stronger Internet for all Americans by responding to major incidents, analyzing threats, and exchanging critical cybersecurity information with trusted partners around the world,"[5] was created to ensure readiness in the case of a major cyberattack. However, in the late 1980s this was not a top priority within national security. In February 1991, the White House asserted that data theft "is a serious strategic threat to national security,"[6] but it was not until 1996 when President Bill Clinton established the first commission on critical infrastructure that identified infrastructures vulnerable to both physical attacks and cyberattacks—specifically, infrastructures that use computer systems, making them especially vulnerable to hackers.

The late 1990s gave rise to concern about the millennial change from the year 1999 to 2000 and how the change would affect electronic devices. The issue, referred to as Y2K, resulted in the president signing the Year 2000 Readiness and Responsibility Act, and spending billions of dollars in preparation for the change.[7] However, in the end, there were very few major problems associated with Y2K. Using the information gathered during the Y2K preparedness phase, the government was able to examine cybersecurity issues prior to the clocks changing from 1999 to 2000 and address potential problems before they occurred.

In the aftermath of September 11, 2001, President Bush charged a committee with creating a strategy for cybersecurity and named Richard Clarke as the National Cybersecurity Advisor to examine the vulnerabilities in cyberspace and the interest of terrorist groups in recruiting individuals with advanced cyber capabilities. Following the attacks of 9/11, Osama bin Laden told an Arab newspaper "hundreds of Muslim scientists were with him" that would use their technological skills against "the infidels."[9] Furthermore, Omar Bakri Muhammad, a supporter of the now-deceased Osama bin Laden, claimed that al-Qaeda had the technology to launch a cyberattack and should use those skills to defend and fight in the name of Islam. Muhammad went on to list the New York, London, and Tokyo stock markets as optimal targets and said: "I would not be surprised if tomorrow I hear of a big economic collapse because of somebody attacking the main technical systems in big companies."[10] Since 9/11, terrorists have continued to increase their knowledge and skills in cyberspace.

THINK ABOUT IT 2.2

War Games

The 1983 movie *War Games* tells the story of a young computer hacker (David Lightman, played by Matthew Broderick) who, on a quest to play a video game that had not yet been released, accidently accesses the North American Aerospace Defense Command's (NORAD) computer system. His hacker curiosity kicks in, and as he explores the computer system, he accesses the game mainframe and chooses to play a game, Global Thermonuclear War, between the United States and the Soviet Union. Lightman does not realize that the computer has been specially programmed and does not understand the difference between reality and fantasy (the computer believes that global war is about to begin and overrides all of NORAD's codes in order to launch nuclear missiles on the Soviets).

Lightman's exploits into the NORAD system result in mass chaos, and he is hunted and apprehended by the FBI. However, his unique knowledge of the computer system allows him to assist NORAD directors (and the program's creator) in trying to stop the computer from playing the game and releasing missiles on the Soviet Union. The seemingly innocent curiosity of Lightman's actions comes close to resulting in the actual release of nuclear missiles and the potential beginning of World War III.[8] Although not intending to be malicious, the hacking incident could have had severe physical repercussions.

What Would You Do?

1. What would you do if your curiosity about something led to a national security threat? How do you think this would play out in a post-9/11 world?
2. Watch *War Games* and discuss what can be learned from the movie. What vulnerabilities (as mentioned in Chapter 1) are still prevalent today? How can we prevent activities such as the ones in the movie from occurring?

Definitions

Cybersecurity is a term that is often used broadly. The conceptualization of this broad, and at times vague, term is cause for discussion. Like many aspects of the criminal justice system, how cybersecurity is defined often depends on the individual or entity doing the defining. Definitions vary across government organizations, nation-states, academics, and the private sector, leading to confusion about what actually constitutes cybersecurity. The conceptualization is a continuous and evolving issue. Some definitions concentrate more on defining cyberspace, while others have more of a security focus. The term cybersecurity is frequently used in policy titles and directives, but the use of the word has lagged behind in terms of accurately defining what it means. In other words, the term is being utilized without a clear meaning of what constitutes cybersecurity. We explore a variety of definitions below.

The conceptualization issue can be addressed in multiple ways; however, Agresti suggests that as the meaning of security is somewhat established, it is the term *cyber* that must be defined.[11] From a criminal justice standpoint, this could encompass tactics of the perpetrator(s) and protection techniques as well as the jurisdiction (cyberspace) in which the criminals are operating.

Definition of Cybersecurity

One of the first legislations to include specific cybersecurity provisions was created in direct response to the terrorist attacks on September 11, 2001, and the subsequent anthrax attacks that fall (Anthrax, a bacterial disease, weaponized in powder form and able to cause severe respiratory distress, was sent via U.S. mail to multiple television studios and congressional offices on Capitol Hill. The attack resulted in five deaths and a renewed fear of biological attacks). In an amendment to this document, Subtitle E of the Homeland Security Act of 2002 (Cybersecurity Programs) was added. SEC 242 includes definitions of cybersecurity services and cybersecurity threat (See Table 2.1) but not cybersecurity by itself.[12]

TABLE 2.1 • Defining Cybersecurity

Document/ Agency	Term	Definition
Homeland Security Act 2002	Cybersecurity Services	Products, goods, or services used to detect or prevent activity intended to result in unauthorized access to, manipulation of, or impairment to the integrity, confidentiality, or availability of an information system or information stored on or transiting an information system, or unauthorized exfiltration of information stored on or transiting an information system
Homeland Security Act 2002	Cybersecurity Threat	Any action that may result in unauthorized access to, manipulation of, or impairment to the integrity, confidentiality, or availability of an information system or information stored on or transiting an information system, or unauthorized exfiltration of information stored on or transiting an information system
Executive Order 13636	Cybersecurity Information Sharing	Timely production of unclassified reports of cyber threats to the U.S. homeland that identify a specific targeted entity. The instructions shall address the need to protect intelligence and law enforcement sources, methods, operations, and investigations
Executive Order 13636	Cybersecurity Framework	Prioritized, flexible, repeatable, performance-based, and cost-effective approach, including information security measures and controls, to help owners and operators of critical infrastructure identify, assess, and manage cyber risk, focus on identifying cross-sector security standards and guidelines applicable to critical infrastructure, provide guidance that is technology neutral and that enables critical infrastructure sectors to benefit from a competitive market for products and services that meet the standards, methodologies, procedures, and processes developed to address cyber risks
Cybersecurity Enhancement Act of 2014	Cybersecurity	On an ongoing basis, facilitate and support the development of a voluntary, consensus-based, industry-led set of standards, guidelines, best practices, methodologies, procedures, and processes to cost-effectively reduce cyber risks to critical infrastructure
Craigen, Diakun-Thibault, and Purse (2014)	Cybersecurity	The organization and collection of resources, processes and structures used to protect cyberspace and cyberspace-enabled systems from occurrences that misalign de jure from de facto property rights

Cyberthreats are the top priority of multiple federal agencies. The National Security Agency (NSA) is charged with providing security to the United States via interception of signals intelligence and decrypting threats both physical and cyber. The FBI has 60 cyber squads that work together with other federal, state, local, and private-sector agencies to increase cybersecurity. Their ability to improve cybersecurity depends on a better understanding of cyberthreats and vulnerabilities in the United States.

The former director of the CIA, General Michael Hayden, asserted that there is a cybersecurity knowledge gap between the youthful generation that has grown up with technological advances and the older generations who do not have the knowledge or understanding of the Internet or technological capabilities. This gap results in a vulnerable population, ripe to be targeted by cybercriminals.

In 2013, President Barack Obama approved Executive Order 13636: Improving Critical Infrastructure Cybersecurity. EO 13636 also details elements of cybersecurity information sharing and cybersecurity framework (Table 2.1), but again, cybersecurity is not specifically defined. In this document, the biggest cyberthreat discussed is that to critical infrastructures, including the electric grid system, banking/finance, and transportation.

A year later, the Cybersecurity Enhancement Act of 2014, which did define cybersecurity (as shown in Table 2.1), was passed with the goal of

> providing for an ongoing, voluntary public-private partnership to improve cybersecurity, and to strengthen cybersecurity research and development, workforce development and education, and public awareness and preparedness, and for other purposes.

Furthermore, in regard to cybersecurity, this document amended the National Institute of Standards and Technology Act (NIST; 15 U.S.C. 271) to extend the role of the Secretary of Commerce so that he or she may continuously develop new methods of cybersecurity (see Appendix 2A). Specifically, the secretary of commerce should continuously develop new methods of cybersecurity that follow industry-led standards, guidelines, best practices, methodologies, procedures, and processes. The goal is to reduce the risk cyberthreats pose to critical infrastructures, such as power grids or water supplies. This is important because if cybercriminals were to attack our power grid, for example, they could cause major damage throughout the country. Anything that uses electric power (street lights, banking systems, transportation) would be affected.

Government policy doctrines are not the only writings that do not clearly define cybersecurity. Academic writings are full of varying and, at times, contradicting definitions. This contentious issue, as discussed by Craigen, Diakun-Thibault, and Purse, may lead to confusion and is often "subjective, and at times, uninformative."[13] In their research, Craigen and his team reviewed multiple definitions of cybersecurity in order to find recurring themes in the conceptualization in order to produce a "new, more inclusive, and unifying definition of cybersecurity" that would be applicable across "academia, industry, and government and non-government organizations."[14]

Definitions reviewed by this research team ranged from extremely general, as found in the Committee on National Security Systems' 2010 conceptualization,

"The ability to protect and defend the use of cyberspace from cyber-attacks," to very detailed, as defined by the Department of Homeland Security (DHS). The DHS definition reads:

> The activity or process, ability or capability, or state whereby information and communications systems and the information contained therein are protected from and/or defended against damage, unauthorized use or modification, or exploitation.[15]

After reviewing the literature, nine current definitions were chosen to help construct a new definition of cybersecurity.

Upon review, the research team was able to identify five dominant themes within the cybersecurity conceptualization literature:

1. Technological solutions
2. Events
3. Strategies, procedures, and methods
4. Human engagement
5. Referent objects (of security)

Using a focus group of academics and cybersecurity experts, the research team proposed and had critiqued multiple newly proposed definitions of cybersecurity. Based on this information, Craigen and his team produced a comprehensive definition of cybersecurity:

> Cybersecurity is the organization and collection of resources, processes, and structures used to protect cyberspace and cyber-space enabled systems from occurrences that misalign de jure from de facto property rights.[16]

CASE STUDY 2.1

The Original Hacker: Kevin Mitnick

Kevin Mitnick is famous in the hacker subculture. Growing up in Los Angeles in the 1970s, Mitnick's curiosity and extensive memorization ability paved the way for his interest in cyberspace. While in high school, Mitnick learned how to phone phreak. Phone phreaking allows an individual to exploit the telephone system, making calls for free. He quickly switched to the more complex world of hacking, gaining access to classified/protected information, with relative ease.

Mitnick went on to study computers in college. He quickly was able to identify the vulnerabilities in the school's computer system and gained complete administrative privileges. While today that would be cause for expulsion, Mitnick was given the opportunity to stay in school and complete a project in order to avoid

(Continued)

(Continued)

punishment. This specialized project was to examine the vulnerabilities of the system that Mitnick had already illegally accessed and then update the security of the school's system. In one of the first examples of "white-hat hacking," Mitnick assisted the school and graduated cum laude with honors.[17]

Mitnick continued to hack into systems, knowing that it was wrong but enjoying the challenge. As he detailed before a congressional hearing years after he had retired from hacking, Mitnick asserted,

> I have gained unauthorized access to computer systems at some of the largest corporations on the planet, and have successfully penetrated some of the most resilient computer systems ever developed. I have used both technical and non-technical means to obtain the source code to various operating systems and telecommunication devices to study their vulnerabilities and their inner workings.[18]

In the mid-1990s, Mitnick went from a seemingly unknown hacker to "cyberspace's most wanted" and landed on the front page of the *New York Times*. Charged with 14 counts of wire fraud, eight counts of possession of unauthorized access devices, as well as interception of wire or electronic communications, unauthorized access to a federal computer, and causing damage to a computer, Mitnick pleaded guilty to all charges.[19] He was sentenced to 3 years, 10 months in prison. While incarcerated, he was viewed as such a threat (it was believed that he could whistle into a phone and set off a nuclear missile) that he was placed in solitary confinement. Upon his release, Mitnick was placed on probation for 3 years, one of the conditions being he could have no access to computers.

After successfully completing his probationary period, Mitnick went on to use his skills to positively enhance security. He now runs Mitnick Security, a security service specializing in penetration testing.

For further reading on Kevin Mitnick's story, see *The Art of Intrusion* and *The Art of Deception*.

Cybersecurity Policies

As previously mentioned, President Obama signed into effect Executive Order 13636: Improving Critical Infrastructure Cybersecurity with the goal of increasing the cybersecurity measures to each of the 16 sectors identified by Presidential Policy Directive-21. Order 13636 states the framework will "identify areas for improvement that should be addressed through future collaboration with particular sectors and standards-developing organizations."[20] President Obama had identified cyberattacks as the number-one threat facing the United States. As cybersecurity measures continue to sophisticate, so do the methods of penetration. The National Cybersecurity and Communications Integration Center is charged with 24/7 information sharing of cyberthreats with both the public and private security sector agencies in order to reduce both probability of and the damage caused by cyberattacks.[21]

Cybersecurity information sharing with the private sector is extremely imperative, as critical infrastructures are extremely vulnerable to cyberattacks and 80% of U.S. critical infrastructure is owned by the private sector. These infrastructures include dams, hospitals, railways, airlines, and power plants, all of which are susceptible to cyberattacks. As the cyberthreat increases, collaboration between public and private sectors can strengthen the role that cybersecurity plays in detection and mitigation. Private security corporations have much to offer to the understanding of cybersecurity. These firms are often equipped with individuals (red teams) comprised of white-hat hackers (nonmalicious hackers for hire) who possess the skills necessary to expose vulnerabilities in the system and to provide cybersecurity solutions because they understand how cyberattacks are perpetrated.

CASE STUDY 2.2

FusionX

FusionX, a private cybersecurity firm, offers their services to companies and government organizations in an effort to reduce the vulnerability of their systems. FusionX identifies threats to their clients by hacking into their system and attempting to "model and replicate sophisticated adversary attacks."[22] Also known as a red team, or ethical hackers, the goal of FusionX is enhanced security. Using a team of professionals skilled in the art of hacking, FusionX is hired to identify vulnerabilities in computer security and to offer solutions to these problems. Using private-sector resources such as FusionX may help to increase cybersecurity to critical infrastructures. Along with their skilled team of computer experts, FusionX offers the following services:

- Annual enterprise vulnerability assessments
- Tactical penetration texting activities
- On-demand application (including mobile) security assessments
- Recurring external vulnerability assessment scans
- Spearphishing and other employee awareness exercises
- On-demand incident response and threat analysis support
- Infrastructure security design support
- Annual risk management program reviews
- On-demand access to subject matter experts
- Annual security awareness training programs

What Do You Think?

1. What are the benefits associated with hiring someone from the private sector to perform security assessments on computers? Are there risks associated with it?
2. If you were the CEO of a major corporation, what would you do to ensure that your vulnerable information was not passed to individuals with malicious intent?

Overview of Cyberspace Intrusions

There are many ways that computer systems can be infiltrated and infected. Since the 1980s, when computer viruses became increasingly prevalent, companies have spent millions of dollars to protect their systems from malicious intrusions. One of the most famous first intrusions, Moonlight Maze gained notoriety due to the complexity involved in the attack. In 1998, a computer technician at ATI Corporation noticed a strange connection at 3 a.m. A computer at the company was connecting to Wright-Patterson Air Force Base; however, the computer account's owner was not using the system.

Upon investigation by the Air Force CERT, the attack was traced to Russia and was found to be one of multiple attacks using business and university computer systems as proxies to obtain information. These coordinated attacks were given the name Moonlight Maze. The Moonlight Maze attacks resulted in the theft of thousands of documents containing information on military technologies. The attacks infiltrated "military, governmental, educational, and other computer systems in the United States, United Kingdom, Canada, Brazil, and Germany."[23] These attacks were significant, as they were some of the first to illustrate how vulnerable our technology is to malicious infiltration.

Today, malicious software (malware) is readily available for purchase and/or download. This software is often designed with a specific purpose, and often the host computers are unaware that they have been hit with an attack. Some of the more common forms of cyberspace intrusions are detailed next.

Network-Based Attacks

A network intrusion occurs when a computer system is accessed without permission. Such intrusions may go unnoticed depending on the level of firewalls and security associated with the system. Network-based attacks are attractive because (1) they may often go undetected and (2) the perpetrator(s) are often difficult to trace. Two main forms of network-based attacks are untargeted attacks and targeted attacks.[24]

Untargeted attacks are of concern for the public, as the attack indiscriminately chooses who the attack victims are. If one computer or computer system is heavily protected, the intrusion will just move on to the next vulnerable system. One example of an untargeted attack includes distributed denial-of-service attacks in which computer systems are hijacked, often without the owners' knowledge, and used to flood a website (i.e., the website has so many computers attempting to access it that it crashes). Another popular form of untargeted attacks is phishing. A phishing attack is when a mass e-mail is sent to multiple computers requesting that personal information (banking, Social Security number, etc.) be sent to a specific location. A famous example of this is the Nigerian prince scheme in which victims were solicited to give their banking information or make a small payment in return for a large payment from a Nigerian prince looking to share his wealth. Of course, the victims lost whatever money they paid, resulting in substantial profit for the perpetrators of this scheme.

Another form of network-based attacks is a targeted attack. Targeted attacks differ from untargeted attacks as they single out a specific business, organization, or user's system to infiltrate. Targeted attacks are not random; the victim is deliberately chosen and targeted. The perpetrator may have a personal reason for the attack or could be hired by someone to orchestrate the infiltration. Even more alarming is that the perpetrator could be an insider—someone working for the company being victimized. Insiders are especially problematic as they do not have to hack into a system because they have legitimate access to it. For example, a disgruntled employee at a power plant would have access to the systems and even the passwords protecting the infrastructure. If this individual shared the information with someone with malicious intent, the damage could be catastrophic.

CASE STUDY 2.3

Vitek Boden

In the spring of 2000 in Queensland, Australia, over 800,000 liters of raw sewage was spilled from the sewage treatment plant along the Sunshine Coast suburb and the Hyatt Regency hotel, resulting in the death of marine life. "The creek water turned black and the stench was unbearable for residents," said Janelle Bryant of the Australian Environmental Protection Agency. This was not an accident but a malicious, intentional attack on the Maroochy Shire Treatment Plant. The Maroochy water plant briefly thought the problem was created by some internal system error, but as they began to eliminate possible internal problems, they eventually realized that the problems were due to an external hacker.

In his late 40s, Vitek Boden was out of a job and looking for employment from the Maroochy Shire Council. Boden had previously been employed by Hunter Watertech, a business which installs supervisory control and data acquisition (SCADA) equipment for the Council at multiple businesses, including the Maroochy Shire Treatment Plant. When he was not hired by the Council, Boden took action. Using only a laptop computer, a two-way radio, and his personal knowledge of the SCADA systems operation, he infiltrated the system 46 times over a 3-month period from the comfort of his vehicle. Boden was able to gain access to the sewage system's mainframe and to modify the system so that communication between computers was shut down and alarms were not triggered. His attacks ranged from mild to shutting off every alarm, which in turn allowed for sewage to be released undetected.

Authorities eventually caught Boden, who had the laptop and equipment in his car. He was charged with 30 counts of computer hacking, theft, and environmental damage. He was sentenced to 2 years of incarceration as well as having to reimburse the Maroochy Shire Council for all clean-up expenses resulting from his crimes.[25, 26]

What Do You Think?

1. What lessons can be learned from the case of Vitek Boden?
2. Do you think that his punishment will act as a deterrent to stop others from committing similar crimes?

Wireless Attacks

There are great benefits to wireless services, such as ease of access, the ability to be more flexible, and increased productivity. However, with these benefits also come added security risks. Wireless networks are often less secure than traditional online networks. Businesses often advertise free Wi-Fi as a way to draw in customers. These open-access networks are easy for hackers to access. Some of the vulnerabilities and attack methods associated with wireless attacks as discussed by Morgan are detailed below:[27]

1. **Human Error**: Individuals who do not have a clear understanding of inner workings of the system can make errors in setup leading to vulnerabilities in the system.
2. **Rogue Access Points**: Rogue access points are created in two ways: (1) the individual who installed the wireless network does so within the confines of

another network—that is, a rogue access point (backdoor) into the original system may be created; or (2) hackers with malicious intent can also plant an access point to allow access via that backdoor at a later time. A backdoor access can be as simple as programming a special password that would allow the hacker into the system without the owner's knowledge.

3. **Noisy Neighbors**: As wireless signals are sent via radio waves, they can experience interference with other sources also using radio waves (e.g., baby monitors, cordless phones, other routers). This can have an effect on the speed or even the accessibility of the network. Noisy neighbor incidents can be accidental, but they can also be orchestrated maliciously by an individual using other wireless devices to deliberately interfere with the network.

4. **Man in the Middle**: In this form of attack, the malicious party intercepts a message; he or she can gather information, alter the message, attach a virus, etc., and then send the message on to the intended recipient. The intended recipient would have no idea that the message has been intercepted by a third party (see Figure 2.1).

FIGURE 2.1 ● Man-in-the-Middle Wireless Attack Diagram

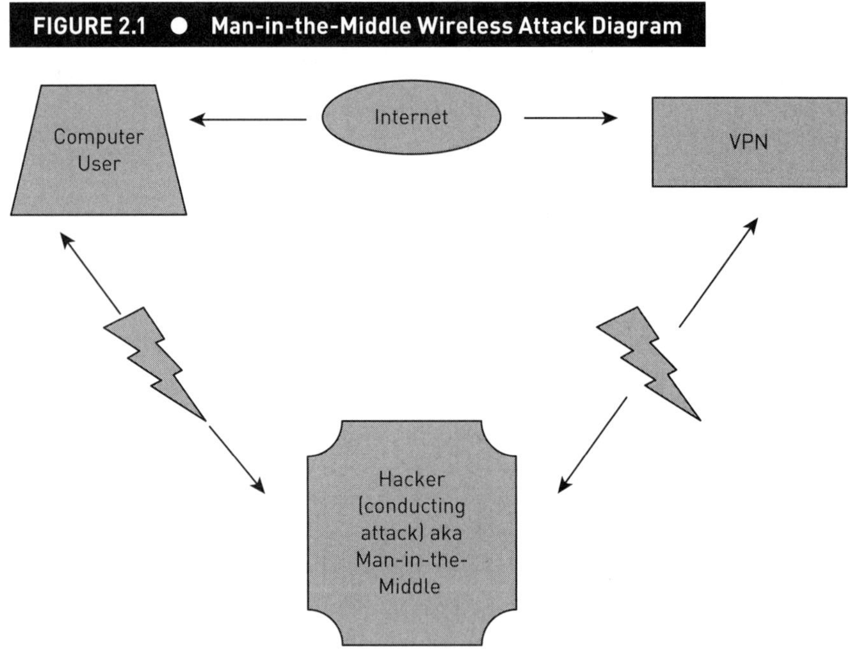

Man-in-the-Middle Attacks

Man-in-the-Middle attacks are increasing in popularity, and there are six main techniques used by fraudsters to hack into an Internet connection and manipulate or steal data:[28]

1. **Wi-Fi Eavesdropping**: The fraudster hijacks the Wi-Fi connection and intercepts the communication. Public Wi-Fi connections are especially vulnerable. There are several ways in which criminals can hijack a Wi-Fi connection. They can create a fake Wi-Fi node, which tricks individuals into connecting to that node. The fraudster can also intercept the communication of Internet users by hacking an unencrypted connection or hacking the Wi-Fi password. To protect users, passwords should be secure and public networks shouldn't be used for checking bank accounts, e-mail, and other sensitive information.

2. **Man in the Browser**: This is also referred to as a *banking Trojan*. The Trojan operates in the background of the computer by modifying banking transactions. The customer may see the correct amount to be transferred on the screen but the browser display is incorrect. The display shows what the customer intended to do, but in reality, the Trojan has manipulated the transaction. For instance, the customer intended to pay $1,000 toward credit card debt. The Trojan instead sent all the money in the account of the customer to a different account held by the fraudster. The screen will show the correct intended transfer of $1,000 and the correct amount of money in the accounts, but when the customer goes to the bank to get money, the bank account will be empty. Even a printed PDF from the online banking site may show that everything is correct, but it's an illusion. The screen is not always correct. A Trojan can manipulate the screen and make it look like everything is fine when in reality all the money has been stolen.

3. **Man in the Mobile**: Criminals increasingly hack into mobile devices and monitor user activity, such as text messages and apps, to obtain passwords and account authorization information. For instance, if the user texts passwords or the last four digits of the Social Security number, the criminal could then use the information to access banking accounts or other financial information.

4. **Man in the App**: Almost anything can be done via apps, including depositing checks, buying and selling stock, arming the house alarm, preheating the car, and so on. Unfortunately, anybody can develop apps and put them in the app store. This, of course, includes criminals who develop apps with built-in malware such as Trojan horses. In addition, many apps are not secure from hacking, and fraudsters are diligent to abuse any such security flaws. For instance, many people use mobile apps for online banking. If the customer installed an app with a Trojan, the criminal could then access all information typed in by the customer and the bank account.

5. **Man in the Cloud**: File-sharing tools such as Google Drive, DropBox, and Microsoft OneDrive have become popular among businesses and academics for collaborative work. They are also popular among individuals who are sharing files, such as music. Clouds have vulnerabilities related to session management that are easily exploited by hackers. For instance, DropBox and other services don't require signing in every time a user accesses the account. Also, synchronization of the files is often automatic without a sign-in requirement. This makes it very easy for criminals to access the shared

files. If these files contain confidential or sensitive information, it can have devastating consequences. Or imagine the files have information about a pending patent or technical specifications only known to the company. This information would be accessible, and criminals could sell it to companies who may reverse-engineer a product. Industrial espionage is rampant, and cloud-based services create substantial risks for companies.

6. **Man in the Internet of Things**: Our connected devices, such as alarm systems, cars, thermostats, appliances, and TVs, have basic operating systems that can be hacked and manipulated by fraudsters. Hackers can take over the steering of a connected car, airplane, or ship, turn off your house alarm, and change how your appliances work. The assumption that these devices don't need sophisticated cybersecurity measures is not only false—it's dangerous. Imagine someone taking over the control of a car and driving it over a bridge. That could be the future of assassinations. The hacker could be in a different country, hired and paid to kill a person via a car accident. As your daily life, including your home, becomes more connected to the web, and therefore more connected to potential criminals, this problem will grow.

LEGAL ISSUE 2.1

HACKING . . . WITH A BODY COUNT?

As seemingly improbable as it may seem for a hacker to take over someone's car and cause it to crash, it is not unheard of. Imagine driving down the interstate when your car stereo starts to blast, your windshield wipers turn on, and on the car's display screen appears a picture of two individuals wearing hoods and masks. They have hacked into your car's control system, and they are in complete control of your vehicle. They tell you such from the vehicle's display screen and then disappear as your car suddenly starts to slow down and comes to a complete stop. Other cars, including 18-wheeler trucks, begin to back up behind yours. Then your car starts up again, but after you accelerate, your car begins to veer off the road. You attempt to slam on your breaks; however, you find they are no longer functioning and you slam into a ditch.

This seems like something out of a movie, but for Andy Greenberg it was a frightening reality. Although Greenberg volunteered to be a guinea pig for the experiment, he didn't know what to expect. For the past few years, hackers Charlie Miller and Chris Valasek, funded by a DARPA grant, have been experimenting on hacking into car vehicle systems. Scenarios such as these, which are often referred to as *zero-day exploits*, are a very possible reality of the future of cybercrime. As carmakers are leaning more toward the digitalization and wireless features in automobiles, more and more vehicles are becoming susceptible to hacking. However, few manufacturers, and even fewer consumers, are viewing this as a viable threat. But according to Miller, "If consumers don't realize this is an issue, they should, and they should start complaining to carmakers. This might be the kind of software bug most likely to kill someone."[29]

Due to the seriousness of this issue, Congress has begun to examine issues surrounding car hacking. In 2015, Senators Ed Markey and Richard Blumenthal introduced a bill to tighten regulations on car manufacturers in order to reduce the risk that the car system can be hacked. The attention brought by Markey and Blumenthal to this problem prompted security professional Josh Corman to recommend five steps for automobile manufactures to do in order to increase automotive cybersecurity:

1. Safer design to reduce attack points
2. Third-party testing

3. Internal monitoring systems
4. Segmented architecture to limit the damage from any successful penetration
5. The same Internet-enabled software updates that PCs now receive[30]

As this cybersecurity issue is making headway in Congress, criminal justice professionals should be prepared to encounter this problem within the field. How will criminal attempts at hacking into vehicle systems affect law enforcement and those working in the court system? Discuss issues that may arise if this problem continues to develop.

Securing Your Wi-Fi in a Wireless World

One way that individuals can increase their personal cybersecurity is by ensuring their networks are secure, especially when it comes to wireless networks. According to Mitnick, "New security loopholes are constantly popping up because of wireless networking. The cat-and-mouse game between hackers and system administrators is still in full swing."[31]

There are two main steps for securing devices at the corporate level: (1) policy and (2) submarine network policy. Where policy is concerned, cybersecurity should be enforced, involve security from the beginning, keep "junk" away from the network, and involve periodic reviews to ensure protocol is being followed.

As for submarine network policy, three steps are recommended: (1) segment everything possible, (2) microsegment again, and (3) ensure each "air-tight compartment" can be breached without causing the system to "sink."[32] To fulfill these steps, corporations should ensure that policy is realistic and achievable. Furthermore, they should operate in an environment that acts, in practice, like there is no such thing as a "no Wi-Fi environment." Finally, if possible, always wire infrastructure.

Lastly, to ensure cybersecurity, money must be spent. It can be costly to hire the right people and to spend on training, human resources, and awareness, but these are necessary costs. Experienced personnel should be hired to configure and secure devices that are currently in use, and to train staff members on cybersecurity protocol.[33] Spending money on these tools up front can help save companies from spending even more if their cybersecurity is breached.

Summary

This chapter is designed to give readers a basic understanding of the concept of cybersecurity. Cybersecurity was a national security concern prior to September 11, 2001; however, it has received much more attention since the 9/11 attacks. Definitions of cybersecurity are often vague and, at times, contradicting. Various definitions are explored throughout this chapter.

The chapter also highlights main timeline points as cybersecurity developed and continues to develop. The role of the private sector in cybersecurity measures is examined, and common cyberspace intrusions are identified. After completion of this chapter, students should feel comfortable moving into more detailed chapters of cyberspace disruptions and prevention techniques.

Key Terms

Discussion Questions

1. Describe and differentiate between the various definitions of cybersecurity. What are the most common characteristics found across definitions?
2. Discuss the evolution of the term cybersecurity. What are the strengths and weaknesses of each term? What do you feel should be included in a definition of cybersecurity?
3. Differentiate between different forms of cyberspace intrusions. What role does human involvement/error play?
4. Describe what is involved in a man-in-the-middle attack. Which form do you think is the most threatening? Why?
5. What are practices you engage in that put you at risk for hacking, and what could be the possible consequences?
6. What is the role of the private sector in cybersecurity? What risks are involved with using private security groups?

Internet Resources

FusionX
http://fusionx.com/

Mitnick Security
https://www.mitnicksecurity.com/
https://twitter.com/kevinmitnick
https://www.facebook.com/kmitnick007

Further Reading

Mitnick, K. D., & Simon, W. L. (2002). *The art of deception: Controlling the human element of security.* Indianapolis, IN: Wiley.

Mitnick, K. D., & Simon, W. L. (2005). *The art of intrusion: The real story behind the exploits of hackers, intruders and deceivers.* Indianapolis, IN: Wiley.

Digital Resources

Want a better grade?

Get the tools you need to sharpen your study skills. Access practice quizzes and eFlashcards, at **study.sagepub.com/kremling**.

Appendix 2A: Specific functions of the Secretary of Commence as outlined in Section 2(c) of the NIST Act[34]

In carrying out the functions specified in subsection (b), the Secretary, acting through the Director may, among other things—

1. construct physical standards;
2. test, calibrate, and certify standards and standard measuring apparatus;
3. study and improve instruments, measurement methods, and industrial process control and quality assurance techniques;
4. cooperate with the States in securing uniformity in weights and measures laws and methods of inspection;
5. cooperate with foreign scientific and technical institutions to understand technological developments in other countries better;
6. prepare, certify, and sell standard reference materials for use in ensuring the accuracy of chemical analyses and measurements of physical and other properties of materials;
7. in furtherance of the purposes of this chapter, accept research associates, cash donations, and donated equipment from industry, and also engage with industry in research to develop new basic and generic technologies for traditional and new products and for improved production and manufacturing;
8. study and develop fundamental scientific understanding and improved measurement, analysis, synthesis, processing, and fabrication methods for chemical substances and compounds, ferrous and nonferrous metals, and all traditional and advanced materials, including processes of degradation;
9. investigate ionizing and nonionizing radiation and radioactive substances, their uses, and ways to protect people, structures, and equipment from their harmful effects;
10. determine the atomic and molecular structure of matter, through analysis of spectra and other methods, to provide a basis for predicting chemical and physical structures and reactions and for designing new materials and chemical substances, including biologically active macromolecules;
11. perform research on electromagnetic waves, including optical waves, and on properties and performance of electrical, electronic, and electromagnetic devices and systems and their essential materials, develop and maintain related standards, and disseminate standard signals through broadcast and other means;
12. develop and test standard interfaces, communication protocols, and data structures for computer and related telecommunications systems;
13. study computer systems (as that term is defined in section 278g–3(d) [2] of this title) and their use to control machinery and processes;
14. perform research to develop standards and test methods to advance the effective use of computers and related systems and to protect the information stored, processed,

and transmitted by such systems and to provide advice in support of policies affecting Federal computer and related telecommunications systems;

15. on an ongoing basis, facilitate and support the development of a voluntary, consensus-based, industry-led set of standards, guidelines, best practices, methodologies, procedures, and processes to cost-effectively reduce cyber risks to critical infrastructure (as defined under subsection (e));

16. determine properties of building materials and structural elements, and encourage their standardization and most effective use, including investigation of fire-resisting properties of building materials and conditions under which they may be most efficiently used, and the standardization of types of appliances for fire prevention;

17. undertake such research in engineering, pure and applied mathematics, statistics, computer science, materials science, and the physical sciences as may be necessary to carry out and support the functions specified in this section;

18. compile, evaluate, publish, and otherwise disseminate general, specific and technical data resulting from the performance of the functions specified in this section or from other sources when such data are important to science, engineering, or industry, or to the general public, and are not available elsewhere;

19. collect, create, analyze, and maintain specimens of scientific value;

20. operate national user facilities;

21. evaluate promising inventions and other novel technical concepts submitted by inventors and small companies and work with other Federal agencies, States, and localities to provide appropriate technical assistance and support for those inventions which are found in the evaluation process to have commercial promise;

22. demonstrate the results of the Institute's activities by exhibits or other methods of technology transfer, including the use of scientific or technical personnel of the Institute for part-time or intermittent teaching and training activities at educational institutions of higher learning as part of and incidental to their official duties; and

23. undertake such other activities similar to those specified in this subsection as the Director determines appropriate.

Threat Factors—Computers as Targets

Learning Objectives

1. Differentiate between viruses, worms, and Trojan horses.
2. Explain the threat viruses pose to computers and computer users.
3. Explain the threat worms pose to computers and computer users.
4. Explain the threat Trojan horses pose to computers and computer users.
5. Describe countermeasures to threats that target computers and mobile devices.

Cyberattacks are cheap and unconstrained by geography and distance to the target. Let's compare a bank robbery with the ransomware attack on a bank. The goal of the attackers is the same: get money from the bank and get away without leaving evidence. A bank robber has to stake out the bank, learn about the employees' behavior, learn about when money is taken to the bank and picked up from the bank, and whether the bank has a security guard—and if so, what the routine of the guard is. A bank robber often also needs an accomplice to stay outside and check for police and/or drive the getaway car. The bank robber then has to plan the attack, carry it out without any incidents, and get away with the money. The bank robber has to stack the money in a safe but accessible place. The robber eventually starts spending the money. Very often, banks now have money that is marked, which would make it easier to catch the bank robber. The whole process is very time consuming and risky. Bank robbery is a serious felony, and police will spend significant resources to catch the criminal.

Now compare the bank robbery with a ransomware attack on a bank. The attacker does not need help from others. All that is needed is a computer and network connection. The cyberthief hacks into the bank and encrypts the data. The bank now cannot operate its business because they can't access their data, including customer accounts. The cyberthief sends a message to the bank manger telling him or her that if the bank wants their data decrypted they must pay a ransom of $100,000 in bitcoins (a digital currency untraceable by law enforcement). If the bank refuses to pay, the data will stay encrypted. Typically, the cyberthief sets a deadline to put pressure on the victim. The bank can try to decrypt their own data by hiring experts or with the help of law enforcement, but that may not be possible. The cyberthief simply has to wait. He or she does not have to be physically present or even near the bank and could be in a different country. There is also little risk of detection because there are usually no traces. Attribution of the attack—that is, finding the person who committed the attack—is very difficult and even in major attacks often not possible with certainty. For instance, even though the U.S. government believes that Russia hacked the Democratic Party during the 2016 election campaign and possibly interfered with the election, there is no hard evidence linking Russia to the security breaches. Thus, in a ransomware attack it is highly unlikely that the attacker will get caught. These differences between a traditional bank robbery and a cyberattack on a bank demonstrate why cybercrime has drastically increased and will likely continue to increase. They also demonstrate the difficulty cybersecurity specialists in the government and private industry face when dealing with cybercrime.

CASE STUDY 3.1

The Top 10 Data Breaches[1]

1. Yahoo—2014

   The hackers stole information from 500 million account holders.

2. FriendFinder Network—2016

   FriendFinder is the mother company of about 49,000 dating websites. In 2016, data from 412 million users was breached going back as far as 20 years.

3. MySpace—2016

   The company "lost" 360 million user passwords.

4. Experian—2012

   More than 200 million Social Security numbers were breached after the credit reporting company acquired the data firm Court Ventures.

5. USA Voter Database—2015

   Voter information from 191 million people dating back to 1990 was stolen.

6. LinkedIn—2012

   In 2016, LinkedIn admitted that 165 million accounts had been breached.

7. Nasdaq Stock Exchange—2012

   Attackers stole more than 160 million credit and debit card numbers.

8. eBay—2014

   Fraudsters gained access to 145 million user accounts.

9. Heartland Payment System—2009

   Magnetic strip information from 100 million credit cards was stolen.

10. VK—2016

    The Russian version of Facebook was breached and 100 million accounts were breached.

What Do You Think?

1. Think about what user information each of these companies hold. What are the negative consequences for the victims of the data breach for the different companies?

The Evolution of Cybercrime

Phases of Convergence

There are three phases of convergence in the evolution of cybercrime. In Phase 1 of convergence, technology is separate from people. It's also referred to as *sneakerware* because people had to physically take a floppy disk or other external hard drive and walk to a computer to transfer a malware onto the computer. The first Macintosh virus, Elk Cloner, was part of a video game for computers inserted via a floppy disk.

In Phase 2 of convergence, man is leveraging technology—that is, man is using technology. In this phase, fraudsters developed the first e-mail-born viruses, such as the ILOVEYOU and the Melissa virus, which spread via e-mail attachment. Everyone who opened the attachment infected their computer.

In Phase 3 of convergence, technology replaces people. The first malware that fell into this phase was Code Red discovered in 2001. Code Red attacked Microsoft computer systems and spread to other systems by using HTTP requests. The Code Red worm does not respond to the owner's commands, but rather it operates independently by creating a backdoor into the operating system of the computer. The computer owner does not know what the worm will do with the computer. The original Code Red initiated a denial-of-service (DoS) attack on the White House. All machines infected with the Code Red virus started to send requests to the White House web server at the same time, overwhelming the server. People who had computers infected with Code Red not only had an infected machine but they were potentially also suspected of committing a crime (i.e., the DoS attack) on the White House.[2]

Phase 3 of convergence was also the beginning of the era of cyberspying. People do not have to be physically present in one country to spy out information on computers in another country; instead, they can infiltrate computers and steal information by using computer programs such as Trojan horses. This chapter discusses viruses, worms, and Trojan horses in detail and provides examples for each.

Reference Report

CIA Report on Russian Hacking of Democratic Party

https://www.intelligence.senate.gov/sites/default/files/documents/ICA_2017_01.pdf

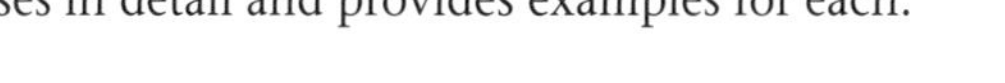

Main Targets in Information Technology

Cybercrimes are a growing problem in need of new solutions. A whopping 74% of businesses are expected to be successfully hacked in 2017. By 2020, the economic cost of cybercrime is expected to go above $3 trillion. Increasingly, nation-states are committing the attacks, which results in more sophisticated attacks

THINK ABOUT IT 3.1

Russian Cyberspies and the 2016 Presidential Election

U.S. intelligence agencies seem to agree that Russia's President Vladimir Putin and state-sponsored hackers were involved in hacking incidents against the Democratic Party in late 2016 during the presidential election. A report by the Office of the Director of National Intelligence from January 2017 states that the evidence strongly implicates Russia as the origin country of the hackers and cyberspies.[3] Another report released by the FBI in December 2016 also concludes that Russia interfered with the election process by stealing and releasing classified information, including confidential e-mails.[4]

Just like the Russians infiltrated the computers of the Democratic Party, the FBI and CIA also had to get their information from insiders or by spying on the Russians. Russia believes that the insider information came from one of their agencies. In January 2017, Sergei Mikhailov, the head of Russia's Federal Security Service, was arrested for treason for passing information about Russian hacking to the CIA.[5]

What Would You Do?

1. How has the Internet changed the ability of political espionage?
2. Read the CIA Report on the Russian Hacking of the Democratic Party. What evidence does the report present?

and attacks on important infrastructures.[6] There are three main targets in information technology: software, hardware, and the network. Table 3.1 provides some examples of the vulnerabilities of software, hardware, and networks. Throughout this book we explain these vulnerabilities and countermeasures in detail.

TABLE 3.1 ● Vulnerabilities of Software, Hardware, and Networks

	Software	Hardware	Network
Attacks	• Infected download links of software or software updates • Malicious apps • Drive-by downloads	• Manufacturing backdoors • Backdoor creation • Access to protected memory • Hardware modification • Inducing faults • Counterfeiting products	• Denial-of-Service Attacks • The Man in the Middle • Browser • Brute Force • SSL • Scan • Domain Name Servers • Backdoor[7]

	Software	Hardware	Network
Devices	• Computers • Computer networks • Smart devices	• Access control systems • Network appliances • Industrial control systems • Surveillance systems • Components of communication infrastructure	• Computers • Modem • Router
Countermeasures	• Anti-virus software • Security patches • Data backup • Software screening	• Tightly control production • Use detection measures to discover compromised hardware[8]	• Network-based mitigation • Host-based mitigation • Proactive measures[9]

Cybersecurity is concerned with three main issues: (1) confidentiality of the data, (2) integrity of the data, and (3) availability of the data. Confidentiality refers to keeping private information private. This includes classified government documents, such as the engineering of the latest fighter planes, but also trade secrets and patents, such as wind turbines. If other governments or companies can steal such data, they could also build such fighter planes and develop defense systems. Integrity of the data means that the data are correct. If criminals can manipulate data, people can be injured or killed. For instance, if cybercriminals could manipulate the software that runs a power plant, the power plant could stop working or blow up, causing power outages and injury or death to the workers. Availability means that persons who need access to the system actually have access at all times. If there were an attack on the power plant, people might be able to stop a disaster if they continue to have access to the system. But if they are unable to access and control the system, they would have no opportunity to stop the attack.[10]

These main components of cybersecurity—confidentiality, integrity, and availability—are the main targets of cybercriminals. They try to steal confidential data, manipulate data, or make data unavailable. The tools used to accomplish these goals range from computer viruses and malware to cyberwar and cyberterrorism. Computers can be the target of cybercrimes, but they can also be a tool for cybercrimes. For instance, hackers may target a computer or computer network to gain access to data or disrupt the functioning of the computer (see Chapter 4). At the same time, computers are used as a tool by hackers to break into the network system of a company or to engage in crimes such as cyberstalking or pornography (see Chapter 4).

There are three main threat clusters: (1) technological, (2) sociopolitical, and (3) human-machine. In the technological cluster, computers are the target of the cybercrime—mainly malware, such as viruses and worms. The sociopolitical cluster includes crimes where computers are used as a tool, such as phishing or identity theft. The human-machine cluster focuses on computer infrastructure and vulnerabilities created through our dependence on computers and networks. For instance, many people use the Internet to make money. This includes bloggers, news agencies, advertising agencies, video producers, financial planners, etc. Their ability to work depends on an open Internet environment. This open environment, of course, also aids criminals because it makes it easy to commit crimes against computers and with the help of computers.[11]

This chapter discusses the different types of cyberthreats against computers and countermeasures to these cyberthreats. The following chapter continues the threat analysis by focusing on computers as a tool to commit cybercrimes.

Computers as a Target

Computers are used to execute commands, such as calculating a value, sending information to another computer, or performing whatever tasks the user needs. As a student, you instruct your computer to open a Word document, write into that document, save the document, and send it to your professor. Some software that runs on your computer may disrupt its performance. Imagine you are trying to open the paper you started writing the day before but all you get is an encrypted, unreadable Word document. It's possible that you downloaded malicious software (malware) that encrypted your computer and makes it impossible for you to access your documents. The term *malware* combines the words *malicious* and *software*. A malware is a computer program or piece of software written by someone with a malicious or criminal intent. It is a code written to destroy, disrupt, or steal data, or do other damage to a computer or network. Malware fulfills two main functions: spread itself and cause damage. Malware typically spreads itself via e-mail attachments embedded in web pages, file sharing, infected CDs or DVDs, or by scanning a computer or network for exploitable vulnerabilities. For instance, a user may click on a web page link to download software needed to run a specific program, such as Adobe Flash. That link to Adobe Flash may contain a malware that infects the computer. The damage that such malware can cause ranges from trivial to very serious. Trivial damage may be a message that pops up on the screen every time the user starts the computer. But the damage can also be debilitating by destroying files, taking the computer hostage, or stealing data and passwords to facilitate other crimes, such as identity theft. One of the most common damages is using the computer as a slave to send spam to other computers, to host illegal data, to attack other computers, or to extort others. Not all malware will become active right away. Some malware can be activated remotely or is programmed to activate after a certain amount of time so that it can spread without being noticed right away.[12]

Threats to Mobile Devices

Whereas malware has traditionally targeted computers and computer networks, the lightning-speed spread of mobile devices has become a new and fruitful market for malicious code developers. Similar to computers, mobile devices are vulnerable to all sorts of malware, including viruses, worms, and Trojan horses. There are five main reasons for the increase in threats to mobile devices.[13] First, the increase in smartphones has led to a significant drop in the prices users pay and a substantial increase in the number of smartphones people own. In addition to smartphones, there has also been a growth in the health tracker industry, and devices such as Fitbit or Garmin Vivofit have become very popular. Even smartwatches are no rarity: Pebble, Apple Watch, and Samsung GearS2 may be the most popular models. In addition to smartphones, smartwatches, and health trackers, many people also have a tablet, such as a Kindle or an iPad. All of these devices can communicate via Wi-Fi and Bluetooth. Their ability to communicate with each other is of great convenience for the users and also for criminals who are trying to steal data, hijack a mobile device, or manipulate the device in other ways. For instance, if a criminal infects one device with a malware, the infection may spread to the other devices and other people's devices.

Second, malware intrusion has mainly concentrated on Android devices due to their open-source technology. Androids' open-source technology is based on Linux kernel and developed by Google. This open-source technology enables developers to freely create and add applications, features, and updates. Unfortunately, this also enables criminals to distribute malicious applications and updates. Since there are no centralized updates, Android devices are not regularly updated with security software and are therefore highly vulnerable to malware intrusions.

Third, smartphone users are storing much information on their devices, including financial information, credit card numbers, user names and passwords, pictures, etc. Many people use the app "Wallet," which enables them to pay with the phone. Others use a personal finance or budgeting app such as "Mint" where they record all of their expenses and income. For criminals, this is easy-to-steal information, which can then be used for financial gain, identity theft, and to spread the malware to other devices.

Fourth, smartphone hardware has become increasingly sophisticated, and so has the capability of smartphone operating systems. These increased capabilities are helpful for developers of applications and make smartphones much more useful for customers, but malware writers also profit from this opportunity. They can develop more sophisticated malware and infiltrate a smart device without the owner ever noticing.

Finally, programming software for smartphones is similar to that of PCs. Malware developers can simply transfer from the PC environment to the smartphone.[14]

There are many different forms of malware, and each has its own way to behave, be triggered, and spread.[15] This chapter focuses on three main forms of malware threats: computer viruses, Trojan horses, and worms. All three have in common that they are used to disrupt computer networks or create advanced persistent threats. As the following case study shows, even sophisticated companies are vulnerable to a malware attack. These threats posed by viruses, worms, and Trojan horses are discussed in more detail in following sections.

CASE STUDY 3.2

Democratic Election Campaign—Hackers Steal Campaign Information

For over a year, hackers attacked political entities that supported the democratic election campaign. An official said, "If they wanted to get into a system, they got into the system." A private investigator who had been hired by the campaign found several data breaches, some of which had substantial negative consequences for the campaign.[16]

The most detrimental attack was the hacking of the Democratic National Committee (DNC), where the hacker Guccifer 2.0 stole nearly 20,000 e-mails, including private e-mails. The e-mails and other information, such as financial contributions, were then fed to WikiLeaks, which published them on July 22, 2016. The e-mails stem from seven members of the DNC, including communications directors, finance directors, and key senior advisers covering a period of January 2015 until May 2016. WikiLeaks provided a searchable database of these e-mails, and information from the e-mails quickly became public.[17]

The e-mails revealed that the DNC chairwoman, Debbie Wasserman Schultz, had exchanged e-mails with a variety of people and entities in an effort to discredit Bernie Sanders and help Hillary Clinton win the Democratic Party endorsement. The DNC is supposed to be a neutral entity supporting each candidate equally and without bias. As a consequence of the leaked e-mails, Debbie Wasserman Schultz resigned from her position and the DNC issued an apology to Bernie Sanders, who had been disadvantaged in the preliminary elections.[18]

A few days later, investigators of the Democrats found that hackers had hacked into the analytics data program and stole data about voters. The hackers had access to the data for approximately 5 days. The Clinton campaign stated that no personal voter information was stolen and that the hackers did not get into the internal campaign servers, which are independent from the analytics data program.[19]

What Do You Think?

1. Discuss the possible motives of the hackers.
2. Do you believe that all e-mails of all election campaigns (Republicans and Democrats) should be public so that the voters have full knowledge, or should these e-mails remain secret? Discuss pros and cons.
3. Discuss whether leaked e-mails from your private account could damage your own reputation. How can you protect the privacy of your e-mails?

Viruses, Worms, and Trojan Horses

Viruses

A virus is a "small software program designed to spread from one computer to another and to interfere with computer operation."[20] A virus is a code that will duplicate itself into a host program when it is activated. Every company has at least one employee who will click on anything and open any file he or she receives. Not surprisingly, hackers are well aware of that, and so 90% of all cyber intrusions start with a phishing e-mail.[21] Virus files are typically executable files—that is, a file that the computer directly executes. They typically end in .exe. This may be a hidden extension, however, to prevent users from becoming suspicious. Users cannot read executable files. Once the user opens or runs the program, the virus spreads further and infects other programs or the entire computer. Imagine you downloaded a music file from the Internet that was infected with a virus aiming to disable your Excel files. When you run your Excel program, the virus is activated and starts to destroy your Excel files.

One of the first to experiment with computer viruses was Fred Cohen, who developed self-replicating miniprograms in the 1980s and warned early about the risks associated with these programs. Cohen compared computer viruses to a disease:

> As an analogy to a computer virus, consider a biological disease that is 100% infectious, spreads whenever animals communicate, kills all infected animals instantly at a given moment, and has no detectable side effects until that moment. . . . If a computer virus of this type could spread throughout the computers of the world, it would . . . wreak havoc on modern government, financial, business, and academic institutions.[22]

IMAGE 3.1 • Computer Virus

©iStockphoto.com/joxxxxjo

Cohen was able to show that viruses can attach themselves to other programs and cause denial of services (i.e., interrupting service or making a program unusable). He defined a virus as "a program that can infect other programs by modifying them to include a possibly evolved copy of itself."[23] Programs that are infected by a virus can then also spread the virus. Cohen also was one of the first to write about the dangers of the lack of security systems by companies, institutions, and individual users. At the time, very few institutions were aware of the real threat, and there was no system that could have stopped a virus.[24] Even though the development of antivirus programs also began in 1987 with Bernd Fix, the real advances didn't start until 1991 with Norton Antivirus. At that time, viruses developed much faster and were well ahead of antivirus programs. Since 1987, antivirus programs have been making significant progress, but they continue to trail the development of new viruses by cybercriminals.[25]

There are three main types of viruses: (1) shell viruses, (2) add-on viruses, and (3) intrusive viruses. Shell viruses form a shell around the original code and the original host program with the purpose to take over the functions of the host program. Add-on viruses attach to the original code, changing the startup information of the program. The viral code then executes before the original code, interfering with the program that the user attempts to run. Intrusive viruses overwrite the original code, which can make the host program dysfunctional.[26]

One of the most destructive viruses in the United States was the "ILOVEYOU" virus, which caused damages of about $10 million. The virus was attached to an e-mail with the subject line "ILoveYou" and fooled users around the globe. The e-mail said, "Kindly check the attached LOVELETTER coming from me," and had an attachment named "Love-Letter-For-You.txt.vbs." The .vbs extension was hidden so that the users only saw a text file. Users who opened the attachment activated the .vbs file (virus) and the virus then sent itself to all contacts in the users' Outlook address book. According to estimates, the virus affected over 15 million computers within 10 days. This is about 10% of all computers connected to the Internet worldwide. The ILOVEYOU virus was a simple virus in that it did not attempt to hide. It was very obvious to the users that something was wrong with their computer.[27]

Since then, viruses have evolved and become more sophisticated. Viruses are now able to operate in stealth to avoid detection. This is called an *advanced persistent threat* (APT). APTs are "cyber attacks executed by sophisticated and well-resourced adversaries targeting specific information in high-profile companies and governments, usually in a long term campaign involving different steps." Originally, APT only referred to cyber intrusions against military units, but APTs are now targeting a wide range of industries and governments. APTs can be distinguished from traditional threats by their characteristics. Table 3.2 shows the differences between traditional attacks and APT attacks.[28]

TABLE 3.2 ● Traditional Attacks Versus APT Attacks

	Traditional Attacks	APT Attacks
Attacker	Single hackers or a loose community of hackers	Highly targeted attacks with a clear objective
Target	Typically individual computers or devices, nonspecific	Skilled and highly organized and resourced hackers
Purpose	Profit, fame, challenge	A long-term campaign with persistent attacks
Approach	Single run, mostly easy to detect	Stealthy and evasive attack techniques that can stay undetected

Source: Chen P., Desmet L., Huygens C. (2014) A Study on Advanced Persistent Threats. In: De Decker B., Zúquete A. (eds) *Communications and Multimedia Security*. CMS 2014. Lecture Notes in Computer Science, vol 8735. Springer, Berlin, Heidelberg.

An example of an APT is an attack by one of the most advanced Chinese cyberhackers called "Deep Panda." Deep Panda targets government officials, defense contractors, think tanks, and financial institutions with the goal to gather sensitive information. The hackers use the Windows PowerShell scripts to intrude the computer systems. For the administrator, it often goes unnoticed because the scripts that include the malware look like scheduled tasks that are performed routinely. Once executed, the malware is installed without leaving any artifacts.[29] According to news agencies, an attack on the U.S. Office of Personnel Management computers compromised the information of 4 million current and former employees of the federal government. For several months, the hackers copied several gigabytes of data undetected. Even after the Cyber Incident Response Team found the intrusion, it took them 2 months to lock the intruders out of the system. The response

IMAGE 3.2 • Credit Card Theft

Pixabay.com

team stated that the hackers are continuing to try to get back into the system.[30] Both traditional and APT attacks pose five main risks for private computer users, companies, and government entities: (1) disable computers and mobile devices, (2) send spam, (3) provide access to computers, (4) steal personal information, and (5) hijack the user's web browser.[31]

Risks Created by Viruses

1. Disable computers and mobile devices

   Some viruses can cause the computer or mobile device to stop functioning properly. Disabling devices carries great risks for companies and people. These devices may disable alarm systems in people's homes or businesses, or they can disable the defense network of the government and the military. One such incident occurred in 2008 when a virus disabled the defense network of the Department of Defense (DoD). The virus was transferred to a DoD computer via an infected USB flash drive brought in from the outside by an authorized user. The virus invaded classified and unclassified networks and gave control of the computer system to the author of the virus. It took 14 months and $1 billion to recover from the attack, and the true extent of the compromise remains unknown.[32]

2. Send spam

   Viruses are often capable of accessing the address book of the infected computer or mobile device and sending spam messages with itself attached to friends, family, and colleagues of the victim. If these users opened the attachment in the belief it came from a friend, they infected their own computer or mobile device. This is also a common scheme through Facebook. Users may receive an e-mail from a "friend" with a picture or video attached and are asked to open the file. The file contains a virus, and the e-mail did not come from their Facebook friend.

3. Provide access to computers

   Viruses may be written with the purpose to give the malicious writer control over the computer or mobile device. Control over the device can serve the purpose of stealing data, controlling certain functions of the computer, or manipulating files on the computer, such as encrypting files or changing the security settings. If an outside person changes the security setting, the owner of the device may be locked out. Imagine a hospital being locked out of their computer system. Without access to medical records, patients cannot receive treatment.

4. Steal personal information

   Criminals often target computers to gain information they can use to steal someone's identity, steal his or her money, or get information from the computer that would help them make money. For instance, a criminal may try to get information about stocks before the market opens to make certain bids that will be financially beneficial. This type of trading is illegal, of course.

5. Hijack the user's web browser

   Viruses can also hijack a computer's web browser. By default, the devices download messages without users having to open the message and initiating the download. Users can prevent this problem by disabling automatic downloads of text messages and e-mails. The person controlling the computer or mobile device can push automatic messages to the victim or users found in the device's address book.[33]

Risks to Mobile Devices

As discussed above, the risks created by viruses are not only risks to computers or networks but also to other electronic devices, such as smartphones, drones,

IMAGE 3.3 ● Computer Locked

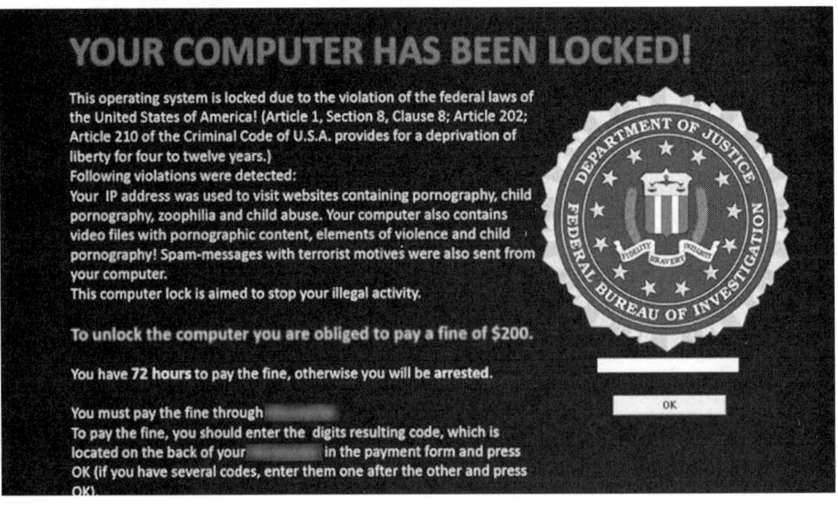

Picture of a Ransomware Attack by Motormille2, https://commons.wikimedia.org/wiki/File:Ransomware-pic.jpg. Licensed under CC BY-SA 4.0, https://creativecommons.org/licenses/by-sa/4.0/legalcode

home security cameras, baby monitors, and other devices that use Bluetooth or are connected to the Internet. Smartphones and Bluetooth devices, such as health trackers like Fitbit, have been swarming the market, and many users are constantly connected to the Internet. This technology has also become a popular target of cybercriminals who understand the opportunities to exploit device vulnerabilities. Smart devices have several vulnerabilities, including web browsing, Wi-Fi, multimedia message service (MMS), short message service (SMS), Bluetooth, applications, and e mails. Malicious code writers have developed viruses that target mobile devices. These viruses are generally referred to as MMS viruses. Similar to computer viruses, these MMS viruses can disrupt phone service, steal information, block data, track the user's movement, force text messages to friends and others in the address book, etc. Users may never find out that their mobile devices are infected and unwittingly spread the virus to other devices, including computers via USB or Bluetooth connection. Some researchers have warned that devices such as Fitbits could contain a virus, and if the user connects it to a company computer to charge it via USB cable, the virus could spread into the computer network of the company. Although this is currently a hypothetical scenario, it certainly presents a serious danger. Another threat that MMS viruses pose is their ability to randomly scan the phone network and contact mobile phone users who are not in the address book.[34] MMS viruses can infect large numbers of smartphones. For instance, the virus "Zombie" infected over one million smartphones in China and created costs of about $300,000 per day. The virus was designed to send automatic text messages.[35] See Table 3.3 for examples of types of viruses.

TABLE 3.3 ● Types of Viruses

Type	Example	How it works
File Infector Virus	Jerusalem Cascade	Infect program files, such as .com or .exe
Boot Sector Virus	Disk Killer Michelangelo	Infect the system area of the disk—the boot record.
Master Boot Sector Virus	NYB Unashamed	Infect the system area of the disk—the boot record. But the location of the viral code is different. Typically saves a legitimate copy of the master book sector in a different location.
Multipartile Virus	Anthrax Tequila	Infect boot records and program files.
Macro Virus	Melissa NiceDay	Infect data files.

Source: Based on information from Symantec.com. *What is the difference between viruses, worms, and Trojan horses?* (n.d.). Retrieved from https://support.symantec.com/en_US/article.TECH98539.html.

CASE STUDY 3.3

The First Viruses

Elk Cloner: The First Apple Virus

The first virus reported on an Apple computer was called the Elk Cloner. Created in 1982 by 15-year old Richard Skrenta, the Elk Cloner was developed for the Apple II operating system and stored on a floppy disk. When the user inserted an infected floppy disk, the virus would become resident on the computer and spread by infecting other floppy disks used on that computer. The virus did not cause any actual damage, but rather it caused users to see a message on the screen every 50th time they started their computer. The message was:

> Elk Cloner: the program with a personality. It will get on all your disks. It will infiltrate your chips. Yes it's Cloner! It will stick to you like glue. It will modify ram too. Send to the Cloner![36]

Brain: The First PC Virus

In 1986, brothers Basit Farooq Alvi and Amjad Farooq Alvi developed the first computer virus for PCs running MS-DOS. The virus was called "Brain." The Brain changes the boot sector of a storage media, such as a floppy disk, and when the computer boots, the virus infects the computer. At the time, floppy disks were used to start up a computer. Thus, a virus on a floppy disk was a sure way to infect the computer, and once the virus was on the computer, it stayed in its memory and infected newly inserted floppy disks. The Brain virus was mainly a nuisance because it caused work to be lost and sent perplexing messages to the users of infected computers. These boot sector viruses disappeared when floppy disks were no longer used to start up a computer.[37]

Worms

In his 1975 science fiction novel *The Shockwave Rider*, John Brunner was the first to use the term *worm*, calling it *tapeworm*. In his novel, Brunner describes a computer-dominated world in which the hero, Nick, creates a tapeworm with an intent to destroy all secrecy by the government. Brunner introduces the worm as a "continental net, a self-perpetuating tapeworm." This was the first time the idea of using a tool to manipulate information in a computer network was used. This was long before the actual Internet developed. The term worm was later adopted by computer experts and defined very similar to Brunner's definition.[38]

A worm "is a self-replicating virus that does not alter files but resides in active memory and duplicates itself."[39] Worms live and replicate within the operating system that is invisible to the computer user. Users typically encounter the worms when their computer starts to slow down substantially due to the resources taken up by the worm during self-replication.

Whereas viruses need some form of intervention from the computer user, such as opening an e-mail attachment or link, worms can spread without the help of the user. Worms also do not need a host program to spread. Worms exploit system vulnerabilities (i.e., weaknesses or flaws in the computer operating system or management of the system) to intrude a computer or network. Once the worm is inside the computer, it replicates and causes damage similar to viruses, such as destroying or stealing data, sending e-mails to other computers by using the address book, and infecting other computers. Worms replicate via network connections.[40]

LEGAL ISSUE 3.1

THE MORRIS WORM

The inventor of the first real computer worm was Cornell graduate student Robert Tappan Morris, the son of then-head researcher of the National Security Agency (NSA), Robert H. Morris. Around 6 p.m. on November 2, 1988, Morris released the first worm into a Unix-based computer system that was part of the research network (i.e., early Internet). The Internet had come under attack for the first time. The worm fulfilled two main functions: (1) infect as many computers as possible and (2) be difficult to discover and stop. Within 12 hours, the worm overwhelmed approximately 6,000 computers, reducing their functionality substantially. At the time, this was 10% of all computers on the network. The Morris worm created much confusion and consternation within the community of researchers and the military because the military computers were also connected to this network. By Wednesday night, researchers at the University of California–Berkeley and Massachusetts Institute of Technology had managed to copy the worm and started to analyze it in an attempt to stop it. Morris, who had not intended to cause that much damage and panic, put an anonymous post on the network outlining how to stop the worm from spreading. Unfortunately, the network was so overloaded at that point that few people actually received the message. By Thursday morning, some researchers also started to post information on how to stop the worm. This incident demonstrated for the first time the vulnerability of the network and laid the groundwork for cybersecurity. In the aftermath of the Morris worm, the National Computer Security Center held a workshop on the exploitation of the Internet and produced a report that detailed how the program worked and fixes to the vulnerabilities of the Unix system.

Morris was charged with having violated the Computer Fraud and Abuse Act of 1984 and received probation. Morris argued that he was only experimenting with worms and had no intention of actually causing harm.[41]

What Do You Think?

1. Do you believe that Morris had the intent to commit a crime by distributing the worm? If you were his defense attorney, what would you argue? If you were the prosecutor, what would you argue?
2. Some people argue that hackers like Morris should be rewarded for demonstrating the vulnerabilities of computer systems. What do you think?

Removing a worm from an infected computer is very difficult because the worm is intertwined with the system. If antivirus or antimalware software does not remove the worm, users may have to do a clean install of the operating system.[42]

Similar to viruses, worms are not only a threat to computers but also to Bluetooth devices such as mobile phones, health trackers, wireless surveillance cameras, connected-drive cars, and similar devices. Research suggests that Bluetooth worms spread quickly to other devices.[43] The first mobile worm, called Cabir, was discovered in 2004 and infected Nokia devices via unsecured Bluetooth connections during the 2005 10th World Athletic Championships in Helsinki. Cabir accessed the contacts in the user's phone and sent itself to other users.[44]

Worms create several risks to computers and mobile devices, including (1) risks to the integrity of the computer system, (2) risks to maintaining confidentiality of information on the computer, (3) risks to the availability of computer files, and (4) Internet slowdown.[45] Table 3.4 provides a list of the five most destructive worms.

TABLE 3.4 ● The Five Most Destructive Worms

Worm	Year Released	Origin	Damage
Mydoom	2004	Russia	$38 billion
Sobig	2003	United States	Crashed internet gateways and e-mail servers $37 billion
ILOVE YOU	2000	Philippines	10% of the World's PCs $15 billion
Conficker	2007	Ukraine	Infected millions of PCs $9.1 billion
Sasser	2004	Germany	Infected critical infrastructures $18 billion

Source: Based on information from wildammo.com. (n.d.). *10 most destructive computer worms and viruses ever.* Retrieved from http://wildammo.com/2010/10/12/10-most-destructive-computer-worms-and-viruses-ever/.

Risks Created by Worms

1. Integrity of the computer system

   Some worms will cause the pop up of messages such as "I think (user's name) is a big, stupid jerk!" This worm was called the WM/97 Jerk worm. After the message was displayed, users could continue to work. Other worms may not only show a message but also lock the computer when the message disappears.

2. Confidentiality of information on the computer

   The user should be the only one who has access to the computer and information stored on the computer. Some worms breach this confidentiality. For instance, the Koobface worm infected computers of users who clicked on a link to update their Adobe Flash. Once inside the operating system, the Koobface worm started to send advertisements for software and recorded the clicks of the user and web searches, which were then sold to the malicious authors of the Koobface worm. This type of worm is also used by criminals who engage in identity theft to steal passwords, credit card numbers, or tax returns.

3. Availability of computer files

   Worms can interfere with users' access to their files by making files unavailable, damaging files, or slowing down the computer. For instance, the Michelangelo worm upon activation began damaging computer files by overwriting the information in these files.

4. Internet slowdown

   In January of 2016, the Slammer worm caused network interruptions across the United States, Asia, and Russia. The worm also infected the network of news provider ABC and caused hundreds of cash machines of the Bank of America to be unavailable. The Slammer further disabled websites of major credit card companies and shut down more than 900 systems in the DoD. Worms such as the Slammer can have very serious impacts on network systems and national security.[46]

Trojan Horses

A Trojan horse is a malware that is "disguised as, or embedded within, legitimate software. It is an executable file that will install itself and run automatically once it is downloaded."[47] Stated differently, a Trojan horse is a program that poses as a legitimate program but performs unknown or unwanted functions. The term *Trojan horse* stems from the Greek Trojan horse that carried an army inside its body. It was used by the Greeks to invade the city of Troy. The Greeks presented a Trojan horse as a present to the city. When Trojan soldiers pulled the horse inside the city gates, it provided the Greeks with an opportunity to destroy the city. The Greek army waited inside the horse until it was dark and then struck down Troy's army in a surprise attack. Similarly, Trojan horses are typically used as delivery systems for crimeware such as keystroke-capturing software. This software can then be used to monitor what people type, especially passwords and user names. Social engineering is the most common way to infect a computer. Social engineering is fooling someone into giving out personal information. Once the user has activated the Trojan, the malware can delete, block, modify, or copy data from the computer. A Trojan horse may also disrupt the performance of the computer or network. Unlike viruses and worms, Trojans are not capable of self-replication.[48]

The first Trojan for Android mobile devices was discovered by Kaspersky Lab in 2010. The Trojan was named Trojan-SMS.AndroidOS.FakePlayer.a because it masqueraded as a media player application. Since 2010, there has been a rapid increase in the development of mobile Trojans especially targeting open-source devices.[49]

Trojan horses create five main risks for computers and mobile devices: (1) deleting files, (2) using the computer to infect other computers, (3) watching users through the webcam, (4) logging keystrokes, and (5) recording user names, passwords, and other personal information.[50] See Table 3.5 for a list of the types of Trojan horses.

TABLE 3.5 ● Types of Trojan Horses

Trojan Horse	Damage	Type
NVP	Modified the system file of Macintosh computers so that all typed vowels disappeared.	Joke Trojan
Feliz	Displayed image warning users not to run any programs.	Joke Trojan
AOL4Free	Claimed to give users free access to AOL and then wiped out every file from the infected hard drive.	Joke Trojan

(Continued)

TABLE 3.5 ● (Continued)

Trojan Horse	Damage	Type
ProMail	Claimed to be a freeware e-mail program and then stole user data.	Data Theft Trojan
SubSeven	Deletes, modifies, and copies files. Steals information.	Remote Access Trojan
Back Orifice	Accessing personal computer files.	Remote Access Trojan

Source: Based on information from etutorials.com. *Types of Trojan Horses.* (n.d.). Retrieved from http://etutorials.org/Misc/computer+book/Part+2+Dangerous+Threats+on+the+Internet/Chapter+8+Trojan+Horses-+Beware+of+Geeks+Bearing+Gifts/TYPES+OF+TROJAN+HORSES/.

Risks Created by Trojan Horses

1. Deleting files

   One of the main problems with Trojan horses is that files are deleted or corrupted in another way. This, of course, is not only inconvenient but can cause great problems if it affects work files that can't be recovered.

2. Using your computer to infect other computers

   A Trojan horse planted in a computer may access the user's address book and send phishing e-mails to other people with the Trojan horse attached to the e-mail. Users who open the attachment unknowingly download the Trojan horse onto their computer. Once on the computer, it accesses the address book and the process starts over. This way, the Trojan horse can spread to more and more computers. For instance, the Trojan horse "Sub7" or "SubSeven" was developed to attack computers running on a Windows 9.x platform. What makes Sub7 so dangerous is the ability of the malicious writer or another person to remotely control the program and issue any command to an infected system. There are a variety of commands that can be given, such as "send an e-mail to the attacker after installation," or "melt server after installation." This ability makes Sub7 a very flexible Trojan. Some of the less dangerous but very irritating things that the hacker can do is reversing mouse buttons, restarting Windows constantly, or changing desktop colors. Sub7 can also cause very serious damage to an infected system, however. This includes stealing data, taking control of text messaging, and overwriting or destroying files.[51]

3. Watching users through their webcam

   Trojan horses can also be used to spy on people via spyware. An author who infects a user's computer with a Trojan horse may watch the user through the webcam and possibly watch their security system or children, daily routines, or other things. This type of software is also available for commercial purposes. For instance, online programs may use the commercial type of software such as "Proctor" to watch students while they are taking exams.

4. Logging users' keystrokes

A keylogger Trojan records users' keystrokes, saves them to a file, and sends them to the author of the malicious software. The goal is to get information such as passwords, credit card numbers, or documents. Some keylogger software is more advanced and able to monitor for specific activity, such as opening a web browser pointing to a specific website (e.g., banking or credit card site). Keylogger programs are also available as commercial software for parents or employers to monitor children's or employees' online activity.[52]

5. Recording usernames, passwords, and other personal information

In 2011, a Chinese Trojan horse hijacked the computer of the Japanese parliament intending to steal data. It is possible that the Chinese hackers were able to download passwords and other information stored on the government computer. These types of attacks are especially of concern for industrial companies and intellectual property, as stealing such information can result in companies going bankrupt. For instance, if a hacker could steal the blueprint for building a certain machine and then build the machine cheaper, the company that invented the machine could lose all its business.[53]

CASE STUDY 3.4

The U.S. Government Firewall Virus

The U.S. government firewall virus is part of the Reveton family (Trojan/Win32.Reveton), which hijacks computers and demands a ransom to unblock the computer.[54] This is also referred to as *ransomware*. Ransomware is "a type of malware that severely restricts access to the computer, device, or file, until a ransom is paid by the user."[55] The U.S. government firewall virus blocks the computer, encrypts files, and displays the following message that appears to be from the U.S. government.

THE FIREWALL OF THE UNITED STATES COMPUTER BLOCKED

This computer has been blocked to Americans by the US Government Firewall

Illegally downloaded material

(audio, videos or software)

has been located on your computer

By downloading, those were reproduced, thereby involving a criminal offence under Section 106 of Copyright Act.

The downloading of the copyrighted material via the Internet or music sharing networks is illegal and is in the accordance with Section 106 of the Copyright Act subject to a fine or imprisonment for a penalty of up to 3 years.

Furthermore, possession of illegally downloaded material is punishable under Section 184 paragraph 3 of the Criminal Code and may also lead to the confiscation of the computer, with which the files were downloaded.

To perform the payment, enter the acquired GreenDot MoneyPack code in the designated payment field and press the "OK" button.

The U.S. government, of course, has not blocked the user's computer, but rather the computer was infected with a Trojan horse and the cybercriminals are trying to extort money. The user can remove the malware by using software such as Hitman Pro.[56] This is not true for all ransomware, however. In some cases, even the FBI is not able to remove the malware.

(Continued)

(Continued)

Ransomware attacks were first reported in Russia in 2005. There are ever new scams, and ransom attacks have become common around the globe. One of the most "successful" ransomware attacks was conducted with CryptoLocker. CryptoLocker infected hundreds of thousands of PCs because it was able to spread across computers connected to a network.

Most ransomware attacks on private users ask for $100 to $300 because that seems to be a sum users are willing to pay to get their data back. Attacks on companies or hospitals tend to ask for a lot more because the stakes for the victim are much higher. For instance, if a company cannot access its computers for several days, they may lose a lot of money. Cybercriminals are well aware of this predicament and use it to extort large sums of money. However, users carry the risk that even if they pay the ransom, there is no guarantee that the computer will be fully functional again. If the criminals demand payment via credit card, they may then also steal that information and additional financial losses to the victim may be incurred.[57] A proven firewall and antivirus software helps avoid such intrusions. In addition, users should use other prevention methods discussed in the next section.

What Do You Think?

1. If you were the victim of a ransomware attack, what negative consequences would that cause for you?
2. What safeguards do you currently use to protect yourself against ransomware attacks? How can you improve your safeguards?

Preventing Malware Intrusions

There are several effective countermeasures users can employ to prevent infection of their computer with a malware.

Antivirus Software

Antivirus software is "a class of program that will prevent, detect and remediate malware infections on individual computing devices and IT systems."[58] Antivirus software programs recognize malware and prevent it from entering the computer by checking programs and comparing them to known malware. Viruses, worms, and Trojan horses are nothing more than a malicious code, and antivirus software detects these malicious codes. This is referred to as *signature matching*. Every virus has a specific signature, and antivirus software programs include a database of these virus signatures. The more comprehensive the database, the more likely is the detection of a virus. Unfortunately, no antivirus software is able to detect all viruses because the code must be known. Thus, new unknown malicious codes cannot be detected. In order to get the best possible protection, the user must update the software regularly and install patches to keep the database current because malware writers change the programs and develop new threats.[59]

Antivirus software is an inexpensive way to provide up-to-date protection for computers. There is a wide variety of antivirus software on the market. Some of the most popular ones are Avira, Bitdefender, McAfee, Norton Antivirus, and Sophos. Every antivirus program has its pros and cons. Good antivirus programs effectively recognize malware with real-time and on-demand scanners, are easy to install and use, and can scan files, such as e-mail attachments. They can also scan within compressed files quickly. Good antivirus software also does a heuristic check of the program for bad behavior to detect new unknown malware. Some antivirus software can repair a virus infection but typically only if the host file is not damaged.[60] In addition to antivirus software, computers should also be protected by a firewall.

Firewall

A firewall is "a software program or piece of hardware that helps screen out hackers, viruses, and worms that try to reach your computer over the Internet."[61] Firewalls are an important part of cybersecurity. Companies who are using a firewall to protect their network must determine what type of Internet traffic they will allow for inbound and outbound traffic. The firewall must be configured in a way that it only allows approved traffic to pass. Any changes to the protocol should be approved and security logs should be reviewed regularly. A firewall is also important for private users, and users should be very careful to allow a website to open that was blocked by the firewall.[62] Unfortunately, firewalls are not a fail-safe solution to criminals. Criminals may access a computer or network by using a virtual private network to get into another target, such as a power grid. For instance, the North American Equipment Council reported that a computer worm had penetrated their data storage system by migrating through the company's corporate network.[63]

Thoughtful User Behavior

Some cybersecurity experts argue that technology has outpaced people in the sense that people use sophisticated technologies without any education about how a criminal views the technology and its potential for abuse. In the absence of such education, people make naturally bad decisions because it's easy to use technology insecurely and difficult to use it securely.[64] The following are rules users should follow to avoid infecting their computer or mobile devices with malware.

1. Users should refrain from opening e-mail attachments that are unexpected or unsolicited, as these attachments are a common strategy to spread malware. Many of these attachments appear to come from friends, official agencies, or companies such as Microsoft, Adobe, etc. For instance, Microsoft does not send attachments for security updates. These attachments are hoaxes. Similarly, users should not open links in e-mails.

2. Unsolicited CDs and DVDs can also contain malware. Users can check a CD or DVD with their antivirus software to make sure it does not contain malware. This strategy does not guarantee a clean CD or DVD, however. Criminals who write malware try their best to stay ahead of antivirus developers.

3. Websites that offer free services such as TV live streams can be a trap, and great caution is warranted. Websites such as hahasport.com may ask users to update their Adobe Flash or some other media player if they want to stream TV for free. The provided link to the update is a link to a malware. Once the user clicks on the link, the malware infects the computer or mobile device.

4. Threats also stem from applications such as Pokémon Go. Users may download a fake application that contains a malware instead of the actual program. It is also possible that users give inadvertent permission to access their phone or Google account.

5. Weak or repetitive passwords are also a liability because malware can steal passwords. If a person uses the same password for several accounts or applications and it gets stolen, the criminal then has access to all of these accounts.[65]

Each of these rules makes it more difficult and cumbersome to use technology. Thus, many people choose to continue to ignore these rules and use technology insecurely. Cybersecurity would make great advances if it would make it easy to use technology securely and difficult to use it insecurely. That is very complicated, however, and we are not close to such breakthrough development.

THINK ABOUT IT 3.2

Pokémon Go, Cybercriminals, and Cybersecurity

The Pokémon Go fun, developed by Niantic Labs, started in July 2016 in the United States, Australia, and New Zealand, and then spread quickly across the globe. The current frenzy over the Japanese gaming app has not only inspired users to catch Pokémons but also cybercriminals to attack users. The game has substantial vulnerabilities. One of the threats was downloading the app from an unverified provider and falling victim to a malicious app that could delete or steal information, install spyware on the device, or take remote control of the device. Cybercriminals are able to use the actual app and turn it into a malware. Another issue revolved around the software used in the app. Apple iPhone users, due to a software bug, granted the app full permission to their Google account. The users were not informed about this issue when agreeing to the terms and conditions. Users who gave permission were advised that they should uninstall the app and revoke the permission to access Google.[66]

What Would You Do?

1. What safeguards do you use before you download an app? As a reference article, read "Pokémon Go: When Cyber Security Breaches Real Life" at https://www.bluecatnetworks.com/blog/2016/07/25/pokemon-go-cyber-security-breaches-real-life/
2. Pokémon Go uses location data to guide users to the Pokémons. How could criminals abuse these location services?

Encryption

Encryption is the obfuscation that is fast when you know the secret but very slow when you don't. Encryption of data is still the most effective way to protect it from being stolen. It is also called *cryptography*. Even though the NSA has the capability to crack encrypted data, it is very difficult and resource intense. Also, some suggest that even the NSA cannot decrypt data encrypted with an Advanced Encryption Standard.[67] Proper encryption encompasses five components: (1) attribution, (2) integrity of data, (3) nonrepudiation, (4) infinity, and (5) scrambled text. Attribution refers to a digital signature providing proof of authorship. The signature may be used to provide legal proof of a person's communications and activities. It is imperative that only the person who has authority to sign can actually do so. If someone could posture as the signatory, the system is not secure. Imagine that the DoD receives a request for data about their latest stealth fighter plane from the president of the United States. In actuality, the request for information comes from a Chinese hacker working for the Chinese government with the intent to steal the data and reverse engineer the fighter jet. This type of cyberespionage is very common and can become a threat to national security.

Integrity of data "refers to protecting information from being modified by unauthorized parties."[68] Only information that is correct also has value. In addition, if data is manipulated, this can prove very costly. Imagine that the CIA sends information to the president of the United States about a possible nuclear attack against the United States by North Korea. In reality, the information was manipulated and there is no nuclear threat. The president could potentially authorize a preemptive strike against North Korea, which could lead to a war.

Nonrepudiation, also called *availability*, means that persons authorized to access information always have access to the information. One of the main cyberattacks today includes the denial to information for authorized persons. There are two main ways to deny access: denial-of-service (DoS) attacks and distributed denial-of-service (DDoS) attacks. In a DoS attack, the attacker may flood the network and overload it, which then makes it impossible for the authorized user to access the network and information. In a DDoS attack, the attacker typically accesses an innocent person's computer to attack other computers by overwhelming them with data requests. In that sense, the attacker distributes the data from one or several computers that the attacker took control of prior to the attack by exploiting a security vulnerability of the computer.[69] One of the largest DDoS attacks of its kind, if not the largest, was called the Mirai botnet. The Mirai botnet brought down much of the Internet in the United States and Europe, including Twitter, Netflix, Reddit, and CNN, in October 2016. The Mirai botnet was distinct from other attacks because it took advantage of the vulnerabilities of the Internet of Things (IoT). The IoT includes iPads, health trackers, smartwatches, and other consumer goods connected to the Internet. The sheer amount of IoT devices that have flooded the computer market has greatly increased the access of hackers to personal information and the ability of hackers to hijack the devices to carry out a DoS attack. These goods often have much less security than computers and are therefore easy to access by a hacker, making the attack much larger.

Infinity means that there should be such a great number of combinations to guess the encryption key that it would take around 1.5 million (18 zeros) years. This number would practically be infinity.[70]

The final condition is that the text must be scrambled by using a mathematical algorithm. The scrambled text is also referred to as *ciphertext*. "Keys" are used to encrypt and decrypt the text. To encrypt the text, a public key is used. This key is known to everyone and is distributed to the public. Since this public key can only encrypt the text (scramble the text) but not decrypt, it does not need to be kept secret. A private key, however, must be kept private because it decrypts the text—that is, it makes it readable. The private key should only be known to the person receiving the message.[71] If other people obtained the private key, they could read the text that was meant to stay private. For instance, messages sent by military leaders to their troops need to be kept secret or the safety of the troops could be in danger. If the enemy knows how the Navy SEALs are going to free a person, they could get killed during their mission.

Figures 3.1 and 3.2 illustrate how encryption and decryption work.

FIGURE 3.1 ● Encryption

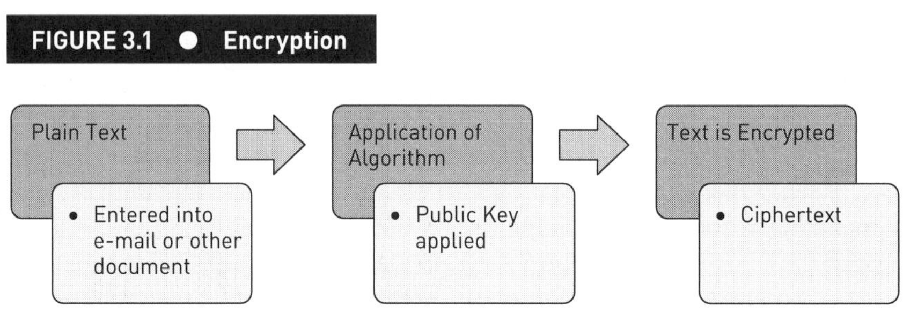

The process of decryption is basically the reverse:

FIGURE 3.2 ● Decryption

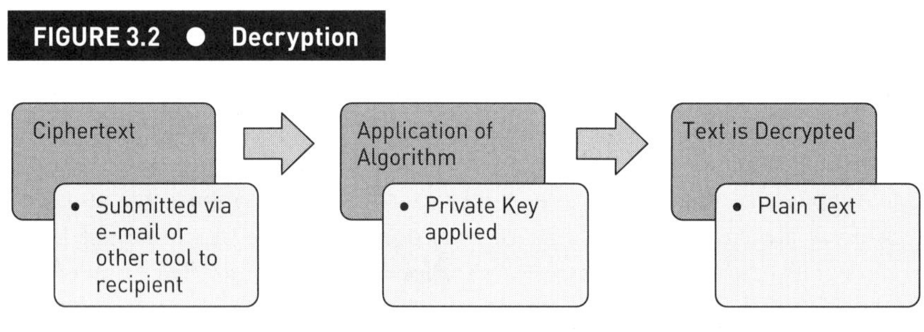

WHAT CAN YOU DO?

Encrypting Your Computer

1. MacOS

If you own a Macintosh computer, you can easily encrypt your data.

- Open System Preferences
- Click on Security and Privacy
- Click on FileVault
- Turn on the File Vault
- You will receive a recovery key (DO NOT LOSE IT)
- To turn the Encryption off, you will need the key

2. PC

If you own a PC and you have Windows 10 Professional, you can use the software BitLocker, which is already built in.

- Control Panel

System and Security

- BitLocker Drive Encryption

If you own a PC and you don't have Windows 10 Professional, you can use the software VeraCrypt.

- Download VeraCrypt

- Follow the instructions on the screen

Future Developments

One of the most promising technologies in cybersecurity is biometrics, which is "the measurement and statistical analysis of people's physical and behavioral characteristics."[72] Biometrics is based on touch and movement information, and mainly used for identification and access to computers and mobile devices. Every person has unique characteristics and behaviors. Fingerprints have long been used by police to identify suspects in a crime. Fingerprints have also been used by companies to control who has access to certain areas. Thus, fingerprints can also be used for access to computers and mobile devices, and several companies, such as Apple, already offer that option. Another biometric option is behavioral data. Every person has a different way of typing, and software can recognize typing behaviors to determine whether the person who is typing is the actual owner. The use of the mouse is also distinct between people. Touchscreens are also being employed for user identification. Researchers have found that people touch different parts of a touchscreen. A software called SilentSense combines touching behavior (pressure, area, duration, position) with reaction of devices (rotation and acceleration).[73] This type of technology is still developing, however, and hackers will likely find ways to disable or fool such systems.

Summary

Chapter 3 explains the difference between viruses, worms, and Trojan horses, and details the purposes for which they are being used. The chapter also provides insight into advanced persistent threats and denial-of-service attacks, such as the Mirai botnet. Finally, Chapter 3 provides an overview of basic cybersecurity measures that everyone can use to protect their computer and data. The use of malware has evolved into a multibillion-dollar business, and every *Fortune* 500 company is well aware that they are a constant target of hacker attacks and will likely have a data breach. Cybersecurity specialists state that 100% protection is impossible, and much depends on preparedness for a major attack. This is also true for major infrastructures, which are largely owned by private companies. A distributed denial-of-service attack on the power grid of Los Angeles, for example, could lead to great damage to the city. For instance, without power, there are no alarms and automatic doors would stay open. People could be looting and burglarizing houses. They could use the chaos of darkness to commit a variety of crimes. The Mirai botnet not only made headlines in the general public and among cybersecurity professionals because it took down much of the Internet of North America, but because it used the IoT (e.g., iPhones, video cameras, webcams, etc.) as botnets for the attacks. With the growing number of the IoT, the threat to private companies and critical infrastructures also increases. Cybersecurity measures are available, but technology always depends on human decision-making—the human factor. Part of the security challenge is to educate people about cybersecurity. The other challenge is to convince companies to build their IoT with good cybersecurity measures in place, but profit often trumps security in a field where time is money.

Key Terms

Advanced Persistent Threat 43
Antivirus Software 56
Biometrics 61
Firewall 55
Malware 39
Ransomware 37
Social Engineering 53
Spyware 54
Trojan Horse 54
Virus 39
Worm 39

Discussion Questions

1. Discuss similarities and differences between worms, viruses, and Trojan horses.
2. Discuss the countermeasures to cyberthreats and how effective they are. What countermeasures would you suggest?
3. Discuss the protections that antivirus software provide and based on what criteria you would choose your antivirus program.
4. Read the reference article on "How to protect your computer networks from ransomware" (https://www.justice.gov/criminal-ccips/file/872771/download). Which of the measures described in the article are you using? Will you change your behavior based on what you have learned?
5. Discuss what mobile devices you own and what the threats to your devices are. How can you protect your devices from cyber intrusions?
6. Look at the ratings of different antivirus software programs and discuss the categories used to rank the programs. From what you have learned in the chapter, which categories are most important?

Internet Resources

Department of Defense
http://www.defense.gov/About-DoD

United States Computer Emergency Readiness Team
https://www.us-cert.gov/

The Best Antivirus Protection of 2017
http://uk.pcmag.com/antivirus-reviews/8141/guide/the-best-antivirus-protection-of-2017

Best Antivirus Software and apps 2017
http://www.tomsguide.com/us/best-antivirus,review-2588-6.html

Further Reading

Arachchilage, N. A. G., & Love, S. (2014). Security awareness of computer users: A phishing threat avoidance perspective. *Computers in Human Behavior, 38,* 304–312.

Durkota, M. D., & Dormann, W. (2008). *Recovering from a Trojan horse or virus.* Retrieved from https://www.us-cert.gov/sites/default/files/publications/trojan-recovery.pdf

Wechsler, P. (2016). *China's unit 61398 pulled from the shadows.* Retrieved from http://businessresearcher.sagepub.com/sbr-1775-98146-2715481/20160201/short-article-chinas-unit-61398-pulled-fromthe-shadows

Digital Resources

Want a better grade?

Get the tools you need to sharpen your study skills. Access practice quizzes and eFlashcards, at **study.sagepub.com/kremling**.

Threats to Cybersecurity by Criminals and Organized Crime

Learning Objectives

1. List the different crimes in which computers are used as a tool.
2. Explain what consumer crimes are, and differentiate between the different types of consumer crimes.
3. Discuss how the Internet has contributed to pornography, trafficking in persons, and mail-order bride services.
4. Explain the different methods used in cyberbullying and how the media, videos, and gaming impact cyberbullying.
5. Explain countermeasures to cybersecurity threats posed by criminals.

Cybercrimes

If you wanted to cause a lot of trouble, you'd do some banking fraud on payday.[1]

If cybercrimes were thought of as disorganized, lone attacks and small fractions of fraudsters at the beginning of the Internet, cybercrime has quickly evolved into organized crime with organizations headed by crime bosses employing an armada of experienced developers who create ever-more sophisticated malware and attack tactics. This is also referred to as the *digital mob*. Cybercriminals are no longer 16-year-old hackers living with their parents and developing malware in their basements. Cybercriminals today are very sophisticated computer experts with an average age of 35 years. A majority of these cybercriminals are associated with organized crime, also called *Crime Inc.* Cybercrime has become a profession, and

Reference Map

Norse Attack Map

map.norsecorp.com

Crime Inc. operates very similar to legitimate businesses with a highly professional staff and structure. A great part of the substantial growth of cybercrime can be attributed to the great rate of information sharing between criminal groups and the availability of tools used for cybercrimes. For instance, there are starter kits for newbies widely available on the Internet. These starter kits may include malicious codes that new fraudsters can use to commit their first crimes.[2]

Why Do People Commit Cybercrimes?

Cybercrime has various layers. There are hackers, hacktivists, organized crime cartels (Crime Inc.), and nation-states that engage in cybercrime for a variety of reasons. Everyone hacks for a different reason. Some hackers do it for curiosity, some for ideological reasons, and many for financial gain. Some hackers, often younger people, may hack to see if they can get in—it's for the thrill. At the beginning of the Internet and cyberspace, this may have been the most common motivation, but cybercrime has evolved into a high-stakes business with millions of dollars attached. For instance, a hacker can make much money by selling stolen credit cards or health records. There is also a significant increase in the number of cybercrime organizations and their level of sophistication. Industrial cyberespionage of engineering blueprints brings in much money in the underground cyberworld. Financial crimes now make up the largest proportion of their cybercrimes. But there are also people who hack for ideological reasons: They are called *hacktivists*. Hacktivists, such as the group "Anonymous," engage in political action against a certain person, group, or even nation-state. Nation-states are mainly engaging in political and economic espionage. This chapter focuses on criminals and organized crime cartels, and the crimes they commit, including fraud, human trafficking, pornography, and cyberbullying. Chapter 5 continues the discussion of cybercrime by analyzing the crimes and motives of hacktivists and nation-states, such as espionage and the theft of trade secrets.

Fraud and Financial Crimes

Consumer Crimes

Consumer crimes are "deceptive practices that result in financial or other losses for consumers in the course of seemingly legitimate business transactions."[3] Consumer crimes include identity theft, phishing scams, and spam. The Federal Trade Commission (FTC) collects and distributes data on consumer crimes that are reported each year. In 2015, the FTC recorded 3,083,379 consumer complaints. The most common crime in 2015 reported to the FTC was identity theft, with more than 490,000 consumer complaints.[4]

Identity Theft

Identity theft "refers to all types of crime in which someone wrongfully obtains and uses another person's personal data in some way that involves fraud or deception, typically for economic gain."[5] Identity theft can happen to anyone because personal information such as Social Security numbers, bank account and credit card information, and other identifying data can be used by anyone to open new accounts, apply for new credit cards, buy goods on credit, or even take out a loan or mortgage. Identity theft has very serious financial consequences, and it often takes years for the victims to recover. Data thieves also commit very serious crimes, such as money laundering or counterfeiting, in the name of the victim. For instance, in California, a woman pleaded guilty to having deposited $746,000 in counterfeit checks in a bank account created with a stolen identity. The consequences for the perpetrator could have been devastating because counterfeiting checks is a federal crime.

There are various ways for criminals to get the personal information they need. First, they may watch the victims or listen to them provide their Social Security number, credit card, or bank account number to someone in person or over the phone. Second, if the victim throws away credit company letters with preapproved credit cards, criminals could activate these cards, as not all companies have adopted sufficient security measures. Third, criminals may simply steal mail from an open mailbox or out of the trash. Finally, the Internet provides ample opportunities to steal someone's personal information. Weak passwords or the use of the same password for several accounts makes it easy to steal the victim's information. The most common passwords are "12345" and "password." Also, Internet dating sites and chat rooms are popular venues to obtain personal information. In response to this growing criminal activity, in 1998 Congress passed the Identity Theft and Assumption Deterrence Act, making identity theft a federal crime. Offenders may be punished with up to 15 years in prison, a fine, and criminal forfeiture. Unfortunately, victims rarely get compensated for the damages incurred.[6]

WHAT CAN YOU DO?

Counter Measures—Protecting Your Identity

The FTC provides information for consumers on how to prevent identity theft.[7]

- Freeze your credit by contacting the major credit reporting agencies: Equifax, Experian, and TransUnion. Freezing your credit makes it much more difficult for identity thieves to open new accounts under your name, take out a loan or mortgage, and buy goods on credit.
- Keep your financial documents, credit cards, Social Security card, extra keys for your house and car, and other essential documents in a fireproof file box.
- Keep your personal information secure by shredding receipts, credit offers, credit card applications, insurance forms, checks, and other financial statements.
- Keep your personal information secure online by using strong passwords and encrypting your data. Don't share personal information over e-mail or on social networking sites. Use only secure Wi-Fi networks to send e-mails with personal information. Use your private network for bank transactions, etc.
- Use security software on your computer, such as antivirus, antispyware, and a firewall.

(Continued)

(Continued)

- Don't open or respond to spam or phishing e-mails (see the following section).
- Monitor your credit reports for free by using AnnualCreditReport.com.

What Do You Think?

1. Which of these measures have you already implemented?
2. Discuss the purpose of each of these measures and why everybody should implement them.

Phishing Scams

The use of e-mails for personal and business communication has become standard today. Unfortunately, not only are e-mails a prominent tool for cybercriminals to intrude a computer but also to solicit information from unsuspecting users or lure them into visiting fraudulent websites to download software that contains a virus, worm, or other malware. Phishing is also referred to as *brand spoofing* or *carding*. The term *phishing* stems from an analogy that Internet scammers are using to fish for passwords and financial data from Internet users.[8]

IMAGE 4.1 ● Phishing Amex

From: **American Express** <azure_2a60bd72889127115a212c8486279b8c@azure.com>
Date: Fri, Nov 1, 2013 at 11:05 AM
Subject: A message is ready for you to view
To:

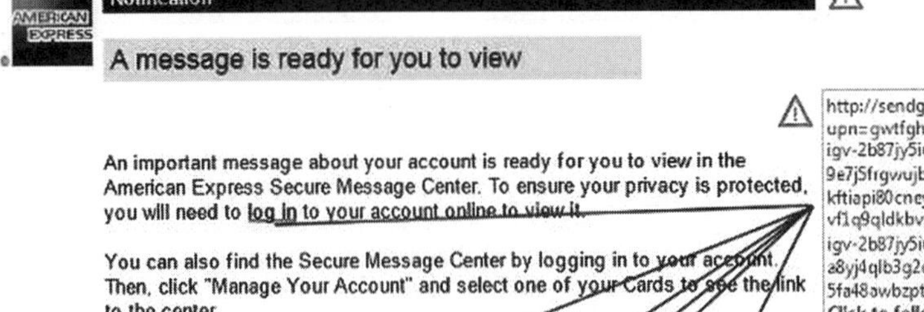

Notification

AMERICAN EXPRESS

A message is ready for you to view

http://sendgrid.me/wf/click?
upn=gwtfghtlm9vmtay-2ftd-2b1zqixfmqetp4b6c-2bahaigv-2b87jy5iu9-2fzkrpbyi-2f3hgameh7cxc4stdibvpo8lny9e7jSfrgvvujb0vhqhtisnn7lmj5-2bhc-2bu96hamyzxnc_adkftiapi80cneyorttzhr7cd75aieib0eg4c3m9h62wpzpqj-2fvvf1q9qldkbvz4lf0r3mgh0togh8j-2bxsvw9r9yvcfrpbyigbl9igv-2b87jy5iu9-2fzkrpbyi-2f3hgameh7cxc4stdibvpo8lnya8yj4qlb3g2cdeplsuclftfqxyiiexl-2bv8j9dm17xppsk-2brkli5fa48owbzptuv4fcl1doul-2fg-3d-3d
Click to follow link

An important message about your account is ready for you to view in the American Express Secure Message Center. To ensure your privacy is protected, you will need to log in to your account online to view it.

You can also find the Secure Message Center by logging in to your account. Then, click "Manage Your Account" and select one of your Cards to see the link to the center.

The message will be available for you to view for the next 90 days.

Thank you for your Cardmembership.

Contact Customer Service | View Our Privacy Statement | Add Us to Your Address Book

This is a customer service e-mail from American Express. Using the spam/junk mail function may not block servicing messages from being sent to your email account. To learn more about e-mail security or report a suspicious e-mail, please visit us at americanexpress.com/phishing. We kindly ask you not to reply to this e-mail but instead contact us securely via customer service.

Copyright 2013 American Express. All rights reserved.

Amex Phishing Details by Intel Free Press, https://www.flickr.com/photos/intelfreepress/14167152169. Licensed under CC BY-SA 2.0, https://creativecommons.org/licenses/by-sa/2.0/legalcode

Phishing scams typically target personal information such as bank accounts and e-mail accounts to use for nefarious purposes. The main threat to victims is identity theft but also loss of credibility and loss of trust. Identity theft can have devastating effects on the victims, who often need years to recover. The Identity Theft Resource Center estimates that it takes on average 600 hours to repair the damage of identity theft.[9]

Phishing is very lucrative for the criminals, and the gangs are well organized, especially in Africa, Eastern Europe, Asia, and the Middle East. Phishing is also popular among organized crime groups and terrorists to create fake IDs, gain employment, and finance their illegal activities. Phishing scams can be difficult to detect because they often look like they are coming from a reliable e-mail account or known contact.[10]

In 2015, the FTC recorded 25,324 consumer complaints about Nigerian/Other Foreign Money Offers.[11]

Take a look at the example below:

From: "CSUSB Technology Support Center <support@csusb.edu> <support@csusb.edu> <support@csusb.edu>" <yalqah1@students.towson.edu>

Date: Jul 2, 2017 12:31 PM
Subject: Confirm
To:
Cc:

We noticed an Unsuccessful login attempt to your mailbox today 2nd July, 2017 from an unrecognized device & location.

Sign-In to Confirm Your Login

Thank you
ITS HelpDesk

The e-mail appears to have come from the university IT department and the *From* line includes valid e-mail addresses. For a student, faculty, or other employee, it may look as though this is something they should respond to. Unfortunately, if they click on the link to "Sign-In to Confirm Your Login," they have invited malware into their computer. Typically, these types of phishing attempts are targeting e-mail account data, which can then be used by the criminal to send spam to other users.

Another example is a malware attack by using the appearance of governmental agencies as senders, such as the Internal Revenue Service (IRS).

Example of a Phishing E-Mail

Dear Steven Yates,

The Internal Revenue Service Antifraud Commission has found 3 fraud attempts regarding your bank account. Someone enrolled your credit card to our Electronic

(Continued)

(Continued)

> Pay System - EFTPS – and tried to pay some taxes. Due to these attempts, some of your money were lost and your remaining founds were blocked. We are sorry for this inconvenience but this the standard procedure in order to try to recover your lost money. Although you may unblock your founds, if needed it, by accessing our webpage through the link provided here. Once again, we are sorry for this inconvenience and we will do our best to recover your money.
>
> The Internal Revenue Service Antifraud Commission

Once the customer clicks on the "provided here" link, he or she gets redirected to a website that looks like a legitimate IRS website. There, the customer is asked to fill in the information needed to verify the account by entering name, date of birth, Social Security number, password, and other personal information. The website is a scam, however, and the customer has just given the scammers everything they need to change the accounts, open new accounts, withdraw money, take out loans, and make other financial transactions. The IRS has a reporting site for such phishing e-mails to encourage customers to report these scams. The IRS also states on their website that they do not use e-mail, text messages, faxes, or phone calls to initiate contact with a taxpayer.[12]

CASE STUDY 4.1

Advance Fee Fraud—Nigerian Phishing Scam

During the 1990s, the dictators of Nigeria (Sani Abacha) and Zaire (Mobutu Sese Seko) were pushed out of power and their assets frozen. These assets included their international bank accounts with millions of dollars. The freeze of those bank accounts led to the birth of the Nigerian Internet scammers who posed as family members of the former dictators. There are a variety of scams, including beneficiary of will, bogus cashier checks, donation solicitations, and fake websites. One of the most well-known is the beneficiary of will. The scammers sent mass e-mails to people telling them that they were the beneficiary in a will and would inherit millions of dollars. The scammer then asked for the personal financial information of the "beneficiary" as proof that they were the actual beneficiary and to wire the money into their bank account. The scammers typically also asked for the victim's Social Security number and date of birth. With this information, the scammers could empty the victim's bank account or steal his or her identity. These Nigerian-based scams have evolved and become more sophisticated, causing millions of dollars in economic damages. In some schemes, victims were lured to Nigeria to meet with fake government officials who promised to make them an investor in a multimillion dollar project. The FBI reports that some of these victims have been imprisoned in Nigeria. The Nigerian government has taken steps against the scammers, but the scam has been ongoing for years and there are ever new twists to it.[13]

What Do You Think?

1. Think about some e-mails you have received that you believe were phishing e-mails. Share your examples with your classmates.
2. Why do people respond to e-mails from a stranger who promises them a large amount of money?
3. What can you do to protect yourself from becoming a victim of advance fee fraud?

WHAT CAN YOU DO?

Countermeasures to Phishing Scams

Companies can protect themselves from becoming a victim of phishing scams by following some basic rules:[14]

1. *Update e-mail policies* to ensure that no single employee or single e-mail can authorize a transaction. The policy must also include oversight procedures for confidential or financial information.
2. *Plan for ID theft after a data breach* by implementing a response plan that everyone follows.
3. *Complete regular updates* to limit vulnerabilities. All software, firmware, operating systems, and applications need patching and updating. Also, companies must complete regular data backups.
4. *Implement Message Authentication* to avoid e-mail spoofing, that is, the forgery of an e-mail header to make it appear as if it is coming from a friend or employee. The domain-based Message Authentication Reporting and Conformance Standard provides protection from e-mail spoofing by reporting such attempts to the companies. This is also called *threat intelligence.*
5. Improve collaboration efforts between public and private sectors to make it more difficult for hackers, mitigate the impacts of attacks, and have a quicker recovery after an attack.

What Do You Think?

Which measures can you as an individual use to protect your devices from hackers?

Spam

According to the CAN-SPAM Act, spam is defined as

> unsolicited commercial electronic mail that includes any commercial emails addressed to a recipient with whom the sender has no existing business or personal relationship and not sent with the consent of the recipient, and commercial electronic mail is defined as any electronic mail message the primary purpose of which is commercial advertisement or promotion of products or service.[15]

Spam typically includes advertisements about lotteries/awards, business proposals, requests for favors, benefits/charity, financial offers, and phishing offers.

E-mail spam has been a persistent problem despite legislation prohibiting spam, such as the CAN-SPAM Act of 2004. According to the CAN-SPAM Act, people who send unsolicited commercial e-mails that violate the provisions of the Act can be punished with fines of up to $16,000 for each e-mail and imprisonment. In 2008, Robert Soloway (i.e., the Spam King) was sentenced to 47 months in a federal prison for sending tens of millions of unsolicited commercial e-mails. Soloway also had to pay $708,000 in restitution to the victims.[16]

Spam messages are not only an annoyance but they cause real economic damage. It has been estimated that spam costs add up to $20 billion in lost time and productivity. There are several criticisms of the CAN-SPAM Act that highlight why the Act has not been very effective in preventing spam. First, some argue that the Act actually helps spammers by laying out exactly how to send spam within the rules. For instance, the Act states that spammers can include an "opt-out" clause for people who receive the message. This actually helps spammers by letting them know whose accounts are active and who reads their messages. Very likely, people who opt out will receive more spam either from the same sender or other senders. And as long as these messages have an opt-out clause, they are legitimate. Spam is also legitimate if the subject line is not deceptive—that is, the subject line clearly indicates that this is an advertisement. Second, a preemption clause in the Act of some state laws that are more rigorous than the federal Act may not be enforceable. Third, law enforcement has to deal with jurisdictional issues. The main question is whether the United States has authority if the spammer operates from another country. Research has found that due to its shortcomings, the Act has not had any significant impact on the amount of spam sent or compliance with the law.[17]

In order to limit the amount of spam that people receive in their mailboxes, e-mail providers such as Gmail, Yahoo, and Hotmail have built-in spam filters. Accurate spam filtering is very helpful for users, but these filters also filter out messages that are legitimate. If users don't check the e-mails that were moved into the spam folder, they may miss important e-mails and miss following up on important e-mail communications. Spammers also work diligently to find ways to outsmart the spam filters.[18]

Banks and Financial Corporations

Botnets

Botnets are defined as a

> collection of infected machines worldwide which receive commands from their botmaster and perform some illegal actions such as Distributed Denial of Service (DDoS) attacks, credential stealing, click fraud, spam sending, bank account and credit card theft and downloading other malwares.[19]

The botmaster controls the botnet using a communication channel called Command & Control (C&C). Botnets use a peer-to-peer (P2P) architecture in which each workstation has the same capabilities and responsibilities. The P2P networks enable the delivery of content, especially software. Thus, in a P2P architecture, the botnet computers not only communicate with the C&C but also with each other. Botnets prevent detection by obfuscating and encrypting information and by fluxing their Internet protocol addresses and domain names.[20]

Botnets infect computers via USB connector or drive-by downloads. Drive-by downloads are of great concern for companies because employees may inadvertently infect a machine by opening malware links hidden on reputable websites. Once the machine is infected, the C&C controls the machine remotely. Cyberattackers target reputable websites to hide their malware because they know that Internet users trust these companies. Another common tactic is to send out infected security patches that companies unsuspectingly install on their machines. These attacks are very effective because very few antivirus programs recognize the malware.[21]

IMAGE 4.2 ● Botnet Attack

Botnet by Tom-b, https://de.wikipedia.org/wiki/Botnet#/media/File:Botnet.svg. Licensed under CC BY-SA 3.0, https://creativecommons.org/licenses/by-sa/3.0/legalcode/

A special target of botnet attacks are banks and other financial institutions. A report by SecureWorks suggests that in 2015 more than 1,500 financial institutions were targeted across more than 100 countries. The vast majority of attacks (80%) targeted financial institutions in the United States. In 2015, hackers stole $12 million for the Banco de Austria in Ecuador. Another popular target includes cloud service providers and tech companies, which suggests that attackers are looking to infect masses of mobile platforms.[22] Cyberattackers learn from their mistakes, becoming more sophisticated with every attack attempt.

Logic Bombs

Logic bombs are

> small programs or sections of a program triggered by some event such as a certain date or time, a certain percentage of disk space filled, the removal of a file, and so on.[23]

A logic bomb may delete part of a code to make a software dysfunctional. Logic bombs are typically installed by insiders—that is, people who work or have worked in the company. Some employees install logic bombs because they are upset about being laid off or because they did not get promoted. Others use logic bombs for their own advantages, such as manipulating a stock price.[24]

Logic bombs can "sleep" for months or years. For instance, an employee who believes he may get fired may install a logic bomb that goes off after 90 days of inactivity of his user account. The purpose is to punish the company for firing him. No damage is done as long as the employee uses his account, but if he gets fired, the logic bomb will "detonate" and harm the company by deleting a critical database or something similar. Logic bombs are very difficult to detect by companies because antimalware often does not recognize the logic bomb. Logic bombs use a custom code specific to the system in which they are installed, and they do not have a signature that can be detected. Since they are installed by people who know the system well, they also know how to circumvent the security measures.[25]

In 2013, cybercriminals wiped out the hard drives of at least three banks and three broadcasters in South Korea. The logic bomb was set to go off around 1 p.m. on March 20 and started erasing data in more than 48,000 computers. The banks suffered a computer network failure. An investigation by South Korea and other countries suggests that the North Korean Reconnaissance General Bureau was behind the attacks.[26]

Viruses

Viruses are also a great threat for banks, as they can wipe out millions of customer accounts and steal personal information of account holders and bank information. A hybrid Trojan, dubbed GozNym or Gozi by IBM, has attacked 22 financial institutions and stolen millions of dollars from victims. The Trojan was planted by Nymain, a group known for its ransomware attacks, where a virus holds the computer hostage until the victim pays a fine. Nymain also rents out Gozi for $400 per week.[27]

Internet-Initiated Sexual Offending and Exploitation

Internet-Initiated Sexual Offending

The Internet has become one of the main tools to meet new friends, catch up with old friends, and find romantic relationships, especially among younger people. Popular media outlets for sexual solicitation are chat rooms, social networking sites (i.e., Facebook, Twitter), and P2P platforms. People who meet online often share very personal information without ever meeting in person. Others may decide to meet after having communicated online. This type of interaction and dating has advantages, especially for people who work long hours or don't go to bars or events where they would meet others. There are also significant dangers of Internet meeting and dating, however.[28]

The anonymity of the Internet facilitates sexual offending because it is a significant resource for sex offenders and people looking for pornographic materials, including production, possession, and distribution of child pornography, sexual solicitation, sex trafficking, snuff films, and mail-order brides. In the past decade, the number of prosecutions and clinical referrals for these crimes has substantially increased, suggesting that these crimes are increasing. Unfortunately, it is very difficult to estimate the true extent of Internet sexual offending because there is no national database integrating the data from the various states and there is a very high dark number—that is, the number of crimes that are not reported. Also, laws vary by state. However, the number of arrests for Internet sex crimes tripled between 2000 and 2009. One of the most researched and discussed Internet-facilitated crimes is child pornography. There are more arrests for sex offenses against children, and the average sentence for child pornography offenses has gotten longer.[29]

Child Pornography

Child pornography "refers to the sexualized depictions of children produced, distributed, accessed or stored via various internet facilitated paths such as web-cams, bulletin boards, email, websites and peer-to-peer networks."[30]

Child pornography always involves the exploitation and abuse of children. Most child pornography involves sexual acts of prepubescent children with adult men. Children are victimized during the pornographic act and afterward by being on the Internet against their will, by knowing that offenders gratify themselves with their pictures and videos, and that they are being used to "groom" other children for sexual abuse.[31]

The Internet provides criminals with a certain amount of anonymity and the ability to pose as a different person. Offenders may use a computer, smartphone, tablet, or other mobile device that can access the Internet. It is impossible to estimate the number of children abused by individual offenders or organized rings. The United States Sentencing Commission believes that there are over 5 million unique pornographic images on the Internet and offenders who possess more than 1 million images. The majority of child pornography websites are hosted in the United States. Many child pornography offenders are pedophiles—that is, they are motivated by their sexual interest in children. Some child pornography offenders are motivated by other reasons, such as addiction to pornography and curiosity.[32]

Access to the Internet, sexual deviance, and antisocial tendencies have been found to be the main explanatory factors of Internet-based child pornography offenses. Research suggests that online child pornography offenders differ from offline offenders. Offline offenders have greater access to children than online offenders. Online child pornography offenders have a greater sexual deviance and are more likely to be sexually preoccupied and have great difficulty with sexual self-regulation. Online offenders are younger, have a higher income, and a higher education level than offline offenders. Finally, online offenders are less likely than offline offenders to have a prior contact offending history.[33]

Online pornography offenders who are interested in adolescents (ages 13–15) are not considered pedophiles. Briggs, Simon, and Simonsen found that there are two types of online offenders who are interested in adolescents.[34] First, fantasy-driven offenders receive gratification simply from the online activities, such as sexual chatting or sharing pornographic materials. They may also engage in exhibitionism online via webcam and have an orgasm while online. They are not likely to initiate a meeting with the adolescent. Second, contact-driven offenders aim to meet the victim in person. They spend significantly less time online, and if they meet in person with the adolescent, there is typically sexual contact. They are not likely to use threat or force.

Offenders typically target children who appear vulnerable, such as children who are unhappy or needy, or are less able to tell someone about their abuse. Online offenders use a variety of strategies to get access to the victim. Offenders are often perceived as upstanding citizens who are well liked and respected in their community. Offenders typically try to befriend the targeted children and gain their trust by spending time communicating with them. They may try to make the child feel "special" and adored. They will establish that their relationship must stay secret, and they may try to isolate the child from his or her friends and family. There is a grooming process that involves desensitizing the child by showing explicit pictures or videos, talking about sexual acts, and violating the child's boundaries.[35]

Offenders may also impersonate someone else to get close to the child. For instance, an offender may enter a chat room under a wrong name, age, place of living, work, etc. 15-year-old Susan may believe that she is chatting with 16-year-old Jonathan, when in reality Jonathan is Will and 50 years old. Even though most people fear that their children will be abused by a stranger who they met on the Internet, most often the offender is a relative or friend, or a person that the parents and children trust, such as a teacher, priest, or nurse. Almost daily, the news media report of a person arrested for possessing and/or distributing child pornography who was popular in his or her community and whom people would not have suspected.

On the darknet, pedophiles can also order "pay per rape" in online streaming. In October 2016, the FBI informed the police in Nanterre, France, that a 71-year-old Frenchman had been participating in child rape via live stream services. In these services, the viewers can direct the rapist's actions by telling the rapist what they want him to do. The 71-year-old was indicted for rape on minors, complicity with torture and barbarism, conspiracy, and possession of child abuse images. For 20 Euro, the pedophile had bought the live stream of child rape streamed from the Philippines using the darknet.[36]

The consequences of child pornography for the victims are lifelong not only because of the abuse at the time but because the pictures of their abuse are on the Internet forever. Victims often say that they feel they are being victimized over and over. Amy, now 39, told her story of abuse by her father. It started when she was 5, after her mother's suicide. He took pictures of her naked and in explicit positions, molested her, and like most other offenders, was never punished. By the time Amy was ready to report him to the police, the statute of limitations had expired. All of the pictures and the proof she had were worthless before the law and continue to haunt her every day. Like so many victims, she suffers from debilitating depression, and even though she has managed to have a successful career and build a family, she lost her childhood and she will struggle with the abuse for the rest of her life.[37]

Some companies, like Google and Microsoft, by blocking web searches for child sexual abuse have led to a 65% reduction in web-based searches for child sexual exploitation material. Increasingly, offenders are using the darknet, the underground web, which allows offenders to stay anonymous and undetected as they are not traceable by police. There are also search engines like Yandex and Baidu, which are hosted outside the United States and do not block child sexual exploitation material. In addition, encryption software has become cheap, sophisticated, and user-friendly, and decoding is difficult for law enforcement agencies, making it increasingly difficult to prove that the suspect shared pornographic images.[38]

In 2009, the Homeland Security Investigations Unit (HIS) began investigating an online forum called *Dreamboard*. Dreamboard was the name of an online bulletin board that distributed images and videos of child sexual abuse. Dreamboard was a private members-only club with members across the globe. By 2013, a total of 72 defendants were charged with the sexual abuse of minors. Operation Dreamboard was one of the most successful law enforcement investigations with regard to child exploitation.[39]

LEGAL ISSUE 4.1

CHILD PORNOGRAPHY

In 2009, Nathanial (Ned) Solon, a Wyoming resident, was arrested for the possession of thousands of child pornography images on his computer. During his trial, Ned claimed that he did not download them, but rather a criminal had hacked into his computer and stored the images there without his knowledge using a Trojan.[40]

What Do You Think?

1. How could the prosecutor prove that Ned knew of the images on his computer?
2. If you were the defense attorney, how could you prove that the images were planted by a hacker?
3. Discuss the difficulties that both the prosecutor and defense attorneys face in cases like this one.

Snuff Films

Snuff films are films where a person or an animal gets tortured and killed, or seems to get killed. Snuff films were long an urban legend—many people talked about them but doubted that they actually existed. This changed when police found the first snuff films and made the first arrests. One of the first websites where people could see still images of shocking things like medical conditions, body parts gnawed up by rodents, or meat-grinder injuries was rotten.com. Compared to the now-available snuff porn and pedophile snuff films, these still images seem harmless. People can now watch live gore videos where people, including young children, are raped and tortured until they die. In 2014, the British police arrested a man who possessed a snuff film in which a teenage girl was raped and strangled. The video was 20 minutes long. He received 8 months in prison. The British government arrested the man after receiving a tip from the Russian Interior Ministry, which had noticed an increase in an upload of child pornography from a UK-based computer.[41]

Russia is one of the main production countries of snuff films, and it is easy to recruit young children from orphanages or rural areas by promising them money or simply a warm meal. In 2000, police searched the residence of Dmitri Vladimirovich Kuznetsov, a 30-year-old Russian, where they found 3,000 videos. Police across Europe have searched hundreds of homes of customers of snuff films.

Customers of snuff films repeatedly ordered videos from Kuznetsov. The British Newspaper the *Guardian* printed an exchange between Kuznetsov and a customer:

> "Promise me you're not ripping me off," says the Italian.
>
> "Relax, I can assure you this one really dies," the Russian responds.
>
> "The last time I paid and I didn't get what I wanted."
>
> "What do you want?"
>
> "To see them die."[42]

The common belief about snuff film viewers is that they are hiding in their basements watching snuff films, but in reality, there are many gore site users with professional jobs, families, and social skills. What most of them have in common is that they keep their hobby on the down low. One gore site user stated: "The people I work with are old blood. They have ties to the Pilgrims," says SAF. "They're conservative." Ultimately, what they all seem to share is a compulsive curiosity about human nature and frailty, and a firm belief that the mainstream media does a disservice by censoring "what's really going on." "We live in the developed world, and we don't have exposure to how people actually treat each other," says Kingfate, a 20-year-old midwestern GoreGrish.com member. "[Gore sites] keep us rooted in reality." Another user tries to justify watching snuff films: "Posting these videos doesn't mean that we condone them," says Niki. "We're just giving people a means to see what's going on. When you hear a bomb has gone off in Moscow, we try to find those images and put them up for people who want to see. And why should we not see it?"[43]

All states have implemented laws against child pornography, sex offenses, and murder, but prosecuting viewers of snuff films is very difficult because they can claim that it was staged. Police officers who work in the Immigration and Customs unit (ICE) not only work to prevent illegal immigration but they are also responsible for preventing unlawful goods being trafficked into the United States. Child pornography is one such illegal good, and ICE officers have found that people who watch and collect child pornography often also collect snuff films. For these officers, watching these films can be very distressing and have serious negative consequences for their life, especially if it involves very young children.[44]

Trafficking in Persons

Trafficking in persons is the

> recruitment, transportation, transfer, harbouring or receipt of persons, by means of the threat or use of force or other forms of coercion, of abduction, of fraud, of deception, of the abuse of power or of a position of vulnerability or of the giving or receiving of payments or benefits to achieve the consent of a person having control over another person, for the purpose of exploitation. Exploitation shall include, at a minimum, the exploitation of the prostitution of others or other forms of sexual exploitation, forced labour or services, slavery or practices similar to slavery, servitude or the removal of organs.[45]

FIGURE 4.1 • Victims and Profits by Region

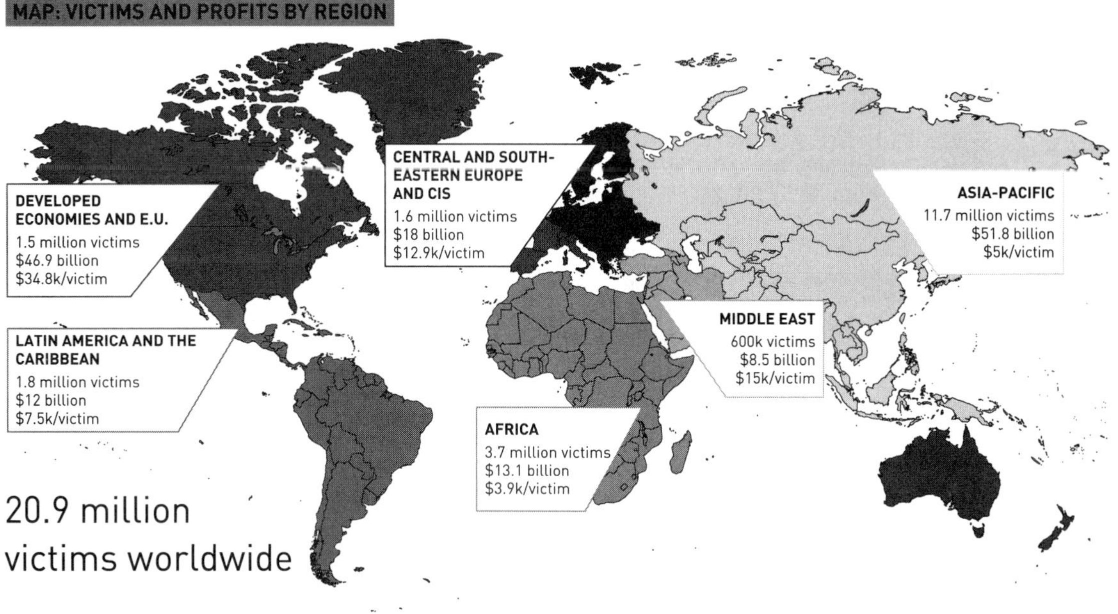

Source: Humanrightsfirst.org.

Human trafficking consists of three main elements: (1) act, (2) means, and (3) purpose. First, the act of trafficking includes the recruitment and transportation of people. Second, the means of trafficking is how it is done, either via the use of force, coercion, deception, or abuse of vulnerability. Finally, the purpose of trafficking is the exploitation of the trafficked person via sexual exploitation, labor exploitation, slavery, or harvesting organs.[46]

The Internet plays a detrimental role in human trafficking, especially the recruitment of victims. Social networking sites like Facebook and MySpace are used by criminals to contact victims and gain their trust, promising them a career as a model, an actress, or becoming the wife of a wealthy man in a desirable destination country. Other traffickers promise gainful employment as nannies, waitresses, or dancers. Once the victims are picked up by the traffickers, the traffickers take their passports and prevent the victims from communicating with their families or friends. Female victims are typically sold into brothels, forced to make pornographic videos, including sadistic practices, sold as slaves, or forced to perform on live Internet sex shows. Male victims are often contacted through employment websites and sold as labor slaves.[47]

The numbers of victims are estimated to be around 20 million globally. About 700,000 victims are trafficked into the United States, and about 50,000 of them are children. Within the United States, more than 300,000 children are at risk of becoming victims of sex traffickers. Most of the sex trafficking victims are between 12 and 14 years old, but they are as young as 5.[48] Parents sell their children or give them to traffickers because they promise them a better life in a wealthy country. Some academics argue that rapid developments in the Internet industry are a direct cause of the demands of pornographic sites, including rapid payment via credit card, database management, and search engines.[49]

The Internet allows the traffickers to hide their identities by encrypting their data, posing as another person, and using wireless technology that is difficult to trace. Traffickers also build networks with other traffickers and consumers who are buying the victims, pornographic materials, or buying sex with the victims.[50] According to the National Human Trafficking Resource Center, the top three trafficking venues are commercial-front brothels, hotels and motels, and residential brothels.[51]

THINK ABOUT IT 4.1

Countermeasures to Child Pornography—Operation Predator and Operation Globe

The Child Exploitation Investigations Unit is part of the HIS, working to protect and rescue children from exploitation by criminals. Their Operation Predator seeks to identify and arrest child predators by using cutting-edge technologies. The agents work with all 61 Internet Crimes Against Children task forces within the United States, Interpol, foreign governments, the National Center for Missing and Exploited Children, and other federal agencies. Since 2003, the agency has made more than 8,000 criminal arrests.

HIS was one of the founding members of the Virtual Global Task Force (VGT), created in 2003. VGT is a collaboration of public and private organizations that fight against child sexual exploitation. Its Operation Globe started in June 2016, and within 6 months, the task force made 20 arrests and identified 30 child victims. Several offenders were prosecuted and sentenced to up to 16 years in prison.[52]

What Would You Do?

1. If you were the chief investigator of HIS, what strategies would you use to investigate child pornography and trafficking rings?
2. What punishment would you propose for the offenders?

Mail-Order Brides

Mail-order brides are women "who with intent to marry, publish in a catalogue. This is done by a woman to marry someone from another country, usually a financially developed country."[53] Mail-order brides are not a new phenomenon. The first settlers in North America would write letters to Europe to find a wife. Later, during World War II, American soldiers exchanged letters with women whom they had never met in hopes of finding a wife. Mail-order bride services have over time turned into a business, however—and a lucrative one. In 2010, mail-order bride agencies made a total of $2 billion in profits, and business continues to grow. Most men who are seeking a wife from another country, and most women looking for a man from another country, use international matchmaking services to help them. The brides typically come from developing countries, such as Cambodia, Thailand, and the Philippines, but also from countries where women don't see the possibility of developing their full potential, such as Russia and other eastern European countries. Before the invention of the Internet, it could take years to find a mate. Males would be presented with a catalog of women and pick a few to write letters to. The exchange of letters could go on for many months or years before a man and a woman would finally meet. Since the 1990s, the Internet has greatly sped up the letter-writing and meeting time, as communication is instantaneous. Now, males and females could also see each other via webcam, and there is much greater access to profiles of potential wives.[54]

Even though the term *mail-order bride* has a demeaning connotation, it is still widely used by the popular media and the academic literature. The reason may be the power differential between the "buyers" (males from a wealthy country) and the "sellers" (women from an economically disadvantaged country). Women are treated as desirable goods because they (other than women from wealthy countries) have not been spoiled by feminism and they will focus mainly on the needs of the husband and children. A common theme among buyers is that Western women are too focused on themselves and fulfillment of their own needs and wants: "I am not happy with the existing relationships. I wanted something different. American women are too individualistic. Downside of feminism . . . I cannot really say that women's liberation and feminism really benefited family life."[55]

The brides are typically looking for a better life and the opportunity to fulfill their needs and wants. If they already have children, they may also want a better life for them. Very often, the brides will also see the opportunity to support their family in their home country, who may be very poor. Other females choose the matchmaker service because they are not a suitable wife in their culture due to age, having children, or being divorced. A few females stated that they had friends who had used the matchmaking service and were now in America.[56]

Most matchmaking services encourage the males to meet the females they have been communicating with quickly, and the Internet is a helpful facilitator through text messaging, FaceTime, Facebook, Twitter, etc. Agencies also offer tour dates where men pay on average $3,000 to $10,000 to attend a social event with many women.[57] The agencies are mainly concerned about their well-paying male clients, and the women are rarely protected from predatory clients.[58] Some agencies offer girls as young as 13 in their catalogues. Some organizations in the trafficking business have been linked to mail-order bride services where adult females are offered as brides. Instead of matching them to a male adult who wants to marry them, the women are sold into sexual exploitation or domestic slavery. Organized crime organizations use fiancé and marriage visas to bring the women into the United States.[59]

Mail-order bride services are regulated by the International Marriage Broker Regulation Act of 2005 (IMBRA). The main purpose of IMBRA was to address the issues of domestic violence and abuse. A report by the Government Accountability Office found, however, that many of the provisions meant to protect women have not been implemented fully. Women continue to be vulnerable to abuse as long as protective measures are not followed and as long as large power differentials between the buyers and sellers exist.[60]

Cyberbullying

FIGURE 4.2 ● Cyberbullying Statistics

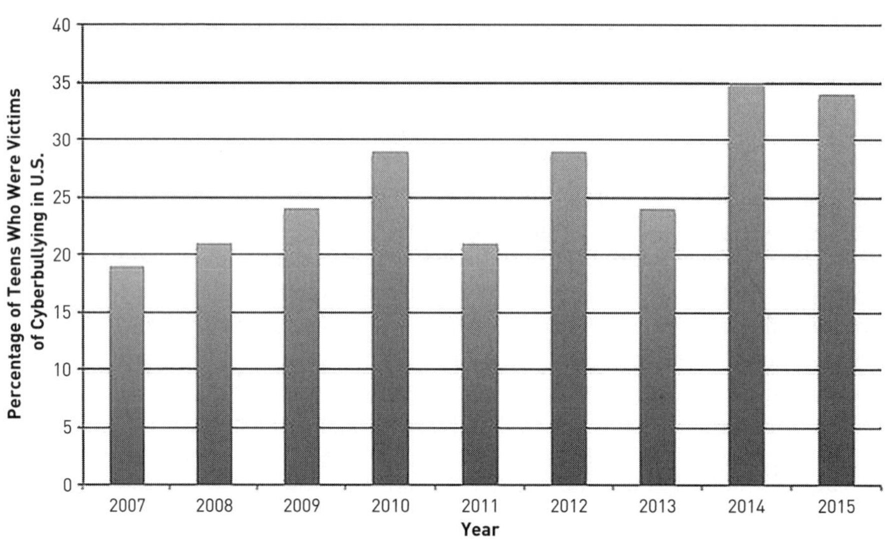

Source: Cyberbullying by Year by Erwcastro1. Licensed under CC BY-SA 4.0, https://creativecommons.org/licenses/by-sa/4.0/legalcode.

Cyberbullying is defined as "intentional, aggressive behavior toward another person that is performed through electronic means (i.e., computers, cell phones, PDAs)."[61] Academics have not yet agreed on whether cyberbullying has to involve multiple instances of aggression or if one instance, such as a single post on Facebook, is sufficient. Proponents argue that due to the large audience and the ability to view the post repetitively, a single post can have the same amount or more damage than repeated physical bullying. Cyberbullying, similar to traditional bullying, takes place within a larger group or community. Often, students are victimized in front of their entire class or school. Cyberbullying has similar negative consequences for the victim as traditional bullying, including depression, aggression, fear, lower life satisfaction, social anxiety, drug use, and suicide.[62] Many victims also experience physical illnesses such as stomachaches, sleep problems, headaches, bedwetting, fatigue, and poor appetite. Victims of cyberbullying may also suffer with negative effects on grades in school and work.[63] Cyberbullying is more complicated, as the offender may be anonymous and completely unknown to the victim. This appears to be the case in about half of the bullying incidents.[64] There are several online behaviors/methods that fall under the category of cyberbullying: (1) Harassment, (2) Cyberstalking, (3) Denigration, (4) Impersonation, and (5) Exclusion.

Cyberharassment

Cyberharassment "involves offensive messages by the perpetrator to the recipient (aka victim); flaming is the exchange of insults in a public setting, such as a bulletin board or chat room." The offender may post untrue or cruel rumors about another person on Facebook, Twitter, chat rooms, or some other social media outlet. This can then be read by all of their friends, classmates, or coworkers. In addition, the offender may send harassing e-mails threatening the victim. Instant messages are also a popular tool for such behaviors. High school students are one of the population groups where cyberbullying is rampant. Studies have consistently demonstrated that about 30% of high school students have received harassing messages. Research suggests that females are more likely than males to engage in cyberbullying. A possible reason is that females generally avoid physical confrontation, and by using the computer they can hide. The use of computers may also encourage more brazen behavior because there is less personal communication involved. An eye-to-eye conversation is very different from sending an e-mail or text. In fact, many people will write things in e-mails that they would not say to another person in a live conversation.[65]

Cyberstalking

Cyberstalking is difficult to define. Most definitions "typically include unwanted and repetitive behaviors which are perceived as intrusive, frightening, threatening, or harassing." Antistalking legislation requires that the offender's behavior cause a reasonable person to be fearful. Research shows that offline stalking and cyberstalking have similarities but also some differences. The most frequent category of cyberstalkers is ex-partners. Men are much more likely to be stalkers than females, and females have much higher victimization rates than males. More men report having been a victim of cyberstalking by a female as compared to offline stalking. It is possible that the online environment attracts perpetrators that otherwise would not engage in harassment. Females typically avoid physical confrontation. The online environment enables them to be confrontational without having to face another person. In general, it appears that the online environment facilitates intrusion-like behaviors. In one out of four cases, offline stalking and cyberstalking overlap—that is, the stalker engages in both behaviors. For instance, a stalker may follow the victim to her workplace and then send her a harassing or threatening text message letting her know that he followed her and will wait for her. The main motives for cyberstalking are jealousy, initiation of a love relationship, and revenge.[66]

Cyberstalking, similar to offline stalking, has substantial negative social, physical, and psychological consequences for the victim. More than half of the victims report feeling helpless, angry, and aggressive. Two thirds of the victims have difficulty sleeping and a feeling of distrust toward others. Many victims also suffer from physical consequences, especially concentration problems, stomachaches, and headaches. Psychological consequences include depression, panic attacks, and social withdrawal. Methods used by cyberstalkers are mainly e-mail, posting messages on social media, and spreading rumors about the victim.[67]

Currently, 49 states have statutes that specifically address cyberharassment, cyberstalking, or both. The states with the most comprehensive legislation are New Hampshire, Oklahoma, Oregon, and Utah. The only state that has no legislation prohibiting cyberharassment or cyberstalking is Nebraska. The Arizona statute covers only cyberharassment and is very vague, possibly too vague to protect victims in a meaningful way. Overall, there is a need for a comprehensive cyberharassment and cyberstalking legislation that details applicable behaviors and punishments.[68]

Online Denigration

Denigration is the posting of harassing messages about the victim aiming to cause harm to the victim. The main purpose of denigration is to damage the reputation of the victim. It is commonly used by students against school employees, such as administrators and teachers. Students who are upset with a school employee may post demeaning messages or "made up information" on social media or inside the school on bulletin boards. Bullies may also create hate websites where they may post pictures and abusive messages.[69]

Online Impersonation

Impersonation is also referred to as *imping,* which is the stealing and revealing of information under another person's name. The offender uses the identity of the target victim and posts unpopular messages on social networking sites. The offender uses the identity of the victim to make the victim a target of harassment by peers.[70]

Online Exclusion

Online exclusion "occurs when victims are rejected from their peer group and left out of technological communications."[71] This is especially common among students. The victims are being isolated by their peers and made an outcast. Exclusion is very effective because people in general, and especially children and adolescents, want to be recognized and liked by their peers. Being excluded from the group can be devastating for a person.[72]

Tools Used

Social Media

Facebook, Twitter, MySpace, WhatsApp, iPhones, and similar tools and devices are widespread communication instruments. They are also used for all types of cyberbullying by sending harassing messages, pictures, and other media. Teenagers who are dating often use text messages to send pictures to each other, some of which may be pornographic in nature. These pictures can then be distributed to any contact in the address book. The purpose of distributing such pictures is to embarrass the victim.[73]

For instance, 13-year-old Hope Witsell had sent a nude picture to a boy she liked. Another girl, who found the picture on the boy's phone, sent it to other students, and the picture made its way to other schools. Hope received harassing and demeaning messages calling her a "whore" and "slut." When the school found out, they suspended her from school for one week. A few days later, on September 12, 2009, Hope hanged herself in her bedroom.[74] Unfortunately, this is not an unusual story and sexting is widespread among school students. Sexting is the "sending or forwarding nude, sexually suggestive, or explicit pictures on a cell phone or online." Research has found that about 24% of 14- to 17-year-olds engage in sexting.[75]

YouTube

The posting of videos of unsuspecting victims taken in showers, locker rooms, store dressing rooms, and in other compromising situations are a growing concern for communities, schools, and law enforcement. Videos can be e-mailed or texted to others, and they can also be posted on YouTube for everyone to see.[76]

Tyler Clementi, a violinist and student at Rutgers University in New Jersey, killed himself by jumping off the George Washington Bridge in September 2010. His roommate had set up a webcam and streamed Clementi having sex with another man, thereby exposing that Clementi was gay. Two days later, Clementi's roommate streamed another video and sent a tweet saying, "Anyone with iChat, I dare you to video chat me between the hours of 9:30 and 12. Yes it's happening again." Some 150 people were watching. The next day, Clementi posted on Facebook "Jumping off the gw bridge sorry."[77]

YouTube has also been used by victims of cyberbullying to record their odyssey. Amanda Todd, a 15-year-old Canadian student, made a soundless black and white video before she killed herself in her parents' home in October 2012. Her video starts with "I'm Amanda Todd. I'm here to tell you about my never ending story." One of her friends asked her to flash on video . . . and she did. That was the beginning of her never-ending suffering. One year after the video, a boy contacted her and told her that he would send the pictures to all of her schoolmates if she did not put on a show. The boy knew her address, friends, family, and school. During Christmas break, police came to her house at 4 a.m. and told her that her flash picture had been sent to everyone. Amanda says she got really sick and depressed, and moved to another school. But the boy found her and started again, telling everyone about her picture. No matter where she moved, he followed her and continued to post harassing and threatening messages. She got beaten by another girl at her school, tried to kill herself by drinking bleach, and when she came home from the hospital she saw this message on Facebook: "She deserved it. Did you wash the mud out of your hair? I hope she's dead." Amanda moved back to her mom's home, but the bullying continued for another 6 months—until she killed herself.[78]

Gaming

Gaming is the "running of specialized applications known as electronic games or video games on game consoles like Xbox and PlayStation or on personal computers."[79]

Gaming has become a giant industry and a way to socialize with players around the globe. These games have evolved into elaborate worlds where players merge with this new reality. Many children and teenagers play games online, engage with other players in guilds and clans, and are therefore also exposed to cyberbullying.[80] There are websites dedicated to gaming, and many of the popular gaming consoles, such as PlayStation and Xbox 360, allow their users to play together with others online. These games have significantly contributed to cyberbullying. The ability to bully another player depends on the interface of the game. Games that allow for chats are more likely to foster cyberbullying than games that only have gaming interactions. Online gaming often requires some type of role playing where players take on the persona of a certain character, such as a bad guy who uses violence to accomplish certain goals set by the game. This type of role playing can be very addictive, and behaviors used in the game can be applied in real life. This includes bullying behaviors. Research has linked prevalence for violent games to hostility and cyberbullying behaviors. This is not surprising considering that aggressive behavior toward other players is rewarded within the game, leading to higher-rank status.[81] In a study of online gamers, 25% of the players reported having been the victims of cyberbullying, and 22% reported that they had bullied someone else once or twice. Males were more likely to be bullies than females, and females and lesbian, gay, bisexual, and transgender players were more likely to report sexual-related incidents of cyberbullying.[82]

Another problem associated with gaming is so-called griefers. Griefers are "those who make use of online games as a way to target children and sometimes even adults while they are taking part in online gaming." Griefers target other gamers purposefully and send harassing messages under the cover of the game. They may say that it's part of the game. Other may abuse the anonymity online gaming offers and gang up with other players against the victim.

Impersonation can also be a tactic in gaming. By stealing another player's password and logging into his or her account, the bully can send harassing messages to the friends of the victim, isolating the victim and making him or her a target. The bully could also change the password, locking the victim out (exclusion) and making it look like he or she does not want to be part of the game anymore. Players may also spread viruses to the target player. By including links in the chats, the victim may inadvertently download a virus that can disable or destroy the player's computer.[83]

CASE STUDY 4.2

Cyberbullying and Suicide

There are many cases of suicide due to cyberbullying that have made the news. Some of these remain in the headlines either because family members started an antibullying foundation or simply because of the horrific details of the case. One of those cases was that of Megan Meier. Meier, a 13-year-old teenager, met 16-year-old Josh online via MySpace. At the time, Megan suffered from attention deficit disorder, depression, and weight issues. Megan and Josh chatted regularly via MySpace but never met in person. Megan believed that Josh really cared about her and believed that she was pretty. Over time, Josh's messages to Megan became hostile and demeaning. He told her he did not want to be friends anymore and "that the world would be a better place without her." Other classmates started to post mean messages about Megan on MySpace. After reading these messages, Megan went into her room and hanged herself in the closet. Investigations by the police found that Josh was actually the mother (Lori Drew) of one of her classmates.[84]

Research on the consequences of cyberbullying shows that 20% of the victims seriously considered suicide. Cyberbullying victims are twice as likely as youth who were not bullied to have attempted suicide. Cyberbullying victims also often had other emotional and social issues. These issues typically contributed to their victimization by making them an easy target.[85]

What Do You Think?

1. If you were the prosecutor, would you charge Lori Drew with a crime?
2. If yes, what crime would you charge her with? Explain. If not, explain why you would not charge her.

Summary

The purpose of Chapter 4 is to provide a good understanding of the most common cybercrimes committed for financial gain. These crimes include ransomware attacks, data theft, pornography, trafficking, and mail-order brides. The chapter also covers cybercrimes committed for reasons other than financial gain, such as cyberbullying, denigration, and impersonation. The consequences for the victims are often lifelong, and victims feel victimized over and over because the images and statements stay online forever. Cyberbullying is now one of the top priorities of the FBI and the National Institute of Justice. There is also much focus on combating child exploitation. The success is limited due to the difficulty of tracing down the perpetrators, jurisdictional issues, and the inability or reluctance of victims to report the crime. There have been increasing efforts in cooperative law enforcement between the United States and Europe. However, as in everything else, demand drives the supply, and as long as there are so many perpetrators demanding child pornography and other forms of child exploitation, the supply will surely continue.

Key Terms

- Botnets 72
- Child Pornography 74
- Consumer Crimes 66
- Cyberharassment 82
- Cyberbullying 82
- Cyberstalking 83
- DDoS Attack 72
- Denigration 82
- Gaming 85
- Griefer 86
- Identity Theft 66
- Impersonation 82
- Logic Bomb 73
- Mail-Order Brides 80
- Malware 65
- Online Exclusion 84
- Phishing 66
- Snuff films 74
- Spam 66
- Trafficking 78

Discussion Questions

1. From what you have learned from the text, discuss how you would prioritize Internet sex crimes if you were the head of the Internet Sex Crime Task Force.
2. Discuss why logic bomb attacks are so difficult for companies to prevent.
3. Discuss how the new media outlets such as text messages, e-mail, Facebook, Twitter, and YouTube are used in cyberbullying and what prevention measures could be taken by schools to protect students from cyberbullying.
4. Discuss how parents can protect their children from Internet-facilitated sex offenses.
5. Discuss how online gaming may be contributing to cyberbullying. What can parents do to protect their children from being victimized?

Internet Resources

Federal Trade Commission: Consumer Information Identity Theft
https://www.consumer.ftc.gov/features/feature-0014-identity-theft

STOP Cyberbullying
http://stopcyberbullying.org/what_is_cyberbullying_exactly.html

Computer Fraud and Abuse Act
https://www.law.cornell.edu/uscode/text/18/1030

Amanda Todd Story Full Documentary
https://www.youtube.com/watch?v=EKFr3TNMJ4k

Office of Sex Offender Sentencing, Monitoring, Apprehending, Registering and Tracking
http://www.smart.gov/sorna.htm

Project Kesher
http://www.projectkesher.org/trafficking.html

Norse Cyber Attack Map (live map)
http://map.norsecorp.com/#/

Operation Predator
https://www.ice.gov/predator

Further Reading

2016 Norton Cyber Security Insights Report. https://us.norton.com/cyber-security-insights

Federal Bureau of Investigation—Internet Crime Complaint Center. https://www.ic3.gov/crimeschemes.aspx

New Bullying Data—and Definition—From the National Crime Victimization Survey. http://cyberbullying.org/new-bullying-data-definition-national-crime-victimization-survey

Digital Resources

Want a better grade?

Get the tools you need to sharpen your study skills. Access practice quizzes and eFlashcards, at **study.sagepub.com/kremling**.

Threats to Cybersecurity by Hacktivists and Nation-States

Learning Objectives

1. Be able to explain local, national, and international threats to cybersecurity.
2. Explain the threats that nation-states pose to cybersecurity.
3. Discuss threats to cybersecurity by terrorist groups.
4. Distinguish between the different types of hackers.
5. Discuss what motivates hackers.

THINK ABOUT IT 5.1

Cyberattacks on the Power Grid

Imagine waking up in darkness, turning on the light switch but no light; looking at the alarm clock but it's off; going in the dark into the kitchen to find the refrigerator without power and the climate control not working; trying to open the garage door but it's not moving; looking out the window and everything is completely dark. This is what happens when a cyberattack takes out the electric system. In 2007, a cyberattack on the electric system plunged 3 million people in Rio de Janeiro into darkness for 2 days. Subway trains and elevators

(Continued)

(Continued)

stopped, traffic signs went off, and the largest energy producing dam, the Itaipu Dam, had to shut down. To this day, the Brazilian government denies that a cyberattack was responsible for the power outage, but cybersecurity experts appear to agree that the power grid was taken down by a denial-of-service attack.[1]

What Would You Do?

1. What do you think would be consequences in your city and your life if power went out for several days?
2. Why would Brazil, and other governments, deny having been the victim of a cyberattack?

The purpose of this chapter is to provide an overview of the different types of threats posed by nation-states and hacktivists. The following three chapters go into greater detail with regard to cyberespionage, cyberterrorism, and the role of the dark web.

Threats to cybersecurity are constant and all encompassing—that is, nobody is safe from becoming a victim, including the FBI and other government agencies. The threats originate from a variety of actors, some from individuals or groups who engage in cybercrime for the "thrill," "challenge," or "money," and others from nation-states and groups associated with nation-states with the intent to destroy important infrastructures such as power grids, water supplies, hospitals, and law enforcement. The dangers of these cyberattacks are manifold, ranging from stealing sensitive data or holding it hostage to the possibility of blowing up a nuclear power plant, killing millions of people.

Reference Article

2015 Internet Crime Report

https://www.ic3.gov/media/annualreport/2015_IC3Report.pdf

According to the FBI's Internet Crime Complaint Center (IC3), the IC3 recorded its 3-millionth complaint on May 10, 2014, at 9:20 a.m. The total number of complaints in 2014 was 269,422 with a total loss of $800,492,073. Every month, the IC3 receives about 22,000 complaints. Considering the fact that only about 15% of victims report these crimes, the extent of cybercrime is enormous.[2] Some reasons why so few victims report the crime, even if they lost a considerable amount of money, include the low probability that the criminals will get caught and convicted, and the public exposure that could reduce trust in a company or organization. This is especially true for businesses for which the theft of data would put people's privacy at risk, such as retailers, banks, and hospitals.

Threats to Cybersecurity

Threats to cybersecurity originate from three sources: (1) local threats, (2) national threats, and (3) international threats. According to the Department of Homeland Security (DHS), a cyberthreat "refers to persons who attempt unauthorized access to a control system device and/or network using a data communications pathway."[3] Cyberthreats originate mainly from hacktivists, hackers, foreign governments, military units, terrorists, industrial spies, and organized crime groups.

Reference Table

The DHS has developed a GAO Threat Table, which provides a short description of each cyber threat group.

https://ics-cert.us-cert.gov/content/cyber-threat-source-descriptions

Local Threats

Local threats are threats that originate from inside the company or organization. These insider threats are very difficult to combat. Insider threats are defined as "harmful acts that trusted insiders might carry out; for example, something that causes harm to the organization, or an unauthorized act that benefits the individual."[4] An insider threat manifests itself as "human behavior that departs from compliance with established policies, regardless of whether it results from malice or a disregard for security policies."[5] Insiders are people who are current or former employees of a company. These current and former employees have much knowledge about how the company operates, the computer systems, vulnerabilities, and accessibility. Insiders can also be people who have in other ways, possibly as contractors, obtained information about the company that enables them to break into the computer system. They often either know login information and passwords or have friends inside the company who may provide them with access to the computer systems. According to national surveys, these insiders are the second-greatest threat to a company's cybersecurity, only trumped by hackers.[6]

Some of the most common insider cybersecurity crimes are accessing and/or stealing sensitive information, fraud, violation of copyright laws, and negligent use of classified information. The most serious insider cybercrimes include cyberespionage, sabotage, terrorism, embezzlement, extortion, bribery, and corruption.

Most companies are ill prepared for insider threats because they are mainly concerned about attacks into their computer system from the outside and therefore protect only their network border.[7] Companies also believe that it takes substantial computer skills to steal or expose information, or delete or alter data. This is not necessarily true when all it usually takes to get into a data bank is a password. Employees often trust each other and may share passwords and other information that should not be shared. Companies also often give all employees unrestricted and unnecessary access to information. Even employees with low skills can easily steal, leak, or sell information that is highly sensitive.

Types of Insider Threats

There are three main types of insider threats: (1) malicious insiders, (2) exploited insiders, and (3) careless insiders. Malicious insiders are the least common but the most costly because they strategically cause data breaches, often with the goal to cause great damages. Exploited insiders are people who are "tricked" by others into giving up access information or into accessing information themselves and giving the information to an external party. Careless insiders may delete or expose sensitive information by accident, by either pressing a wrong key or other mistakes.[8]

FIGURE 5.1 ● Insider Threat

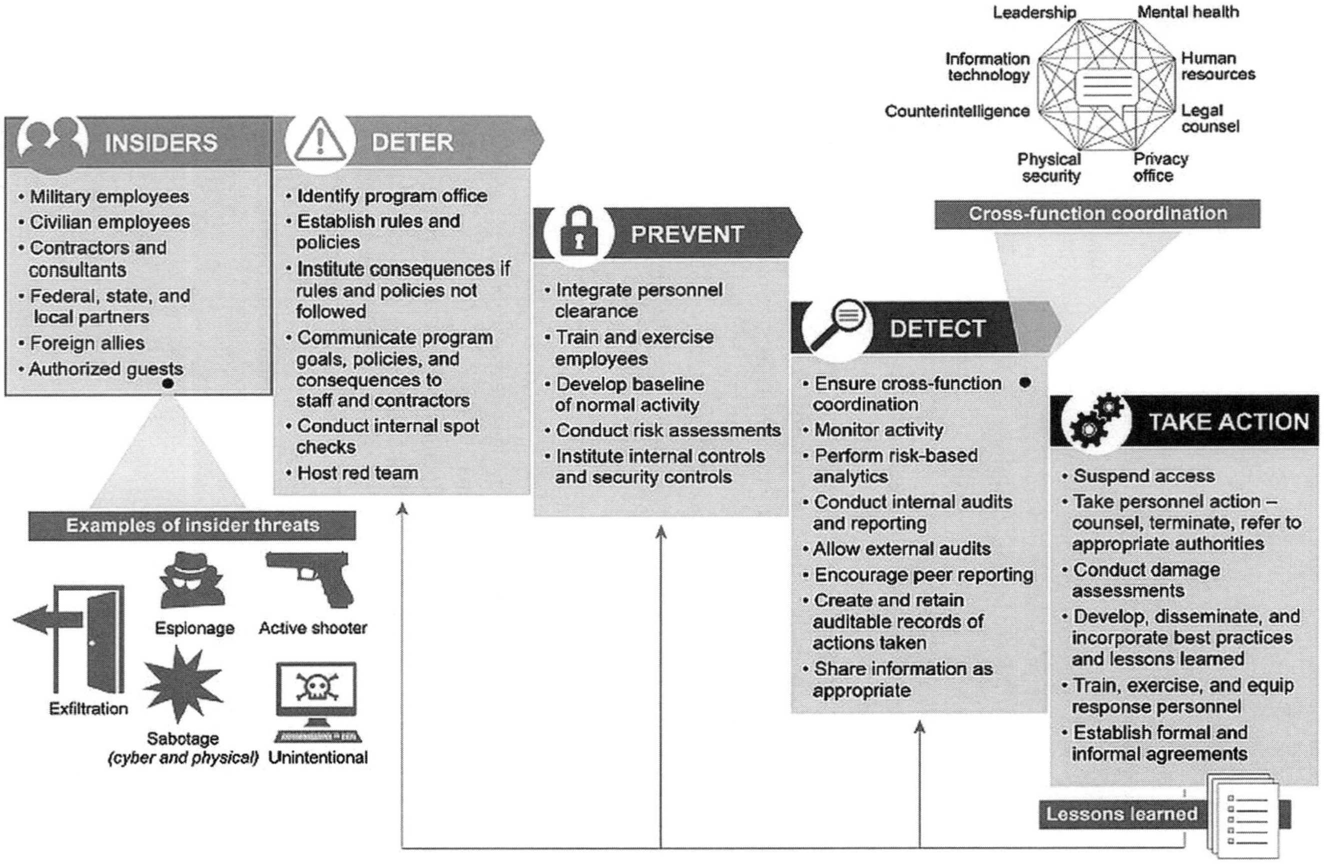

INSIDERS

- Military employees
- Civilian employees
- Contractors and consultants
- Federal, state, and local partners
- Foreign allies
- Authorized guests

Examples of insider threats

Exfiltration
Espionage
Active shooter
Sabotage *(cyber and physical)*
Unintentional

DETER

- Identify program office
- Establish rules and policies
- Institute consequences if rules and policies not followed
- Communicate program goals, policies, and consequences to staff and contractors
- Conduct internal spot checks
- Host red team

PREVENT

- Integrate personnel clearance
- Train and exercise employees
- Develop baseline of normal activity
- Conduct risk assessments
- Institute internal controls and security controls

DETECT

- Ensure cross-function coordination
- Monitor activity
- Perform risk-based analytics
- Conduct internal audits and reporting
- Allow external audits
- Encourage peer reporting
- Create and retain auditable records of actions taken
- Share information as appropriate

Cross-function coordination

Leadership
Mental health
Information technology
Human resources
Counterintelligence
Legal counsel
Physical security
Privacy office

TAKE ACTION

- Suspend access
- Take personnel action – counsel, terminate, refer to appropriate authorities
- Conduct damage assessments
- Develop, disseminate, and incorporate best practices and lessons learned
- Train, exercise, and equip response personnel
- Establish formal and informal agreements

Lessons learned

Source: Government Accountability Office.

The Computer Emergency Response Team at Carnegie-Mellon University has noted that traditionally insider threats only included current or former employees, but with growing business networks and partnerships, insider threats now also include business partners and other trusted persons.

LEGAL ISSUE 5.1

CORPORATE ESPIONAGE—INSIDE SECURITY BREACH AT AMSC

American Semiconductor Corporation (AMSC), a developer of wind turbine control software, was the victim of insider theft through one of their software engineers, Dejan Karabasevic. Karabasevic was solicited by AMSC's biggest client, the Chinese-based company Sinovel Wind Group, China's second-biggest wind energy company.

Sinovel made a deal with Karabasevic to steal the proprietary source code for the purpose of reverse engineering the software. The theft of the source code allowed Sinovel to engineer their own hardware to operate the wind turbines, and AMSC lost its biggest customer. Subsequently, AMSC stocks dropped by 84% from $370 to $5 per share and 600 employees lost their jobs.[9]

AMSC sued Sinovel in a Chinese court. In the midst of the court proceedings, AMSC was attacked by hackers using an advanced malware. It is likely that the attack was carried out by the People's Liberation Army Unit 61398 in an effort to get information about AMSC's legal position and strategy.[10]

In April 2015, the Beijing Intermediate People's Court dismissed the charges against Sinovel's U.S.-based subsidiary, Sinovel Wind Group (USA) Co., Ltd., but not its Chinese parent, Sinovel Wind Group Co., Ltd. The U.S. government charged two of Sinovel's executives and Karabasevic with conspiring to steal and actually stealing trade secrets, copyright infringement, and wire fraud. Sinovel argues that they are not subject to prosecution in the United States because they are based in China. This also includes Sinovel USA.[11]

What Do You Think?

1. Why did the U.S. government only serve Sinovel's U.S.-based subsidiary, Sinovel Wind Group (USA) Co., Ltd., and not its Chinese parent, Sinovel Wind Group Co., Ltd.?
2. If you were the attorney general for the U.S. government, how would you counter the argument by Sinovel that they cannot be prosecuted in the United States?
3. If you were AMSC, what would you learn from this incident and what strategies would you use to prevent insider threats in the future?

National Threats

National threats originate from individuals inside the United States aiming to attack local or national governments and infrastructures. These individuals are often displeased with the government and/or specific causes (i.e., antiabortion activism, animal rights activism, environmental activism).

Displeasure With the Government

Individuals who are displeased with the government may work independently or join together to form an organization. They typically launch cyberattacks in opposition of certain initiatives, bills, or laws. These groups are comprised

IMAGE 5.1 ● Anonymous

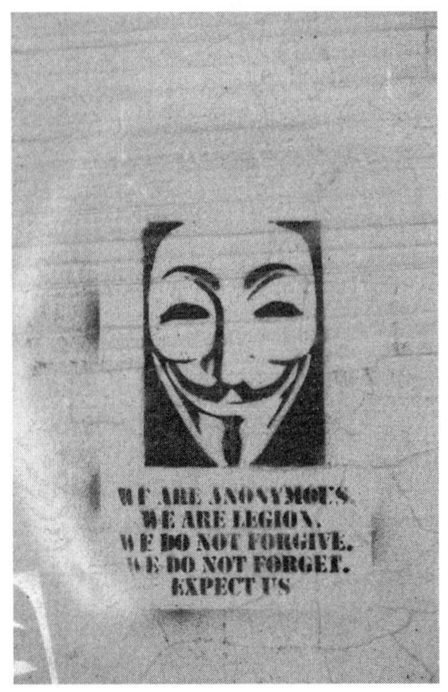

of individuals from different countries with a loose and decentralized demand structure. They operate mainly on ideas, and attacks may be planned and carried out by a few members. They operate in secrecy and have great media awareness. These groups are often motivated by the defense of freedom, free speech, privacy, individuality, and meritocracy.[12]

One of the most well-known hacker groups is "Anonymous," a global hacker community. As a protest to the Canadian antiterror bill, Anonymous launched a denial-of-service-attack on the web servers of the Canadian federal government. Anonymous flooded the website with requests, which resulted in a shutdown of the website.[13] In 2016, Anonymous took down a number of websites of the North Carolina state government as a response to House Bill 2 (HB2), also known as the "Bathroom Law," which is commonly regarded as an anti-LGBT law. HB2 requires people to use public bathrooms as per the gender of their birth.[14] Anonymous has attacked several other state governments and the federal government in opposition to political decisions that threaten civil rights. For instance, Anonymous has backed political activities such as the release of secret diplomatic cables by WikiLeaks and Occupy Wall Street. Members of the groups also hacked the U.S. Justice Department after the arrest of Internet hacktivist Aaron Swartz for state breaking and entering. Swartz had downloaded journal articles from JSTOR (an online journal article depository) using his Massachusetts Institute of Technology account and posted the articles on the Internet. The FBI charged him with wire fraud and violation of the Computer Fraud and Abuse Act of 1986. Swartz was facing a fine of $1 million and 35 years in prison. In protest of this prosecutorial overreach Anonymous launched a denial-of-service attack (DOS) against the Department of Justice. Swartz committed suicide on January 11, 2013, while under the federal indictment.[15]

Specific Causes

There are numerous groups who launch cyberattacks trying to accomplish specific causes. These groups include the White supremacists, left environmentalists, animal liberation groups, and antiabortion groups. These groups can pose significant threats to critical infrastructures. For instance, the Earth Liberation Front has long opposed nuclear power plants and has been a continuing threat. If they were able to hack into a power plant control system and remotely operate the system, the consequences could be devastating. Another threat is attacks against Internet service providers (ISPs). In 1996, a hacker, allegedly a member of the White supremacists, disabled a Massachusetts ISP and destroyed parts of their record-keeping system. He signed with the threat "you have yet to see true electronic terrorism. This is a promise."[16]

Antiabortion groups are also quite active, using cyberattacks against abortion clinics and doctors. In April 2016, an antiabortion group hacked into the participant list of a Bowl-a-Thon sponsored by the National Network of Abortion Funds (NNAF), which raises funds for abortions and advocates for political and social change. The antiabortion group then sent e-mails with anti-choice propaganda to the registered participants. In addition, the antiabortion group flooded the NNAF website with fake donations intended to cause a DoS attack. As a result of the flooding of the website, the payment card processing site went down and people were not able to register. The goal of the DoS attack was to stop the ability to fundraise for the Bowl-a-Thon.[17] These are only a few examples of cyberattacks for specific causes. These attacks can have substantial negative consequences for organizations and the government, and people who depend on services provided by these organizations.

CASE STUDY 5.1

Edward Snowden—Going Dark

Edward Snowden, an American computer professional, worked for the CIA until 2013 when he leaked several thousand documents with National Security Agency surveillance information about U.S. citizens and foreign governments and citizens to WikiLeaks. Snowden's revelations not only showed the complete surveillance of Americans but a large part of the globe. Snowden, who is hiding in Russia from U.S. law enforcement (for charges of treason), also published his advice for keeping private information protected.

Snowden provided four tips on how to keep your data private:

1. Encrypt your phone calls and text messages. Using the free app Signal, customers can prevent anyone from listening to their conversations.
2. Encrypt your computer hard drive. If someone steals your computer, he or she would have all of your private information, including your address, children's pictures, and possibly your Social Security number, bank account numbers, and other information that would allow the criminal to steal your identity, harm your kids, or harm you in other ways.
3. Use a password manager to create and store unique passwords. If someone steals your password and you have used it for several purposes, which most people do, criminals can access all of that information. For instance, if you use the same password for your different banking accounts or credit cards, the thief would be able to access all of your bank accounts.
4. Use two-factor identification, such as using a password and a fingerprint or other physical device. This makes it significantly harder for criminals to access your data. The U.S. government already uses multifactor identification for digital accounts as part of the White House initiative "kill the password." This initiative funds several private projects working on the development of password alternatives.[18]

International Threats

International threats originate in individuals outside the United States. International threats take three main forms: (1) nation-states hacking or spying on trade and other secret information, (2) advanced hackers aiming at large corporations, and (3) terrorists looking to identify and exploit vulnerabilities in our infrastructures and to infiltrate military and government systems.

1. *Nation-states hacking or spying on trade and other secret information*

Nation-states pose a significant threat to the United States as they are educated and well-funded operatives with very specific targets and strategies. These states do not need to have the most sophisticated technology, especially if they are capable of launching a large number of attacks in a short period of time. These states may use brute-force attacks because they are inexpensive and relatively easy to carry out. One of the most persistent threats originated in China. China's military cyber unit 61398 has been credited with hacking attacks on hundreds of companies across more than 20 industries that have strategic value for China.[19] According to the DHS, Chinese military attacked 23 natural gas pipeline operators over a 6-month period, from December 2011 until June 2012. The Chinese cyberspies stole information that could sabotage U.S. gas pipelines by controlling and altering the operation of the pipelines.[20] The cyberthreat posed by nation-states is discussed in more detail in later sections.

2. *Advanced hackers aiming at a large corporation*

Advanced hackers are typically motivated by financial or political goals. Hackers who target financial institutions have turned increasingly to corporate espionage aiming to steal data that can be sold to third parties or used for insider trading. Financially motivated hackers may also engage in identity theft and money laundering. For instance, in 2015 nine men were arrested by the FBI for stealing sensitive data from the New York Stock Exchange for financial gain. Over a time frame of 5 years, dozens of rogue stock traders sent requests to hackers, working from the Ukraine, asking for specific news releases that were to be published. The stock traders used the information from the news releases for illegal insider trading purposes, that is, to buy and sell stock for illegal profits. Overall, the illegal profits totaled over $100 million for traders and hackers.[21]

There are also politically motivated advanced hackers, also called *hacktivists*, who target large corporations. Hacktivists "form a small, foreign population of politically active hackers that includes individuals and groups with anti-U.S. motives" The DHS classifies them as medium-level threats of carrying out damaging attacks. Hacktivists typically focus on isolated attacks for a specific cause.[22] Hacktivism may overlap with left- and right-wing online terrorism. For instance, in 2016, the Islamic State (IS) announced that they were targeting Facebook and Twitter as retaliation against the shutting down of militant Facebook and Twitter accounts. The IS message shows the CEO of Facebook, Mark Zuckerberg, and Twitter CEO, Jack Dorsey, with bullet holes and the statement:

- To Mark and Jack, founders of Twitter and Facebook and to their Crusader government. You announce daily that you suspended many of your accounts, and to you we say: Is that all you can do? You are not in our league.[23]

The message adds that for every account that is shut down, IS members will open 10 new accounts. A few weeks earlier, Twitter had announced the closure of more than 125,000 IS-related accounts. Research has shown that accounts that were shut down and then reopened had far fewer visits and much lower levels of activity. Twitter has also changed its terms of use to make it more difficult to reestablish such accounts by requiring a verified phone number or e-mail address.

Cyberattacks on big companies are typically well covered by the media, such as data breaches at Sony Corp., Target, and eBay. But cybercriminals increasingly target midsize companies with 500 to 2,500 employees. These companies are often unsuspecting because they believe that they are not of value for cybercriminals. That assumption is false, however. Cybercriminals perceive them as easy targets because these midsize companies typically do not have sophisticated cybersecurity technology and skilled staff. In 2014, more than half of the 26,000 targeted attacks took aim at midsize companies. Midsize companies, similar to large companies, store private information of customers and sensitive business information, including intellectual property. Data breaches can have serious consequences for those whose data was stolen and for the attacked business. The loss of the company's good reputation and customer loyalty may be the most costly for these businesses. Research on the economic costs of data breaches shows that it takes these businesses much time and effort to acquire new customers and reestablish their brand name. The reason for the lack of sophisticated cybersecurity measures relates to the costs. For many midsize companies, the costs of hiring a cybersecurity expert and purchasing software are too high. Thus, they may assign the cybersecurity responsibilities to their IT department, which is often already overworked and ill equipped to address cybersecurity threats.[24]

CASE STUDY 5.2

The Hacked Company Graveyard

"The larger the organization, generally, the greater its ability to absorb short-term impact."[25] Cyberattacks can not only cost companies time and money but they can literally kill a company. Small companies are much more vulnerable to such effects than large companies. The following are four examples of companies that either filed for bankruptcy or were bought off by another company.

1. Code Spaces

   Code spaces specialized in digital storage and project management. A hacker deleted all of the stored data, and the company went bankrupt in 2014.

2. Mt Gox

   Mt Gox was the biggest bitcoin exchange company. In 2014, the company went bankrupt after 850,000 bitcoins were stolen. The CEO Mark Karpeles was later arrested for embezzlement—that is, stealing the bitcoins.

3. DigiNotar

   DigiNotar experienced a hacking attack in 2011. Following the attack, the company

(Continued)

(Continued)

began issuing fraudulent certificates, which eventually led to its demise.

4. HBGary

HBGary was a small cybersecurity company. It got hacked by the group Anonymous and e-mails were stolen. A lack of trust in the company to provide effective cybersecurity resulted in its acquisition by the firm ManTech.

What Do You Think?

1. For each company, discuss some cybersecurity measures these companies should have implemented to prevent the breach or mitigate damages.

3. *Terrorist Threats to Infrastructures and Military and Government Systems*

Cyberterrorism has been defined in a variety of ways and is discussed in greater detail in Chapter 7. For the purpose of this chapter, cyberterrorism

- involves using computer networks and technologies as a means for conducting attacks, and targets critical national infrastructures or governmental assets, has a psychological, social, political or religious motive, causes harm to individuals or groups, or physically damages infrastructures or assets.[26]

Cyberterrorism attacks typically target the government or critical infrastructures, and they often take the form of denial-of-service attacks, cyberespionage, and cyberwarfare. Since the first cyberattacks in the early 90s, cyberterrorists have become much more sophisticated in their attacks. For instance, in 1997, communication of the U.S. Federal Aviation Administration with their control tower was shut down for 6 hours by a hacker from Massachusetts. In 2006, the Bureau of Industry and Security at the U.S. Commerce Department had to disconnect their computers from the Internet due to a cyberattack. The cyberattack successfully disabled employees to do their work.[27]

Cyberterrorism attacks on national infrastructures are an even greater threat. There is an abundance of targets, which, if attacked, could cause substantial damages to the U.S. population and economy. Especially vulnerable infrastructures are energy systems, emergency services, telecommunications, banking and finance, transportation, and water systems. In 2004, cyberterrorists attacked police emergency services, which resulted in fake calls and deployment of police to fake locations. In the case of a double attack, a cyber- and physical terrorist attack, police may not be able to respond quickly if they are deployed elsewhere.[28]

The Department of Defense is well aware of the threat posed by attacks against critical infrastructures, but more than 90% of networks and infrastructures are operated by the private sector and vulnerabilities are often not addressed comprehensively due to time constraints, costs, or lack of understanding of the risk.[29] Cyberterrorism is covered extensively in Chapter 7.

CASE STUDY 5.3

Inside the Office of Personnel Management Cyber Attack

The Office of Personnel Management (OPM) holds the confidential information for government officials, including their fingerprints, Social Security numbers, and background checks. In 2015, cyberhackers stole 5.6 million fingerprints from OPM. With the increasing use of biometrics to secure data, stealing fingerprints can have great negative consequences. Biometrics, and especially fingerprints, are now used for Apple iPhone identification or home security as well as some government labs. Currently, the use of biometrics is still very limited, but that could change in the future. The main problem with the theft of fingerprints is that whereas Social Security numbers and credit cards can be reissued, fingerprints cannot be changed. Many suspect that Chinese hackers are behind the attack, but there has been no official statement. As discussed in earlier chapters, attribution of cyberattacks to the actual criminals is very difficult, even with the most technologically advanced resources.[30]

In 2015, OPM published a report that detailed which measures will be taken to ensure the security of the data. The report is accessible via https://www.opm.gov/cybersecurity/cybersecurity-incidents/opm-cybersecurity-action-report.pdf.

What Do You Think?

1. What makes our government vulnerable to cyberattacks?
2. Which measures is OPM taking to increase cybersecurity and avoid breaches of confidential information?

THINK ABOUT IT 5.2

Setting Up a Cyberheist

On February 4, 2016, the Bangladesh Central Bank noticed that they had been hacked and the fraudsters had stolen almost $1 billion. How exactly did the hackers set up this cyberheist? There were five steps the criminals had to accomplish. First, during the initial "setup," they had to establish bank accounts, which would later be used to hold the stolen money. In this case, the accounts were created in 2015 and left for more than a year. In addition, insiders at the bank inserted the password token for the Society for Worldwide Interbank Financial Telecommunication (SWIFT) server and left it there for several months to enable the criminals to access the server, plant a malware, and then issue fake transfer orders. This was the second step, the "intrusion." The intruders planted six types of malware to capture keystrokes and screenshots. Another malware delayed the detection of the transactions. The intrusion was made possible by actions of bank officials, some knowingly and some negligently. According to the investigators, several bank officials had knowingly created vulnerabilities to the bank's security system, and other employees had unwittingly helped in the heist by being negligent. For instance, IT technicians had connected the SWIFT system to the Internet, which made it accessible to anyone from the outside. In addition, the malware was

(Continued)

(Continued)

specific to the Bangladesh server system. The creation of such malware would not be possible without the help of insiders from the bank. The third step was the right "timing." February 4, a Thursday, was just a few days before February 8, the Chinese New Year. This was the most important day for the fraudsters because the casinos would have large amounts of money due to the celebrations by the Chinese. There would be much money in the bank at that time, allowing the criminals to steal a large amount of money in one day. The fourth step was the token for the hardware, which had been left inserted for several months, and a credential used by bank officials. The criminals either received the credential from a bank official or captured credential passwords from the keystroke-capturing malware. The intruders placed 35 fake orders for a total of $1 billion. Of these 35 transactions, 30 were stopped by the Federal Reserve Bank of New York, but five transactions, each being about $20 million, went through. One transaction was moved through a bank in Sri Lanka and was stopped there because a bank clerk noticed a typological error in the order. A typological mistake in such an important order is very unusual and the transaction was stopped. The other four transactions were moved through a bank in the Philippines, however, who did not notice the error. The $81 million was then withdrawn from the bank and laundered through a net of prearranged criminal networks. Most of the money disappeared in Manila's loosely regulated casino system. This was the last step, the "subversion." Seven Filipino banks have been accused of money laundering. By December 2016, the Bangladesh Central Bank had only recovered about $15 million. The rest remains lost in Manila's casino bank system.[31]

What Would You Do?

1. You can assume that the bank officials who knowingly helped the criminals were paid for their assistance. Do you think that everybody has a price—that is, that everybody can be bought to do illegal acts if the money is right?
2. If you were the CEO of the bank, how could you assure the security of the money in your bank? Research strategies against insider threats and propose some solutions.

Hackers

Evolution of the Term Hacker

The term *hacker* originates from the verb *hack*, a word that first appeared in the English language around 1200. It means "to cut with heavy blows in an irregular or random fashion."[32] The Jargon File, a computer programmer glossary launched in 1975, lists eight definitions that span a wide range of definitions of the word hack that have developed since then. Some of these are:

1. "Originally, a quick job that produces what is needed, but not well."
2. "An incredibly good, and perhaps very time-consuming, piece of work that produces exactly what is needed."
3. To bear emotionally or physically. "I can't hack this heat!"
4. "To pull a prank on."[33]

The term *hacking* is nowadays used for a variety of purposes and by a range of organizations, and has become an integral part of our popular culture: From advertising agencies who want to "growth hack," psychologists who want to "hack the happiness molecule," and companies like Yahoo who were recently "hacked," there appears to be an expanding and changing meaning of the word hacking.[34]

Thus, the words hacker and hacking are not limited to computer technologies or to negative actions. It was the Massachusetts Institute of Technology (MIT) that first used the term hacking in relation to solving a tech problem.[35] The term hacking had no negative connotation at that time but rather meant working on a tech problem in a more creative way. There are numerous definitions of the term hacker. The Jargon File lists eight definitions for the word hacker. Seven definitions have a positive connotation, and only the last one defines hacking as something malicious. The first definition defines hacker as "A person who enjoys exploring the details of programmable systems and how to stretch their capabilities, as opposed to most users, who prefer to learn only the minimum necessary." A second definition states that a hacker is "One who programs enthusiastically (even obsessively) or who enjoys programming rather than just theorizing about programming." The last definition defines what we now call the bad guys or criminal hackers: "A malicious meddler who tries to discover sensitive information by poking around. Hence password hacker, network hacker. The correct term for this sense is cracker."[36]

The Hacker Community

Sociological research shows that hackers congregate in global hacker communities defined by the network. They consider themselves to be part of an intellectual elite because they have greater computer-related abilities than the average person. Hacker communities function similar to other social groups by providing expertise, support, and training opportunities via regular communication but also by publishing in journals and organizing conferences—something we consider academic activities. Hacker communities also have certain characteristics that distinguish them from other social groups. Typically, hacker communities are male dominated and work anonymously and secretly. The members may never meet each other or know each other's true identities, but they often have a common cause. To hide their true identity, members may create several public identities that serve the purpose of masking their real identity. Hackers may also have "handles," such as Hack-Tic, Faustus, or Mercury, to hide who they are. Even though anonymity and secrecy are a necessary part of their life and work, they have to share and publicize information to gain recognition within the hacker community and get credit for their "hack." Not all hackers are equally capable, and gaining status in the hacker community requires proof of successful hacks. Thus, hackers may keep trophies from successful hacks (i.e., documents, etc.) or sign their hacks to prove what they accomplished and for their own satisfaction. These trophies and signatures can become a liability if the police find them in a search because these trophies constitute hard evidence of their involvement in a criminal act. Gail Thackery, Arizona's top cybercrime cop stated, "What other groups of criminals . . . publish newsletters and hold conventions."[37]

"Black Hats," "White Hats," and "Gray Hats"

There are many myths and stereotypes about hackers. Many believe the stereotype of the lone hacker. In reality, many hackers belong to hacker communities, and many conventional crime groups and nation-states are now using technology for their criminal acts. Researchers have classified hackers into "black hats," "white hats," and "gray hats." Even though these categories are presented as distinct, it is likely that hackers cross over into another category when they believe it is necessary.

Black Hats The black hats are the "bad guys," and they receive most of the media attention. They are criminals who intercept online communications, steal information and data, plant malware in computers, or engage in consumer scams such as phishing. Black hats are typically motivated by personal gain or by a certain cause. For instance, stealing personal data such as credit card information can be used to buy goods or services and even taking out a mortgage or loan. At other times, black hats may plant malware because they oppose the website content or business. They may also cause economic damage to major national infrastructures.[38]

Black hats may work together to accomplish their goal by communicating about Internet security of industrial systems and successful strategies on breaking these security measures. Even though hackers have broken into industrial control systems of utility companies for decades, little is known about how the hackers are getting into the systems. The main reason for the lack of information is the underreporting by companies of these acts. Most companies never report a security breach because it would likely result in negative publicity and damage to their reputation. One known strategy of hackers is to look for accident reports of industrial control systems and exploit the weaknesses apparent in these reports. It is also known that the attackers are generally way ahead of the defense or cybersecurity measures.[39]

According to Kaspersky Lab, attacks on critical national infrastructure such as power plants or water supply systems are the greatest threat. One of the reasons why these infrastructures are vulnerable is that important security updates aren't always performed if it means interrupting service. For instance, if a power plant that provides power to millions of people needs to shut down for several hours, it will cause great problems for those who are without power. Since the power plant company is well aware of the negative consequences of shutting down, they are reluctant to do so for the purpose of installing security updates. The power plant company may also have to pay fines for shutting down service. Some companies also use cheaper systems or older systems to save costs, which are significantly more vulnerable to security breaches.[40] Black hats look for and take advantage of such vulnerabilities.

White Hats White hats are regarded as "ethical hackers." They use their abilities for legal purposes by researching vulnerabilities in software products and disclosing them to the companies who developed the software. White hats are often hired by companies to test computer security systems and help improve cybersecurity measures. Some companies pay "bounties" or "prices" for discovering and revealing security vulnerabilities. With the increasing complexity of web applications, white hats may also be asked to do "social engineering." Social engineering is "any act that influences a person to take an action that may or may not be in their best interest." Examples of social engineering are attempts to gather personal information by pretexting as another person ("impersonation"), sending e-mails pretending to be a reputable source such as the IRS ("phishing"), or soliciting information via the telephone ("vishing" or "phone spoofing").[41]

Gray Hats Gray hats typically work independently to expose security vulnerabilities or practices that endanger individuals' private data. They may be considered hackers for hire, engaging in both black- and white-hat hacking; they go where the money is. Gray hats may have good intentions, but by hacking into a security system without permission they commit illegal acts that are punishable by law. Also, gray hats may expose the company's security flaw to the public rather than privately to the company itself, thereby causing negative publicity and concerns among customers. Gray hats may help law enforcement in cases where white hats may refuse to assist. One of the most discussed cases was the Apple iPhone case in 2016.[42]

The Internet and the Transparent Citizen

The Internet has contributed greatly to the collection and storage of personal data. Anyone can look up where registered sex offenders live in their neighborhood or whether their new date has ever been arrested and convicted of a crime. Employers can order background checks and search social websites like Facebook for private information from their applicants or current employees, such as weekend activities. This information can have detrimental effects on someone's career. The possibilities are endless, and the ability of citizens to keep private information private becomes more difficult as new technologies and services develop. It is almost impossible to be invisible, even for people who are very careful.

In this sense, then, we have become "transparent citizens," and our reliance on the Internet as a social and business portal has exposed us to a growing number of cyberthreats including data breaches, tax fraud, cyberespionage, political hacktivism, and identity theft. The number of cyberthreats increases as more and more people and businesses use the Internet. Marketing companies collect customer profile information to send targeted advertising, banks offer online banking services, Amazon offers shopping for almost anything, and students can read textbooks online. All of these online activities require registering an account that holds your personal information.[43] Social websites like Facebook and Twitter let people share their life stories, everyday events, social activities, family pictures, love stories, break ups, etc. Even if the profile is made "private," the data is still on the Internet and the server of some company or in the cloud—accessible to law enforcement and criminals. It may have never been easier to reconnect with a long-lost friend, but it has also never been easier for law enforcement to conduct surveillance and for criminals to gather information.[44]

LEGAL ISSUE 5.2

PRIVACY VERSUS SECURITY

The Apple iPhone Case[45]

The rise of the transparent citizen also encourages anonymity of individuals or organizations that don't want to expose their private information.[46] Some may choose to create fake Facebook accounts to be able to participate in certain social or business groups that require a Facebook account. Others may go completely offline or only use tools and goods that are absolutely necessary, such as video conference calls or a smartphone. One of the main debates is about the issue of privacy versus security. Whereas law enforcement and the FBI argue that they should be able to access anyone's phone calls, e-mails, and other communications, tech companies (i.e., Apple, Facebook) and privacy rights advocates are saying that building a "backdoor" into devices for law enforcement use will also open the door for criminals. The iPhone case of the San Bernardino shooting divided the nation along those lines: privacy versus security. Apple insisted on keeping iPhone data private and refused to develop software that would break the iPhone encryption of the San Bernardino shooter. The FBI eventually hired professional hackers who were paid a flat fee to find a software flaw in Apple's iPhone that could be used to hack the phone. The FBI used at least one gray-hat hacker, which raises eyebrows among those who consider gray hats unethical hackers.

Now that the FBI has the tools to break into iPhone 5s that run OS9, one of the main questions is whether they should tell Apple what the software flaw is. A White House working group is addressing this question. Supporters of giving Apple the information state that the economy and government of the United States more than that of any other country depend on the digital infrastructure. Businesses and government agencies must be able to communicate information safely, and vulnerabilities are vulnerabilities for all. If the FBI can pay a hacker to break the iPhone, so can governments of hostile countries who want to harm the U.S. economy and government. Thus, it is in the interest of the United States to provide information about vulnerabilities to the companies that produce software. Opponents of giving Apple the information state that if they give Apple the information, Apple will fix the problem, making it more difficult or possibly impossible for law enforcement to catch the next terrorist or criminal. It's an ongoing debate that is unlikely to end.

What Do You Think?

1. If you were the CEO of Apple, how would you have responded to the request to unlock the iPhone of the San Bernardino shooter?
2. List pros and cons for the company and your customers.

What Motivates Hackers?

One of the most popular tourist attractions in Bali, Indonesia, is the Ubud Monkey Forest. The forest has about 600 species of wild monkeys who have been around tourists their entire lives. Their experience from interacting with the tourists has taught them some invaluable lessons. First, get the bananas the tourists likely bought at the entrance. If they don't give out the bananas easily, attack. Tourists get bitten by monkeys in the forest on a daily basis. Second, steal something valuable from the tourists and only return it for a ransom, either bananas or something else. The monkeys learned to be extortionists and may also have gone through some "training" by the forest guards. The following is a review from a tourist who visited the monkey forest.

> Even though the place itself had truly amazing views, the total experience was really negative because of the aggressive, trained-to-steal monkeys! It was really obvious, that there was always a guy next to the stealing monkey to "help" you to get your stuff (glasses, cameras, mobiles etc.) back, but it was evident that the monkeys seemed to know the guys and practi cally handed the stuff back to them—and you payed the "savers" for their "effort."[47]

This is not an unusual occurrence but rather normal at Ubud Monkey Forest. The monkeys are extortionists, and they also seem to know who to target. What motivated the monkeys to attack and steal? Were they evil monkeys, or did they just want something? How did they decide which people to attack?

This question is very similar to the question of what motivates hackers. Herbert Thompson developed the term *hackernomics* and defined it as "social science concerned chiefly with the description and analysis of hacker motivations, economics, and business risk."[48] Thompson developed five laws that apply to hackers. First, hackers are not evil people, but rather they attack because they want something. Very similar to the extortionist monkeys, hackers look for weak targets and exploit their vulnerabilities.

We may not be able to secure all systems against evil people, but we can protect systems against hackers looking for an easy target.

Second, security is not about security—it is about mitigating the risk of an attack. The absence of metrics on cyberattacks, targets, and damages has led to an overreliance of known and recent risks. The greatest threats, however, are the unknown risks.

THINK ABOUT IT 5.3

Why Do People Have a House Alarm?

Most people who have a home security system want to protect themselves from burglars and other possible criminals. Most people are also well aware that a home security system will not stop a criminal who really wants to get into the house. But it will deter criminals who are looking for an easy target.

What Would You Do?

1. Discuss the similarity between having a home security system and a cybersecurity system.
2. Discuss the motivations of a burglar and a hacker. What are similarities and differences?

Third, the greatest damages are not caused by genius hackers but by simple failures. For instance, simple failures include the opening of attachments not knowing whether these attachments include a malware. Another simple failure is the use of weak passwords, such as "password" or "1,2,3,4,5." Simple failures also stem from giving out passwords to other people.

TABLE 5.1 ● The 25 Most Common Passwords in 2016

1. 123456	14. 666666
2. 123456789	15. 18atcskd2w
3. qwerty	16. 7777777
4. 12345678	17. 1q2w3e4r
5. 111111	18. 654321
6. 1234567890	19. 555555
7. 1234567	20. 3rjs1la7qe
8. password	21. google
9. 123123	22. 1q2w3e4r5t
10. 987654321	23. 123qwe
11. qwertyuiop	24. Zxcvbnm
12. mynoob	25. 1q2w3e
13. 123321	

Source: 25 most common passwords in 2016 and how quickly they can be cracked. (2017, January 17). Retrieved from http://www.networkworld.com/article/3158213/security/25-most-common-passwords-in-2016-and-how-quickly-they-can-be-cracked.html.

Even though most data breaches are due to simple failures, motivated hackers can be very creative to accomplish a desired goal. For example, hackers were very diligent to find a strategy to crack CAPTCHAs. CAPTCHA stands for *Complete Automated Public Turing Test to Tell Computers and Humans Apart*. Thus, CAPTCHAs are programs designed to distinguish between a machine and a human. They have been used to authenticate users on websites such as banks, Google, and many other companies. The original CAPTCHA consisted of distorted text and numbers that cannot be read by machines. CAPTCHAs were invented by Luis Van Ahn when he was a graduate student at Carnegie Mellon University.[49] When CAPTCHAs were first used for authentication, cyberhackers tried to develop code that would read the distorted text. But that was not a successful strategy. Soon, other types of CAPTCHAs entered the market. One of the popular recent ones is the identification of pictures with certain characteristics, such as street signs or storefronts.

IMAGE 5.2 ● Captcha

Really?! by Matthew Ollphant, http://bit.ly/2pQWyh6. Licensed under CC BY-ND 2.0, https://creativecommons.org/licenses/by-nd/2.0/legalcode

When the hackers realized that a program was not a good solution, they came up with a solution that targeted the vulnerabilities of computer users: pornography. The hackers would bait a person with a pornographic image, but in order to get to the next image, the person had to fill in five CAPTCHAs. These CAPTCHAs were used in real time from websites/user accounts they were trying to access to steal confidential information. The hackers even had a quality-control mechanism built in. They would send the same CAPTCHA to different people and compare the answers to ensure that the answer was indeed correct. This strategy was a full success for the hackers.[50]

Fourth, without proper education and training, people naturally make bad decisions with regard to cybersecurity. Using technology securely is much more difficult than using it insecurely, and most users tend to ignore security guidelines when they really want something. The main issue to date is how to implement security into devices so that people will naturally use secure processes.

Fifth, most attackers don't have to crack some impenetrable security control to get into a system, but rather they use weak points to get access. Weak points may be employees who are not trained well in cybersecurity. For companies, the human factor is a main vulnerability, and more and more companies mandate cybersecurity training for their employees. This is also encouraged by the increased regulations and auditing of companies by regulators. Companies have learned that a hacker "may" get access to their computer system, but auditors "will" check on whether the regulations are being followed. The penalties for violating these rules can be hefty.[51]

LEGAL ISSUE 5.3

CALIFORNIA'S BREACH NOTIFICATION STATUTE

In 2003, California passed the first breach notification statute in the United States. The statute requires companies to inform people whose confidential information has been stolen. For instance, Yahoo was required by law to notify the millions of users whose account information had been breached in the 2013 and 2015 cyberattacks. Since 2003, California has amended the statute three times, with the latest amendment having been added in 2015. The 2015 amendment clarifies a number of terms. First, *personal information* now also includes data from automated license plate recognition systems, such as those used on toll roads. Second, the term *encryption* refers to "unusable, unreadable, or indecipherable to an unauthorized person through a security technology or methodology generally accepted in the field of information security." A final change was made to the actual notification letter, which must now have the title "Data Breach" and answer the following questions: "What Happened,"

(Continued)

(Continued)

"What Information Was Involved," "What We Are Doing," "What You Can Do," and "For More Information."[52]

What Do You Think?

1. What information do you consider "personal information"? Take a look at the statute to see if it covers all the things that you consider personal.
2. Discuss the purpose of requiring companies to notify people whose data has been breached.
3. What do you think has been the impact of the statute on companies?

Summary

The purpose of this chapter is to provide an overview of origins of the term hacker, different types of local and international threats posed by nation-states and hacktivists, and to discuss what motivates hackers. One of the greatest challenges for public and private agencies is the threat posed by insiders and hacktivists who commit targeted attacks, often with the goal to damage the company. Just as human behavior is a vulnerability, it is also an asset. White-hat hackers are working together with public and private agencies to protect individuals, companies, and critical infrastructures from hacktivists and nation-states. They work together with law enforcement to catch cybercriminals and gather evidence necessary to convict these criminals.

Key Terms

Black Hats 102
Brute-Force Attack 96
Cyberthreat 90
Cyberterrorism 90
Denial-of-Service Attack 90
Gray Hats 102
Hackernomics 105
Hacktivist 90
Impersonation 103
Insider Trading 96
Insider Threats 91
Internet Service Provider 94
Malware 93
Phishing 102
Phone Spoofing 103
Social Engineering 103
Transparent Citizen 103
Vishing 103
White Hats 102

Discussion Questions

1. Discuss how you can protect yourself from scams, such as the payroll scam discussed at the beginning of the chapter.
2. Discuss why victims of cybercrime are reluctant to report the crime to the police. How may this reluctance impact future decisions of cybercriminals? If you were the chief of law enforcement on a special unit for cybercrime, what would you do to increase the reporting of cybercrimes by victims?

3. Discuss the similarities and differences between local threats, national threats, and international threats to cybersecurity. If you had a company, how would you protect the company from cyberthreats?
4. Distinguish between black hats, white hats, and gray hats.
5. Discuss whether hacking could be considered "breaking and entering."
6. Look at the GAO threat table (see link provided) and discuss which groups you think pose the greatest cyberthreat. Explain your answer.

Internet Resources

Comprehensive National Cybersecurity Initiative
http://nsarchive.gwu.edu/NSAEBB/NSAEBB424/docs/Cyber-034.pdf

Internet Crime Complaint Center
https://www.ic3.gov/default.aspx

WikiLeaks
https://wikileaks.org/

Security Through Education
http://www.social-engineer.org

Further Reading

A Cyberattack on the U.S. Power Grid. http://www.cfr.org/cybersecurity/cyberattack-us-power-grid/p38941

Cyberespionage Is Reaching Crisis Levels. http://fortune.com/2015/12/12/cybersecurity-amsc-cyber-espionage/

Digital Resources

Want a better grade?

Get the tools you need to sharpen your study skills. Access practice quizzes and eFlashcards, at **study.sagepub.com/kremling**.

6 National Security

Cyberwarfare and Cyberespionage

Learning Objectives

1. Explain the motives of cyberwarfare.
2. Discuss the threats posed by economic and political cyberespionage.
3. Describe what cyberintelligence is and how it can be an effective tool in cybersecurity.
4. Discuss why denial-of-service (DoS) attacks are a substantial threat to national security.

In 2007, Israel hijacked Syria's Air Defense System to destroy a suspected nuclear materials site. The control of cyberspace by Israel via the use of malware was detrimental in accomplishing the mission. Some academics have referred to this as *cyberwarfare*. The RAND organization defines cyberwarfare as follows:

> Cyberwarfare involves the actions by a nation-state or international organization to attack and attempt to damage another nation's computers or information networks through, for example, computer viruses or denial-of-service attacks.[1]

In March 2007, agents from Israel's national intelligence agency, Mossad, swept the house of Ibrahim Othman, the head of the Syrian Atomic Energy Commission. They extracted computer files detailing Syria's nuclear program and left without a trace. These files would help Israel a few months later in their attack of a suspected nuclear materials site. Israel had grown suspicious of the Syrian atomic program because Syria had been trying to buy nuclear research reactors from Russia and Argentina in 2006. Due to pressure from the United States and Israel, the deal never materialized, but Syria continued to pursue its nuclear ambitions. The files extracted by the Mossad showed color pictures of a top-secret nuclear reactor inside a building under construction in the northeastern desert of Syria. Israel also found evidence that Syria had support from North Korea in their attempt to build an atomic bomb. Israel's Prime Minister Olmert and the Mossad began working on a plan to destroy the nuclear reactor. Israel's goal was to keep a low signature on the attack and minimize the potential of a response from Syria. Israel did not want to publicly corner Syrian's president Bashar al-Assad for violating his obligations to the International Atomic Energy Agency by building an atomic bomb. Assad had avoided a military confrontation with Israel in 2006, and Israel was hoping that he would do the same if Israel did not claim credit for the attack. Thus, the best strategy was to disable Syria's Air Defense System and leave as little evidence as possible. On September 5, 2007, several F-15s and F-16s entered the Syrian airspace and dropped 17 tons of explosives, destroying the nuclear reactor. Syria's response was as hoped by Israel. The Syrian Arab News Agency publicized an article stating that Israeli aircraft had entered the Syrian airspace but were forced to leave by Air Defense units. Syria also denied that they were working on an atomic bomb. They stated that the destroyed building was an unused military building.[2] How did Israel bypass the Syrian Air Defense System? The question has never been conclusively answered, but people from the U.S. aerospace industry and retired military officials believe that Israel used a program similar to the U.S. network attack system "Suter." This system hacked Syria's defense communication network and took control of the sensors that would spot their airplanes. By directing the sensors into directions where there were no airplanes, the system was effectively disabled without shutting it down.[3]

One of the oldest reasons for threats of harm by nation-states is power. Power historically depended on physical strength, or in the context of nation-states, on military strengths. The United States, Russia, China, and Europe have traditionally been the strongest actors in world politics due to their military strengths. These nations are also economically very powerful.

The emergence of cyberspace has contributed to a change in world politics because small actors and nation-states can pose serious threats to the largest powers.[4] In other words, cyberspace has reduced the power differential between nation-states and between nation-states and nonstate actors. This is also referred to as *power diffusion*. Small actors can cause significant damage by using power that comes from the access to information. Controlling the flow of information has become one of the greatest challenges for governments, companies, and private actors. For instance, gaining information about a certain military mission could put lives in danger and threaten the success of the mission. Imagine if Osama Bin Laden, the former leader of Al-Qaeda, had been able to access information about Operation Neptune Spear, the military operation carried out by the U.S. Navy SEALs, during which Osama Bin Laden was killed. The operation likely would have been unsuccessful. Similarly, imagine a crime organization gaining access to bank information, including customers' bank accounts, credit cards, loans, 401(k) plans, etc. The potential damage is difficult to grasp even for experts. It does not take great resources to launch cyberattacks to create, process, and transmit information because most information is accessible on computers, in clouds, or on other devices. The convenience of having important information at your fingertips also creates significant threats if the information falls into criminal hands, however. This chapter discusses the cyberthreats created by cyberwarfare, cyberespionage, cyberintelligence, and cybersabotage, and the various nation-states posing the greatest threats to cybersecurity.

Cyberwarfare

The attack by Israel on Syria at the beginning of this chapter demonstrates the potency of cyberattacks in conventional warfare. A similar attack could be launched against the United States by enemy states such as North Korea and Iran with an attempt to bomb major infrastructures or buildings.

Cyberwarfare generally includes cyberespionage and cybersabotage. According to Major General James D. Bryan of the U.S. Army, more than 40 nation-states have declared their intention to develop cyberwarfare capabilities. Cyberattacks have become a potent political instrument. The political motives vary by region and group, but a common goal is the protection of national sovereignty and power. Cyberattacks typically aim to gather sensitive information or destroy military or economic targets. These attacks occur mostly outside the public view, and many people may be quite unaware of the threat posed by cyberattacks. Cyberattacks do not make the news with dramatic images of bombings or fleeing civilians. Cyberattacks happen silently, and many governments and companies, especially financial institutions or hospitals, may not report attacks in fear of losing customers. The most pervasive cyberthreat may be the theft of intellectual property. This is a very serious problem, as the competitiveness of the U.S. economy and the effectiveness of the U.S. military depend on the integrity of intellectual property. The Department of Defense estimates that every year, intellectual property larger than what the Library of Congress can hold is stolen from businesses, universities, and government departments and agencies.[5]

Nation-State Threats by Region

This section examines three regions in this world in more detail to provide a better understanding of motives and the threat level posed by the actors in these regions. The cyberspace and technological advances in cyberespionage and cybercrimes have added a new layer to international relations and national security, increasing its complexities. Nation-states are interdependent in the global economy, and they work together closely to accomplish economic growth. At the same time, there is much distrust between nation-states with regard to political goals and the use of cyberattacks. Very often, it is impossible to clearly identify the attacker, and many attacks go undetected. Governments are well aware of these issues and thus spy on each other. The interconnectedness of these nation-states, however, also serves as a major deterrent to an outright cyberwar, as that could have devastating economic and political consequences. In this sense, warfare by cyberspace is not so different from warfare at land, sea, or air. There are many factors that discourage cyberwarfare similar to conventional warfare. Thus, cyberattacks focus mainly on the collection of sensitive data and disruption of services.[6]

Syrian Electronic Army

The Syrian Electronic Army (SEA) was established in May 2011, shortly after the prodemocracy protests erupted in March 2011. The SEA states that the protest against the Assad regime was the main reason for its creation. The Assad regime is led by President Bashar al-Assad who became president in 2010 after his father died. His father had been in power for more than 25 years, and his presidency and that of his son are assured by loyalists in the military, the security forces, the Baath party, and the Alawite sect, who had amended the constitution to enable Bashar al-Assad to take the throne.[7] Another reason for the existence of the SEA is the anti-Assad stance of many Western and Arab media channels and their responsibility for the killing of thousands of members of the Syrian Arab Army. The SEA states that they support the Assad regime, but they are an independent group.

> We are not an official side and do not belong to a political party. We are Syrian youths who responded to the call of duty after our homeland, Syria, was subjected to cyberattacks. We decided to respond actively under the name of Syrian Electronic Army SEA.[8]

The SEA's claim that they operate independent of the Syrian government has been dismissed by most researchers and government agencies because it would be impossible to operate within government-controlled areas without the government knowing and directing their actions.

The SEA has mainly targeted oppositional groups to collect information by using malware and Trojan horses such as Blackshades, DarkComet, Fynloski, Rbot, Xtreme RAT and Zapchast. The SEA sends the collected information to a Syrian government-controlled Internet protocol (IP) space, and in some instances, the SEA publishes the collected data. For instance, in 2012 the SEA published 11,000 names and passwords from opposition members. In another instance, the SEA stole sensitive customer information from several telecommunication providers used by opposition members. The SEA also hacked Facebook and Twitter accounts as well as major U.S. newspapers, including the *Washington Post*, the *New York Times*, and the *Onion*. SEA has posted false information on the hacked websites serving as Assad's international media and propaganda tool. Some of these posted messages were that "the Prince of Qatar was subjected to an assassination attack" and "Erdogan orders terrorists to launch chemical weapons at civilian areas."[9]

Chinese

Over the past decade, the Chinese government has reorganized their military forces, the People's Liberation Army (PLA), to focus increasingly on cyberwarfare. By combining cyberwarfare and intelligence units into a new Strategic Support Force, which is also called 3PLA as the third department of the PLA, China is believed to have more than 100,000 cyberwarfare hackers and highly trained personnel to focus more on warfare using integrated networks and satellites. The National Security Agency (NSA) has stated that the 3PLA is China's most aggressive cyberspying agency. Through their own operations, the NSA has estimated that 3PLA members are responsible for more than 30,000 cyberattacks against U.S. defense networks. About 500 of these attacks were found to be "significant intrusions" of defense networks, which means they posed a serious threat. China also engages in economic espionage against the United States and other countries. However, China also has significant vulnerabilities, and its ability to absorb stolen data is questionable. China prioritizes political information control over cyberdefense strategies. Even though China aggressively pursues cyberspying and cyberattacks, it does not have the same capabilities as the United States with regard to surveillance and infiltration of networks. The revelations by Edward Snowden have exposed the comprehensive data collection by the NSA and its ability to discover cyberoperations by China and prevent devastating intrusions. The United States and China have close economic relationships, and it is unlikely that either side will start a cyberwar, as that would result in very high costs that neither is willing to pay. The Internet has brought great economic growth for both countries, and continuing this growth depends on keeping the Internet as open as possible. A major cyberwar would likely result in closures, and neither side has an interest in reduced interoperability.[10]

Russia and Eastern Europe

Russia is considered one of the most advanced cyberespionage powers. Similar to China, Russia has developed military units specializing in the development and use of cyberweapons. It is, however, believed to be more advanced with regard to the sophistication of their cyberweapons. Another important difference is that Russia uses its cyberweapons mainly to supplement more aggressive forms of warfare, especially against the Ukraine and Estonia.[11]

On December 23, 2015, a cyberattack on the power grid of the Ukraine left as many as 80,000 people without power for about 6 hours. The Ukraine suspects that the malware "KillDisk" that shut down the power grid was based in Russia and was possibly backed by the Russian government.[12] Russia and the Ukraine have been in a conflict over territories since early 2014 when Russia seized the Ukraine's Black Sea peninsula Crimea and raised the Russian flag. Following this, Russian military forces took control of several cities in the east of the Ukraine. Since that time, Russian and Ukrainian military forces have been fighting over the territory, and cyberattacks have become an important part of this conflict. Russia also used DoS attacks against servers in Estonia to disrupt the service of major websites and communication systems.[13]

Contrary to Chinese cybercriminals, Russian cybercriminals make substantial efforts to hide their identities and objectives. Russian cybercriminals are very capable, and they continuously change their strategies and attack patterns to evade detection. For instance, Russian cyberhackers may go to great lengths to make it seem as if the attack is coming from Asia or some other region.[14]

CASE STUDY 6.1

North Korea and the Sony Hack

In 2014, Sony Pictures Entertainment had planned to release the movie *The Interview*, a satire about a plot to assassinate the president of North Korea, Kim Jong-un. In the weeks before the release of the movie, Sony experienced several cyberattacks believed to be the work of hackers from North Korea working for the government. The movie had received low reviews prior to the cyberattacks, but the publicity that surrounded the cyberattacks led to an increased interest in the movie. After the cyberattacks, President Obama, for the first time, publicly attributed the attacks to the North Korean government as an act of retaliation against Sony and raised the issue of foreign obstruction of First Amendment rights in the United States. It raised the question whether the government has a responsibility to protect corporate networks and constitutional rights of citizens against attacks by other nation-states.

The hackers, who called themselves Guardians of Peace (GOP), released documents from the Sony computer network over several weeks. These documents included financial documents, health documents of employees, internal e-mails, and private information about actors. They demanded that Sony halt the release of the movie. The GOP also threatened movie theaters that intended to show the movie with violent attacks. On December 17, Sony announced that the movie premier was suspended. Two days later, the FBI announced that North Korea was behind the attack, and on January 2, 2015, President Obama signed an executive order for new sanctions against several North Korean organizations. Obama also criticized Sony for having suspended the release of the movie.

North Korea has used carefully calculated provocations against South Korea and the United States for decades. The formation of the General Reconnaissance Bureau and cyberunits (Units 91 and 121) in 2009 has greatly increased the ability to utilize cyberspace for these provocations. The government actively recruits talented students as early as middle school and has devoted entire training schools and universities to cybertraining.[15]

What Do You Think?

1. What do you think were reasons by Sony to halt the premier?
2. Why do you think President Obama stated that Sony's response was a mistake?

Cyberespionage

Most people think of James Bond, flashlights that turn into weapons, cars that can shoot rockets, and impossible stunts to save the country when they hear the word *espionage*. Cyberespionage looks nothing like a James Bond movie. To the contrary, the actions and actors often stay hidden in cyberspace. The varying geographic masking methods increase anonymity, making it difficult to assign blame to a certain actor.

Computers were made to spy and offer unique opportunities for cyberespionage. Encryption and going dark are not new inventions, but rather go far back into history. Most codes were developed by the military to conceal messages to their army or allies. For instance, the Greeks used a naval flag system during the Peloponnesian War, and the Romans used a complex "box cipher" system that stood for different letters. One of the most important inventions was that of a telegraphing code, which was first introduced by French inventor Claude Chappe in

IMAGE 6.1 ● Cyberespionage

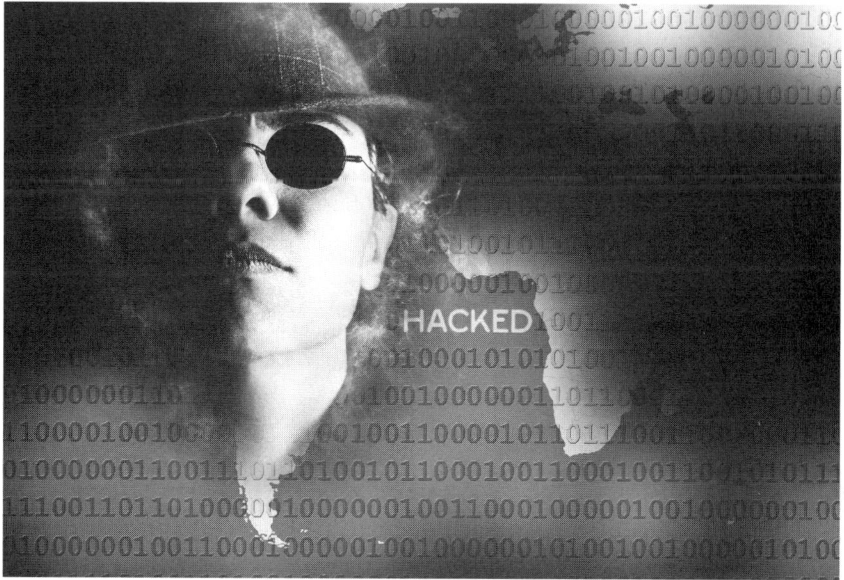

Pixaby.com

1792. During the Napoleonic era, telegraphing was used to carry signals from Paris and London to the naval bases. The first "software" was the Morse code developed by Samuel F. B. Morse. The Morse code made telegraphing much easier by using dots and dashes. The most common letters had the easiest codes—that is, the letter E was a dot and the letter T was a dash. Telegraphing also quickly gave rise to new methods of communication such as the circulation of news and gathering of data. This is very similar to the Internet about 1 century later.[16]

During World War I and World War II, coded radio messages were used to communicate. The famous enigma machine, developed by the Germans, was the machine that could turn typed messages into undecipherable codes. The decoding of the messages required that the receiver had the exact same settings as the sender machine. According to Prime Minister Churchill, the ability of the British code breakers based in Bletchley Park laid the groundwork for winning the war. The British tried to keep their code-breaking success a secret because if the Germans found out that the British could read their messages, they would likely develop a better coding machine.[17]

At the beginning of the Cold War, Igor Gouzenko defected from Russia with 109 documents that outlined the Russian spy ring in Canada and the United States. In addition, the documents included the codes used by Russia to communicate their secrets and secret weapons. The United States and Britain now had the ability to spy on the Russian atomic program.[18] Thus, spying on other countries' military and defense systems has a long tradition, which is intimately related to the development of codes and breaking of codes. Governments have always put forth great effort into espionage, and the Internet has opened the gates to new forms of spying.

The United States has been the most advanced country with regard to computers, hardware, and software, and as such, the United States understands better than any other country how computers can be exploited for cyberespionage and sabotage because U.S. scientists pioneered the techniques. More recently, other countries have started to catch up, such as China and Russia, and are trying to assert their power.

Cyberespionage can be classified into economic and political espionage. Thus, holding those who intruded the network responsible is a daunting task. A report by Verizon on data breaches shows that 86% of breaches had a financial or espionage motive.[19]

There are four main issues:

1. Malicious software can be developed and used by actors with limited and large resources, and without developing specific tools. This makes it difficult to associate certain tools with certain actors.
2. Hackers across the Internet share tools and techniques, making it very difficult to distinguish between hackers.
3. Nation-states and crime organizations sometimes use independent hackers to avoid being associated with a cyberattack.
4. Actors route Internet traffic through different countries, making it appear to come from another country.

On July 4, 2009, North Korea or pro-North Korean groups attacked government computers in the United States and South Korea, and jammed several government agency websites, including the Department of the Treasury, the Secret Service, the Federal Trade Commission, and the Department of Transportation. The DoS attacks used computer botnets in several countries, including Estonia, Great Britain, and Russia, to overload the targeted computer systems and shut them down. There was no direct link to North Korea, but there were several hints. The program was based on a Korean-language browser and operated through the Chinese network used by North Korea's cyberunit because North Korea does not have a sophisticated Internet. The U.S. government did not have enough evidence to publicly blame North Korea, however.[20]

In the past 2 years, one of the greatest threats has emerged from the Islamic State in Iraq and Syria (ISIS) and their operators who use the Internet and social media to launch attacks, propagandize, and recruit members. ISIS uses social media as their platform to support terrorism. On December 2, 2015, Syed Farook and his wife, Tashfeen Malik, killed 14 people and injured 22 during a mandatory employee training session and Christmas holiday party at Farook's workplace in San Bernardino. Syed and Tashfeen were on the run for 4 hours before being shot by police officers during a gun battle. The shooters had automatic rifles with lots of ammunition and bombs. Before they ran from the crime scene, they planted three pipe bombs, which they tried to detonate later. Fortunately, none of the bombs went off. While on the run, the couple posted messages on social media sites pledging their allegiance to ISIS. Tashfeen had also posted messages prior to December 2 stating that she was upset that her husband had to participate in a holiday that Muslims don't celebrate.[21]

In response, several social media outlets, including Facebook and Twitter, are actively working to prevent terrorists from spreading their ideologies by shutting down accounts. In 2016, Twitter shut down 235,000 terrorist accounts, raising its daily suspension rate by 80%. Twitter has also improved its response time to new terrorist accounts, shutting them down faster. The FBI had called out Twitter for assisting terrorists in the planning of attacks. Twitter, who prides itself on freedom of speech, eventually gave in to the public pressure.[22] Similarly, Facebook shut down accounts associated with Hamas, the Palestinian Sunni Islamic fundamentalist group, in 2015. Twitter had already done so in 2014.[23] The question of whether social media websites should shut down accounts associated with terrorists had long been discussed in the media and the government. Some government officials had asked the Federal Communications Commission (FCC) to shut down terrorists' accounts posted on Facebook and other social media. In a hearing, the FCC stated that it neither had jurisdiction over Facebook or other social media, nor did they intend to intervene. The chair of the FCC, Tom Wheeler, also stated, however, that he would call Mark Zuckerberg and discuss the issue.[24] The question of who has jurisdiction to shut down websites continues to be a major challenge. Cyberspace has no borders, and thus, jurisdiction is not clearly defined. The challenges associated with jurisdiction are discussed further in Chapter 10.

Economic Cyberespionage

The U.S. Commercial Code defines economic espionage as an act that

> occurs when an actor, knowing or intending that his or her actions will benefit any foreign government, instrumentality or agent, knowingly: (1) steals, or without authorization appropriates, carries away, conceals, or obtains by deception or fraud a trade secret; (2) copies, duplicates, reproduces, destroys, uploads, downloads, or transmits that trade secret without authorization; or (3) receives a trade secret knowing that the trade secret had been stolen, appropriated, obtained or converted without authorization. (Section 101 of the Economic Espionage Act, 18 USC § 1831.)[25]

Economic cyberespionage is typically carried out by state-affiliated actors, nation-states, and organized crime groups seeking sensitive information about trade secrets, such as intellectual property, proprietary technologies, and sensitive scientific information. Large amounts of stolen data can be transferred very quickly and without any physical meetings.[26]

The theft of industrial information can have great negative consequences for U.S. military capabilities and national security. The transfer of military applications to hostile nations such as Iran and North Korea could endanger the lives of military personnel and military missions. The theft of trade secrets could undermine U.S. economic growth by endangering innovation and the creation of new jobs and profits. New ideas and new technologies are the backbone of the economic strengths of the United States, and thus, this information is highly sought after by foreign nations intending to harm the United States and its citizens.[27] The most persistent threats have been economic cyberespionage attacks from Russia and China, who view themselves as strategic competitors and link their intelligence operations and economic interests. In September 2015, China and the

United States signed a bilateral agreement to refrain from cybertheft. Despite this agreement, James R. Clapper, former director of National Intelligence, has no confidence that China will honor the agreement. He stated, "Malicious cyber activity will continue and probably accelerate until we establish and demonstrate the capability to deter malicious state-sponsored cyber activity."[28] For China, the control of cyberspace is strategically important because it helps redress the military imbalance between China and the United States. Ally states also spy on U.S. corporations and military organizations to obtain sensitive information that could give them an advantage in the global market.[29]

LEGAL ISSUE 6.1

MISAPPROPRIATION OF INFORMATION OR ESPIONAGE?

The Economic Espionage Act of 1996 makes it a federal crime to steal or interfere with trade secrets. Trade secrets are treated as property, which means that intellectual property is considered a trade secret. This includes publications, research, presentations, music, videos, etc. You are a student, so imagine after one of your classes that your professor forgets to log out of his classroom computer. While walking by the computer, you notice that it is still on, and you decide to shut it down for him. But before shutting it down you download his lectures and exams. You start selling the notes and exams to other students via Facebook, Twitter, and other social media outlets. Discuss whether lectures, notes, and exams from your professors are protected by the Economic Espionage Act. Discuss whether you have engaged in a crime, and if so, what crime.[30]

Political Cyberespionage

Political espionage is typically used to gain access to sensitive information and/or to fatally damage a network. It is motivated by the "collection and provision of sensitive information from the United States government to other entities or agencies abroad."[31] Gaining access to sensitive military information can severely diminish military capabilities and defense systems. Shutting down a government website can prevent access to important information. Access to information equals power in the world of politics, where power is the ability to get others to do what they otherwise would not. This includes harboring sensitive information; gathering, transmitting, or losing defense information; photographing or sketching any defense installation; and disclosing classified information.

The Threat of Insiders

On June 6, 2013, the British Newspaper the *Guardian* publicized details about the surveillance program by the NSA. The publicized information had great consequences in that it exposed the systematic surveillance of millions of U.S. citizens and foreign government officials by the NSA. The classified information was leaked by Edward Snowden, a former employee at Booz Allen Hamilton, a management and technology consulting firm to the U.S. government in defense, intelligence, and civil markets. Snowden was promptly charged with espionage for leaking classified information to the press. Since then, Snowden has been hiding

CASE STUDY 6.2

GhostNet

GhostNet was one of the most successful programs with regard to political cyberespionage. The malware-based network GhostNet, which consists of over 1,295 infected computers in 103 countries controlled by China, had real-time control over the infected computers. This control included computers of the ministry of foreign affairs in numerous Asian countries, countries in the Middle East, but also in Europe. In total, about 30% of the infected computers were high-value diplomatic, political, economic, and military targets. The modus operandi included several hard-to-detect technologies and tools. It is unknown what information was stolen and how the information was used.[32]

in Russia, which has given him temporary asylum and protects him from extradition to the United States.[33]

In this case, the identity of the insider became known very quickly, but often it is very difficult to find the insiders who stole the data. For instance, Dongfan Chung, an engineer working for Rockwell and Boeing, worked as an insider spy for the Chinese aviation industry between 1979 and 2006. Chung worked on the B-1 bomber and other programs. The police found 250,000 pages of sensitive documents in Chung's house, and he was sentenced to 15 years in prison for possession with the intent to benefit the People's Republic of China. There was no direct evidence that Chung had actually provided the stolen information to China. With the help of current technologies, this type of data handling would be much easier. All 250,000 pages would have fit on one CD and a small external hard drive, and could have been easily distributed to China.[34]

LEGAL ISSUE 6.2

THE FOURTH AMENDMENT

The Fourth Amendment states:

> The right of the people to be secure in their persons, houses, papers, and effects, against unreasonable searches and seizures, shall not be violated, and no warrants shall issue, but upon probable cause, supported by oath or affirmation, and particularly describing the place to be searched, and the persons or things to be seized.[35]

In order to listen to private phone calls, the police need a search warrant. Imagine that the government had been listening to your conversations, reading your e-mails, and monitoring what websites you visit. You had downloaded a movie on a free streaming channel and distributed the movie to your friends via e-mail. You had therefore violated copyright law. The NSA gave the evidence about your download and distribution to your local sheriff's office who arrested you a few days later.

What Do You Think?

1. How would you defend yourself in court?
2. Did Edward Snowden cause irreparable harm, or did he reveal illegal conduct of the government?

Cyberintelligence

Cyberintelligence is "the collection and analysis of information that produces timely reporting, with context and relevance to a supported decision maker."[36] Cyberintelligence relies on data collection about events or incidents relevant to issues in the cyberdomain, especially cybersecurity. This type of intelligence includes information about cyberactivity or geopolitical events. For instance, data collected about a planned DoS attack on a computer network can be used to counter the attack or limit the damage of the attack. Cyberintelligence reduces the uncertainty about planned attacks and enables a timely and efficient implementation of cybersecurity policies. It also enables public-private partnerships and effective operational and investment decisions. The goal of gathering intelligence is to be proactive toward cyberattacks rather than reactive. Once the data is stolen, the damage is done. Proactively preventing the theft of data or other cyberattack is a more effective cybersecurity strategy. For instance, in 2015, a report by Kaspersky Lab, a Russian software maker, exposed a spyware integrated into hard drives of Toshiba, Seagate, and other top brand names. The program developed by the NSA installs the spyware every time the computer is turned on. This is called *disk drive firmware*. This firmware gives the NSA the ability to spy on millions of computers around the globe. The goal of the NSA is to gather information about foreign governments and possible cyberattacks. Peter Swire, one of Barack Obama's committee members of the Review Group on Intelligence and Communications Technology, cautioned that these cyberespionage acts can upset allies and hinder the sale of U.S.-made technology to other countries. The goals of intelligence agencies to provide security conflicts with the desire to keep the public's trust.[37]

Cybersabotage

Before the Internet, sabotage acts targeted physical property, and the actor had to be physically present and often relied on physical violence. The success of acts of sabotage was unreliable. If someone wanted to sabotage the railway, they had to go to the railway, cut the wires, and tear down telegraph posts. The creation of cyberspace has changed the face of sabotage by changing tools, techniques, and strategies of acts of sabotage. If someone wanted to sabotage the railway today, he or she could hack into the railway computer system and manipulate the software that runs the train system. The hackers could also erase the hard drives of the computer network, stopping all trains from running and causing trains to derail. Cybersabotage can accomplish goals that would typically require force or violence.[38]

Sabotage is defined as

> the act of hampering, deliberately subverting, or hurting the efforts of another. It is most often an issue in the context of military law, when a person attempts to thwart a war effort, or in employment law, when disgruntled employees destroy employer property. Cyber-industrial sabotage activities, such as hacking, usually relate to industrial secrets that have commercial value to competitors. In some countries, computer sabotage may be

FIGURE 6.1 ● Cybercriminals Targeting a Computer System

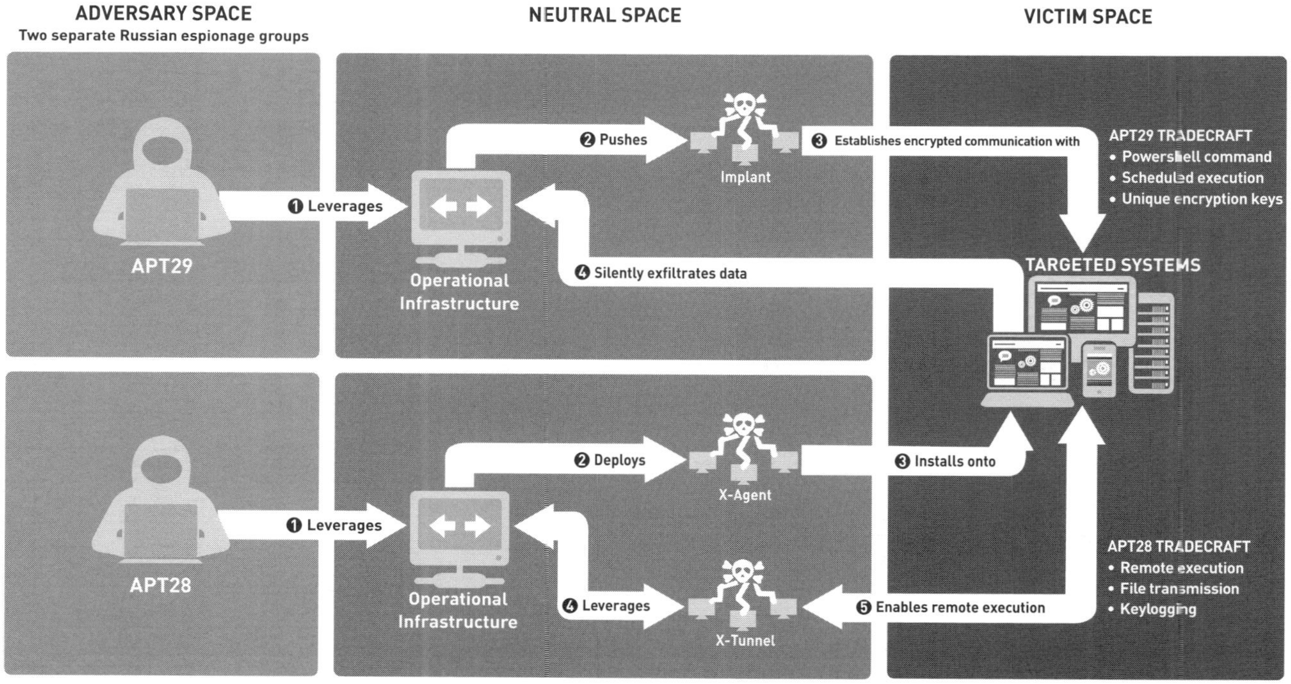

ADVERSARY SPACE
Two separate Russian espionage groups

NEUTRAL SPACE

VICTIM SPACE

APT29
❶ Leverages
Operational Infrastructure
❷ Pushes
Implant
❸ Establishes encrypted communication with
❹ Silently exfiltrates data

APT29 TRADECRAFT
- Powershell command
- Scheduled execution
- Unique encryption keys

TARGETED SYSTEMS

APT28
❶ Leverages
Operational Infrastructure
❷ Deploys
X-Agent
❸ Installs onto
❹ Leverages
X-Tunnel
❺ Enables remote execution

APT28 TRADECRAFT
- Remote execution
- File transmission
- Keylogging

Sources: U.S. Department of Homeland Security NCCIC; Federal Bureau of Investigation.

> regarded as a breach of civil law rather then [*sic*] criminal law, but there are laws clearly defining cyber-crime as a criminal offense.[39]

Cybersabotage is carried out by governments, militaries, hacktivists, and other actors. It doesn't require a large force to hack into computers and manipulate software. In 2013, the Obama administration publicly accused China of having hacked into the U.S. government's computers and computer networks of defense contractors. The motive may have been to gather data that would allow China to sabotage U.S. computer systems and infrastructures. One of the most common techniques used in cybersabotage acts is DoS attacks.[40]

Denial-of-Service Attacks

DoS attacks are "any attacks intended to compromise the availability of networks and systems. Both network and application attacks are designed to overwhelm systems, resulting in performance degradation or interruption of service."[41] The purpose of DoS attacks is to prevent the normal operation of a computer system or other digital system, such as mobile phones. There are four general types of DoS attacks: (1) line-of-sight devices, (2) worm programs, (3) flood attacks, and (4) subversion of intrusion detection systems. First, line-of-sight programs use devices that temporarily or permanently disable digital circuits either at close or long range. For instance, a high-intensity radio frequency gun can disrupt digital circuits at close range (approximately 1 m) and an electromagnetic pulse cannon works long range (approximately 1 km). Both types of devices aim to stop the operation of a computer or other digital system. Second, worm programs slow down computer systems by taking up significant resources for their self-replication. It is possible for worms to grow to such extent that they disable the computer or digital system all together. Third, a flood attack is a concerted effort to overwhelm the computer system with connection requests. When a system gets overwhelmed with incomplete connection requests, it cannot process genuine connection requests. The flood of connection requests has filled up the memory of the computer system and no new connections can be made.[42] Fourth, subversion of intrusion detection systems are "hidden software or hardware artifice that create a 'backdoor' known only to the attacker."[43] This hidden system undermines the control of the computer system because the system can be accessed by the attacker at any time without being noticed.

CASE STUDY 6.3

Rutgers State University—DDoS Attack

On September 28, 2015, Rutgers University experienced the consequence of another DDoS attack. Their online platforms were shut down, IT services were interrupted, and the campus Wi-Fi network and e-mail services stopped working. Classes and exams were cancelled, and students were not able to submit their assignments or enroll in classes. In 2014, Rutgers had invested $3 million in a security update, which resulted in a tuition increase of 2.3%.

In a petition, students requested a part of their tuition be returned due to the consequences of the attack on their education. One student summarized the concerns of the students: "Since I came to college, I expected at least decent internet speeds, and while it usually holds up, we get DDoS attacks every time an exam rolls around. Now I would not say anything, yet I feel the need to tell all the students to join together to either get a refund or to make Rutgers change something on their own time. Why? Because Rutgers spent over 3 million on upgrading the network, yet only $160,000 actually went to physical upgrades.[44]

What Do You Think?

1. Discuss the impact of DoS attacks on universities and the students attending them.
2. What solution would you propose if your university was attacked and you had no Internet access for 2 weeks?

Summary

This chapter provides an overview of cyberwarfare, cyberespionage, and cybersabotage. It also includes the consequences of these crimes and the role of social media. Economic espionage causes significant damage to the economy. The theft of intellectual property could drive companies into bankruptcy, forcing people out of work. The theft of military secrets is even more disconcerting, as enemy states would know how our military operates, how our fighter jets operate, and possibly even be able to reverse engineer our military technologies. This not only makes our technologies vulnerable to cyberattacks but also potentially ineffective in a time of war. Espionage and sabotage are not new tools, but the way they have evolved in this era of cyberspace has made them even more dangerous. The United States, of course, also spies on other countries and is possibly the most powerful spy. It is difficult to predict how cyberespionage and cyberwarfare will change the U.S. defense policy, but we know for certain that it will change.

Key Terms

Discussion Questions

1. Discuss the greatest threats posed by DoS attacks. Think about potential targets and the damage an attack on those targets could cause.
2. Discuss the motives behind cyberespionage programs.
3. Explain why outright cyberwarfare from China and other nation-states against the United States is rather unlikely.
4. Discuss the purpose of the Economic Espionage Act (1996). How can the Act be used to fight cyberespionage?

Internet Resources

National Counterintelligence and Security Center
https://www.ncsc.gov/index.html

NSA Day of Cyber
https://www.nsa.gov/resources/students/nsa-day-of-cyber/

Economic Espionage Act (1996)
https://www.law.cornell.edu/uscode/text/18/1831

Further Reading

Center for Security Policy. (2011). *Cyber threats to national security. Dealing with today's asymmetric threat.* Retrieved from https://www.asymmetricthreat.net/docs/asymmetric_threat_5_paper.pdf

Makovsky D. (2012, September 17). The silent strike: How Israel bombed a Syrian nuclear installation and kept it secret. *New Yorker.* Retrieved from http://www.newyorker.com/magazine/2012/09/17/the-silent-strike

Yépez, A., & Dixon, D. (2016). *Cybercrime and threats are growing in 2016.* Retrieved from https://www.rsaconference.com/blogs/cybercrime-and-threats-are-growing-in-2016

Digital Resources

Want a better grade?

Get the tools you need to sharpen your study skills. Access practice quizzes and eFlashcards, at **study.sagepub.com/kremling**.

Cyberterrorism

Learning Objectives

1. Define the difference between cyberterrorism and other forms of cybercrime.
2. Discuss the role of the media in the (mis)understanding of what constitutes cyberterrorism.
3. Understand the vulnerability of critical infrastructures to cyberterrorism.
4. Differentiate between the four steps of the emergency/risk management process.
5. Apply the risk management procedure to critical infrastructure.

THINK ABOUT IT 7.1

The Future of Terrorist Attacks

On November 26, 2008, the city of Mumbai, India, experienced a terrorist attack by the Lashkar-e-Taiba (LeT) that would go on for 60 hours and cost the lives of 172 people. LeT is a Pakistan-based terrorist group with the declared goal of liberating Kashmir and breaking up India. India is ruled by the Hindu, and the LeT, being a Muslim group, opposes the majority government. There has been a long history of antagonism between the majority Hindu population and the minority Muslim population, which has caused much violence and terrorist attacks. What made the attack in Mumbai in 2008 different was the expansive use of technology by the terrorists and their ability to use information from live TV, Internet news, and social media to make their attack so prolonged and deadly. This was not a suicide attack as 9/11 or many others, but rather

(Continued)

(Continued)

a no-surrender attack targeting foreigners and the local elite. The attack demonstrated how the Internet and information technologies can be turned into deadly tools by terrorists, and it provides a glimpse of future terrorist attacks, greatly impacting law enforcement responses to such attacks.

The attackers had arrived by sea on a hijacked sailing boat after killing the crew of the boat. The attackers were heavily armed with AK-56 automatic rifles, hand grenades, and several highly explosive improvised explosive devices. The 10 attackers split into four groups, each having a different target, and began their highly sequential and mobile attack on high-impact targets in the city of Mumbai. The targets had been strategically selected to attract as much international attention as possible and kill as many people as possible in a short period of time. The main targets were two large luxury hotels (the famous Taj Mahal Palace Hotel and the Oberoi-Trident Hotel), the main train station, a hospital, a Jewish residential complex, and the stock exchange (India's Wall Street). The first group of two attackers began their attacks in the train station and then continued to the Cama & Abless Hospital where they continued to kill mostly Indian citizens. This team of two killed one third of the victims before they were stopped by police. One of the attackers was killed and the other captured.

The second team of attackers attacked a Jewish commercial-residential complex where they took 13 hostages, killing five of them. The third two-man team stormed the luxury Oberoi-Trident hotel where they started shooting inside the lobby and continued their attack for 17 hours, killing 30 people. The largest attacker group went to the famous Taj Mahal Palace Hotel where they would move their way up through the corridors shooting guests along the way. The attackers monitored news media, social media like Facebook and Twitter, and used their own technology, including cell phones, satellite phone, and Skype, to stay ahead of the police. The command central gave constant instructions to the attackers about where the police were, where to go next, and other strategic information. The attackers confused India's police by calling them and making demands in exchange for releasing hostages, making it appear as if this was a hostage situation.[1]

At 11:08, the Indian government asked all people to stop posting updates on Twitter. "ALL LIVE UPDATES - PLEASE STOP TWEETING about #Mumbai police and military operations," a tweet says. Eventually, police ended the attack, but the attack by the LeT provided a daunting picture of what future terrorist attacks may look like and how social media may impact attacks. Thus, the significance of the Mumbai attacks for future terrorist and other attacks lies in the sophistication and effective use of information technology (IT). This type of advanced technological attack will likely become more common and make it more difficult for law enforcement, and likely result in more victims.

What Would You Do?

1. What do you think an act of cyberterrorism would look like?
2. The term encompasses both the words *cyber* and *terrorism*. What actions and results are needed for an attack to be considered cyberterrorism?
3. Can the effects of cyberterrorism affect more than just the virtual world?

Cyberterrorism Defined

Barry Collin, while working as a research analyst at Palo Alto's Institute for Security and Intelligence in the 1980s, first coined the term *cyberterrorism*, defining it simply as the convergence of terror and cyberspace.[2] Cyberspace is relatively easy to define, but defining terrorism, especially in a cyber context, poses a greater challenge. As Conway relates, "Cyberspace is a place in which computers function and data moves. However, terrorism is harder to define."[3] Though on paper it may seem relatively simple, the conceptualization of cyberterrorism has serious implications and requires elaboration to be usefully applied.

The term *terrorism* refers to a tactic. Yet there are multiple definitions of what constitutes an act to be terrorism, even within the borders of the United States. According to the FBI, terrorism is

> the unlawful use of force or violence against persons or property to intimidate or coerce a government, the civilian population, or any segment thereof, in furtherance of political or social objectives.[4]

The CIA defines terrorism under Title 22 of the US Code, Section 2656f(d), this way: "The term 'terrorism' means premeditated, politically motivated violence perpetrated against noncombatant targets by subnational groups or clandestine agents."[5]

And the U.S. Department of Defense defines terrorism as:

> the calculated use of unlawful violence or threat of unlawful violence to inculcate fear; intended to coerce or to intimidate governments or societies in the pursuit of goals that are generally political, religious, or ideological.[6]

Just as there is no universal definition of terrorism in the United States, there is also not an internationally recognized definition of terrorism. The Organization of the Islamic Conference has repeatedly vetoed the inclusion of the phrase *armed struggle for liberation and self-determination* in the definition, leaving the United Nations without an agreed-upon definition of terrorism.[7]

This becomes even more problematic when the technique of terrorism is moved to the cyber realm. Just as not all acts of fear-inflicted violence are terrorism, not all activities of terrorists in cyberspace constitute cyberterrorism. Cyberterrorism, like terrorism, is a *tactic* used by terrorists, and one main element of that tactic is to create fear in a population, something that is more difficult to accomplish in cyberspace.

Mirroring the conceptual problems of the term terrorism, researchers have defined cyberterrorism in various ways as well. Moving from Collin's basic idea of cyberterrorism being "the convergence of terrorism and cyberspace," Denning suggests that the best way to define cyberterrorism is to combine the definitions of terrorism, adding emphasis to *cyber*. In testimony before a Special Oversight Committee, she defined cyberterrorism as being

> generally understood to mean unlawful attacks and threats of attacks against computers, networks, and the information stored within when done to intimidate or coerce a government or its people in furtherance of political and social objectives.[8]

Notably, this definition includes the *threat* of attack. Although threat of attack is common in many definitions of terrorism, in the case of cyberterrorism, it seems unlikely that a threat alone would produce the mass fear and devastation necessary for an event to be considered cyberterrorism.[9]

There is much confusion concerning what a cyberterror attack would look like, but Denning argues that it would likely "lead to death or bodily injury, explosions, plane crashes, water contamination or severe economic loss." It is results such as these that would result in the fear necessary for an event to be considered cyberterrorism. However, using the definitions provided by U.S. federal agencies, Pollitt suggests a more precise definition, regarding cyberterrorism as

> the premeditated, politically motivated attack against information, computer systems, and data which results in violence against noncombatant targets by sub national groups or clandestine agents.[10]

Such attacks can target places that were once thought to be safe from terror attacks.

The Role of the Media

The media also contribute to the misunderstanding of what constitutes cyberterrorism. News media tend to "hook" the public with catchy headlines rather than ensuring that there is a good operational definition of cyberterrorism.[11]

A 2002 Canadian headline provides one example of how the term cyberterrorism is used inappropriately: "Canadian boy admits cyberterrorism of his family."[12] This was not a case of cyberterrorism but merely a child who sent e-mails to his family that reportedly "terrorized" them.

In 2007, an Internet report led with the headline: "World's first cyberterrorism trial." Although the individuals on trial were alleged al-Qaeda operatives, their use of the Internet to raise funds for al-Qaeda does not constitute cyberterrorism.[13] Another online headline in 2008 read: "Brazilian man charged in cyber-terrorism case." In reality, he was charged with selling computers infected with malicious software, also not a true case of cyberterrorism.[14]

Finally, an April 10, 2014, report out of the United Kingdom read: "Iran: The world's worst cyber—terrorists-for now." The article detailed the cyber capabilities of Iran, but not in regard to cyberterrorism.[15]

CASE STUDY 7.1

Defining Cyberterrorism Within the Academic Context

A recent focus group examined what would constitute an act to be considered cyberterrorism. The focus group involved 30 participants from a range of government agencies and professionals, and examined in depth the conceptual framework that encompasses the definition of cyberterrorism. The proposed conceptual framework included six elements:

1. Target
   a. Critical National Information Infrastructure computer system
   b. Critical infrastructure
   c. Civilian population

2. Impact
   a. Mass disruption or serious interference with critical service operations
   b. Causes fear, death, or bodily injury
   c. Severe economic loss
3. Method of Action
   a. Unlawful means
4. Domain
   a. Cyberspace
5. Tools of Attack
   a. Network warfare
   b. Psychological operation
6. Motivation
   a. Political
   b. Ideological
   c. Social

The investigators of this focus group argue that defining and understanding the concepts of cyberterrorism are critical for security. Differences among participants on the semantics of a definitional framework were reported to be "not that critical," as 18 participants agreed fully with the conceptual design and the remaining 12 agreed with "some recommendations."[16]

What Do You Think?

1. Based on the suggestions of the focus group participants, devise a detailed definition of cyberterrorism.
2. Provide examples of what would and would not qualify, who the perpetrators could possibly be, and what would be involved in such an attack.

Combining the definitions presented by Denning, Pollitt, and Parker,[17] and accounting for Ahmad et al.'s six elements, as well as taking into account Jackman's concern with the conceptualization of violence (Legal Issue 7.1), within this textbook, cyberterrorism will be defined as

> an intentional act, committed via computer or communication system and motivated by political, religious, or ideological objectives, against information, data, or computer systems/programs, intended to cause severe harm, death, or destruction to civilians.

Cyberterrorism can be a technique employed by those engaging in information warfare, but not all information warfare is cyberterrorism. This statement can also apply to the distinction between cybercrime and cyberterrorism as "the intent, perpetrators and harm of each can be vastly dissimilar."[18] As illustrated in Figure 7.1, terrorists are more likely to attack critical infrastructures or engage in cyberwarfare than the average cybercriminal. For an event to be classified as cyberterrorism, experts have argued that the damage resulting from the attack should be somewhat catastrophic.

FIGURE 7.1 ● Differentiating Cybercrime From Cyberterrorism (one example)

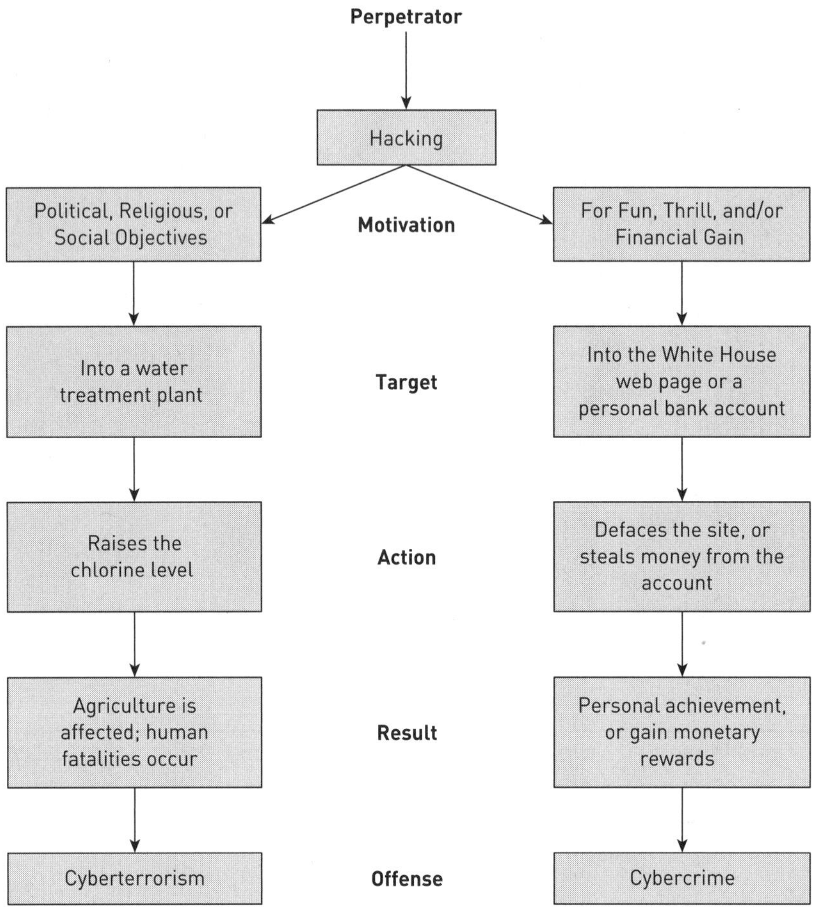

Source: Parker, A. (2010). The conceptualization and misconceptualization of cyberterrorism. In D. Antonius et al. (Eds.), *Interdisciplinary analysis of terrorism and political aggression* (pp. 293–310). Newcastle upon Tyne, England: Cambridge Scholars Publishing.

LEGAL ISSUE 7.1

THE ROLE OF VIOLENCE

What is the role of violence in cyberterrorism? Within the academic definitions of terrorism, over 80% of definitions indicate violence as a necessary element. However, how does violence, and subsequently fear of harm/violence, translate in cyberspace? Furthermore, how would the presence of violence affect the prosecution of cyberterrorists?

Jackman has elaborated on the issues surrounding the conceptualization of violence. She asserts that there are four main issues that have affected society's perception of violence. The first is the idea of physical violence. Often, acts of violence that result in "psychological, material, and social injuries" are ignored. Second, the conceptualization of violence is usually limited to "physical behavior and threats of physical behavior." The third issue is the idea of failure to resist by the victim, and the last is the concentration on interpersonal violence, or the concentration on acts which have "individually identifiable agents and victims and immediate and certain outcomes."[19] In the virtual realm, these four points come under scrutiny when examining the conceptualization of violence as it applies to cyberterrorism.

In most cases of traditional cybercrime, investigations are conducted by banks or antifraud departments, not by traditional law enforcement. However, if an act results in violence, which may be the case in events of cyberterrorism, law enforcement may have to respond to the report.

What Do You Think?

1. What role do you think violence plays in cyberterrorism?
2. How will this affect the investigation and prosecution of cases of cyberterrorism?
3. What training do you think will be necessary for criminal justice professionals to handle such a task?

Evolution of the Threat

As cyberterrorism has arguably yet to occur, there are diverse opinions about the actual probability of attack and the actual amount of damage that could result. It has been suggested that concern about cyberterrorism is "overblown" and that

> neither the 14-year-old hacker in your next-door neighbor's upstairs bedroom, nor the two- or three-person al-Qaida cell holed up in some apartment in Hamburg are going to bring down the Glen Canyon and Hoover dams.[20]

On the other side of the argument, some researchers suggest that cyberterrorism represents the future of terrorism and can pose a grave threat to national security, as terrorists are increasing their knowledge of technology and are actively recruiting individuals with IT skills and training. As technology rapidly advances, some commentators believe that cyberterrorism may soon manifest as a deadly threat, a threat that left unexamined could leave law enforcement unprepared to detect, prevent, and respond.

A 1991 National Research Council report forecasts that "tomorrow's terrorist may be able to do more damage with a keyboard than with a bomb."[21] However, terrorists typically do not adopt new methods of attack unless they have knowledge of and trust in the technique. Following the attacks of 9/11, Osama bin Laden told an Arab newspaper, "hundreds of Muslim scientists were with him who would use their knowledge . . . ranging from computers to electronics against the infidels."[22] Furthermore, Omar Bakri Muhammad, a supporter of the late Osama bin Laden, claimed that al-Qaeda has the technology to launch a cyberattack and "Islam authorizes the use of all technologies for offensive purposes when Islam is under attack." Muhammad went on to list the New York, London, and Tokyo stock markets as optimal targets, and said: "I would not be surprised if tomorrow I hear of a big economic collapse because of somebody attacking the main technical systems in big companies."[23] Since 9/11, terrorists have continued to increase their knowledge and skills in cyberspace.

Technology Use by Extremists

The use and exploitation of technology by extremist groups is not a new concept. Groups such as Aum Shinrikyo in Japan and al-Qaeda in the Middle East have used technology for recruitment, propaganda dissemination, and fundraising. The ease of access to the Internet and the anonymity it allows makes technology an attractive tool for terrorists. The use of technology by these groups has evolved from basic surveillance to advanced use of the deep web and darknets (see Chapter 8) to avoid detection. The following section outlines the evolution of use by three different groups.

Al-Qaeda

As previously mentioned, al-Qaeda has been extremely vocal in their plans to incorporate technology into their future attacks by not only using technology but targeting those infrastructures that are most vulnerable to cyberattack. Al-Qaeda has been known to recruit individuals with IT or computer backgrounds, and as the skills necessary to hack into computer systems are declining, and the sophistication of tools to do the hacking is increasing exponentially, the threat of a cyberattack continues to increase. The United States has seized computers from this group and found information on U.S. critical infrastructures (dams and power plants) in the computers' data bases.[24]

Boko Haram

The Nigerian terrorist organization Boko Haram, also known as Jama'atu Ahlis Sunna Lidda'awati wal-Jihad, has also embraced the use of technology to further their cause. Until 2015, Boko Haram did not have much of a social media presence, but that changed when a Twitter account was established for the group on January 18, 2015.[25] Boko Haram has since used this and other social media platforms to spread propaganda and publish pictures of their militants in action.

Perhaps the most famous use of the Internet, predominantly YouTube, by Boko Haram was, and still is, the coverage of the kidnapping of Chibok girls. On April 14, 2014, Boko Haram kidnapped 276 girls from a school in Chibok, Borno State, Nigeria. Only about 50 girls were able to escape. Later that year, the leader of Boko Haram used video coverage to show that the girls were still alive, and he detailed his plans to sell them into the slave market. The majority of the girls are still being held by Boko Haram, and images of them occasionally appear on social media affiliated with Boko Haram and on YouTube.[26]

The Islamic State (also known as ISIS/ISIL/Daesh)

The terrorist organization most well known for their use of the Internet and social media is the Islamic State (IS; also referred to as the Islamic State of Iraq and Syria [ISIS], the Islamic State in Iraq and the Levant [ISIL], and Daesh). IS has embraced the use of technology in a way that has never been done by any previous terrorist network. They have spent hundreds of thousands of dollars on propaganda and encouraged the use of social media by both their members and their followers.[27]

Using social media for recruitment has been extremely successful for IS. Although social media accounts can be shut down, new accounts can be created just as fast as the government shuts them down. Some report up to 90 tweets per minute, as one specific recruit reported that along with daily social media contact she also received over 200 videos of IS-related killings and 500 requests for her to travel to the Islamic State.[28] Social media allows IS supporters to be reached around the world, with the United States ranking fourth in pro-IS tweets, falling only behind Saudi Arabia, Syria, and Iraq.[29] Both the San Bernardino, California, terrorists and the Orlando, Florida, Pulse Nightclub terrorist had active social media pages with pro-ISIS propaganda displayed.

Using social media to recruit supporters has resulted in multiple lone-wolf terrorist attacks in the United States. These individuals are not directly affiliated with IS but have been self-radicalized via online forums and propaganda. Furthermore, as they have not had direct contact with IS, they are, at times, more difficult to track, as in the cases in Florida and California. IS praises such actions, as these attacks help further IS's cause at no cost to the organization.

Targets of Cyberterrorism

Probable Versus Possible

Although it is evident that terrorists have embraced the use of technology for recruitment and propaganda distribution, it is often debated whether terrorists truly have the skills and capabilities necessary to launch a cyberterror attack resulting in massive destruction. Weimann's take on this poses a chilling hypothetical:

> Perhaps terrorists do not yet have the know-how to launch cyber attacks or perhaps most hackers are not sympathetic to the goals of terrorist organizations. However, should the two groups join forces, the results could be devastating.[30]

After 9/11, the government began to examine the threat of cyberterrorism in more depth. The National Association of Regulatory Utility Commissioners (NARUC) identified eight targets that could be vulnerable to a cyberterror attack. These include the following:

1. Information and Communication
2. Electronic Power Systems
3. Gas and oil (production, transportation and storage)
4. Banking and Finance
5. Transportation
6. Water Supply Systems

7. Emergency Services
8. Governmental Services[31]

The U.S. government has become more concerned about the potential threat of cyberterrorism. Although some of the infrastructures identified by NARUC may seem unlikely targets for terrorists, experts caution not to underestimate the threat. The concern is shared internationally that cyberterrorists will use the electrical grid system to attack critical infrastructure. Stephen E. Flynn, a professor of Homeland Security at Northeastern University in Boston, Massachusetts, identified the electrical grid to be one of the top Homeland Security concerns. Flynn also asserts that the electrical grid is a significant target because it is not just a U.S. infrastructure. He elaborates that "the grid is a North American grid," as a significant part of the United States receives power from Canada and, more modestly so, from Mexico.[32]

CASE STUDY 7.2

The 2003 New York City Blackout

Just 2 years after the attacks on September 11, 2001, a major power outage caused massive damage in New York City, seven other states, and Canada. New York, still at a heightened alert after the 9/11 attacks, first feared the power outage was an act of terrorism. Thousands of people were stuck underground on the subway. Cell phone towers were not working, and air travel was disrupted. The outage, which occurred at approximately 4 p.m., caused major disruptions with rush-hour traffic, as traffic lights were disabled. Furthermore, due to the widespread outage, those who did not have cash on hand were unable to purchase food, water, or other supplies. Hospitals were overflowing with patients, and some hospitals even lost their backup power.

The incident turned out to be due, in part, to a natural disaster and in part to a man-made accident. A tree branch fell on a power line, which began the outage; however, manual errors contributed to the widespread outage affecting over 50 million people across Detroit, Cleveland, Toronto, and parts of New Jersey, Pennsylvania, Connecticut, and Massachusetts.[33]

IMAGE 7.1 ● View of the 2003 Blackout From Space, Compared to a Typical Evening (Left)

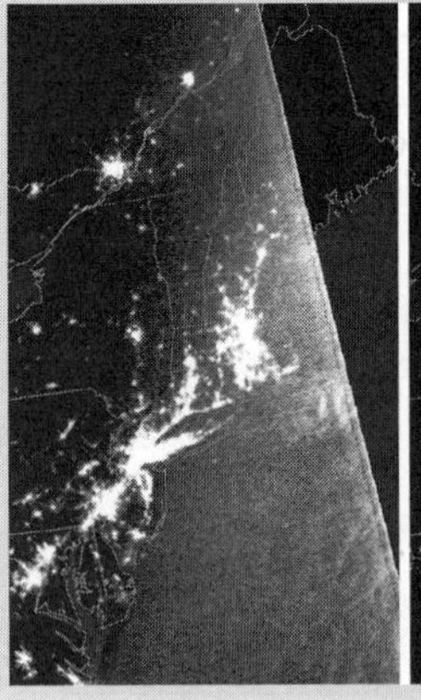

NOAA/Getty Images

What Do You Think?

1. The 2003 power outage was a nonmalicious incident. How would a malicious attack on the power grid be different?
2. Why is the power grid an attractive target to terrorists?
3. How likely is a cyberterrorism attack on the power grid?
4. What can be done to prevent it?

Vulnerability of Critical Infrastructures

Cyberterror attacks may be conducted in a variety of ways, including:

1. destroying machinery through computer manipulation;
2. interfering with information technology, including critical infrastructures; and
3. using computers to override control systems, including power plants and dams.[34]

Our nation's critical infrastructures can be extremely susceptible to cyberterrorism. After the first World Trade Center bombing and the Oklahoma City bombing, then-president Clinton signed into action the President's Commission on Critical Infrastructure Protection. This directive aimed for a 5-year plan to protect all critical infrastructure, defined as:

> A framework of interdependent networks and systems comprising identifiable industries, institutions (including people and procedure), and distribution capabilities that provide a reliable flow of products and services essential to the defense and economic security of the United States, the smooth functioning of government at all levels, and society as a whole.[35]

Following the attacks on September 11, 2001, the USA PATRIOT Act redefined critical infrastructures as

> systems and assets, whether physical or virtual, so vital to the United States that the incapacity or destruction of such systems and assets would have a debilitating impact on security, national economic security, national public health or safety, or any combination of those matters.[36]

Currently, there are 16 sectors of critical infrastructure identified by Presidential Policy Directive 21. These sectors include the chemical sector; commercial facilities sector; communication sector; critical manufacturing sector; dams sector; defense industrial base sector; emergency services sector; energy sector; financial services sector; food and agriculture sector; government facilities sector; health care and public health sector; information technology sector; nuclear reactors, materials, and waste sector; transportation systems sector; and the water and wastewater sector.[37] Because of their reliance on technology and their necessity to our way of life, all sectors are vulnerable to cyberterrorism.

The USA PATRIOT Act also differentiated between critical infrastructures and key assets. Unlike critical infrastructures, which by definition would result in "a debilitating impact," key assets are an aspect of critical infrastructure, and although an attack upon a key asset would result in some damage, it would not completely upset the country's ability to function. Examples of key assets include national monuments or any other structure that may function as a symbol of the United States.

Risk Management

As terrorists have yet to venture deeply into the realm of cyberterrorism, it is necessary to assess the vulnerability of targets, identifying what is possible versus what is probable. In order to do this, risk management techniques can be applied within the cyberspace arena. The four steps in the risk/emergency management process—mitigation/prevention, preparedness, response, and recovery (Table 7.1)—should be examined in order to best prepare for and possibly prevent cyberterrorism.

TABLE 7.1 ● Risk Management Steps According the Department of Homeland Security

Mitigate	Heightened inspections, improved surveillance, public health/agriculture testing, immunizations, and law enforcement operations to deter/disrupt illegal activity and apprehend perpetrators.
Prepare	Continuing process. Involves efforts to identify threats, determine vulnerabilities, and identify required resources.
Respond	Implement policies for federal, state, local, and private-sector support. Address long-term, short-term, and direct effects of an incident, including immediate actions to preserve life, property, and the environment.
Recover	Helping people and the community return to normal, if possible. This can include development, coordination, and execution of service and site restoration.

Source: Based on U.S. Department of Homeland Security. (n.d.). *National infrastructure protection plan.* Retrieved from https://www.dhs.gov/national-infrastructure-protection-plan.

In order to properly address these steps, three aspects must be taken into account to determine risk: (1) the threat, (2) the asset, and (3) the vulnerability. Simply put: Risk is equal to the threat of attack, multiplied by the asset at risk and the vulnerability.

Risk = Threat × Asset × Vulnerability

As previously mentioned, risk is equal to the threat of attack multiplied by the asset at risk and the vulnerability.[38] In order to calculate the risk of a cyberterrorism attack, you must understand what constitutes a threat, an asset, and a vulnerability. These are outlined by U.S. Homeland Security Presidential Directives 7 & 8 and summarized as follows.[39]

Asset Value Assessment

The asset, or resource (either infrastructure or people), that needs protection must be assessed to determine (1) what the value of the potential target is and (2) how would contact with the target be made. In the case of cyberthreats, how protected is the virtual operating system from infiltration and/or attack? In order to do this, the functions and processes associated with the target must be understood. Finally, each potential target (asset) should be assigned a score ranging from 1 (very low) to 10 (very high), indicating the amount of destruction that would result from an attack on the asset.

Threat Assessment

In order to examine the threat aspect of risk assessment, it should be understood that risk can come from two sources: natural disasters and man-made disasters. In the case of man-made disasters, these can be divided into intentional and accidental. In the case of cyberterrorism, the threat would be an intentional man-made attack. The role of the perpetrator is key in this, as natural disasters as well as accidental disasters do not have the malicious intent that is present within intentional attacks.

Collins and Baggett detail a common method for evaluating the threat associated with intentional attacks, examining five factors: (1) existence, (2) capability, (3) history, (4) intention, and (5) targeting.[40] Existence is the reality of the threat. Does it actually exist, and if so, by whom? Capability is the availability of necessary weapons or techniques to attack the target. Are the weapons readily available, or must they be developed? History examines the past actions of the threat. Who have they targeted in the past and how? Intention examines the goal(s) of the perpetrator. What are they hoping to achieve by their actions, and would an attack against the target help to further their agenda? Finally, targeting looks at whether the threat has investigated infrastructures similar to the target, and if so, in what capacity. This method can be used for both general and specific threats. Once the threat level has been assessed, the vulnerability of the target must be considered.

Vulnerability Assessment

The last step of the risk assessment process is the vulnerability assessment, which examines weaknesses in the target and tries to address how to mitigate such weaknesses. In the case of cyberterrorism, the vulnerability assessment is mainly concerned with weaknesses in the cybersecurity of the infrastructure and how susceptible it would be to a cyberattack. Specifically, the accessibility of the target's cyber systems must be examined and the usefulness of the threat accessing such systems should be evaluated. Evaluators should consider examining what damage can be done by infiltrating the cyber systems and assessing how easy it is to do. Does the system allow for chemical, biological, radiological, nuclear, and explosive (CBRNE) weapons to be accessed? What safe measures are in place to protect and prevent access to the weapons? Is there a physical presence monitoring the activity in cyberspace, or are only safeguards and firewalls being used? And what is the damage potential should the system be breeched and fall victim to a malicious intentional attack?

Damage Potential

The precise potential damage from an act of cyberterrorism is unknown, as a true act of cyberterrorism has yet to occur. And although the actual likelihood of a cyberterror attack has been debated, it is necessary to understand the *potential* attack damage when evaluating vulnerability. Two main forms of damage include the physical damage resulting from a cyberattack and the economic damage.

Both are equally serious and not mutually exclusive of each other. To examine the potential for damage, damage from nonmalicious attacks can be used as a comparison tool. For example, using the 2003 blackout as a comparison tool for a malicious attack on the power grid may allow for a better understanding of what could result from cyberterrorism. Once damage is assessed and considered in the aspect of vulnerability, risk assessment can be conducted. By quantitatively assessing risk, mitigation and preparedness measures can be implemented if deemed necessary. Once the risk is assessed, three options are possible:

1. Accept the risk and take no action.
2. Install some preparedness measures (firewalls, etc.).
3. Completely harden the cyber infrastructure so that penetration is unlikely.

The likelihood of such an attack against critical infrastructure has been questioned in the past; however, the case of Vitek Boden presented in Chapter 2 illustrates that physical damage can occur from a cyberattack. Another example that highlights the vulnerability of our critical infrastructures to cyberattacks happened in 2007. An 11-year-old boy was able to access and control the Norfolk Southern railway system, doing so because "he wanted to see trains." His breach into the system shocked the company, and the resulting damage was catastrophic. For over 3 days, the entire system was shut down and cost the railway millions in damages.[41]

THINK ABOUT IT 7.2

Critical Infrastructure Risk Assessment

Assume you have been hired by the government to assess the risk of cyberterrorism to a local critical infrastructure. How would you go about doing this? What barriers could/would you face? Who would you need to work with in order to complete your project?

Discuss these issues with your classmates in small groups.

What Would You Do?

Choose one of the 16 critical infrastructure sectors outlined earlier in the chapter. Designate a specific infrastructure (building, plant, individual, etc.) within that sector. As a group, use the risk management procedures to determine the risk of cyberterrorism for that infrastructure. Make sure to outline how the asset, threat, and vulnerability assessments were conducted. Based on your findings, devise a plan for mitigation, preparedness, response, and recovery from an attack of cyberterrorism.

Summary

Defining cyberterrorism is a hotly debated and contentious issue. Some claim that cyberterrorism doesn't exist; others use the term to describe any use of the Internet and technology for terrorism, and the term is often misused by the media to gain attention. Cyberterrorism is first and foremost a tactic, which can be used to inflict massive destruction and damage. However, the skills necessary to perpetrate such an attack are specialized and rare, which may be why an actual cyberterror attack has arguably not yet occurred.

Even though such an attack has not yet occurred, the probability or possibility of such an attack must be considered. Risk management techniques should be put in place to assess vulnerabilities and protect infrastructures. As the world continues to move in a technological direction, the threat of cyberterrorism becomes a more realistic possibility, and criminal justice professionals should be prepared for the threat.

Key Terms

- CBRNE weapons 139
- Critical Infrastructure 137
- Cyberterrorism 128
- Homeland Security Presidential Directives 138
- Key Assets 137
- Lone-wolf terrorist 135
- Mitigate 138
- Prepare 138
- Presidential Policy Directive 21 137
- Recover 138
- Respond 138
- Risk Management 138
- Violence 129

Discussion Questions

1. Is the role of physical violence necessary in events of cyberterrorism? Why or why not?
2. Why are critical infrastructures so vulnerable to cyberterrorism?
3. How has terrorist use of technology evolved from the 1990s until today? What should we do to respond to this?
4. Risk = ________________ × ________________ × ________________
5. What do you believe to be the most important element of the risk management process? Why do you think so? What, then, is the role of the other two components?

Internet Resources

Department of Homeland Security: Critical Infrastructure Sectors
https://www.dhs.gov/critical-infrastructure-sectors

The Cyberterrorism Project
http://www.cyberterrorism-project.org/

Cyberterrorism Defense Initiative
http://www.cyberterrorismcenter.org/

National Cybersecurity Preparedness Consortium (NCPC)
http://nationalcpc.org/

Further Reading

Chen, T. M., Jarvis, L., & McDonald, S. (Eds.). (2014). *Cyberterrorism: Understanding, assessment, and response*. New York, NY: Springer-Verlag.

Colarik, A. M. (2006). *Cyber terrorism: Political and economic implications*. Hershey, PA: Idea Group.

Parker, A. M. S. (2010). Cyberterrorism: An evaluation of the preparedness of North Carolina local law enforcement. *Security Journal, 23*(3), 159–173.

Verton, D. (2003). *Black ice: The invisible threat of cyber-terrorism*. New York, NY: McGraw-Hill.

Weimann, G. (2015). *Terrorism in cyberspace: The next generation*. New York, NY: Columbia University Press.

Digital Resources

Want a better grade?

Get the tools you need to sharpen your study skills. Access practice quizzes and eFlashcards, at **study.sagepub.com/kremling**.

An Evolving Threat

The Deep Web

Learning Objectives

1. Explain the differences between the deep web and darknets.
2. Understand how the darknets are accessed.
3. Discuss the hidden wiki and how it is useful to criminals.
4. Understand the anonymity offered by the deep web.
5. Discuss the legal issues associated with use of the deep web and the darknets.

> The action aimed to stop the sale, distribution and promotion of illegal and harmful items, including weapons and drugs, which were being sold on online 'dark' marketplaces. Operation Onymous, coordinated by Europol's European Cybercrime Centre (EC3), the FBI, the U.S. Immigration and Customs Enforcement (ICE), Homeland Security Investigations (HSI) and Eurojust, resulted in 17 arrests of vendors and administrators running these online marketplaces and more than 410 hidden services being taken down. In addition, bitcoins worth approximately USD 1 million, EUR 180,000 in cash, drugs, gold and silver were seized.
>
> **—Europol, 2014**[1]

THINK ABOUT IT 8.1

Surface Web and Deep Web

Google, Facebook, and any website you can find via traditional search engines (Internet Explorer, Chrome, Firefox, etc.) are all located on the surface web. It is likely that when you use the Internet for research and/or social purposes you are using the surface web. The surface web only accounts for about 4% of all the Internet—the rest is found on the deep web, sometimes also referred to as the deep net. The deep web is not accessible through traditional search engines. In order to access the deep web, special considerations are needed, including private URL addresses or, for some areas, darknets (specialized software).

What Would You Do?

1. The deep web offers users an anonymity that the surface web cannot provide. What would you do if you knew that your electronic footprints could not be traced?
2. Why would this be appealing to criminals?
3. What problems does anonymity create for law enforcement and other criminal justice professionals?

The Surface Web

Before discussing a seemingly unknown aspect of the Internet, it is necessary to define what the majority of users consider to be the Internet: the surface web, or the public web. Like its name, the surface web contains any and all websites accessible via traditional search engines, such as Google. The surface web is accessible to anyone with Internet connection and is hosted by browsers such as Internet Explorer, Firefox, and Google Chrome. According to some sources, there are over 4 billion indexed web pages on the surface web; however, many search engines do not have the capacity to access all pages.[2] On average, Google accesses 16% of the surface web, while other search engines are able to access even less.[3]

Criminals do operate on the surface web but are more vulnerable to being discovered than if they operate on the deep web. Examples of crime on the surface web include the stealing of personal information and data for financial gain. However, even more deceptive are surface websites that operate as legitimate businesses but are marketing counterfeit goods. As illustrated in Chart 8.1, millions of dollars in counterfeit goods are seized every year by the U.S. government. Much of this is sold online via websites that are constantly changing their Internet protocol (IP) addresses. Unknown to the buyer, the goods are counterfeit and are being sold illegally, taking advantage of the easy access online shopping provides.

CHART 8.1 ● Counterfeit Goods Seized by the United States: 2014

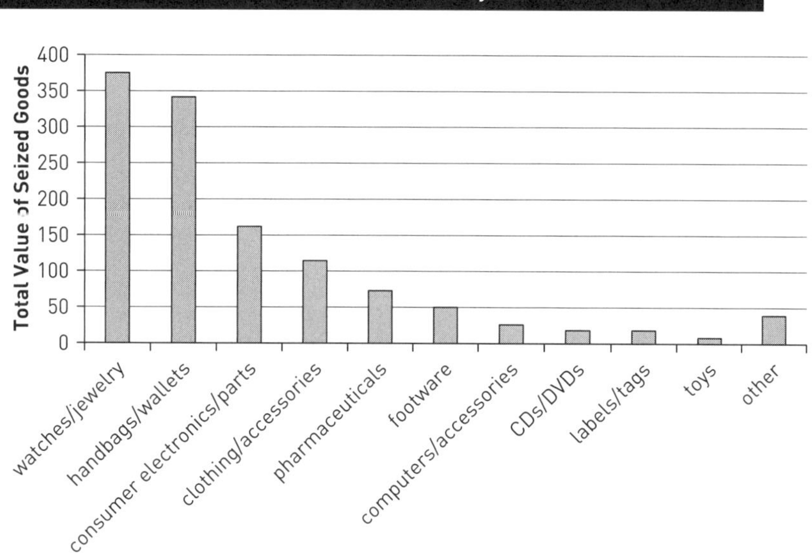

Source: Based on data from Bain, M. (2015). *Counterfeit watches and jewelry are the new counterfeit handbags*. Retrieved from http://qz.com/376249/counterfeit-watches-and-jewelry-are-the-new-counterfeit-handbags/.

The Deep Web and Darknets

Although the surface web seems vast and infinite, it is only a small piece of the Internet compared to the deep web. The surface web is often compared to the tip of the iceberg (see Figure 8.1) of the Internet, as the deep web is 400 to 500 times bigger than the surface web.[4] Moreover, there is an anonymity associated with parts of the deep web, specifically on the dark web. There is much confusion between the deep web and the dark web. These terms are often used interchangeably, but these two areas are not the same. The dark web is just a small portion of the deep web. Both are inaccessible from the surface web, and many general Internet users are unaware of their existence.

The deep web consists of all data behind firewalls. Surface websites use "crawlers" to browse the web in a systematic and automated manner. Deep websites cannot be found via these crawlers. Deep websites can include passcode protected websites, websites that are not searchable, sites that are not linked to other programs (in which the URL must be typed in), medical databases, business Intranets, and darknets (dark web).[5]

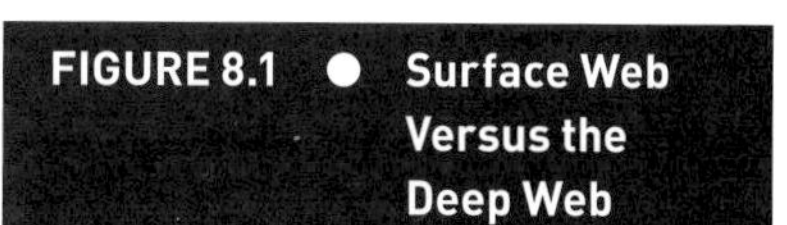
FIGURE 8.1 ● Surface Web Versus the Deep Web

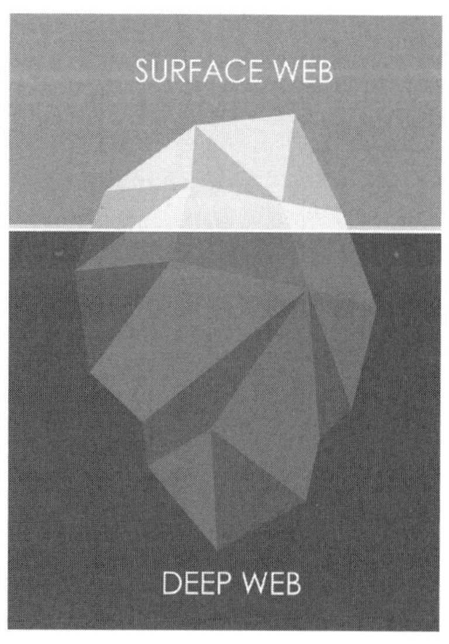

© iStockphoto.com/traffic_analyzer

FIGURE 8.2 ● Deep Versus Darknets (Dark Web)

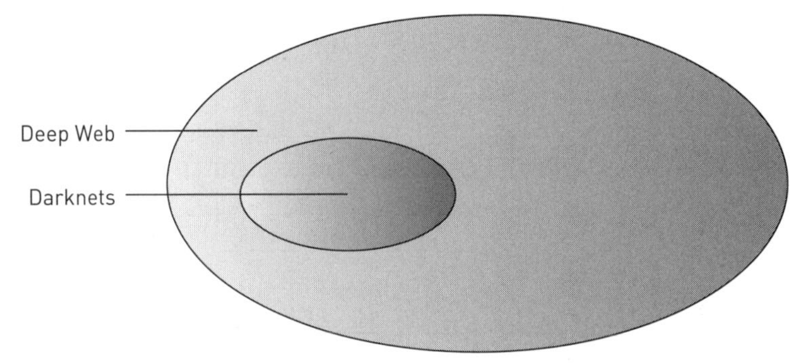

Darknets (also referred to as dark web) make up a small part of the massive deep web (see Figure 8.2), and this is where the majority of criminal activities on the deep web occur. There are two main forms of darknets: peer-to-peer networks (used for file sharing) and large anonymous networks.[6] We concentrate on the large anonymous networks in this chapter.

Due to the anonymity provided, many criminals may feel more comfortable operating in the darknet market than on the surface web or even in the physical world. One reason for this is the lack of law enforcement presence on the deep web. It is extremely difficult to track the digital footprints of criminals on the deep web (see Chapter 9 and the discussion of guardianship for more). Another reason for the high prevalence of criminal activity on the deep web is the ease of accessibility.

Accessibility

Accessing darknets is relatively easy, although it cannot be done via surface web search engines (i.e., Google). There are multiple portals for the darknet, including Freenet, I2P, and The Onion Router. To access the darknet, one must first download one of these platforms. Freenet describes itself as "a peer-to-peer platform for censorship-resistant communication and publishing. Browse websites, post on forums, and publish files within Freenet with strong privacy protections."[7]

The Invisible Internet Project (I2P) advertises that "The I2P network provides strong privacy protections for communication over the Internet. Many activities that would risk your privacy on the public Internet can be conducted anonymously inside I2P" and that it is "an anonymous overlay network—a network within a network. It is intended to protect communication from dragnet surveillance and monitoring by third parties such as ISPs."[8]

Although both of these provide sufficient access to darknets, the most popular portal for access is The Onion Router.

The Onion Router

The Onion Router (aka ToR) was originally developed by the U.S. Naval Research Laboratory as a method of anonymous communication. It can be downloaded for free, and the website asserts:

> Tor is free software and an open network that helps you defend against traffic analysis, a form of network surveillance that threatens personal freedom and privacy, confidential business activities and relationships, and state security.[9]

In regard to security, ToR

> protects you by bouncing your communications around a distributed network of relays run by volunteers all around the world: it prevents somebody watching your Internet connection from learning what sites you visit, and it prevents the sites you visit from learning your physical location.[10]

The number of ToR users around the world is increasing (see Chart 8.2), as many find benefit to the anonymity provided by the server. Once hidden within the layers of ToR, individuals can browse the darknets while their privacy is protected. Sites on the ToR network end in .onion, but if you were to type the web address into Google, the website would not be found. According to the ToR website, people use this platform for multiple *noncriminal* reasons, as outlined in Table 8.1.

TABLE 8.1 • Benefits of ToR Use

Who Is Using ToR?	Why? (Activity)
People Without Malicious Intent	Surf the net in privacy, protect themselves and their families
Businesses	Research competitions, keep strategies secret, internal accountability
Activists	Report abuses and violations from dangerous locations; whistleblowing
Media	Protect sources, resources, and report from areas where it is dangerous
Military/Law Enforcement	Protect communications, investigations, and intelligence

Source: Based on information from torproject.org.

Although many use ToR for legitimate purposes, darknets are known to attract criminals due to the anonymity they provide. Criminals can sell their illicit goods under the protection provided by the deep web.

CHART 8.2 ● Worldwide Onion Router (ToR) Users

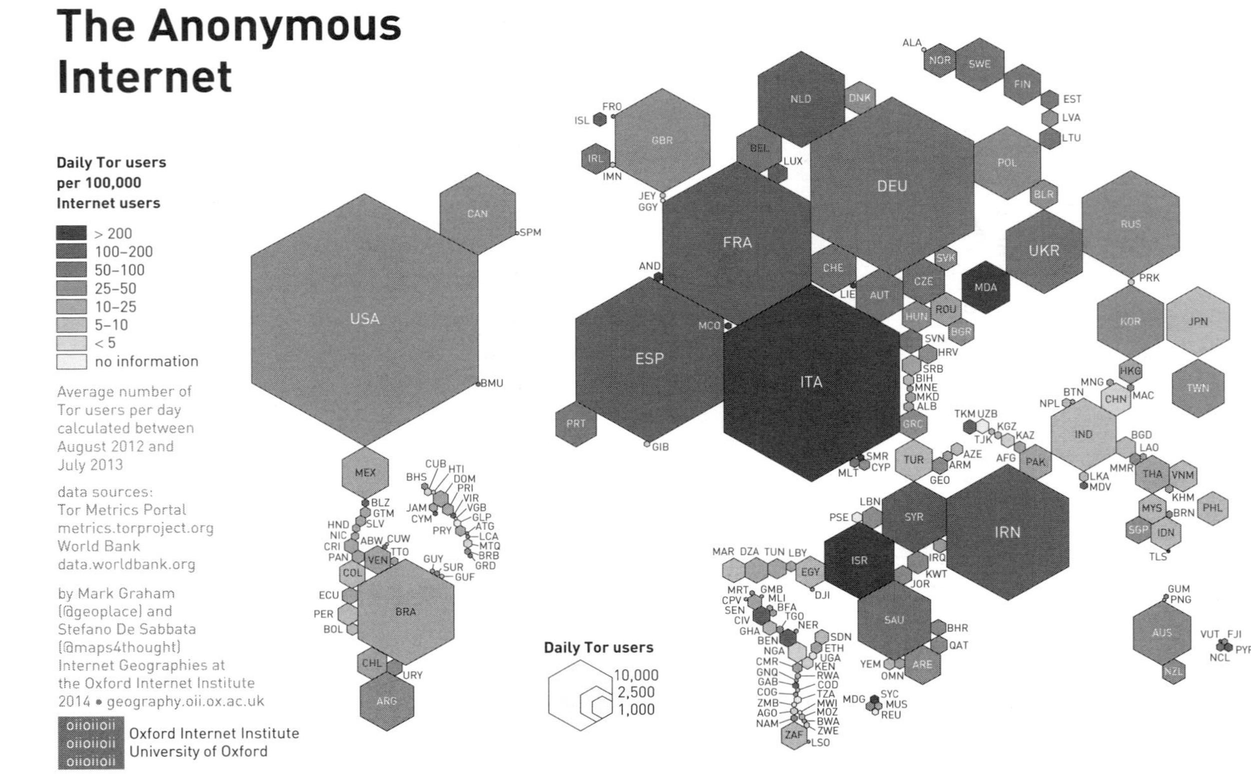

Source: The Anonymous Internet by Mark Graham and Stefano De Sabbata, https://commons.wikimedia.org/wiki/File:Geographies_of_Tor.png. Licensed under CC BY-SA 4.0, https://creativecommons.org/licenses/by-sa/4.0/legalcode.

Products Available

As previously mentioned, both legal and illegal products and services are available on the deep web. Social media sites such as Facebook are accessible on the deep web. Research tools and databases are also located on the deep web. Some of these include JSTOR (an academic search engine), the National Oceanic and Atmospheric Administration, and NASA.[11] In countries where access to social media and/or academic materials/news is restricted or all together prohibited, the deep web offers a place where oppressed populations can retrieve and share information.

Other blogs and chatrooms are available on the deep web. Although not criminal, they may be groups that enjoy certain fetishes or activities and do not feel comfortable sharing that information on the surface web. Fan fiction, from sci-fi to Harry Potter, also finds a home on the deep web. Although some of these groups may not be viewed as mainstream, they are not illegal. The majority of illegal products on the deep web are found in black market darknets.

Via ToR or other specialized browsers, deep web users can access darknet marketplaces. Virtually every type of illegal goods, services, and information is available in darknet markets. Drugs, guns, credit card information, specialty items (Ebola-tainted blood, nuclear materials), and banned books/guides are all available for sale. Moreover, contract killings, human trafficking sales, and videos of human experiments are also products found via darknets. Sites with counterfeit products, as mentioned in the section on the surface web, have also found security on darknets. Once an individual accesses the darknet, they need only go to the hidden wiki in order to find links to any and/or all of these products.

THINK ABOUT IT 8.2

Black Market Blood

In the height of the West African Ebola crisis in 2014–2015, many hospitals could not keep up with the number of individuals being admitted. Resources were scarce, and many were left without proper health care. Due to this, some turned to black markets to buy the blood of survivors. This blood, known as convalescent serum, was believed to have antibodies that could prevent or possibly treat individuals with Ebola, much like modern vaccines.[12]

However, the blood of survivors is not the only blood for sale on the black market. One darknet site was offering Ebola-infected blood for sale by the gallon. Based on what we know about the Ebola virus, there is a 72-hour incubation period before symptoms begin to appear, and once they do, the disease can spread very rapidly.

What Would You Do?

1. Why would someone sell Ebola-infected blood?
2. What damages could occur if someone with malicious intent purchased the blood?
3. What issues does this pose to national and international security?

The Hidden Wiki

The hidden wiki is a popular way to search the darknets. It acts as a search engine for illicit goods, products, and services. The hidden wiki, just like traditional wikis, can be edited by anyone. This means that criminals can anonymously post links to their black market pages, and anyone on the darknet can access them.

Links on the hidden wiki may include websites that feature instructions for illegal activities such as bomb making or the production of methamphetamines. There are recruitment sites for jihadi organizations, assassins for hire, and sites that allow shoppers to purchase stolen credit card information. Darker aspects of some darknets may include violent pornography, snuff films, child pornography, and sadistic videos. Sites that show torture and human experimentation are also operating in the dark arena. Unfortunately, when there is a demand for a product, there is usually someone willing to supply it, and the anonymity provided on darknets can be very appealing to some suppliers.

Some of the most popular products advertised on the hidden wiki are drugs. Drug marketplaces run rampant on darknets. Silk Road (and the subsequent Silk Road 2.0) is arguably the most well-known .onion site for the drug market. As shown in Image 8.1, any and all drug products and paraphernalia are available via Silk Road.

The Silk Road

The darknet Silk Road takes its name from the historical Silk Road, which, during the 19th century, was a trade route from China to Central Asia and then later into Europe. The road was traveled well by merchants selling silk, iron, gold, fruits, spices, and exotic animals. Although the road was a popular trade route, there are still many secrets to the original Silk Road that have yet to be uncovered.[13] The secretiveness of the historical Silk Road is one reason why using the name for the darknet marketplace is so applicable.

The darknet Silk Road runs like a black market eBay-type site for drugs, drug paraphernalia, and other goods and services. Potential buyers can read reviews on the products, the shipping, the seller's reputation, and more. Prices are listed in bitcoins and are shipped to remote addresses or post office boxes. During its prime operating period, Silk Road advertised more than 13,000 listings for controlled substances from vendors in the United States, Germany, the Netherlands, Canada, the United Kingdom, Spain, Ireland, Italy, Austria, and France.[14]

Vendors on Silk Road reportedly made over $1.2 million per month in 2011–2012 and more than doubled that in 2013. The ease of setting up a shop via Silk Road is another reason the site is so appealing. Potential sellers need only to fill out an online form and click a link to pay 150 bitcoin in order to become a vendor on Silk Road. According to one seller, "The opportunity to make money online is far greater than selling locally; even without moving lots of weight."[15] And as much as the vendors make, the operators who ran Silk Road profited with close to $92,000 per month in commissions alone.

IMAGE 8.1 ● Silk Road Marketplace Screenshot

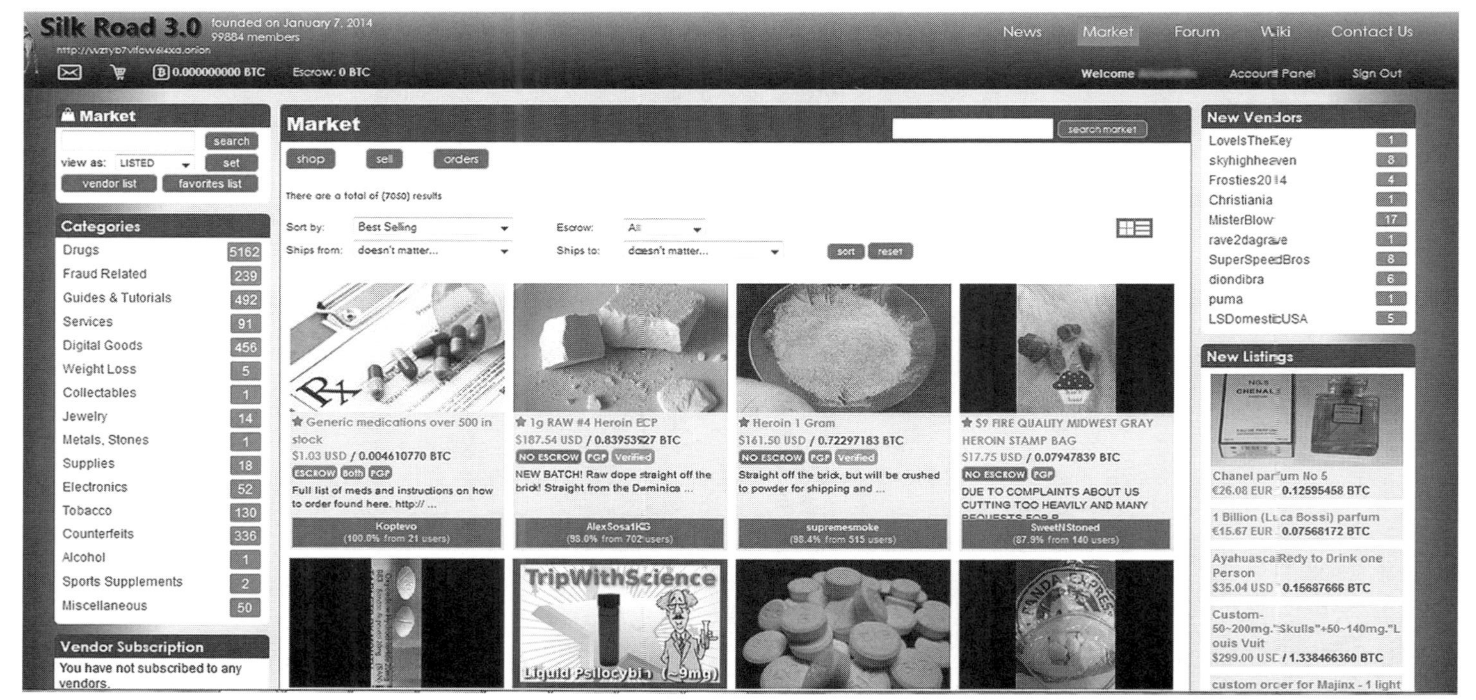

The success of Silk Road vendors is due mostly to the reputation they built for themselves based on product quality and customer reviews. As stated by one seller in research conducted by Van Hout and Bingham in 2014,

> reputation on Silk Road is what keeps the vendors in business. Your reputation is open to all. The seller who wants good business on Silk Road has to try and make every customer happy. Customer service has never been this good on the street market.[16]

One of the main issues with the quality of the product is ensuring that bad and/or tainted products are not sold. Although customers rate the quality of the drugs purchased, at least six overdose deaths have been tied to products purchased on Silk Road. Three victims overdosed on heroin, two from a synthetic form of LSD, and one from health issues triggered by drug use.[17]

Federal agencies have shut Silk Road down multiple times, but as hundreds of .onion addresses lead to the Silk Road, new links pop up once the site has been compromised. Law enforcement actions are discussed in detail later in the chapter.

THINK ABOUT IT 8.3

Dread Pirate Roberts and the Silk Road

The name Dread Pirate Roberts is usually associated with the movie *The Princess Bride*. However, it is also the pseudonym adopted by Ross Ulbricht, the creator of Silk Road. Ulbricht earned a master's degree in material science and engineering, and was also an Eagle Scout. As the creator of Silk Road, he earned over $13 million in commissions off the sale of illegal goods and services.

In 2013, after a multijurisdictional interagency operation, Ulbricht was arrested and charged with multiple offenses. In 2015, he was found guilty of seven offenses: distributing narcotics, distributing narcotics by means of the Internet, conspiracy to distribute narcotics, engaging in a continuing criminal enterprise, conspiring to commit computer hacking, conspiring to traffic in false identity documents, and conspiring to commit money laundering.[18]

Ulbricht was sentenced to life in prison and had to forfeit $183,961,921. Although Ulbricht received an extremely harsh sentence, online darknet drug markets, including Silk Road 2.0, still continue to flourish.

What Would You Do?

1. What does this tell criminal justice professionals about the role deterrence plays in crime in cyberspace?
2. How does this case affect the perception of the applicability of traditional criminal justice methods and theory to crime conducted online?
3. As a criminal justice professional, what would you do to ensure that the actions of Ulbricht were not replicated?

Payment: Cryptocurrency

Since bank accounts and credit cards contain personal information and are easily traceable, a different form of monetary transaction is necessary for darknet purchases. Cryptocurrency, or currency that exists only in the digital arena (you cannot physically hold digital money), is one way that purchases on the deep web can be made in anonymity. Used for both legitimate purchases and illegal ones, cryptocurrency has been evolving since 2009. Two of the most popular forms of cryptocurrency are bitcoins and dash.

Bitcoins (BTC or ฿)

Bitcoins, abbreviated BTC or with the symbol ฿, is a digital currency created in 2009 by an individual using the pseudonym Satoshi Nakamoto. Bitcoins can be used for online, seemingly anonymous, transactions; however, they are not issued by a bank. Bitcoins are also popular with hackers because this currency only exists online and is not controlled by a central authority nor subject to regulation, and therefore untraceable. This makes it very useful for criminals such as drug traffickers and hackers who are extorting money via malware infections (ransomware).

Bitcoins can be obtained in many ways, the simplest being through purchase. Bitcoin exchanges allow for the transfer and purchase of the online currency. Bitcoins can also be obtained via "mining." Mining involves solving complex mathematical puzzles every 10 minutes. The person who solves the puzzle first receives approximately 25 bitcoins, although the amount can vary. Bitcoins are held in a virtual wallet associated with an encrypted IP address. Bitcoin transactions are recorded to ensure users can only spend their Bitcoins once. Although this may seem like a security issue, the blockchain that stores the transaction information has protections so the identities of those involved in the transactions are not identifiable.[19]

One issue with bitcoins is that this currency is not nearly as stable or predictable as real currency, such as the dollar or euro. The exchange rate of bitcoins is highly volatile. When first created, one U.S. dollar could purchase 1,309 bitcoins. In 2010, a programmer in Florida, experimenting with bitcoins, sent 10,000 BTC overseas to an individual in London to purchase pizza (valued around $25). Today, that pizza would be worth £1,961,034 ($2,443,945.39).[20] When the FBI shut down Silk Road as discussed previously, the value of bitcoins changed substantially. Since then, the bitcoin has fluctuated but consistently increased in value. As of February 1, 2017, the exchange rate for one bitcoin was 967.40 U.S. dollars.[21]

IMAGE 8.2 • Bitcoins (BTC or ฿)

© iStockphoto.com/skodonnell

Many legal businesses do not accept bitcoins; however, this is starting to change. In the illegal marketplace, especially on darknets, it is a preferred payment method because it is completely anonymous and bitcoins can be transferred anywhere in the world safely and quickly.

Dash

Dash is another form of online digital currency. Modeled off of bitcoins, dash claims to improve on bitcoins by offering an enhanced level of security. According to dash's official webpage, with bitcoins it is possible to trace a transaction back to see the parties involved. Furthermore, because the bitcoin transactions are one-on-one, with miners being used to confirm validity of payment, a permanent record of all transactions is established.[22]

Dash eliminates this security issue by implementing a two-tier security network. With dash, a third party is not necessary to protect identities, as it uses masternodes (decentralized networks) to scramble data. Due to this, the wait to be approved for a transaction (a wait commonplace in transactions using bitcoins) is eliminated and transactions are almost instantly confirmed.[23] Many online sites, both on the deep and surface webs, have not yet implemented the use of dash as it is new and subsequently less well known than bitcoins. However, if the use of decentralized masternodes proves to be effective, dash may become the safer and faster option for online cryptocurrency.

Law Enforcement Response

Due to its popularity, Silk Road garnered the attention of the Drug Enforcement Agency. When the founder of Silk Road was arrested in October 2013, Silk Road was shut down (Image 8.3) and $25 million worth of bitcoins were seized. However, not long afterward, a copycat site known as Silk Road 2.0 emerged. When federal agents attempted to close it down, a backdoor was established by Silk Road administrators, allowing people with the password to enter the site.

An ongoing battle between federal law enforcement and dark web administrators has emerged, with law enforcement shutting down the site and administrators reopening Silk Road on a new .onion page. However, due to the attention received from federal agencies, other darknet drug markets have emerged. Some of the more popular alternative sites include Agora, Evolution, and Andromeda.

IMAGE 8.3 ● Silk Road Seizures

Federal Bureau of Investigation

As federal law enforcement became more aware of the darknet drug markets, they began cracking down on the sites. In 2014, agencies from around the world got together to shut down deep web black markets in an action known as Operation Onymous.

Operation Onymous

On November 6, 2014, law enforcement, collaborating together and coordinated via Europol, took down multiple darknet drug marketplaces, including Silk Road 2.0. Seventeen countries—the United States, Bulgaria, Czech Republic, Finland, France, Germany, Hungary, Ireland, Latvia, Lithuania, Luxembourg, Netherlands, Romania, Spain, Sweden, Switzerland, and the United Kingdom—were involved in this collaborative effort. According to reports, over 400 .onion domain names associated with at least 27 darknet sites were seized and shut down.[24] In one of the biggest moves of law enforcement against darknet sites, the FBI arrested the alleged operator of Silk Road 2.0, Blake Benthall, and filed a civil complaint in New York.[25]

The civil complaint against the 27 darknet sites includes allegations of (1) selling illegal narcotics, (2) selling fake or stolen credit cards, (3) selling counterfeit currency, and (4) selling fake IDs, including passports.[26] An undisclosed number of bitcoins was also seized. Besides Benthall, 17 others were also arrested, although their identities were not revealed. Benthall, charged with multiple counts including narcotics trafficking, confessed to being involved with Silk Road 2.0. He is currently incarcerated at an unidentified location.

Anonymous and "Vigilante Justice"

As law enforcement is attempting to infiltrate darknet websites, the group Anonymous (see Chapter 5) is taking down darknet sites as well. In acts that could be considered hacktivism, or in some cases vigilante justice, Anonymous is able to penetrate parts of the deep web that law enforcement may not.

In February 2017, Anonymous shut down the over 16,000 .onion sites, including the darknet page Freedom Hosting II. Anonymous left the following message, defacing the site's access page:

> Hello, Freedom Hosting II, you have been hacked
>
> We are disappointed . . . This is an excerpt from your front page 'We have zero tolerance policy to child pornography.'-but what we found while searching through your server is more than 50% child porn . . .
>
> Moreover you host many scam sites, some of which are evidently run by yourself to cover hosting expenses.
>
> All your files have been copied and your databases have been dumped. (74GB of files and 2.3GB of database)
>
> Up until January 31st you were hosting 10613 sites. Private keys are included in the dump. Show full list (hyperlink)
>
> We are Anonymous. We do not forgive. We do not forget. You should have expected us.

> Thank you for your patience, you don't have to buy data ;) we made a torrent of the database dump download here (hyperlink)
>
> Here another torrent with all system files (excluding user data) download (hyperlink)
>
> You may still donate to BTC (bitcoins) to 14iCDyeCSp12AmhVfJGxtrzX-DabFop4QtU and support us.
>
> If you need to get in contact with us, our mail is fhosting@sigaint.org
>
> We repeatedly get how we got into the system. It was surprisingly easy. Here is how we did it: HOW TO HACK FH2 (hyperlink)
>
> Edit: couldn't reply to Clearnet – new mail
>
> Edit2; database dump added
>
> Edit3: added instructions on how we got into the system
>
> Edit4: system files added[27]

Anonymous is well known for their activism against ideas they do not support. They are not against the use of the web for criminal activities, but it is the type of activity (in this case, child pornography) that they act against. This is not the first time Anonymous has acted against darknet sites. In 2011, the predecessor of Freedom Hosting II (the original Freedom Hosting) hosted over 50% of darknet sites, including sites containing child pornography. Anonymous hit the site with denial-of-service attacks and the site was eventually removed by the FBI.[28]

THINK ABOUT IT 8.4

Online Vigilante Justice

Freedom Hosting II broke the law by posting child pornography links on its website. Before law enforcement could respond, the hacktivist group Anonymous hacked into the site, and in an act that could be described as vigilante justice, closed the forum down.

The term *vigilante* refers to "a member of a volunteer committee organized to suppress and punish crime summarily (as when the processes of law are viewed as inadequate),"[29] or someone who punishes certain behavior without the authority to do so.

What Freedom Hosting II was doing (allowing links to child pornography to be posted on their site after explicitly saying they would not do so) is against the law; however, so is hacking.

Should the actions of Anonymous be ignored by law enforcement, as their actions shut down more serious criminal activity, or should they be prosecuted as well, regardless of the good that came out of their criminal behavior?

What Would You Do?

1. Should the actions of Anonymous be protected?
2. Is there past precedent for such actions?
3. How would this affect other cases of vigilante justice, especially those cases that are not so nonviolent?

Terrorist Presence on the Deep and Dark Web

> The government does things like insisting that all encryption programs have a back door. But surely no one is stupid enough to think the terrorists are going to use encryption systems with a back door. The terrorists will simply hire a programmer to come up with secure encryption scheme.
>
> **—Kevin Mitnick**[30]

Cybercriminals are not the only criminal entity who have a presence on and can benefit from the anonymity provided by the deep web. Terrorist organizations can use the deep web as a place to hide their activities. Once anonymous, terrorist organizations can distribute propaganda, train and exchange information with hackers, post training videos, detail how to make nuclear bombs, buy and sell weapons, purchase false identification, and communicate without detection.[31]

Some examples of known terrorist presence on the dark web include an al-Qaeda online forum (ek-Is.org), a weapons marketplace (vlp4uw547agp52is.onion), and an identity marketplace (Web.g6lfrbqd3krju3ek.onion). Chin and his colleagues uncovered a deep web page, "Encyclopedia of Training and Preparedness," which included a set of lessons titled "The Nuclear Tutorial for the Mujahedeen." This tutorial contains over 450 pages of instructions for future jihadists and includes discussion of both nuclear and electromagnetic bombs.[32] Other training manuals and instructions for waging jihad against Western countries have also been discovered. Terrorist organizations use the dark web to reach out to followers, supporters, donators, sympathizers, and others who may contribute to the success of their organizations, as pictured in screenshot Image 8.4.

IMAGE 8.4 ● Screenshot of a Darknet Site for Funding Islamic Extremism

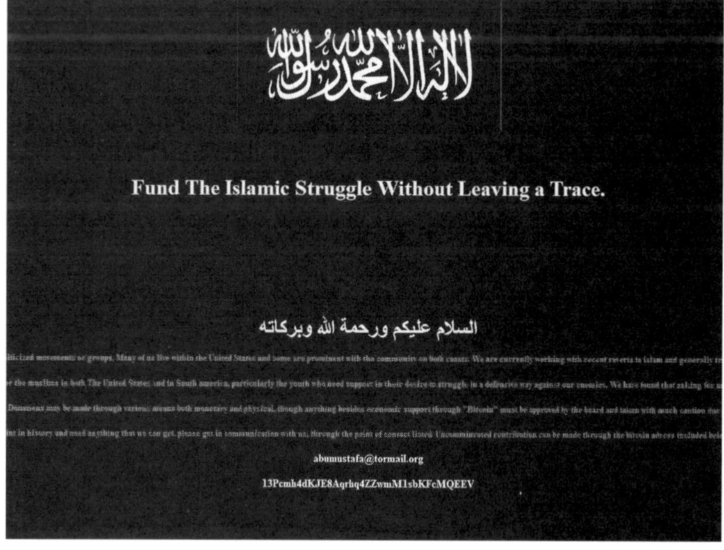

Fund The Islamic Struggle Without Leaving a Trace.
السلام عليكم ورحمة الله وبركاته
abumustafa@tormail.org
13Pcmh4dKJE8Aqrhq4ZZwmM1sbKFcMQEEV

CASE STUDY 8.1

ISIS and the Threat of the Darknet

It is well known that the Islamic State in Iraq and Syria (ISIS; also referred to as ISIL, the Islamic State, and Daesh) has an established presence on the surface web. ISIS has used online chatrooms, forums, and social media in an unprecedented fashion to distribute propaganda, recruit supporters, and to fundraise. However, there is rising concern that ISIS may also have a viable presence on the darknet.

It has been reported that ISIS hosts a "help desk" on the darknet to assist supporters in carrying out attacks. According to the report, the helpdesk operates 24 hours a day, with six operators to answer questions via a series of forums that ISIS supporters can go to for information on how they can support the extremist movement.[33] These chatrooms are not the only way that ISIS could exploit darknet resources for their cause. As previously mentioned, there are mercenaries and assassins for hire. ISIS has ample money to be able to hire these individuals to act on behalf of the organization. Furthermore, hackers for hire can be used to commit cyberattacks that steal data, and ISIS can turn around and sell the data for a profit.[34]

ISIS could use the darknet to coordinate attacks, make plans, and discuss potential targets. Training in cyberskills (hacking, staying hidden, encryption) is also available via darknets.

What Do You Think?

1. How could ISIS use such information to further their goals?

Legal Issues

The Constitution has long established the right to freedom of speech (First Amendment) and the protection against unwarranted search and seizure (Fourth Amendment). However, these issues are often questioned in regard to the Internet in general and especially the deep web. Moreover, due to the borderless arena that is the Internet, users of the deep web and its darknets should be aware of the legality associated with the country in which they are residing and that from which the website is hosted. What is legal in some countries may not be legal in others. The founding fathers were not anticipating the borderless, limitless jurisdiction of the web when they wrote the Constitution, so the U.S. Supreme Court has had to reexamine these issues to evaluate their applicability in cyberspace.

In regard to freedom of speech, the First Amendment reads:

> Congress shall make no law respecting an establishment of religion, or prohibiting the free exercise thereof; or abridging the freedom of speech, or of the press; or the right of the people peaceably to assemble, and to petition the Government for a redress of grievances.[35]

The U.S. Supreme Court elaborated on this by saying that these rights do not include situations that pose a "clear and present danger":

> A situation created which someone deems to require a governmental limitation on Constitutional First Amendment freedoms of speech, press or

> assembly, such as shouting "fire" in a crowded theater (speech), printing a list of the names and addresses of CIA agents (press) or gathering together a lynch mob (assembly).[36]

However, it is unknown as to what would cause a clear and present danger in cyberspace. Much of the information contained on darknets may be legal; however, what someone chooses to do with that information may not be. The Electronic Frontier Foundation (EFF) is an advocacy group that works to protect the right to free speech online, including the freedom to exchange ideas and opinions without the fear of prosecution. They also work to protect the right to anonymity on the Internet, especially on the deep web.

Anonymity is not guaranteed within the First Amendment, but it has been interpreted by the U.S. Supreme Court. Individuals can speak and write anonymously, as long as it does not violate the law. In the 1995 case of *McIntyre v. Ohio Elections Commission* 514 U.S. 334, the court ruled:

> Protections for anonymous speech are vital to democratic discourse. Allowing dissenters to shield their identities frees them to express critical minority views . . . Anonymity is a shield from the tyranny of the majority. . . . It thus exemplifies the purpose behind the Bill of Rights and of the First Amendment in particular: to protect unpopular individuals from retaliation . . . at the hand of an intolerant society.[37]

Since this 1995 decision, opportunities for anonymous speech and writing have increased substantially. See Legal Issue 8.1 to discuss how this interpretation may or may not apply to cyberspace.

The Fourth Amendment has also come under question in regard to online criminal activity, specifically in regard to search and seizure. The Fourth Amendment reads:

> The right of the people to be secure in their persons, houses, papers, and effects, against unreasonable searches and seizures, shall not be violated, and no warrants shall issue, but upon probable cause, supported by oath or affirmation, and particularly describing the place to be searched, and the persons or things to be seized.[38]

The Fourth Amendment was interpreted in 1914 in *Weeks v. United States* 232 U.S. 383, to include that any evidence seized during an illegal search was considered "fruits of the poisonous tree" and was not admissible in federal court (the Exclusionary Rule). The Exclusionary Rule was extended to apply to the states in 1961, *Mapp v. Ohio* 367 U.S. 643.[39]

The main Fourth Amendment/Exclusionary Rule issues in regard to the deep web are (1) how is probable cause established in cyberspace, (2) must warrants be issued to search cyberspace, and (3) if a search is found to be illegal, what online evidence should be excluded, or considered "fruits of the poisonous tree"?

In 2009, the U.S. Supreme Court examined search and seizure in cyberspace in the case of *U.S. v Wellman* 716 F. Supp. 2d 447. Wellman was accused of obtaining child pornography via peer-to-peer Internet sites. An online search revealed that the IP address attached to the pornography was associated with Wellman's computer. Based on this, a judge issued a warrant to search Wellman's home. The search of the home revealed more child pornography, both on the computer's hard drive and on DVDs, and Wellman was subsequently arrested.[40] This case presents an interesting perspective: Should evidence obtained in cyberspace be admissible to show probable cause and obtain a search warrant for a physical location?

LEGAL ISSUE 8.1

ANONYMITY AND THE FIRST AMENDMENT

In 1995, with the case of *McIntyre v. Ohio Elections Commission*, the U.S. Supreme Court interpreted how the First Amendment applied to anonymity. By holding that "protections for anonymous speech are vital to democratic discourse. Allowing dissenters to shield their identities frees them to express critical minority views . . . Anonymity is a shield from the tyranny of the majority. . . . It thus exemplifies the purpose behind the Bill of Rights and of the First Amendment in particular: to protect unpopular individuals from retaliation . . . at the hand of an intolerant society," the court protected anonymous speech and writing as long as it did not break the law.

On the deep web and its darknets, anonymity is a given—that is, established once an individual signs in to the ToR network or another deep web browser. The EFF works to protect the rights of online anonymity. However, this is increasingly difficult when many of the darknet sites contain information that may lead to illegal behavior. Review what EFF has published on their webpage about anonymity (https://www.eff.org/search/site/anonymity) and then discuss the following questions:

1. How has the deep web changed the way that First Amendment rights may be interpreted?
2. Should darknet sites be able to publish information that is not criminal in and of itself, and if so, should they be held responsible if a darknet user decides to use the information in an illegal or malicious way?
3. What role does EFF play in defending the right to anonymity, both on the surface and on the deep web?

Summary

The evolution of the deep web and its subsequent darknets has expanded at an unprecedented pace. The deep web is not criminal in and of itself; however, the anonymity provided, especially on darknets, makes it an attractive tool for criminals. Furthermore, the use of hidden IP addresses and cryptocurrency allow for increased anonymity when operating on the deep web. These benefits also make darknets extremely attractive to terrorists for use in propaganda distribution, recruitment, and fundraising. As the deep web and darknets continue to expand and evolve, the criminal justice system must be able to adapt to the legal issues that may arise from this cyber jurisdiction. It remains to be seen how the Supreme Court will interpret free speech and search and seizure in cyberspace, especially as it pertains to the deep web.

Key Terms

Discussion Questions

1. What is the difference between the surface web, the deep web, and darknets?
2. What is cryptocurrency, and how does it work?
3. Discuss the evolution of darknet marketplaces and products that are available.
4. How does the deep web, and subsequently darknets, make investigating and prosecuting cybercrime difficult?
5. Discuss the changing role of the First and Fourth Amendments in regard to actions on the deep web.

Internet Resources

The Onion Router (ToR)
https://www.torproject.org/

The Official Webpage for Dash
https://www.dash.org

The Electronic Frontier Foundation
https://www.eff.org

Court Cases

United States of America v. Any and All Assets of the Following Dark Market Websites Operating on the TOR Network, Including But Not Limited To The ".Onion" Addresses of the Websites, the Servers Hosting the Websites, and Any BitCoins or Other Digital Currency Residing on Those Servers: Silk Road 2.0; Alpaca; Black Market; Blue Sky; Bungee 54; Cannabis UK; Cloud Nine; CStore; DeDope; Executive Outcomes; Fake ID; Fake Real Plastic; Farmer1; Fast Cash!; Hackintosh; Hydra; Pablo Escobar Drugstore; Pandora; Pay Pal Center; Real Cards Team; REPAAA'S Hidden Empire; Smokeables; Sol's Unified USD Counterfeit's; Super Notes Counter; The Green Machine; TOR Bazaar; and Zero Squad, And all property traceable there to, Defendants-in-rem. (14 Civ. 8812 [JPO])

McIntyre v. Ohio Elections Commission 514 U.S. 334

Weeks v. United States 232 U.S. 383

Mapp v. Ohio 367 U.S. 643

U.S. v Wellman 716 F. Supp. 2d 447

Digital Resources

Want a better grade?

Get the tools you need to sharpen your study skills. Access practice quizzes and eFlashcards, at **study.sagepub.com/kremling**.

Cybersecurity Operations

Learning Objectives

1. Understand the role criminological theory can play in cybersecurity operations.
2. Discuss the issues associated with guardianship in cyberspace.
3. Differentiate between traditional criminal subcultures and the hacker subculture.
4. Understand the concepts of cybersecurity operations from the local, federal, and private-sector viewpoint.
5. Discuss the importance of interagency operation and collaboration in regard to cybersecurity operations.

Many threats and issues within cybersecurity have been addressed thus far in the text. Unlike traditional forms of criminal behavior, the crimes associated with cyberspace are relatively new and constantly evolving. Because of this, traditional law enforcement operating procedures may or may not have an effect on cybercriminality. This chapter examines current criminological (theoretical) operations as well as law enforcement operations at the state, local, and private-sector levels to assess their applicability to detection and deterrence of cyberthreats. Law enforcement training will also be discussed.

Theoretical Operations

The field of criminology has long been devoted to the exploration of why individuals engage in criminal behavior. Criminology has, for the most part, been applied to traditional crimes and has only recently begun to explore its applicability to cybercrimes. Unlike traditional crimes, which occur in a specific location/jurisdiction(s) and are thus subjected to the rule of law of that specific jurisdiction(s), cybercrimes operate in a virtual environment with undefined and seemingly infinite jurisdictional boundaries. As such, there is debate about what laws, if any, should be applied to cybercrimes and what deterrent effect those laws would have, as enforcement would be subject to the cooperation between multiple jurisdictions. As such, the role of traditional criminological theory takes a different role when applied to the cyber realm.

Routine Activity Theory

Developed by Cohen and Felson in 1979, routine activity theory (RAT) examines trends that are necessary for crime to occur.[1] Specifically, when three factors occur together at the same time and in the same space, crime is increasingly likely to occur. The three factors include

1. a motivated offender,
2. a suitable target, and
3. lack of a capable guardianship.[2] (See Figure 9.1.)

FIGURE 9.1 ● Routine Activity Theory Diagram

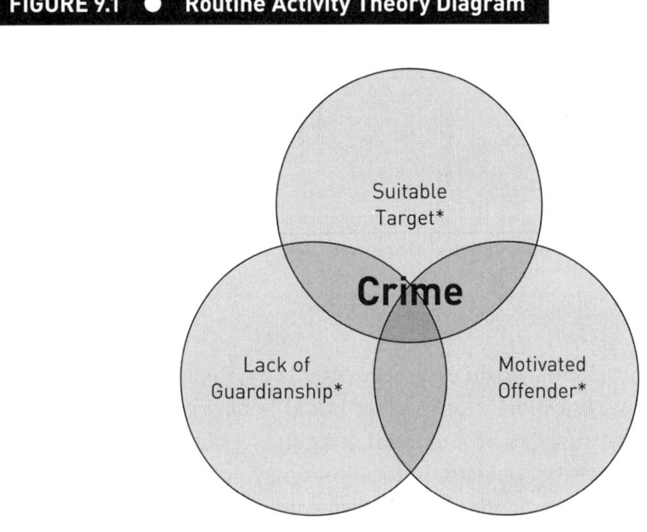

* Occurring together in time and space.

Cohen and Felson argue that the motivated offender is a given. Without a motivated offender, there would be no crime. Likewise, the suitable target is seemingly a given as well, for a motivated offender will move to a new target should a suitable target not exist. As such, the most important component in RAT is the presence or absence of capable guardians.

Role of Guardianship

Guardianship plays a major role in the prevalence of crime, according to RAT. Lack of guardianship increases the possibility that crime will occur. Although guardianship is often a physical presence of a person/people, law enforcement officer, group of people, family at home, etc., it can also occur with a nonhuman presence as well. A well-lit street or a security camera can provide just as much guardianship as a security guard.

Providing guardianship becomes more complicated when applied to cyberspace. Operating in a seemingly invisible, borderless jurisdiction lessens the role that law enforcement or any presence of a person plays in providing guardianship. Moreover, security measures that would increase guardianship in the physical world (or, for example, a tall fence) are not always visible in the cyberworld (a strong firewall). Thus, it is unknown if, by increasing security measures in cyberspace, attackers would actually be deterred, as those security measures may not be visible.

Researchers have found mixed results as to the applicability of RAT in cyberspace. Although it has been argued that RAT is equally applicable to cybercrimes as it is to street crimes,[3] there is not a universal consensus among criminologists about this.[4] Moreover, the necessity of "convergence in time and space" is questionable due to the unique characteristics of the cyber jurisdiction. Furthermore, lack of guardianship can differ from perpetrator to perpetrator based on the skills that individual possesses to get around cybersecurity measures. Finally, because guardians may be "invisible" in the cyber realm, it is difficult for potential criminals to weigh the cost of engaging in cybercrime, as they may not be aware of the intense security, or lack thereof.

Learning Theory

Another perspective that is popular when examining why people engage in certain behavior is learning theory. The idea that people learn to behave in certain ways based on imitating the behavior of those they are close to applies to both criminal and conventional behaviors. Babies learn to walk and talk by imitating their parents or others they spend a great deal of time with. The application of learning theory to criminal or deviant behavior was introduced by Edwin Sutherland. Sutherland, known as the father of criminology, named his theory differential association theory.

Differential Association Theory

Differential association theory (DAT) asserts that criminal behavior is learned via intimate personal groups. Specifically, Sutherland proposed nine points to his theory, which were published in the 4th edition of his textbook *Principles of Criminology*:

1. Criminal behavior is learned.
2. Criminal behavior is acquired through interactions with other persons via communication.
3. Behavior is learned in intimate personal groups.
4. Learning includes techniques, rationalizations, and attitudes.

5. General attitudes and motives are learned by viewing the legal code as either favorable or unfavorable.
6. A person becomes delinquent when there is an excess of definitions favorable to crime over definitions that are unfavorable.
7. Differential association can vary in duration, frequency, and intensity.
8. The process of learning criminal behavior parallels those of any other learning process.
9. Criminal behavior is an expression of general needs and values but isn't explained by those needs and values because noncriminal behavior is also an expression of those values and needs.[5]

Applying the concepts of DAT to cybercrime can be difficult, as oftentimes hackers do not learn their skills in the traditional manner; it is often a developed talent. However, once that talent is developed, either white hat tendencies or black hat tendencies may occur, and those can be based on the excess of definitions favorable to either conventional or unconventional hacking behavior (point 6). The learning environment may also be different for cybercrimes, as learning may occur in online chatrooms or webinars where the identity of the "teacher" may or may not be known. Hacking techniques can also be learned via other hackers—that is, the hacking subculture, including hacking conventions such as DEF CON (discussed later in the chapter).

Subculture Theory

Subculture theories began in the 1950s and 60s while examining the prevalence of youth gangs. Defined, a subculture is "an ethnic, regional, economic, or social group exhibiting characteristic patterns of behavior sufficient to distinguish it from others within an embracing culture or society."[6] Within the fields of criminal justice and criminology, subcultures may include the prison subculture, the criminal subculture, the courtroom workgroup, etc. Many subcultural theories consider low socioeconomic status (SES) as a predominate marker for engaging in crime. For example, Albert K. Cohen examined gang culture in the 1950s to determine how certain subcultures may begin. Based on his research, his subcultural theory of delinquent boys includes eight main propositions:

1. A society shares values and will emphasize certain values over others.
2. Status in society can become an approved goal or value.
3. Lower class is less likely to have opportunities to achieve these goals.
4. Schools and other institutions often evaluate individuals based on these goals.
5. Lower class youths become frustrated that they do not have the opportunities afforded to others.
6. Lower class youth rebel so they can keep status as a goal.

7. These "rebels" create a new value system that is unconventional compared to traditional societal values.
8. This "delinquent solution" is passed on from generation to generation, fostering the subculture.[7]

Like the other traditional criminological theories previously discussed, the application of subculture theory to cybercrime is questionable. There is a lack of evidence that supports that cybercriminals have a low SES compared to the general population. Therefore, although traditional theories examine subcultures deriving from such neighborhoods and the lack of opportunities allocated to members of low SES neighborhoods, in regard to cybercriminality it may be beneficial to examine a subculture that may help train future cybercriminals: the hacker subculture.

The Hacker Subculture

What is a "hacker subculture"? What differentiates it from other subcultures? Is it criminal? These are questions that must be addressed when determining the role theory can play in cybersecurity operations.

A hacker subculture may consist of like-minded individuals who enjoy computer programming, information technology, hacking, and the like. Included with a subculture may be hacker slang, or words common within the subculture. Some common words or phrases within a hacker subculture include the following:

Dumpster Diving: Rummaging through the trash bin on another computer.

Easter Egg: Undocumented, nonmalicious surprise installed on a program by the creator.

Payload: Part of malware that executes the attack.

Rootkit: Tool used by black hats to conduct undetected intrusions.

Script Kiddie: May be seen as an outsider in the hacker subculture. An individual who doesn't have the skills to hack on his or her own so uses prewritten programs to do so.

Wardriving: Driving around trying to access unprotected Wi-Fi networks.[8]

A hacker subculture is not equivalent to a criminal subculture. White-hat hacking organizations may create a subculture where values, norms, techniques, and ideas are shared in order to further the security of our technology. These norms often differ from the conventional societal norms but are not necessarily criminal. When hacking was first discussed in the 1980s, the topic was taboo and hackers were viewed as a different population. The Hacker's Manifesto illustrates this using two voices: one of the hacker and one of authority/society. Although the term *hacking* has become more mainstream today, there are still aspects of the subculture that are not well known to the general population. For example, the annual DEF CON meeting brings together hackers of all kind in an event that is "can't miss" within the hacker subculture.

DEF CON Convention

DEF CON, which began in 1993, is one of the oldest and largest hacker conventions worldwide. Annually held in Las Vegas in late summer, the convention boasts numbers from 15,000 to 18,000 attendees. The convention attracts white hat, black hat, and all hackers in between, as well as curious individuals, law enforcement, and recruiters from federal agencies and the private sector.

DEF CON hosts an array of tech sessions, speakers, demonstrations, and competitions. Registration is at the door, cash only (no need to be using credit cards around a bunch of professional hackers!), and open to anyone; however, the majority of participants come to learn new technology and hacking. Videos of sessions from previous DEF CON conventions can be accessed via their official site (https://defcon.org/).[9]

CASE STUDY 9.1

The Hacker's Manifesto

by The Mentor

Written January 8, 1986

Another one got caught today, it's all over the papers. "Teenager Arrested in Computer Crime Scandal", "Hacker Arrested after Bank Tampering" . . .

Damn kids. They're all alike.

But did you, in your three-piece psychology and 1950's technobrain, ever take a look behind the eyes of the hacker? Did you ever wonder what made him tick, what forces shaped him, what may have molded him?

I am a hacker, enter my world . . .

Mine is a world that begins with school . . . I'm smarter than most of the other kids, this crap they teach us bores me . . .

Damn underachiever. They're all alike.

I'm in junior high or high school. I've listened to teachers explain for the fifteenth time how to reduce a fraction. I understand it. "No, Ms. Smith, I didn't show my work. I did it in my head . . . "

Damn kid. Probably copied it. They're all alike.

I made a discovery today. I found a computer. Wait a second, this is cool. It does what I want it to. If it makes a mistake, it's because I screwed it up. Not because it doesn't like me . . . Or feels threatened by me . . . Or thinks I'm a smart ass . . . Or doesn't like teaching and shouldn't be here . . .

Damn kid. All he does is play games. They're all alike.

And then it happened . . . a door opened to a world . . . rushing through the phone line like heroin through an addict's veins, an electronic pulse is sent out, a refuge from the day-to-day incompetencies is sought . . . a board is found. "This is it . . . this is where I belong . . . " I know everyone here . . . even if I've never met them, never talked to them, may never hear from them again . . . I know you all . . .

Damn kid. Tying up the phone line again. They're all alike . . .

You bet your ass we're all alike . . . we've been spoon-fed baby food at school when we hungered for steak . . . the bits of meat that you did let slip through were pre-chewed and tasteless. We've been dominated by sadists, or ignored by the apathetic. The few that had something to teach found us willing pupils, but those few are like drops of water in the desert.

This is our world now . . . the world of the electron and the switch, the beauty of the baud. We make use of a service already existing without paying for what could be dirt-cheap if it wasn't run by profiteering gluttons, and you call us criminals. We explore . . . and you call us criminals. We seek after knowledge . . . and you call us criminals. We exist without skin color, without nationality, without religious bias . . . and you call us criminals. You build atomic bombs, you wage wars, you murder, cheat, and lie to us and try to make us believe it's for our own good, yet we're the criminals.

Yes, I am a criminal. My crime is that of curiosity. My crime is that of judging people by what they say and think, not what they look like. My crime is that of outsmarting you, something that you will never forgive me for.

I am a hacker, and this is my manifesto. You may stop this individual, but you can't stop us all . . . after all, we're all alike.

Source: The Mentor via Phrack.[10]

Law Enforcement Operations

Theoretical operations can be, and are, used by law enforcement to help look for patterns in behavior and trends in crime rates, and from there they can attempt to mitigate and prevent crime from occurring. Within cybersecurity operations, law enforcement is having to reexamine protocol to shift operation from a physical jurisdiction to cyberspace. As previously discussed, our nation's cybersecurity requires cooperation between all levels of law enforcement, federal down to local. This section outlines the roles played by different federal agencies as well as local agencies in cybersecurity operations.

Federal Agencies

The role of communication and collaboration between federal agencies was reexamined after the events of 9/11 when it was found that there had been communication issues between the CIA and the FBI concerning intelligence on the 9/11 hijackers. Multiple agencies play a role in our nation's cybersecurity, and leading the way is the National Security Agency.

National Security Agency (NSA)

The NSA is primarily responsible for intelligence interception and interpretation/decryption. The mission of the NSA is:

> The National Security Agency/Central Security Service (NSA/CSS) leads the U.S. Government in cryptology that encompasses both Signals Intelligence (SIGINT) and Information Assurance (IA) products and services, and enables Computer Network Operations (CNO) in order to gain a decision advantage for the Nation and our allies under all circumstances.[11]

Via National Security Directives, the NSA has been granted the permission to secure all systems that handle classified information and intelligence. The main arena in which they operate is cyberspace. Not only does the NSA intercept intelligence and detect foreign threats, they also work to mitigate and prevent attacks on U.S. government networks.[12]

Department of Homeland Security

The Department of Homeland Security (DHS) was created in a major reorganization effort after the attacks of September 11, 2001. Multiple agencies were moved under the umbrella of the DHS. Although the NSA takes the lead in protecting government networks, DHS is primarily responsible for the protection of civilian computers. There are five core missions to the DHS, which include

1. prevent terrorism and enhance security,
2. secure and manage our borders,
3. enforce and administer our immigration laws,
4. safeguard and secure cyberspace, and
5. ensure resilience to disasters.[13]

In regard to the cybersecurity mission, DHS works in tandem with local and tribal agencies in order to secure cyberspace and critical infrastructures. Specifically, the department works to

1. analyze and reduce cyber threats and vulnerabilities,
2. distribute threat warnings, and
3. coordinate the response to cyber incidents to ensure that our computers, networks, and cyber systems remain safe.[14]

Agencies under the umbrella of the DHS with special divisions that focus on cybercrime include the U.S. Secret Service (USSS), U.S. Immigration and Customs Enforcement (ICE), and Law Enforcement Cyber Incident Reporting.

The USSS is responsible for both the National Computer Forensics Institute (NCFI) and the Electronic Crimes Task Force (ECTF). The ECTF focuses on international cyber theft, while NCFI is dedicated to training criminal justice professionals in ways to combat cybercrime. ICE is responsible for the Homeland Security Cyber Crimes Center, which provides technical services for both domestic and international cybercrime investigations as well as running a digital forensics lab. Law Enforcement Cyber Incident Reporting details the who, what, when, where, why, and how of cyberincident reporting. This assists law enforcement in knowing what to report and to whom.[15]

Federal Bureau of Investigation

The FBI is "the lead agency for investigating cyberattacks by criminals, overseas adversaries, and terrorists" as was designated under Presidential Policy Directive 41.[16] In line with this, the FBI believes that

1. prevention and management of cyber incidents is a shared responsibility among the government, private sector, and individuals;
2. all incidents should be approached through a united federal government strategy that best uses the skills, authorities, and resources of each agency;
3. the response will be based on an assessment of the risks posed to U.S. security, safety, and prosperity, and will focus on enabling the restoration and recovery of the affected entity; and
4. the government will respect the privacy, civil liberties, and the business needs of victims of cyber incidents.[17]

The FBI also works with local agencies via their 93 established Computer Crime Task Forces located nationwide.

Local Agencies

The first responders to most catastrophic events are usually at the local level, although a substantial proportion of incident detection and investigation is conducted at the federal level.[18] It has been reported, however, that preparation for terror attacks is often detected at the local level during routine operations.[19] Local and federal agencies, therefore, must work cooperatively to address cybersecurity threats to all vulnerable infrastructures. Differences in systematic operations and training can create difficulties with information sharing between agencies.[20] Cooperation is vital, and local law enforcement should receive appropriate instruction and training in detecting, preventing, and responding to a range of significant security threats.

The techniques used by law enforcement to detect, prevent, and respond to crime have evolved over the centuries based on changes in technology and society.[21] Kelling and Moore describe three eras of local-level policing: "the political era" (1840s to early 1900s), "the reform era" (1930s to late 1970s), and "the community era" (1980s to present).[22] Moving into a post-9/11 reality, Henry[23] argues that the community era is insufficient for handling the current threat of terrorism and that beginning on September 11, 2001, a fourth era began, that of "homeland security."[24, 25, 26]

In this era of homeland security, law enforcement agencies are principally using traditional methods to control crime and gather intelligence to counter terrorism, including threats online.[27] Proactive policies are important for detecting and preventing cyberthreats. Individuals with advanced training in IT are essential components of homeland security planning. Based on his experiences in Oklahoma City and in simulated terrorism exercises, Keating makes four recommendations for law enforcement:

1. Train and equip your first responders, they are the front line meeting the terrorist threat.
2. Search for ways to support teamwork *before* an incident and emphasize teamwork after.

3. Tell the truth, and be candid with the people we are working to protect and serve.
4. Trust the experts to do what they know best.[28]

Moreover, Breen suggests that specific terrorism prevention measures can be applied to cybercrime detection and prevention, including creating cyberterrorism training programs.[29] Carter and Carter suggest that to increase the effectiveness of detection and prevention protocol, officers should collect information on four broad areas in regard to the threat of terrorism:

1. Who poses the threat?
2. Who is doing what with whom?
3. What is the modus operandi of the threat?
4. What is needed to catch offenders and prevent crime incidents or trends?[30]

These principles can be taken and applied to threats in cyberspace as well. By acknowledging where the threat is coming from, who is perpetrating the attack, and why, local law enforcement may be better prepared to mitigate cyberattacks.

The role of local-level agencies in cybersecurity is constantly evolving. Prevention is critical, but agencies must be prepared also to react and respond in the event of a cyberattack. Officers assigned to collect information on potential cybercriminals and targets may be unsure about where to begin. The uncertainty of what a catastrophic cyberattack would entail and how to detect and deter such an attack may leave local agencies unprepared to defend against such threats.[31] As Trim discusses, countering cybercrime requires a forward-learning framework that integrates capabilities and personnel from the public and private sectors.[32] Law enforcement should be prepared to monitor the activities of hackers and cybercriminals. Agencies may be able to use people with cyberskills—perhaps even hackers—to obtain information on planning and preparation for an attack, as well as information about the intentions and activity of perpetrators and vulnerable targets.

Cyberterrorism Prevention Training

Training in new cybertechnologies and skills is also vital. Though law enforcement intelligence activity has expanded over the past 15 years, the majority of personnel still receive minimal training in cyberattacks, and training in cyberterrorism defense is extremely rare. Added training in cyberterrorism prevention can better prepare law enforcement personnel to understand the nature of the threat and, subsequently, how to prevent and deter such attacks.

DHS and the Federal Emergency Management Agency have funded the Cyberterrorism Defense Analysis Center (CDAC) to train public safety officers, law enforcement, state and local government, public utilities, colleges and universities, and health care providers at no cost to the local agencies. CDAC delivers this training through the Cyberterrorism Defense Initiative (CDI). CDI offers a

> comprehensive, integrated series of courses that incorporates best practices, procedures and methodologies for a variety of systems . . . [and] utilizes a blended learning approach that balances classroom lecture, hands-on laboratory exercises, and online supplemental material.[33]

CDI courses include the following:

1. Comprehensive Cyberterrorism Defense
2. Cyberterrorism First Responders
3. Cybersecurity: Prevention, Deterrence, Recovery
4. Cybersecurity: Incident Handling and Response

It has been proposed that to deter cyberterrorism, collaboration between six entities is necessary.[34] As universal jurisdiction (see discussion in Chapter 10) has been suggested as most applicable to cyberterrorism, cooperation between local, federal, and international agencies is essential for detecting, apprehending, and prosecuting cyberterrorists.[35] Hua and Bapna suggest cooperation and collaboration between the following entities in order to enhance cyberterrorism deterrence:

1. The national government
2. Fee-based Internet service providers
3. Organizations
4. Free Internet service providers
5. Citizens
6. International community[36]

The researchers elaborate that to increase cyberterrorism prevention, information sharing is essential. The U.S. government should cooperate not only with national jurisdiction of law enforcement at all levels but the international community and private-sector organizations as well. Employees should be trained in cyberterrorism prevention, and the general public should be educated on Internet use. Furthermore, security should be tightened on both free and fee-based Internet servers. Finally, a legal infrastructure should be established to prosecute cyberterrorism perpetrators.[37]

Private-Sector Collaboration

As previously mentioned, over 80% of our national critical infrastructure is owned by the private sector (all businesses not owned by the government that are "for profit"). As these infrastructures are ideal targets for cyberattacks, collaboration to ensure protection is necessary. The private-sector infrastructures must collaborate with government agencies, and public entities must embrace the knowledge of private-sector security agencies. The role of white-hat hackers in the collaborative effort of cybersecurity is vital.

CASE STUDY 9.2

One Hat, Two Hat, White Hat, Red Hat . . .

As previously discussed in Chapter 5, hacking has become an extremely diverse hobby and/or occupation. Hackers can wear many different hats throughout their career, often starting as black- or gray-hat hackers and then moving toward a legitimate career as a white hat, as was the path of famous hacker Kevin Mitnick (discussed in Chapter 2).

Today, the role of white-hat, or good-guy, hackers is even more pivotal. These individuals possess the skills necessary to protect our computer systems and critical infrastructures. However, there is some confusion about what "red hats" or "red-hat hackers" are. Simply put, red-hat hackers do not exist. This term is often confused due to the Linux Operating System Redhat.

Linux Redhat boasts that it is the world's leader in providing open source, enterprising information technology solutions. Specifically,

> Red Hat Enterprise Linux gives you the tools you need to modernize your infrastructure, boost efficiency through standardization and virtualization, and ultimately prepare your datacenter for an open, hybrid cloud IT architecture.[38]

So although many former hackers may now be legitimately employed via this organization, the hat they wear is definitely white, not red.

The rising number of cyberattacks has resulted in a strong collaborative effort between public and private entities. These public-private partnerships (PPP) are imperative for the cybersecurity of our nation. The Homeland Security presidential directives (discussed in Chapter 7) advocate for increased cooperation between the public and private sectors. Many public-sector executives have asserted that they could not provide the necessary security if it wasn't for the private sector.[39]

This is extremely essential when the security of critical infrastructures and/or key resources is at stake. The Office of Infrastructure Protection (OIP) is responsible for reducing risk and vulnerability to these resources. This can be extremely difficult due to the large number of infrastructures owned by the private sector. Furthermore, the private sector often has more resources to put toward security and may not be subjected to the scrutiny and restrictions that are applied to the public sector. However, the government has the arresting and prosecuting power, which the private sector lacks.[40] In order to provide ample security, the OIP coordinates the efforts of PPP in order to fulfill the three aspects of its mission:

1. to identify and analyze threats and vulnerabilities,
2. to coordinate nationally and locally through partnerships with both government and private sector entities that share information and resources, and
3. to mitigate risk and effects (encompasses both readiness and incident response).[41]

Interagency Operations

As previously mentioned, after 9/11 it became evident that there was a lack of communication between agencies concerning threats to homeland security.[42] The 9/11 Commission Report identified flaws in communication and information sharing that was hindering the security of the country. Post-9/11 has been an era of increased cooperation and collaboration between federal agencies. More so than just federal agencies, for collaboration to be most effective, lines of communication must be open between federal, state, local, tribal, and private-sector agencies. This is especially vital concerning cybersecurity, as the jurisdictional lines are blurred (discussed further in Chapter 10) and all agencies have much to contribute to the detection of crime in cyberspace.

According to former deputy attorney general Mark R. Filip, there are three main challenges to policing cybercrimes:

1. It cuts across national boundaries.
2. It ignores bureaucracy.
3. It targets critical infrastructures controlled by public and private entities.[43]

One way the government has tried to increase information sharing between agencies is the creation of fusion centers. Since 9/11, fusion centers have been established at both the state and federal levels to facilitate information sharing between federal, state, local, tribal, and private-sector agencies. According to the DHS:

> A fusion center is a collaborative effort of two or more agencies that provide resources, expertise, and information to the center with the goal of maximizing their ability to detect, prevent, investigate and respond to criminal and terrorist activity.[44]

Fusion centers are modeled off the National Criminal Intelligence Sharing Plan, which was "founded on the concept of interagency-led policing . . . and encourages law enforcement agencies to support and incorporate intelligence-led policing fundamentals in their efforts."[45]

Currently, there are 72 active fusion centers, many with specific crime specializations, including cybercrime.[46] There is one cybercrime fusion center, located in Pennsylvania, that collaborates with all levels of law enforcement as well as entities such as the National Counterterrorism Center on issues such as cyberespionage and cyberterrorism.[47] As this center is a good starting point for identifying vulnerabilities, all levels of law enforcement must work together to provide guardianship for the vulnerable targets. As one fusion center cannot monitor all the terrorist activity in cyberspace, it is imperative that all local, state, and federal agencies as well as the international community and the private sector work together to protect the critical and vulnerable infrastructures that may be targeted in cyberspace. Law enforcement must be able to adapt their detection and prevention techniques to the era of cyberterrorism. In order to facilitate the most effective detection and prevention in cyberspace, cybersecurity stakeholders should be trained in the virtual techniques.

Target Hardening

"Hardening" a computer system reduces vulnerabilities associated with the computer system and subsequent hardware. This can be done in many ways with the use of advanced security and firewalls. However, even before these extra security measures are installed, computer systems can be hardened by closing all unused portals and removing accounts that will not be used. Once this is done, firewalls can be installed to enhance the security of a computer network.[48]

Firewalls

Firewalls are used to enforce network security policy.[49] They are employed so that only approved programs and users can access specific systems. They help keep out spam, viruses, and other malicious forms of attack. Firewalls can also be programmed to specifically detect malicious intrusions. Intrusion detection systems can be sold alone or configured into a firewall. These configurations allow for more intense scrutiny on network security and breaches. This is extremely important for systems that perform critical tasks associated with infrastructure, such as supervisory control and data acquisition (SCADA) systems.

SCADA Systems

SCADA systems may be appealing targets for cybercriminals. SCADA systems are utilized by many of the nation's critical infrastructures to provide automated control of the functions of the infrastructure. However, the automated nature of SCADA systems leaves the systems vulnerable to attacks, which could include shutting down the systems or taking over control of the infrastructure. It has been reported that al-Qaeda has expressed a "high level of interest" in SCADA systems and has individuals skilled in technology that may have the training to access and override the system.[50]

Security of SCADA systems is often outdated, as SCADA programming can last for decades. This was evident in the Stuxnet case (see Chapter 10). Multiple subsystems and connections are necessary for SCADA systems to run our critical infrastructures. This leaves multiple targets for attack. In order to increase security on the systems, all connections *must* be identified. Connections to other networks or subsystems pose a potential risk, and to assure security, SCADA systems may have to be isolated from all other connections.[51] Furthermore, as SCADA systems have relatively long lifetimes, updates and patches to security features are mandatory to ensure protection. Finally, collaboration with the private sector to examine new techniques or mitigation and threat identification is vital to infrastructure security.

Honeypots, Nets, and Tokens

One way that the private sector can contribute to the detection of cyberthreats is by installing honeypots (or multiple honeypots, then referred to as honeynets) into computer systems. Honeypots have been utilized since the 1980s to track and monitor hackers,[52] and have been suggested as an effective way to counteract cyberterrorism.[53] One reason honeypots can be so effective is because they offer an offensive approach to the threat. Traditionally, cyberthreats were dealt with in a defensive manner, but honeypots change that as they gather information on attack tactics and possible targets prior to attack.[54]

Honeynets set up a fake network identical to the actual infrastructure network system. Because it is not an actual production system, any interaction with the honeynet supports that the action is most likely malicious.[55] Once the attacker enters the honeynet, their attack techniques and potential targets can be monitored (see Figure 9.2).

FIGURE 9.2 ● Architecture of a Honeynet

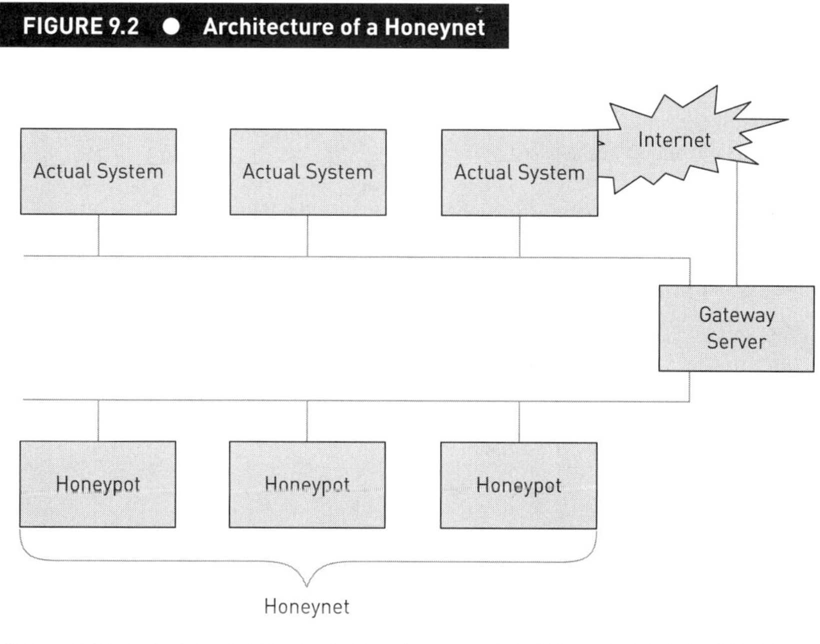

There are risks associated with the use of honeynets, but overall, the benefits of learning the attackers' methodology greatly outweigh the costs.[56] Furthermore, a pilot study on the use of honeypots found that "honeypots are the best known example of defense deception in cyberspace."[57] Using honeynets with the nation's critical infrastructures may help expose the methods that may be used to attack the infrastructures.

Honeytokens, or digital data created specifically to monitor the behavior of potential attackers, may be sent out or placed in visible locations with the goal of the potential cyber perpetrator retrieving the tokens.[58]

Tracking online behavior using technology of honeynets often requires cooperation between multiple individuals and agencies in both the public and private sectors. When policing in the cyber arena, interagency collaboration is crucial.

THINK ABOUT IT 9.1

The Honeynet Project

The Honeynet Project was established in 1999 with the goal of investigating cyberattacks and the latest methods of prevention and detection. The vision is as follows:

> The Honeynet Project is a diverse, talented, and engaged group of international computer security experts who conduct open, cross disciplinary research and development into the evolving threat landscape. It cooperates with like-minded people and organizations in that endeavor.[59]

Currently, chapters of the Honeynet project are located around the world, and every year a security workshop is hosted in a different country. The website also details challenges that have been encountered with cybersecurity.

What Would You Do?

1. Review the Honeynet Project's website at www.honeynet.org and choose one challenge from the navigation sidebar. What is the challenge?
2. Discuss how criminal justice agencies may play a role in combatting the challenge.
3. Work with a partner or in small groups to devise a plan to combat the challenge you chose.

LEGAL ISSUE 9.1

THE FOURTH AMENDMENT

The Fourth Amendment of the U.S. Constitution protects against unreasonable searches and reads:

> The right of the people to be secure in their persons, houses, papers, and effects, against unreasonable searches and seizures, shall not be violated, and no warrants shall issue, but upon probable cause, supported by oath or affirmation, and particularly describing the place to be searched, and the persons or things to be seized.[60]

What Do You Think?

1. Are honeypots/honeynets in violation of the Fourth Amendment's provisions? Why or why not?
2. What current statutes protect the use of honeypots/honeynets?
3. How will this issue impact the future of search and seizure protocol?

Summary

Criminological theory has much to contribute to the study of cybercrimes. However, these theories must adapt to the online atmosphere of the crimes—that cyberspace is a borderless jurisdiction, and elements of learning may differ than that of traditional crimes. Furthermore, the unique nature of the hacker subculture, specifically the criminal hacker subculture, must be understood. Because of the unique nature of the crime, interagency cooperation is imperative to ensure that the best and most appropriate detection and investigation tools are applied. Such operations must include the private sector, as they have knowledge and skills that can greatly contribute to cybersecurity operations. Target hardening is key, and tools such as honeynets allow both public and private entities to gain a deeper look into the tactics and techniques of cybercriminals.

Key Terms

Differential Association 165
Firewall 165
Fusion Center 175
Guardianship 164
Hacker Subculture 167
Honeynet 176
Honeypot 176
Honeytokens 177
Linux Redhat 174
Office of Infrastructure Protection 174
Routine Activity Theory 164
Supervisory Control and Data Acquisition Systems (SCADA) 176

Discussion Questions

1. How can criminological theory play a role in cybersecurity operations?
2. What characterizes the hacker subculture, and how is it different than a criminal subculture?
3. Detail the role of collaboration between local and federal agencies in cybersecurity operations.
4. If you were a member of the local police department, what would be your main concern associated with cybersecurity?
5. How does the private sector contribute to cybersecurity operations?
6. What are the benefits associated with honeynets?

Internet Resources

The Honeynet Project Official Website
http://www.honeynet.org/

Cyberterrorism Defense Initiative
http://www.cyberterrorismcenter.org/

Full text of the 9/11 Commission Report
https://9-11commission.gov/report/

DEF CON official site
https://defcon.org/

Redhat Linux OS
https://www.redhat.com/en

Further Reading

Verton, D. (2002). *The hacker diaries: Confessions of teenage hackers*. New York, NY: McGraw-Hill.

Digital Resources

Want a better grade?

Get the tools you need to sharpen your study skills. Access practice quizzes and eFlashcards, at **study.sagepub.com/kremling**.

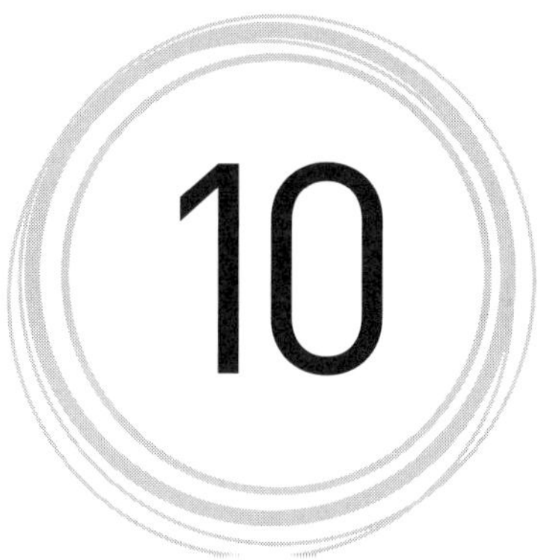

10 Cybersecurity Policies and Legal Issues

Learning Objectives

1. Discuss the purpose of national cybersecurity laws.
2. Describe the purpose of national cybersecurity policies.
3. Discuss the tension between civil rights and national security.
4. Explain the difficulties in creating and enforcing international cybersecurity policies.

In the past decade, our world has become interconnected not only via computer networks but also via the IoT. It is expected that by 2020 there will be 20 billion IoT devices. Most of us carry at least one IoT device with us, but many of us carry several devices, including a smartwatch, a smartphone, a health tracker, an iPad, etc. Our smartphones can now open the front door, turn the house alarm on and off, monitor packages delivered to our door, monitor our children's whereabouts, locate family and friends, access our bank accounts, pay bills, and so on. We will soon be able to drive to school or work in driverless cars, trains, and buses. We will be able to divert energy sources from one town to another. These are incredible technological advances that will greatly improve our lives, but there are also costs attached to these advances—costs that can endanger our lives. Cybersecurity experts are working hard to keep up and develop security measures that will keep criminals from launching cyberattacks, including terrorist acts.[3] Just imagine you are riding in a self-driving bus and the bus is hijacked by a hacker who takes over control of the bus. The hacker could do that from anywhere in the world. He does not need to be near or inside the bus. He could make the bus go faster or change the destination, drive it into other cars or down a cliff. Researchers have shown that it is possible to hack into today's connected

THINK ABOUT IT 10.1

Mirai: A Shot Across the Bow—Distributed Denial-of-Service Attack

IMAGE 10.1 ● Mirai Botnet

Mirai Botnet Linked to Massive DDOS Attacks by Joey Devilla, https://upload.wikimedia.org/wikipedia/commons/3/36/Mirai-botnet-linked-to-massive-ddos-attacks-on-dyn-dns-gif.gif. Licensed under CC BY-SA 4.0, https://creativecommons.org/licenses/by-sa/4.0/legalcode

On October 21, 2016, a massive distributed denial-of-service (DDoS) attack brought down much of the Internet in Europe and the United States. Some of the most popular websites, such as Amazon, Twitter, Reddit, CNN, PayPal, Fox News, the *New York Times*, the *Guardian*, and the *Wall Street Journal,* were unavailable for several hours. This outage also included Amazon's cloud-based service, which has become essential data storage for many large businesses. If businesses can't access their data, they lose money. If health care providers can't access patient records, people could die. Thus, a DDoS attack can have detrimental consequences.[1]

The attack used a botnet named Mirai. Mirai was not the typical botnet made up of computers; rather, it used devices that are part of the Internet of things (IoT) to overwhelm the servers of big companies with service requests until the servers broke down. These devices were mainly home Wi-Fi routers, connected video cameras, and other private home devices. The Mirai botnet was the largest of its kind thus far, but given the enormous growth of IoT devices, it will soon be outmatched by a new botnet. The Mirai botnet of IoT devices bombarded the server of a company called Dyn until the server crashed under the incoming attack traffic. Dyn controls much of the Internet's Domain Name System infrastructure. Experts from Dyn estimated that the Mirai botnet used at least 100,000 endpoint devices (e.g., home video cameras, etc.) and generated more than 1.2 terabytes per second traffic. The Dyn server sustained the pressure for almost an entire day until it broke down. David Fiedler from the Council of Foreign Relations stated:

> We have a serious problem with the insecurity of IoT devices and no real strategy to combat it. The IoT insecurity problem was exploited on this significant scale by a non-state group. Imagine what a well resourced state actor could do with insecure IoT devices.[2]

What Would You Do?

1. Give some examples of what a well-resourced state actor could do with insecure IoT devices.
2. What would be the consequences if a botnet similar to Mirai were to bring down the Internet for more than one week? How would it affect your life if there were no Internet?
3. Think back to prior chapters. What can you do to prevent your IoT devices from becoming infected by malware and being abused in a DDoS attack?

cars and take away the control of the driver. Cybersecurity experts will have to work closely with companies that build self-driving and connected vehicles to make them as safe as possible.

The past decade has seen a rapid increase in cyberattacks by hackers, terrorist groups, nation-states, and other actors. As you have learned in the prior chapters, these attacks have become more sophisticated and dangerous, and are now part of everyone's life. One of the main questions widely discussed is how to make the Internet safer. Some argue that the Internet needs to be strictly regulated; others believe that we need a holistic approach to this issue. The holistic approach includes cooperation between the industry, lawmakers, and cybersecurity specialists. The holistic approach emphasizes that neither technology nor policies in themselves can effectively address the myriad of cyberthreats. Over the past decade, cyberthreats have grown in number and also in sophistication with a widening range of victims, the growth of social engineering, and the increased threat of insiders (as discussed in prior chapters).[4]

The holistic approach encompasses technological, human, and physical factors. All cyberattacks are planned and executed by human beings, and almost all cyberattacks target humans to get access to a computer, server, or network. The Internet has vastly expanded the opportunities for corporations and individuals for business ventures, innovations, and sharing of data, but it has also increased access to individuals and organizations. This access is guarded by humans, who may be the greatest vulnerability with regard to cybersecurity because they must use their good judgment to protect the corporation and the data it holds. The strongest technological security measures cannot prevent an attack if the humans who are operating the technology make bad decisions.[5]

CASE STUDY 10.1

A Holistic Approach to Cybersecurity

A holistic approach integrates technological, human, and physical factors.

1. Assessing vulnerabilities, cyber resiliency, and developing a security baseline

The corporation is not an association of computers and other devices on a network, but rather an association of people who work within a physical domain and who control the technical domain. Part of this assessment is to analyze the security culture of a company, its leadership, HR policies and practices, IT governance, physical defenses, and cyberthreat awareness. This information will provide the security baseline to measure against.

2. Identifying sensitive information

The company must first assess its critical assets that need to be protected. Sensitive information includes trade secrets, customer data, patents, and other aggregate data. A company may not be able to protect all data, so it must determine what receives the highest priority.

3. Determining who has access

After the company has prioritized their sensitive information, they must decide who is

(Continued)

(Continued)

allowed access to the information. Many organizations don't realize how many employees have access to their sensitive information, often without any need for access. Restricting virtual and physical access is imperative because the destruction of computers, devices, or a network would accomplish the same as a DDoS attack—the denial of access to the data.

4. Developing and disseminating ground rules and accountability

The ground rules must lay out precisely what people should and should not do. The accountability rules must clearly state the consequences for negligent and intentional violations. If people are not held accountable, there is also no incentive to follow the rules.

5. Cybersecurity awareness of employees

Employees are the greatest security threat. Most security breaches occur due to negligence. Cybersecurity training mitigates the risk by creating awareness of attack strategies.

6. Addressing the insider threat

Even though most cyberattacks occur due to negligent behaviors, the ones that are malicious cause more significant damage, often by giving away trade secrets and the most sensitive information. The most effective countermeasures are a positive cybersecurity culture and broad monitoring of access to information and employee behavior with regard to downloaded files and badge records. Closely monitoring employee online behaviors clashes with privacy concerns, and many companies do not engage in close monitoring to avoid conflict and attrition of employees. This lack of supervision, however, makes it relatively easier to steal sensitive information or manipulate data.

7. Cyberattack response

Companies must be aware that cyberattacks can happen at any time despite good cybersecurity measures and must prepare for such attacks by implementing a response protocol that everyone in the company follows. One of the first steps of the response protocol should be the assessment of the damage, followed by informing shareholders and partners, and following the response protocol to mitigate damages and restore the normal functioning of the network.[6]

National Cybersecurity Policies

Several laws have been passed in the last few years to more effectively address cybercrime and cybersecurity issues. The main purpose of these was to develop a comprehensive strategy to prevent and mitigate cyberattacks. Further, several new laws require regular assessment of the cybersecurity workforce and recruitment strategies. Another focus has been on streamlining regulations for critical infrastructures.

Comprehensive National Cybersecurity Initiative, 2008

The Comprehensive National Cybersecurity Initiative (CNCI) provided the basis for a comprehensive cybersecurity strategy. The CNCI developed three mutually reinforcing initiatives:

1. To establish a front line of defense against today's immediate threats.

"Creating or enhancing shared situational awareness of network vulnerabilities, threats, and events within the Federal Government—and ultimately with state, local, and tribal governments and private sector partners—and the ability to act quickly to reduce our current vulnerabilities and prevent intrusions."

2. To defend against the full spectrum of threats.

"Enhancing U.S. counterintelligence capabilities and increasing the security of the supply chain for key information technologies."

3. To strengthen the future cybersecurity environment.

"Expanding cyber education; coordinating and redirecting research and development efforts across the Federal Government; and working to define and develop strategies to deter hostile or malicious activity in cyberspace."[7]

On December 18, 2015, President Obama signed the Cybersecurity Information Sharing Act of 2015 (CISA), which creates a cybersecurity information-sharing system for public and private entities. Reporting is voluntary, and the Act guarantees the confidentiality of sensitive information, including the sources and methods of reporting. Four government agencies are working together: the director of National Intelligence, the secretary of Homeland Security, the secretary of defense, and the attorney general. The main task of this workgroup is to develop procedures for the sharing of classified and unclassified cyberthreat indicators and defense mechanisms. They are also responsible for sharing best practices for mitigating cyberthreats.[8] Critics of CISA have argued that Internet users have privacy rights and that their Internet traffic, such as searches and communications, ought to be private, similar to a phone call made from a public phone. The Fourth Amendment guarantees that people are secure from unreasonable search and seizure of their private communications. The question is whether communications sent through a third party are considered private. The government says no because it has been voluntarily disclosed to the third party. This argument, of course, ignores the fact that it is virtually impossible to e-mail another person without using a third-party Internet service provider (ISP).[9]

In addition, the FBI has formed the cyber task force, working to build alliances between governmental agencies and private companies across the United States. The "whole-government approach" is imperative to countering cyberthreats and keeping people safe. Cybercriminals are versatile, using real-world events such as the terrorist attacks in Paris, France, to solicit fraudulent donations, creating fake government websites to get individuals' private information (e.g., tax reporting websites during tax time), or payroll scams where individuals are notified that they need to confirm a change in their employment status. Once the individual logs into his or her account, the criminal has the login information and the ability to steal paychecks and personal information.[10]

Cybersecurity Workforce Act of 2014

The Cybersecurity Workforce Act was signed into effect on December 18, 2014. The Act requires the secretary of Homeland Security to assess the work of the cybersecurity workforce of the Department of Homeland Security (DHS) and

CASE STUDY 10.2

Ransomware—California Hospital Pays $17,000

Ransomware has become one of the most feared threats to cybersecurity. In the context of ransomware, cybercriminals take a computer or device hostage until the owner pays a ransom. The cybercriminals are very effective because if the ransom is not paid, the criminals can steal or delete the content of the computer or device. On February 5, 2016, Hollywood Presbyterian Hospital in Los Angeles noticed that their computer systems had been hacked and that the hackers were interfering with the operation of their computer systems. The hackers had encrypted the data, and even the FBI's attempts to decrypt the data were unsuccessful. Doctors had no access to e-mail and patient records for more than 1 week. The hospital eventually paid 40 bitcoins, which is $17,000, in exchange for the decryption key.[11]

develop a comprehensive strategy to improve the readiness and quality of the cybersecurity workforce. The secretary must conduct such assessment within 180 days of the signing of the law and annually for the following 3 years. The Act focuses on the following issues:

1. "The readiness and capacity of the cyber security workforce to meet its cyber security mission;
2. Where cyber security workforce positions are located within DHS;
3. Which such positions are performed by permanent full-time equivalent DHS employees, by independent contractors, and by individuals employed by other federal agencies;
4. Which such positions are vacant;
5. The percentage of individuals within each Cyber Security Category and Specialty Area who received essential training to perform their jobs; and
6. In cases in which such training was not received, what challenges were encountered regarding the provision of such training."[12]

National Cybersecurity and Critical Infrastructure Protection Act of 2014

The National Cybersecurity and Critical Infrastructure Protection Act of 2014 was also signed into effect on December 18, 2014. The Act enables the secretary of Homeland Security to conduct cybersecurity activities that will defend, mitigate, respond to, or recover from cyber incidents to critical infrastructures such as chemical plants; dams; the Defense Industrial Base Sector; nuclear reactors, materials, and waste; and transportation systems. A cyber incident is defined as

> an incident, or an attempt to cause an incident, that if successful, would: (1) jeopardize the security, integrity, confidentiality, or availability of an

THINK ABOUT IT 10.2

Ransomware

You are the owner of a small business selling home improvement goods. You receive a notice on your computer that your data has been encrypted. That data includes your customer data, payment information, orders, and supplies. It also means that you cannot access the data of your employees. The hacker asks for a ransom of $500.

What Would You Do?

1. Make a list of the benefits and risks of paying the ransom.
2. Make a decision on whether to pay the ransom. Justify your decision.
3. Discuss the implications of these decisions made by small business owners for cybercriminals and cybersecurity.

IMAGE 10.2 ● Ransomware

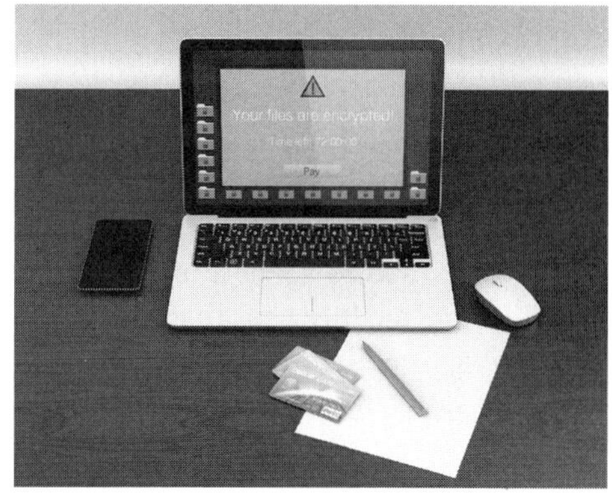

© iStockphoto.com/Chesky_W

information system or network or any information stored on, processed on, or transiting such a system; (2) violate laws or procedures relating to system security, acceptable use policies, or acts of terrorism against such a system or network; or (3) deny access to or degrade, disrupt, or destruct such a system or network or defeat an operations or technical control of such a system or network.[13]

The secretary of state has the responsibility to coordinate federal, state, and local governments, laboratories, critical infrastructure owners and operators, and other entities to accomplish the following goals:

1. "Facilitate a national effort to strengthen and maintain critical infrastructure from cyber threats;
2. Ensure that Department of Homeland Security (DHS) policies and procedures enable critical infrastructure owners and operators to receive appropriate and timely cyber threat information;
3. Seek industry sector-specific expertise to develop voluntary security and resiliency strategies and to ensure that the allocation of federal resources

is cost effective and reduces burdens on critical infrastructure owners and operators;

4. Upon request, provide risk management assistance to entities and education to critical infrastructure owners and operators; and

5. Coordinate a research and development strategy for cyber security technologies."[14]

Even though the past 2 years have seen a surge in cybersecurity laws, overall the law has been slow to catch up with cybercrime and its constant and fast-paced changes. By the time the U.S. government signs a new law, the cybercriminals and nation-state actors have long moved on to new techniques. In addition, corporations are unwilling to invest the money it takes to develop cybersecurity measures and protect the data on their servers. It is typically not until a company has to admit a major attack and the theft of private data that can be used for identity theft that the company begins to implement sophisticated cyberdefense mechanisms.

Some suggest that the government must force corporations to implement a certain cybersecurity standard. Without such policies, corporations will not invest in cybersecurity, and vulnerabilities will remain. Great Britain was the first country to show 20 national banks just how vulnerable they are and force them to implement cybersecurity measures. It announced to the banks that they would be attacked—not by hacktivists or someone else but by hired white-hat hackers. The Bank of England rehearsed a major hacking attack called Walking Shark II by employing 220 hackers to attack the 20 banks.[15]

International Cybersecurity Policies

Cyberspace and cybersecurity defy traditional governance because they are not confined within national borders; rather, they reach across geopolitical boundaries. This raises three main issues:

1. Who can make the law applicable to cyberspace and cybersecurity?
2. What law applies?
3. Who can enforce the applicable law?

In addition, there is a codependence of the government and private sector in which many private assets are detrimental to the public, and their security is of great importance to the government. For instance, many critical infrastructures are privately owned, but the government helps protect them. Proprietary information, such as company research, trade secrets, hardware, and software, is mostly owned by private companies, but the government has an interest in protecting this information. When cybercriminals steal or manipulate data or interfere with company operations, the main challenges that investigators face are anonymity and attribution. The anonymity of cyberspace makes it often impossible to determine who the criminal is and prove it.[16]

LEGAL ISSUE 10.1

THE CYBERWARS IN THE MIDDLE EAST

Most experts in the field seem to agree that the first real cyberwar attack occurred in January 2010 at the Natanz uranium enrichment plant in Iran. This was a new type of attack because it wasn't done by bombing the plant but rather by attacking the software. The attacker, even though it has not been officially admitted, is believed to have been the United States. The malware Stuxnet disrupted the centrifuges of the nuclear power plant while at the same time manipulating the computer control screens to show that everything was normal. But everything was not normal. One after another of the centrifuges spun out of control. By the end of the attack, more than 800 of the plant's centrifuges were destroyed by the malware, bringing to a halt the production of enriched plutonium, which is needed to produce energy but also to build an atomic bomb. It was the potential of building an atomic bomb that had sparked the cyberattack. The attackers were hoping that no one would ever be able to figure out what happened and that the software would stay within the plant. This did not happen, however. Instead, the most advanced cyberweapon at the time spread across the world and became widely available to anyone.[17]

The Counterattack

In a counterattack, Iran, in 2012, attacked the U.S. banking system and substantially slowed down major banking websites of the largest U.S. banks, including the Bank of America, JPMorgan Chase, Wells Fargo, U.S. Bank, and PNC Bank. Some banks' websites were completely inaccessible, making online banking impossible. It is believed that hackers working for the Iranian government used a DDoS attack to overwhelm the servers.[18]

In the aftermath, JPMorgan Chase announced that it spends $850 million per year and employs 1,000 security employees. Despite the large amount of money and security personnel, JPMorgan could not prevent the attack. During the attack, the banks turned to the U.S. government and asked for help, but the government told the banks that this was their problem. The banks turned to Internet service providers such as AT&T and asked them to help. They tried and failed. Eventually, the attack stopped, not because the banks or the U.S. government stopped it but because the Iranians ended it. They could have continued the attack, but they had made their point. The Iranian government had sent a message to the United States that they had the capability to attack and disrupt one of America's most important businesses: the banking industry. The U.S. government had created an offensive cyberunit as part of the military, but they had not built a cyberdefense system that would protect American citizens and corporations from potentially devastating cyberattacks by other nation-states or nonstate actors.[19]

Lessons Learned

When nation-states build a cyberunit, they put their money into creating offensive capabilities so they can attack their enemy. But the lack of cyberdefense systems leaves the corporations and government agencies vulnerable to the simplest attacks. Another lesson was learned by the banks and other corporations. Their takeaway was that if they come under attack, they should not count on the help of the government.[20] This lesson was also learned by Sony when it was attacked by North Korea over the release of the movie *The Interview*, which depicted the assassination of North Korean leader Kim Jong-un. The hackers stole data from the Sony servers, including executive e-mails and private data about actors such as salaries, addresses, etc. The data was then released online via social media, exposing very personal information. Stunned by the sophistication of the attack and threats by North Korea, Sony caved and cancelled the release of the movie.[21]

What Do You Think?

1. Would international agreements help prevent a cyberwar? How would these agreements be similar and different to other international agreements that cover wars, such as the Geneva Convention?
2. Should the U.S. government protect its citizens and corporations, and if so, how could they do that?

Legal Issues

Civil Rights

On November 14, 2015, the Islamic State (ISIS) killed 130 people in a terrorist attack in Paris, France. The terrorists attacked the citizens of Paris in six locations, with the first attacks at 9:20 p.m. outside of the Stade de France, a sports stadium where the French soccer team was playing against Germany. French President Hollande, who was in attendance, was safely evacuated and the stadium secured. The second explosion followed at 9:30 p.m. about 400 feet away from the stadium. Both suicide bombers and one person walking by died during the explosions. At 9:53 p.m., the third suicide bomber launched an explosion in the Rue de la Cokerie, injuring several people. The real attack, however, was yet to come and would last until 12:20 a.m. the following day. The first two targets, La Petit Cambodia and Le Carillon, were hit at 9:25 p.m. Men armed with automatic rifles killed 15 people. They then moved on to Café Bonne Biere, killing another five people. At 9:40 p.m., another single suicide bomber walked into a restaurant, Comptoir Voltair, and detonated his bomb. Several people were injured. Another group of three terrorists stormed the Bataclan concert hall where the U.S. band Eagles of Death Metal played before hundreds of people. The terrorists started shooting into the crowd, killing a total of 89 people. Eyewitnesses would later report that the terrorists shot people who were laying on the floor in execution style. The attack ended at 12:20 a.m. when French police stormed the concert hall. They killed one of the attackers immediately. The other two activated their suicide belts before the police could get to them.[22]

> **Reference Reading**
>
> The Real Story of Stuxnet
>
> http://spectrum.ieee.org/telecom/security/the-real-story-of-stuxnet

Following the attack, FBI director James Comey warned that ISIS may also have cyberwar capabilities, which could be a threat to the United States. He stated, "Destructive malware is a bomb, and terrorists want bombs." There has been an increased presence of ISIS on social media trying to recruit persons, and there is a growing encryption of communication between ISIS and recruits. In an effort to gain intelligence about possible future terrorist and cyberattacks, the FBI has been critical of privacy rights because it leaves the FBI and other law enforcement agencies without information necessary to prevent an attack.[23]

IMAGE 10.3 ● Privacy Versus Security

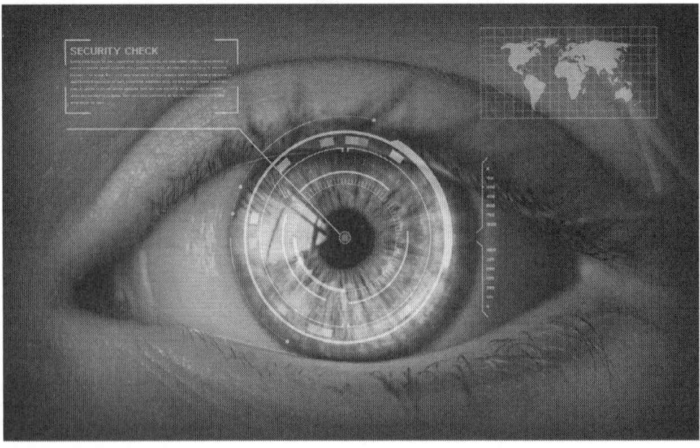

Pixaby.com

Security Versus Privacy

And herein lies the crux of the problem: What is the importance of civil rights and the importance of public safety? Which has priority if both can't be accomplished simultaneously? In 2014, the man behind ShamiWitness, the most influential pro-ISIS Twitter account, was arrested and the account shut down. He had more than 17,700 followers, many of whom were foreign fighters. He helped them before they joined ISIS and praised them as martyrs if they died. The man behind the account was Mehdi Biswas, an executive for an Indian conglomerate in Bangalore, India. Biswas also had Facebook accounts, one for his family and friends where he shared jokes and stories, and one where he promoted ISIS, terrorism, and rape. One of his tweets stated: "@ArjDnn I should thank PKK for recruiting female fighters, especially the ones caught alive by rebels, lol." The PKK is a Turkish separatist group who has been fighting against ISIS in Syria. The PKK has been coordinating their efforts with the American military.[24]

IMAGE 10.4 • Shami Witness Screenshot

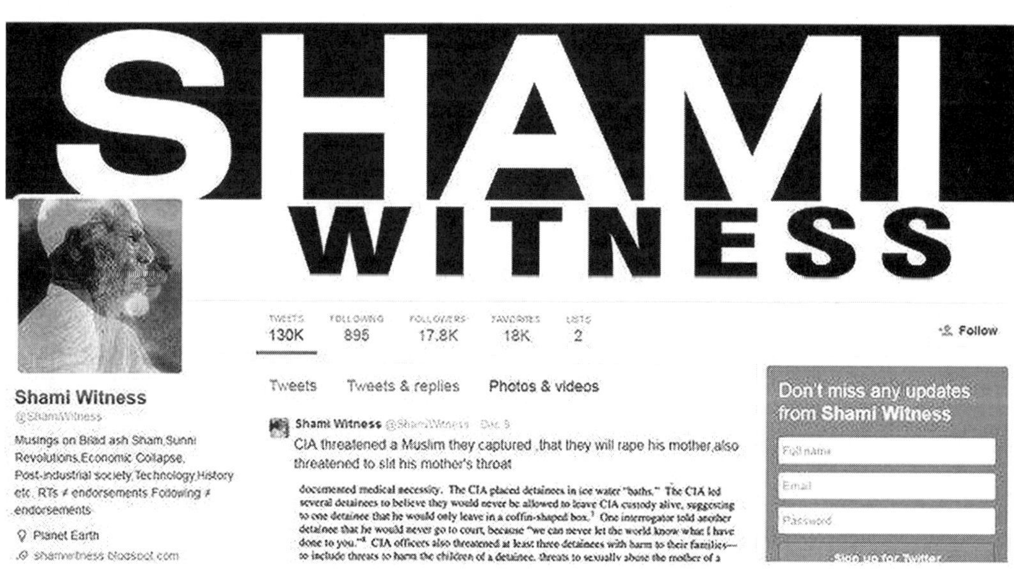

Shami Witness

Biswas also repeatedly tweeted videos of the execution of U.S. aid worker Peter Kassig, who was killed in Syria by ISIS fighters together with dozens of Syrian soldiers. Kassig had served in the Iraq War as an army ranger and later became an emergency medical technician. He founded the Special Emergency Response and Assistance Organization, which delivered medical supplies to northeastern Syria. Kassig was kidnapped by ISIS on October 1, 2013, and held hostage in Aleppo and later in Raqqa together with 23 other Western hostages. Kassig was forced to watch the beheadings of four other hostages in August 2014, and he seemed to know that he would also be killed. In a letter smuggled out in the summer of 2014, he wrote to his parents:

> I am obviously pretty scared to die but the hardest part is not knowing, wondering, hoping, and wondering if I should even hope at all. . . . Just know I'm with you. Every stream, every lake, every field and river. In the woods and in the hills, in all the places you showed me. I love you.

The video distributed by Mehdi shows the body of Kassig and the severed head, indicating that Kassig had been beheaded.[25] British investigators believe that Kassig was killed prior to the beheading because all the other videos showed the actual beheading and also forced the victims to make a statement prior to being killed. Kassig's video was very different, and investigators later saw what appeared to be a gunshot wound on his head.[26]

Mehdi Biswas was arrested by Indian authorities in December 2014. After his arrest, he stated, "No I haven't done anything wrong. I haven't harmed anybody. I haven't broken any laws of my country. I haven't raised any war or any violence against the public.[27]

Biswas's statement reflects a major problem: the right to free speech and privacy versus state interests. Biswas has been charged with cyberterrorism under Section 66F of India's Information Technologies Act. If convicted, he could be sentenced to life in prison. The prosecutor is arguing that Biswas was not simply stating his opinion but supported ISIS and terrorist acts by tweeting pictures and videos, encouraging others to join ISIS, and by becoming a meeting place for ISIS fighters and supporters.[28]

Even though most people in the United States support the right to free speech and the right to privacy, for some, this right, in their eyes, ends when public safety is at stake. The term *terrorism* invokes great anxieties and feelings of helplessness. People don't feel safe anymore in their everyday activities, such as shopping and going to a concert or a festival. There is the general sense that the police should keep the citizens safe, and if that can only happen if citizens give up some of their civil rights, then so be it. This reflects very similar fears and opinions to those after the 9/11 attacks, which had sparked the U.S. Congress to promptly pass the USA PATRIOT ACT.

USA PATRIOT Act

The USA PATRIOT Act, under Section 215, gives the government the authority to collect content records related to telephone activities. The government, specifically the National Security Agency (NSA), defined telephone activities much broader than most people would have expected, however. Specifically, any digital information relevant to an investigation was included under Section 215. This interpretation allowed the government to collect vast amounts of metadata from millions of Americans and billions of people around the world, including European government officials such Angela Merkel, chancellor of Germany. Most data collection under Section 215 falls under the jurisdiction of the U.S. Foreign Intelligence Surveillance Court (FISC or FISA). The proceedings and outcomes of FISA court hearings and decisions are not published, meaning that people do not know what the court does or decides. It is in that sense, then, that FISA is a secret court.[29]

When Edward Snowden leaked the widespread snooping by the U.S. government and the secrecy of the FISA court in 2013, many people, and especially citizens of foreign countries who had been spied on, were outraged. As a consequence, the U.S. government passed the USA Freedom Act prohibiting the bulk collection of digital information. This does not preclude the NSA from collecting foreign Internet content from U.S. companies, however. Under the third-party doctrine, the NSA may collect all information that people voluntarily turn over to a third party. This includes sending e-mails by using a third-party Internet service provider, such as Verizon. It also includes messages on Twitter and Facebook, as they are third parties. The Freedom Act also has not changed much with regard to the FISA court proceedings and the ability of the NSA to thwart encryption. The NSA actively discourages corporations from marketing effective encryption tools to the public because encryption would significantly curtail the NSA's ability to read everything people send over the Internet.[30]

LEGAL ISSUE 10.2

UNITED STATES V. WARSHAK

In 2010, Steven Warshak sued the U.S. government for violating his Fourth Amendment rights. In 2006, Warshak had been charged with 112 counts of conspiracy to wire, mail, and bank fraud, making false statements to banks, conspiracy to commit money laundering, and a variety of other crimes. These crimes were related to the business practices of his company Berkley's, which was known for its product "Enzyte," a male enhancement supplement. The prosecution used thousands of e-mails to prove its case. The e-mails had been obtained from Warshak's Internet service provider. Warshak was convicted of the majority of charges, including fraud and money laundering, and sentenced to 25 years in prison. In addition, a forfeiture hearing was held and the jury found that most of Warshak's assets had been obtained through his criminal activities. The judge ordered that Warshak pay a fine of $93,000, surrender $495,540,000 in proceeds/money/judgment, and $44,876,781.68 in money-laundering proceeds.[31]

Warshak appealed his prison sentence and the forfeiture of his assets, and in 2010 his arguments were heard by the Sixth Circuit Court of Appeals. Warshak argued that using e-mails obtained from his Internet service provider violated his Fourth Amendment Rights against unreasonable search and seizure. In *Katz v. United States*, the Supreme Court established a two-pronged test of the right to privacy: (a) a person has "exhibited an actual (subjective) expectation of privacy" and (b) "that the expectation be one that society is prepared to recognize as reasonable" (p. 347).[32] The Katz decision had not been applied to digital communication, however, leaving much private information open to seizure by law enforcement. The Sixth Circuit for the first time extended the right to privacy to e-mails stored with third parties. Despite the Court's conclusion that the government had violated Warshak's Fourth Amendment rights, it did not overturn his conviction based on the grounds that the law enforcement officers had

(Continued)

(Continued)

acted in "good faith" because they believed that the e-mails were not protected by the Fourth Amendment.[33]

Following the Warshak decision, Congressman Kevin Yoder introduced the Email Privacy Act that would amend the Electronic Communications Privacy Act of 1986 to

> prohibit a provider of remote computing service or electronic communication service to the public from knowingly divulging to a governmental entity the contents of any communication that is in electronic storage or otherwise maintained by the provider, subject to exceptions.[34]

What Do You Think?

1. Discuss the pros and cons of expanding the Fourth Amendment to digital communications.
2. Imagine if the government collected all of your e-mails, posts on Twitter, Facebook, and any other social media website, and charged you with the crime of violating copyright law by sharing music files or downloading pirated software. What would you argue to defend yourself?

Jurisdictional Issues

Universal Jurisdiction

In 2013, the reaction of the Turkish government to a series of protests, called the Gezi protests, across Turkey triggered a number of cyberattacks. The Turkish government had used brute force and tear gas against the protesters. The first cyberattacks came from Anonymous, ColdHaker, and other hacker groups that do not typically act together. The hackers took down the president's website and the website of Turkey's leading party.[35] In 2016, hackers attacked the website of the U.S. Democratic Party, stole e-mails and other confidential information, and released it during the presidential election. Some have argued that this security breach contributed to the loss of the election. This is an arguable position, but the main issue is that such attacks can cause great damage to the economy and democracy of a nation.[36]

There are a number of problems governments across the globe face when such attacks occur. One problem is the issue of attribution. As we have witnessed, it has been very difficult to attribute the cyberattacks to Russia in an attempt to help Trump win the election. Despite all the available resources, intelligence, and technologies, the U.S. government has not been able to present hard evidence, and Russian President Vladimir Putin has denied the attacks. If the cyberattack group does not publicly take responsibility, it is very difficult to determine who the attackers are. Second, a main question is how to react to such cyberattacks and what to do when the attacks originate in a foreign country, making the attackers legally untouchable even if they can be identified. There are no passport checks, border control, or other measures. Thus, traditional governance does not apply. So who makes the laws that apply to cyberspace globally? And how are these laws enforced? Cyberspace also faces the issue of enforcement. If there is a cyberattack, who is responsible for investigating and punishing criminals? Is it the country that was the victim of the attack or the country where the criminal resides? What if the laws with regard to punishment vary substantially between those two countries? This is only a glimpse of the problem of international cybersecurity laws. Not surprisingly, due to the complex nature of cyberspace and geopolitical relations, there is currently no international cybersecurity law. There are, however, some multilateral efforts to tackle cybercrime and cybersecurity.

Budapest Convention on Cybersecurity (2001)

The Council of Europe passed the Budapest Convention on Cybercrime in an effort to establish a uniform law that applies to all signatories. The 50 countries that ratified the convention promised to adopt domestic legislation that would expedite preservation, search and seizure, and interception of data. In addition, the signatories agreed to cooperate with regard to extradition of criminals and access and interception of computer data. Another important part of the convention is the agreement to prosecute cybercrimes committed in the states' territories.[37]

Unfortunately, the Budapest Convention has no teeth—that is, it lacks enforcement mechanisms that would punish violations. It's a symbolic legislation to assure the public that the international community is taking steps to combat cybercrime and the threat of a cyberwar. Unfortunately, adherence to the law is entirely up to the goodwill of the signatory countries, and many countries have taken no steps to implement the provisions of the convention.[38]

Network and Information Security Directive (2016)

In July 2016, the European Union (EU) passed a new Network and Information Security (NIS) Directive establishing the first actual cybersecurity rules. Specifically, the directive regulates network and information security and information sharing. The new NIS directive focuses on critical infrastructures (e.g., energy, transport, health, financial, and digital services) and establishes specific cybersecurity measures. Businesses supplying critical infrastructures are also regulated via the directive and must demonstrate that they have the capability to resist a cyberattack. In addition, the businesses that run or supply critical infrastructures must report all cyberincidents to a national agency. This also includes Amazon and Google and their cloud services. Finally, EU countries have agreed to cooperate on cybersecurity and also build cooperative relationships with service providers.[39]

The main strength of the NIS directive is the ability of the EU to enforce the standards laid out in the NIS directive. Member states have 21 months to implement the standards and an additional 6 months to identify all entities operating critical infrastructures.[40] A major weakness of the directive is its scope. It only applies to countries within the EU. That is a good start, but without a truly international agreement, the impact on cybercrime will be limited.

Issues With Enforcement/Jurisdiction

The response of law enforcement to a terrorist or cyberattack often determines how many people die and are victimized. Cybercriminals and terrorists have been quick to adapt and use available tools such as social media and location services to gain an advantage over law enforcement. The uncontrollable nature of social media poses great challenges to coordinating effective federal and state law enforcement responses to cyberattacks and terrorist acts. The darknet has become the underground Amazon for criminals and nation-states looking for weapons, including cyberweapons such as worms and Trojan horses.[41]

Effective law enforcement responses have been difficult to establish, often due to jurisdictional and geopolitical issues.[42] Every nation-state is a sovereign entity—that is, only law enforcement in that nation has the right to enforce the laws. Similarly, every court only has jurisdiction over crimes that occur in territory under its authority.[43]

If a crime is committed in the United States, only the U.S. government has the right to investigate the crime and arrest the suspect. Even if law enforcement in other countries have an interest in capturing the offender, they cannot simply cross over the border to the United States and arrest the suspect. For instance, Edward Snowden, who released classified information about the U.S. government, is one of the most wanted criminals. Snowden found asylum in Russia, which has declined to extradite Snowden. As much as U.S. law enforcement may want to go to Russia and arrest Snowden, they do not have the right to violate Russia's sovereignty as a nation.[44]

Another problem is that some countries are more developed than others and differ significantly with regard to cybercrime laws. The United States has many more laws against cybercrime than many other nations. If a certain behavior is not a crime in the country where it started, that causes great problems for law enforcement. In 2000, a person from the Philippines released the ILoveYou virus, which damaged files on millions of personal computers around the globe. At the time, there was no law against releasing a virus in the Philippines, and thus, the man had not committed a crime, at least not in the Philippines.[45]

These jurisdictional and geopolitical problems are exacerbated by differences in cultural values between nations. What some nations consider a crime is not considered a crime in others. This difference in political, moral, and constitutional convictions greatly hampers the development of universal enforcement rules. For instance, the U.S. Constitution guarantees the right to free speech and religion. These are not guaranteed rights in numerous other countries. A person in the United States may post a blog with comments that are critical of the Chinese government. In the United States, this is protected speech under the First Amendment. A person in China who reads the blog or even affirmatively responds to the blog may be committing a crime.

Another example relates to sexuality and sexually explicit pictures or pornography. There are many countries in which pornography in all forms is illegal. However, in Europe, the United States, and other countries, many forms of pornography are legal. Someone living in the United States may post pornographic images that are not violating any laws to be viewed by people in nations where such images can result in harsh punishment.[46]

A further problem is that it is very difficult to investigate, prosecute, and punish cybercriminals. Anonymity and identity are the main problems for law enforcement. Even for technologically advanced nations, it is difficult to collect evidence of cybercrimes. The evidence is typically made up of 0s and 1s, and can easily disappear or be changed. The investigator may inadvertently change the evidence simply by examining it, making it useless. For instance, the malicious software may be programmed to self-destruct if accessed by someone other than the criminal. In other cases, the fraudster may erase all logs that would show what happened.[47] Even if evidence of the crime can be collected, this does not necessarily reveal the identity of the criminal. In cases of child pornography, it may be fairly easy to get the evidence, but proving that the person downloaded the images knowingly is significantly more difficult. The suspect can claim that someone else hacked into the computer and stored the illegal images without the user's knowledge.[48] This is certainly possible and does happen. For nations with less-developed technologies, it becomes nearly impossible to determine the identity of the criminal and collect the evidence necessary to punish the fraudster.[49] Even within U.S. law enforcement, the main challenge that has plagued federal and state law enforcement agencies is the development of guidelines to secure the integrity of the agency, improve the training of officers with regard to cybercrime investigations, and develop effective response mechanisms to cyberattacks and terrorist attacks.[50] The investigation of cybercrime is very complex, requiring cybersecurity experts. Traditional law enforcement training does not include such specialized skills. These experts are also highly sought after, and there is an apparent shortage.

LEGAL ISSUE 10.3

LAW OF THE SEA

Some people have suggested applying the law of the sea to cybercrimes. Crimes at sea are similar to cybercrimes in that there is often no clear jurisdiction. In the historical perspective, only a certain part of the sea directly surrounding a nation (a 3-mile radius) was part of the nation's jurisdiction. The rest of the sea was free to all. Thus, there was no regulation of fishing, pollution, natural resources (e.g., oil and gas), and military presence above and under the sea. This began to change at the end of World War I. In 1945, U.S. President Harry S. Truman unilaterally extended the rights to the resources of the sea on the continental shelf. This expansion was in great part due to the pressure from the oil industry, which had realized the enormous potential of underwater oil resources. In 1946, Chile followed the United States in their expansion efforts, and over time, more and more countries expanded their control over the sea. The main industries were oil production and deep-sea fishing but also the search for diamonds and valuable metals. The sea was being exploited as it never had before, which led to conflicts between countries over sea territories, and between countries and environmental activists such as Greenpeace over the pollution of the sea.

On November 1, 1976, the United Nations held their first Conference on the Law of the Sea, but it took until 1982 to adopt the United Nations Convention on the Law of the Sea. The Convention regulates navigational rights, territorial sea limits, economic jurisdiction, legal status of resources beyond national jurisdiction, passing of ships, and preservation of wildlife and seabeds. The Convention also set enforcement rules and is widely regarded as a landmark in international law.

If negotiations between countries fail to resolve a problem, the countries can choose between four options.

1. International Tribunal for the Law of the Sea
2. International Court of Justice

(Continued)

(Continued)

3. Submission to an International Arbitration Procedure
4. Submission to a Special Arbitration Tribunal

In cases where national sovereignty is at issue, states can appeal to the conciliation commission, but they don't have to submit to the decision. However, there is much moral pressure to adhere to the commission's findings.[51]

What Do You Think?

1. Why is the Law of the Sea proposed as a possible solution to jurisdictional issues with regard to cybercrime? Explain.
2. Propose a Law of Cyberspace, including enforcement strategies.

Summary

The last 2 decades could be termed the *decades of the Internet*, as the Internet has developed with lightning speed. The rapid growth of computer technologies, communication infrastructure, and social media has outpaced the legal system and the ability of law enforcement to respond to the dangers posed by the Internet. The main problems for law enforcement and the legal system are attribution, apprehension, and punishment of offenders. Another main issue is the sharing of public assets by private companies and the government, such as critical infrastructures. Protecting companies, individuals, and critical infrastructures is complicated by the fact that cyberspace extends across geopolitical borders and that international coordination on cyber issues is lacking. Even though the EU has begun to cooperate in the fight against cybercrime, the existing conventions are without much force. Different countries have different cultural values, different definitions of crime, and are in different stages of cybercrime preparedness. This is even more complicated at the global level. The trend appears to go toward a regional and national incorporation of treaty-based cybersecurity legal regimes.

Key Term

Discussion Questions

1. Discuss the holistic approach to cybersecurity. What is the focus, and how does it improve cybersecurity?
2. Read "The Real Story of Stuxnet" and discuss the likely consequences of similar attacks on the United States and your life.

3. Discuss the issues related to international jurisdiction, and especially the issue of enforcement of existing international laws. What solutions would you propose?
4. Read Michigan's Cyber Disruption Response Plan. What is the purpose of the plan, and what are the most important steps of the plan?

Internet Resources

United Nations Convention of the Law of the Sea
  http://www.un.org/depts/los/convention_agreements/texts/unclos/unclos_e.pdf

The Real Story of Stuxnet
  http://spectrum.ieee.org/telecom/security/the-real-story-of-stuxnet

State of Michigan Cyber Disruption Response Plan
  https://www.michigan.gov/documents/cybersecurity/120815_Michigan_Cyber_Disruption_Response_Plan_Online_VersionA_507848_7.pdf

Further Reading

Kharraz, A., Robertson, W., Balzarotti, D., Bilge, L., & Kirda, E. (2015). *Cutting the Gordian knot: A look under the hood of ransomware attacks*. Retrieved from https://seclab.ccs.neu.edu/static/publications/dimva2015ransomware.pdf

Nelson, B. (2016). *Children's connected toys: Data security and privacy concerns*. Office of Oversight and Investigations Report. Retrieved from https://www.billnelson.senate.gov/sites/default/files/12.14.16_Ranking_Member_Nelson_Report_on_Connected_Toys.pdf

Wei, J. (n.d.). *DDoS on Internet of Things—A big alarm for the future*. Retrieved from http://www.cs.tufts.edu/comp/116/archive/fall2016/jwei.pdf

Digital Resources

Want a better grade?

Get the tools you need to sharpen your study skills. Access practice quizzes and eFlashcards, at **study.sagepub.com/kremling**.

11 What the Future Holds

Learning Objectives

1. Explain why data is considered to be the new oil.
2. Discuss the risks created by dataveillance.
3. Describe the nature and possible consequences of emerging threats.
4. Discuss emerging perpetrators and their targets.

THINK ABOUT IT 11.1

Pizzeria "Comet Ping Pong" Is a Child Pornography Ring

One of the latest trends has been the posting of "fake news"—that is, news that is made up for the purpose of accomplishing a certain goal or simply for entertainment purposes. On December 4, 2016, an entire Washington, DC, neighborhood was under lockdown due to a fake news story about a pizzeria that was allegedly a child pornography ring run by Hillary Clinton and her campaign manager, John Podesta. The fake story was posted on social media and shared via Twitter and Facebook by hundreds of people, including the son of former national security advisor Lt. Gen. Michael Flynn.

After reading the story, a man decided to take matters into his own hands and entered the pizzeria with an assault rifle, which he pointed at the employees. He fired several shots before he was arrested. People who believe fake news can pose a real danger to society. Fake news stories have always existed, but they were printed in magazines everyone knew were not serious publications. Today, many fake stories are shared by websites and people who look legitimate, which makes them believable and can result in violent threats and bloodshed.[1]

What Would You Do?

1. What do you think motivates people to post fake news?
2. When you read a story, how do you know that it is true?
3. How can you verify that information you receive is accurate?

Data Is the New Oil

The human brain thinks of life in a linear fashion—that is, for each unit added, you get a unit of return. For instance, if a person earns $250 for an 8-hour workday, he or she will earn an additional $250 for each additional day worked. Because people tend to think in linear ways, they also often assume that information technology is expanding in a linear way. This is not the case, however. In the 1970s, Gordon Moore showed how central processing units (CPUs) doubled every 2 years. According to Moore's law, the growth in information technology is exponential.[2] Stated differently, the growth in information technology doesn't grow 1, 2, 3, 4, 5, 6, and so forth, but rather it grows 1, 2, 4, 8, 16, 32, 64, 128, and so forth. Looking at the example of followers on Twitter, they don't grow from 1 in January to 2 in February to 3 in March. Rather, it may take 1 year to get 100 followers, but only 6 additional months to add another 100 followers, and only one month to add another 100 followers. This exponential growth has brought great improvements to people's lives, such as the ability to work from home, develop new businesses such as social media jobs, order products online, make doctor appointments online, buy life insurance, and negotiate loans. The list of online services that has contributed to our life conveniences is endless. And so are the opportunities for cybercriminals.

Before the expansion of information technology, a thief could steal from a few people a day or from one bank or another institution. Cybercriminals can steal from millions or even billions of people, and they can do so repeatedly with the same malicious code in a matter of hours. In 2013, the retail store Target was hacked and 40 million customer credit card accounts including expiration dates and card verification values were stolen. In an attempt to mitigate the damages in customer trust, Target offered a free credit monitoring service. This type of economic damage will continue to grow exponentially as information technology continues to grow.[3] Target is certainly not the only company to be hacked. There are many companies who have fallen victim to cybercriminals, including Yahoo, Sony, JP Morgan, Ashley Madison, Anthem, Blue Cross, and Experian.[4]

Data Mining

One of the latest trends is data mining and data brokerage. Google and Facebook are among the biggest data collection agencies. They are also among the biggest suppliers of data to marketing agencies and, unwittingly, cybercriminals. As discussed previously in this book, Google and Facebook collect everything people post, search for, put in their contacts, calendars, and all other online activities. There is an abundance of companies who buy the data. Even if these companies have no criminal intent for using the data, it is likely that they will get hacked by criminals and the personal data of billions of people will fall into the hands of criminals. The more data of your personal life that are out there in cyberspace, the more vulnerable you are to identity theft and other crimes. The more data that are being collected, the more companies and people will fall victim to cybercriminals, who are becoming ever more sophisticated. Data is the new oil—a hugely valuable, largely untapped asset. Those who manage to tap into that asset will become the new data sheiks.

IMAGE 11.1 • Big Data

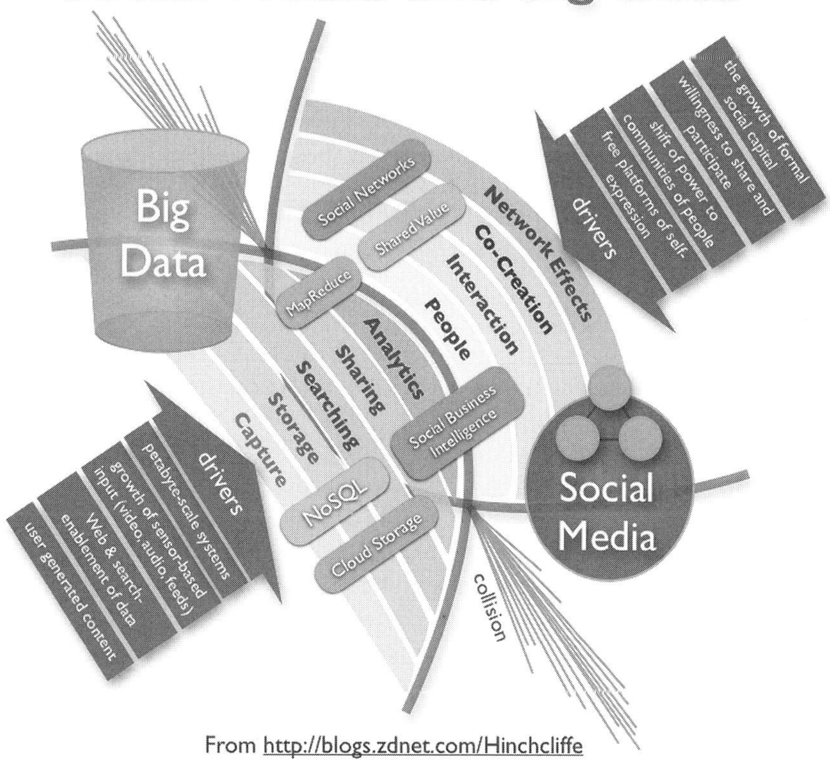

Dataveillance

Outside, even through the shut window-pane, the world looked cold. Down in the street little eddies of wind were whirling dust and torn paper into spirals, and though the sun was shining and the sky a harsh blue, there seemed to be no colour in anything, except the posters that were plastered everywhere. The black-moustachio'd face gazed down from every commanding corner. There was one on the house-front immediately opposite. BIG BROTHER IS WATCHING YOU, the caption said, while the dark eyes looked deep into Winston's own. Down at streetlevel another poster, torn at one corner, flapped fitfully in the wind, alternately covering and uncovering the single word INGSOC. In the far distance a helicopter skimmed down between the roofs, hovered for an instant like a bluebottle, and darted away again with a curving flight. It was the police patrol, snooping into people's windows. The patrols did not matter, however. Only the Thought Police mattered. Behind Winston's back the voice from the telescreen was still babbling away about pig-iron and the overfulfilment of the Ninth Three-Year Plan. The tele-screen received and transmitted simultaneously. Any sound that Winston made, above the level of a very low whisper, would be picked up by it, moreover, so long as he remained within the field of vision which the metal plaque commanded, he could be seen as well as heard. There was of course no way of knowing whether you were being watched at any given moment. How often, or on what system, the Thought Police plugged in on any individual wire was guesswork. It was even conceivable that they watched everybody all the time. But at any rate they could plug in your wire whenever they wanted to. You had to live— did live, from habit that became instinct—in the assumption that every sound you made was overheard, and, except in darkness, every movement scrutinized.[5]

This passage from George Orwell's dystopian novel *Nineteen Eighty-Four* (or *1984*) is not so far from the reality of data surveillance (dataveillance) in the 21st century. His main character, Winston, lives in a surveillance state called Oceania. The omnipresent government of Oceania, whose main objective is unrestrained power, records everything its citizens say, do, and think, and controls their behaviors and thoughts. The threat of being arrested by the Thought Police keeps everyone in line. The main tool of the government is data. They not only collect data on everything, they then manipulate the data to their advantage, rewriting history to their liking. They do this so well that citizens of Oceania cannot distinguish between real data and fake data. This could not happen in the United States—or could it? It may be the government (e.g., National Security Agency) or big corporations like Google or IBM who control data and thereby have the ability to manipulate data. It may also be a combination of the government and legitimate companies such as Google, Internet users, and cybercriminals who will reflect the surveillance Orwell described in his book.

Google

Google Street View cars are driving around the world recording everything, including your house and backyard. The data are then transferred to Google Earth where you can zoom in on your house and backyard, removing all privacy. This is comparable to Orwell's helicopter "snooping into people's windows." You can even download an app on your phone or tablet. Google Earth was originally called Earth Viewer 3D, developed by Keyhole Inc. and funded by the CIA. In 2004, Google purchased Keyhole Inc., renamed Earth Viewer 3D to Google Earth, and made it available to the public for free in 2005. Critics have argued that Google Earth and other Google tools pose great danger to the privacy of people. By typing the name of the location into the search box, customers can get very detailed images, including types of vehicles with license plate numbers parked on a certain street. These concerns are also shared by the governments of a number of countries. For instance, the government of Japan forced Google to reshoot street-level views because the images were enabling viewers to look inside the houses. In Europe, which is substantially more privacy sensitive than the United States, Google had to blur people's faces and car license plate pictures. In Great Britain, a woman filed for divorce after seeing her husband's car in front of another woman's house on Google Street View.[6]

IMAGE 11.2 ● Google Earth Street View

© iStockphoto.com/BanksPhotos

Not only have privacy concerns been raised but also security concerns. Burglars can stake out a neighborhood and houses from their computers that would otherwise be difficult to see due to their remote location or private setting. Even more concerning is the potential ability of terrorists to stake out critical infrastructures, such as the Hoover Dam or nuclear power plants, by using the satellite view. Google has replied to these criticisms saying that its images are several years old and do not show real-time data.[7] However, there have been several incidents where terrorists used Google Earth to attack military bases or used it to plan a terrorist attack. For instance, in the attack on Mumbai, India (see Chapter 7), the attackers used images from Google Earth to plan and carry out the attacks, and used GPS and detailed satellite images to sail from Karachi to Mumbai. They were not sailors and would not have been able to use this route without GPS and the images provided by Google Earth.[8]

In another incident, terrorists used Google Earth images to stake out a United Kingdom military base in Basra, Iraq. The terrorists had printed out detailed photographs from Google Earth that showed the exact location and the layout of the military base. These photographs were seized during a raid of the houses of the insurgents. An intelligence officer from the British Royal Green Jackets battle group stated:

> This is evidence as far as we are concerned for planning terrorist attacks. Who would otherwise have Google Earth imagery of one of our bases? We are concerned that they use them to plan attacks. We have never had proof that they have deliberately targeted any area of the camp using these images but presumably they are of great use to them. We believe they use Google Earth to identify the most vulnerable areas such as tents.[9]

The British base experienced mortar and rocket attacks on a daily basis, and the attacks became more accurate. British officials also claimed that the photographs were being sold to rogue militias.

The fact that so many groups collect data from private citizens, critical infrastructures, the military, and other targets is disconcerting because this dataveillance provides criminals and terrorists with everything they need to attack, and at very low cost. All they need is a computer and high-speed Internet—and both are available en masse.

Manipulation of Data: The Screen Is Always Right

The power of the computer or tablet screen has become so great that people will trust what they see on the screen despite evidence to the contrary. The idea that the information on the screen must be correct is taken at face value—with dire consequences, as you have seen in the story about the pizzeria in Washington, DC, at the beginning of this chapter. In Orwell's Oceania, the government manipulated data by rewriting history to the point where citizens didn't know what day or year it was.

> He sat back. A sense of complete helplessness had descended upon him. To begin with, he did not know with any certainty that this was 1984. It must be round about that date, since he was fairly sure that his age was thirty-nine, and he believed that he had been born in 1944 or 1945; but it was never possible nowadays to pin down any date within a year or two.[10]

You are thinking, "Well, it's a fictional novel." Unfortunately, what seemed like fiction in 1949 has become reality in a variety in ways. Data and what we see on the screen can be changed much easier than imagined. This includes data of law enforcement, governments, health care providers, credit companies, employers, and other agencies holding sensitive personal information. With the increased digitalization of our personal information, the integrity of our data is at great risk. Not all of the data manipulations are due to malicious intent or hacking. Sometimes it's simply a software error. In 2010, California released hundreds of dangerous inmates on unsupervised, irrevocable parole because a computer screen showed the officers that these inmates should be released. Despite the fact that it was clear these inmates were incarcerated for violent crimes such as robbery, rape, gang activities, and murder, the officers believed what they saw on their screen. The idea that the screen must be correct leads people to do things they otherwise would not do.[11]

In another example of the threat of manipulated data, the World Anti-Doping Agency (WADA) released a statement saying that WADA data had been hacked and manipulated before it was released to the public. The data contained information about athletes who had received Therapeutic Use Exemptions (TUE) from WADA to treat an injury. Among these athletes were Olympic gold medalist Simone Giles, tennis icons Serena Williams and Rafael Nada, and cyclists Bradley Wiggins and Chris Froome. The group responsible for the hacking and manipulation calls themselves the Fancy Bears. WADA stated:

> The criminal activity undertaken by the cyber espionage group, which seeks to undermine the TUE program and the work of WADA and its partners in the protection of clean sport, is a cheap shot at innocent athletes whose personal data has been exposed.[12]

In this case, WADA noticed the changes in the data and thus was able to correct the errors. But still, private data was released to the public, and once it is on the Internet, it will stay forever.

Imagine if hackers accessed and manipulated patients' records in hospital data sets with the purpose of making a profit. Would the hospital notice that your record was wrong? Or would they rely on what they saw on the screen? If hospitals and doctors rely on the data on the screen, manipulated records could be deadly for patients if they receive the wrong treatment, medication, or no treatment at all because the screen indicates the patient is not ill. Not only are health care providers digitizing patients' records, they may also store them in a cloud, further increasing the risks of hacking.

Censorship

Manipulation of data is not only used by hackers but also by governments and other groups to influence our thinking and actions. One such tool used to manipulate data and people is censorship: We see what they want us to see. This is not only true for people who live in China but people around the globe. There are many countries that block certain web content, thereby manipulating what people read and know. The Great Firewall of China blocks all content about criticism against the Chinese government, political action, an independent Taiwan, and other undesirable content. While China's censorship may be the best known and most discussed, the censorship of accessible web content is also widespread in the Arab world, Asia, Europe, and the United States.

According to the Committee to Protect Journalists, the 10 most censored countries in 2015 were (in order): Eritrea, North Korea, Syria, Iran, Equatorial Guinea, Uzbekistan, Burma, Saudi Arabia, Cuba, Belarus, and China. Censorship is mainly used by authoritarian governments that have come into power by dint of monarchy, family dynasty, coup d'état, rigged election, or some combination thereof. Some of the leaders have been in power for decades without having an election. For instance, the president of Eritrea, Isaias Afwerki, elected in 1993, has since refused to hold elections and implement the constitution. In North Korea, the leadership has been in the same family since 1948. The current president, Kim Jong-un, took over for his father, Kim Jong-il, in 2011, who had followed his father, Kim Il-sung, who was president from 1948 until 1993.[13]

The purpose of this censorship is to spread the news from the official government information agency and ensure that critical voices are never heard. The citizens in these countries are only allowed to read and hear what the government wants them to believe. This, of course, in itself is a manipulation of facts, but it gets even worse. The governments purposefully falsify information before they spread it. For instance, North Korea announced to the public that president Kim Jong-il died on December 19, 2011. Subsequent investigations, however, indicate that he actually died 2 days earlier, and his date of death was falsified to give the government time to determine who his successor would be. Syria blocks content from oppositional parties of the Assad regime and uses the Internet to spread its own propaganda. When demonstrations against the Assad regime began in 2011, Assad imposed strict regulations on oppositional parties, journalists, and other critical voices. The use of violence against the opposition has since become widespread and progressively worse. Journalists have been tortured and killed, and so have many other people. Criticism of the Assad regime has deadly consequences. The Assad regime not only controls the news media and what content is viewable on the Internet, but they have also disabled mobile phones, landlines, and electricity. This regime, similar to North Korea and China, also uses an army of hackers (the Syrian Electronic Army) to attack those who criticize them. Critics and journalists assert that the control of the Internet has played a substantial role in keeping Assad in power.[14]

Authoritarian governments are not the only ones who manipulate the facts and block websites. Europe and the U.S. government also engage in censorship, mainly targeting hate speech. Europe blocks websites that contain hate speech, European nationalism, and terrorist content. In 2016, the European Union warned Facebook, Twitter, and other social media with regard to hate speech postings:

> If Facebook, YouTube, Twitter and Microsoft want to convince me and the ministers that the non-legislative approach can work, they will have to act quickly and make a strong effort in the coming months.[15]

The United States has been investigating whether Russia is influencing social media and hate speech in the United States. These efforts are funded by a bill of the House of Representatives, H.R. 6393, Intelligence Authorization Act for Fiscal Year 2017, as the U.S. government is concerned about fake news from Russia and how it may impact the beliefs of Americans.[16]

Reference Text

Social Media Cyber Attacks

http://www.databank.com.lb/docs/Social%20Media%20in%20the%20Arab%20World%20Leading%20up%20to%20the%20Uprisings%20of%202011.pdf

What can we believe when what we read and hear is manipulated and falsified? How will we know whether something is true or not? George Orwell predicted this scenario in his novel more than 60 years ago. Maybe it is something inherent in human nature—the desire to make others believe what they believe, the desire to manipulate the facts in a way that has advantages for them, doing whatever it takes to stay in power. The old saying "Power corrupts, and total power corrupts totally" seems to hold true too often. Isn't that what happens in many institutions and businesses? In school, children learn what the state wants them to learn; in the stock market, traders manipulate the stock prices to gain a fortune; people falsify their resumes to get a job; pedophiles call themselves child lovers; and politicians may promise something they know they will never do to get the public's votes. What is dangerous is when people don't realize any longer that information is manipulated in many ways and when people start to believe blindly.

Spoofing

[Spoofing] is a fraudulent or malicious practice in which communication is sent from an unknown source disguised as a source known to the receiver. Spoofing is most prevalent in communication mechanisms that lack a high level of security.[17]

E-Mail Spoofing

E-mail spoofing is the most common type of spoofing. E-mail spoofing is the forgery of an e-mail header pretending to be a legitimate sender, like a business or friend, scamming the receiver into opening the e-mail and downloading malicious software or responding to a solicitation. E-mail spoofing is an easy tool for criminals because the Simple Mail Transfer Protocol (SMTP) does not verify the authenticity of the sender's address. There are e-mail address authentication mechanisms, such as the SMTP service extension and DomainKeys Identified Mail, but they are used very rarely.[18]

The e-mail spoofing process looks like this: A fraudster replaces the actual e-mail header with the e-mail address from a legitimate person you know, such as a family member or friend, work contact, or doctor's office. It may also look like it is coming from the IRS or some other government agency. E-mail spoofing is used for phishing and spam campaigns. The header is meant to encourage the receiver to click on a link or attachment embedded in the e-mail. Imagine you receive an e-mail from the IRS stating that you need to pay $6,000 in overdue taxes or you will be arrested for tax fraud. The IRS would not send such an e-mail, but many people have fallen victim to this scam, paying thousands of dollars to criminals thinking they were paying the IRS.[19]

The IRS posted a warning on their website, stating:

> In recent weeks, a phony e-mail claiming to come from the IRS has been circulating in large numbers. The subject line of the e-mail often states that the e-mail is a notice of underreported income. The e-mail may contain an attachment or a link to a bogus Web page directing taxpayers to their "tax statement." In either case, when the recipient opens the attachment or clicks on the link, they download a Trojan horse-type of virus to their computers. The IRS does not send unsolicited e-mails to taxpayers about their tax accounts. Anyone who receives an unsolicited e-mail claiming to come from the IRS should avoid opening any attachments or clicking on any links.[20]

Stock Market Spoofing

Spoofing can also be used to manipulate the stock market. High-frequency traders place large orders for securities with the intent to change the price. Once the price has changed, the order is cancelled and the trader takes advantage of the new price. In practice, what seems to be an elaborate process happens within milliseconds. The traders can place thousands of buy and sell orders only to cancel them within a few milliseconds. This practice requires very fast Internet connections and computerized trading algorithms. It's basically the computer that is doing the trading rather than a human being. The price only needs to change by a few cents to make millions in profits. For instance, a trader may wish to lower the price of gold because he wants to buy gold. Let's assume the price for 10 grams of gold is $405.028. The spoofer offers to sell gold for $404.90. Other traders also start to lower their price. At that point, the spoofer cancels the offer and starts buying large quantities of gold for the lower price. Since the price was artificially lowered by the spoofer, it will likely go back up, making significant money for the spoofer. Spoofing has substantial impacts on the volatility of the stock market and therefore carries significant dangers with regard to customer trust. If people don't have trust in the market, they refrain from buying and selling stock. Similarly, if traders don't know whether a price is real or artificially changed, they cannot trade with confidence. Traders rely on what they see on the screen, but what if what they see is false? Then trading is no longer a business but a lottery game.[21]

In 2010, the Dodd-Frank Wall Street Reform and Consumer Protection Act made spoofing a federal crime, but it has been difficult to prosecute spoofers. There are many legitimate reasons to cancel an order, making it difficult to determine whether a trader was spoofing. Prosecutors have to wade through huge data sets and use statistical analyses to determine whether a trader was spoofing, and even then it is very difficult to prove.[22]

CASE STUDY 11.1

High-Frequency Trading—"Flash Boys"

In March 2016, a judge asked for the extradition of the British high-frequency trader Navinder Singh Sarao to the United States. The British trader was accused of having a substantial role in the 2010 "flash crash" of the U.S. stock market by engaging in spoofing. In May 2010, the Dow Jones plunged by more than 1,000 points. High-frequency trading has received much attention as one of the contributors of the flash crash. Navinder Singh Sarao allegedly manipulated the stock market by putting in large orders for securities in an attempt to change the price for the securities. Once the price had changed, Navinder would cancel the order and take advantage of the price change. Between 2010 and 2014, Navinder made about $40 million in profits. One year later, he was charged by the U.S. government with wire fraud, commodities fraud, commodities manipulation, and spoofing.[23]

What Do You Think?

1. Spoofing is illegal in the United States but not in Great Britain. If you were the British judge deciding over the extradition of Navinder Singh Sarao, which factors would you consider?
2. Matt Samelson, the chief executive of the consulting firm Woodbine Associates, stated: "Technically it is market manipulation, but some people would call that clever."[24] If you were the defense attorney of Navinder Singh Sarao, what would you argue?
3. Discuss the damages to the stock market, individuals, and companies resulting from high-frequency trading.

Emerging Threats

Internet of Things

The Internet of Things (IoT) includes network-connected devices and sensors, such as connected cars, alarm systems, home thermostats, iPads, Android devices, elevators, health trackers, connected refrigerators, and so forth. There are three major points about future emerging threats. First, as more and more devices become "connected" devices, the "attack surface area" of cyberspace increases.[25] In 2015, Gartner, Inc., forecasted that there would be 20.8 billion devices in use by 2020. From 2014 to 2015, the number of connected devices rose by 30%.[26]

IoT devices have added much convenience to our daily lives, but they are also dangerous because they are "smart" in the sense that they make decisions independent of us and they make decisions about us. For instance, connected cars make decisions when to brake, how to park the car, or which route to give us on GPS. The potential of hacking and manipulating these devices is substantial, and our power to control these devices is small once they have been hacked. Many companies are tempted to release new connected devices as soon as possible and definitely before major holidays such as Christmas. This is understandable, as many companies make a substantial portion of their profit from holiday sales. Unfortunately, in their haste to release the new devices, security often takes a backseat, leaving customers vulnerable to being infected with a malware or even have their identity stolen. Companies may not develop security software and patches for the released product until several weeks or months later. Criminals are well aware of the fact that many new devices will have vulnerabilities that can be exploited rather easily.

IMAGE 11.3 ● Internet of Things

Internet of Things by Wilgengebroed on Flickr, https://commons.wikimedia.org/wiki/File:Internet_of_Things.jpg. Licensed under CC BY-SA 2.0, https://creativecommons.org/licenses/by/2.0/legalcode

Second, cybersecurity resources are stretched thinner with the ever-increasing complexity of new devices. Every few months, new devices are pushed into the market, from tablets to laptops and other connected devices. Increasingly, more devices are interconnected, making cybersecurity more difficult to accomplish. For instance, house alarm systems are connected to smartphones and other devices such as Amazon Echo—a voice-controlled device than can turn on lights, play music, and control other smarthome devices. The next generation Echo will include a built-in screen, allowing users to chat with video and shop online. Cybersecurity resources don't grow at the same rate as these new devices.[27]

Third, the increasing amount of data that we are downloading and uploading on a daily basis makes us more vulnerable to cyberintrusions because we are constantly online and traceable. For instance, the smartphone GPS knows our location at all times. Customers can actively turn off the location service, but many apps don't work without it. Thus, most people have it turned on at all times.[28]

Real-Time Location Services

Real-time location services (RTLS) is a technology that "detects the current geolocation of a target, which may be anything from a vehicle to an item in a manufacturing plant to a person."[29] Location services are used in the military, health care industry, retail, and postal service. There are many industries where RTLS is very important to daily operations. For instance, RTLS is used to track delivery vehicles and optimize routes. The military uses location services to track enemy combatants. Increasingly, these location services are used in phone and tablet features, such as directions (Google Maps), geotagging photographs, gaming (such as Pokémons), and many other apps. Ever since GPS became publicly available in 1983, services that use GPS have grown exponentially. GPS is now used in navigation, clock synchronization, astronomy, sports, and thousands of apps and games. Unfortunately, location services are not only very useful for legitimate businesses but also for criminals. RTLS can be abused for a wide variety of illegitimate purposes, such as stalking, hijacking, and stealing data.[30]

Vulnerable Targets

The app Waze is one of the most popular navigation apps, with more than 50 million users worldwide. Waze relies on traffic reports by users to find the fastest route and avoid traffic jams for users by rerouting them. Due to Waze (and other apps), more people are now able to use shortcuts through residential areas or use surface streets to get around a traffic jam or a construction site on a highway. As convenient as this is for drivers, it can be a great hassle for the residents in the neighborhoods that are now used as shortcuts because of greatly increased traffic. For instance, in some residential neighborhoods in Atlanta, Georgia, traffic increased by 45,000 cars a day. City officials stated that they had no choice but to address the problem by putting restrictions on left and right turns on some major intersections to preserve the sanctity of the residential areas. Other cities and states have similar problems. In Portland, Oregon, city officials blocked streets with barrels. In Sherman Oaks, California, citizens took matters into their own hands by submitting false traffic jams and car crashes in an effort to stop drivers from driving through the neighborhood. Unfortunately for the residents, Waze learned quickly and blocked those residents who had submitted false reports. One giveaway of false reporting is when people are not actually moving, which Waze notices immediately. Another problem is that if one person reports a crash, 10 others will quickly respond that it's not there. Waze and many other apps rely on this type of crowdsourcing. Residents try to use other tools to stop drivers from using a route, such as putting up "No Through Traffic" signs or "Watch for Children" figures. The effect of such strategies is near zero. Even if the traffic through the neighborhood slows down after major construction on a highway is finished, the through traffic remains substantially higher because some drivers adopt the reroute as their permanent route.[31]

GPS Jammers and Spoofers

One main tool used by criminals includes GPS jammers. GPS jammers are illegal to sell, buy, or use in the United States and other countries. This, of course, does not hinder criminals from buying the jammers on the darknet or from websites outside the United States, such as China. A GPS jammer is a radio frequency transmitter that blocks the communication between cell phones, text messages,

GPS, and Wi-Fi systems.[32] Imagine if a GPS jammer blocked the communications of the Los Angeles Police Department, including incoming 911 calls. GPS jammers can cause serious chaos and endanger public safety.

Another tool criminals can use is GPS spoofing by creating false GPS signals. This is possible because the real GPS signals are very weak since satellites are far away. The spoofed (faked) GPS signal is much stronger and thus overlays the real GPS signal. The victims of GPS spoofing may not be able to tell that they are not following the real GPS signal. This can have detrimental consequences for ships, aircraft, cars, drones, and other movable objects guided by GPS.

Naval System

In 2013, the *White Rose of Drachs*, an $80 million yacht, was cruising along the Mediterranean coast. To the captain, it appeared as though the yacht was moving in a straight path when in actuality the yacht had made a turn and was moving in a different direction, and was eventually steered hundreds of meters away from the correct path. How could the yacht's GPS system show that it was on the correct path when it wasn't? The answer is simple: The *White Rose of Drachs* fell victim to spoofing. The screen was wrong; it was being manipulated to make the captain believe that everything was fine. The captain believed what he saw on the screen rather than trusting his senses that the yacht had made a significant turn. But how is that possible?

A research team led by Professor Todd Humphreys from the University of Texas at Austin had built a device that would override the yacht's GPS system with spoofed signals. The device was a blue box about the size of a suitcase that could be moved easily. Humphreys and his team took the device to the harbor and aimed it at the ship. The spoofed signal from the device was much stronger than the real GPS signal coming from a faraway satellite. The stronger signal took over the yacht's navigation system, and Humphreys could now control the ship's direction and what was showing on the captain's screen. Had the hackers been pirates rather than researchers, the passengers and captain may not have lost money but possibly their lives as well.

Humphreys admitted that prior to his experiment he did not think that it would be that easy to take control of a ship. Following his experiment, he urged that

> With 90 percent of the world's freight moving across the seas and a great deal of the world's human transportation going across the skies, we have to gain a better understanding of the broader implications of GPS spoofing.[33]

Further, Humphreys urged the government and private businesses to take this security vulnerability serious, as it could have devastating consequences for national security.

> This experiment is applicable to other semi-autonomous vehicles, such as aircraft, which are now operated, in part, by autopilot systems. We've got to put on our thinking caps and see what we can do to solve this threat quickly.[34]

Global cargo and yachts are not the only ships at risk of hacking and hijacking. Warships also use the GPS system to complete their missions. Imagine if North Korea hijacked an American warship and sank it, or took the soldiers hostage and reverse engineered the ship to build similar warships and use them against the United States. Similarly, cruise ships also use GPS systems and certainly provide good targets for potential criminals.

Aircraft

What is already reality for most ships will soon also be reality for aircraft. The next generation aircraft will be operated by a computer-generated flight path and GPS tracking. Currently, the air control system uses radar and radio systems to guide airlines. The move of the Federal Aviation Administration to a satellite/GPS-based system has many advantages but also carries significant dangers. The advantages include faster route changes due to computerized routing in cases of bad weather. That means fewer delays and cancellations, which currently is a major problem for airlines and passengers because they are costly and cause much inconvenience. The next generation aircraft could also use straighter routes to the destination and cut flight times by 12% to 15%. Airlines would save money on fuel, and passengers would arrive faster. By using GPS, more airplanes could be in the air, and they would be easier to track.[35] Maybe Malaysia Airlines Flight 370 that disappeared on March 8, 2014, over the South China Sea would not have disappeared from radar, and air traffic control would have known right away that it crashed in the ocean. Or maybe air traffic control could have prevented the crash by remotely steering the airplane to a safe landing place, taking control of the plane out of the hands of the pilot. This would have saved many lives, but therein also lies the danger. If air traffic controllers can take over the plane from thousands of miles away, so can criminals who want to hijack a plane for the fun of it or terrorists as a tool of war. How safe are these next generation airplanes from being hacked and remotely controllable similar to a connected car or ship like the *White Rose of Drachs*?

Army Bases

When location services are turned on, cell phones are constantly sending signals of location and attach so-called "geotags" (latitude and longitude) to all pictures. Many people always have their location services turned on because they are using GPS and other services that require location services. This feature on cell phones led to the destruction of four military Apache Guardian helicopters, armed attack helicopters, in Iraq in 2007. Soldiers who had posed in front of newly delivered helicopters posted the pictures on Facebook. Insurgents who saw the uploaded pictures knew exactly where the military base was because the pictures had the geotags embedded. In a surprise attack, the insurgents destroyed the helicopters, costing the military not only millions of dollars but also diminishing the capacity of the soldiers at the military base to fight insurgents.[37]

Women's Shelters

Females who are seeking shelter from their abusive husbands or boyfriends may risk being found if their cell phone's location service is turned on. Their husbands may also use the app "Find My Friends" or "Find My Family" to find out

THINK ABOUT IT 11.2

Dangerous Criminal or Researcher Trying to Save Lives?

According to Chris Roberts, a cybersecurity consultant, the next generation aircraft are similarly as vulnerable as connected cars and ships. Roberts claims that he has hacked the computer systems of several airlines, including Boeing and Airbus, by manipulating the entertainment system and gaining access to onboard control systems, including the engines. Roberts stated that he was able to overwrite code and "thereby caused one of the airplane engines to climb resulting in a lateral or sideways movement of the plane during one of these flights." Roberts was interrogated by the FBI after he exposed the aircraft's vulnerabilities but has not been charged with a crime. No airline has come forward to confirm the manipulations. United Airlines has banned Roberts from flying with United, stating that he violated their policy. At the same time, United claimed, "However, we are confident our flight control systems could not be accessed through techniques he described."

Supporters of Roberts have asked why United would ban Roberts from their flights if they are confident that Roberts could not hack their system. They have also asked other questions, such as: Shouldn't the FBI and airlines be thankful to hackers who encounter security vulnerabilities and disclose them before criminals can cause a disaster? Is this part of trying to manipulate what the public knows and believes? Is it a crime to say what people don't want to hear because it could cost much money to make the technologies safer?

Critics of Roberts have stated that Roberts is a dangerous criminal: "You cannot promote the (true) idea that security research benefits humanity while defending research that endangered hundreds of innocents."[36]

What Would You Do?

1. Is Roberts a dangerous criminal or a researcher who may have saved lives?

where the shelter is located. This puts all women in these shelters at risk. Shelter managers have learned to take the cell phones and disassemble them as one of the first actions to avoid being located. When abusive husbands do find their spouse, it can have deadly consequences. In Arizona, Andre Leteve used a tracking feature on his wife's cell phone, installed by him, to stalk his wife. When he found her and their two children, he killed the children.[38] Cell phone companies allow account holders to activate tracking on all cell phones on the account. The spouse may never know he or she is being tracked. Cell phone providers are required by law to enable GPS tracking on at least 95% of devices in their network. The ability of people to track and stalk each other is an unintended consequence of this federal regulation. The federal tracking requirement certainly has positive sides, too, of course. The ability to track people has helped police find those who went missing. For instance, a 9-year old girl went missing in Massachusetts. The police were able to find the girl, who had allegedly been kidnapped by her grandmother. But carriers also profit greatly from the tracking services because they charge customers for turning on the tracking feature. Carriers state that they do inform all people on the plan that the tracking feature has been turned on. Victims cannot turn the feature off, but carriers do have untraceable devices victims of stalking and domestic abuse can buy.[39]

LEGAL ISSUE 11.1

HEALTH CARE RECORDS ARE WORTH MILLIONS

Cybercriminals increasingly hack into hospital records and other health care providers' computer systems to steal medical records and sell them on the black market. Medical records have become a highly sought-after product among criminals because they include a wealth of personal information such as birth dates, Social Security numbers, billing information, policy numbers, and medical information. This data can be used to create fake IDs and buy drugs and other products that can be sold in the underground market. The data can also be used to create fake policy claims with insurers. Criminals can earn between $10 and $20 for each health record. This is much more than for a credit card number, which sells for about 50 cents to a dollar. Banks typically cancel credit cards immediately when they see unusual activity on a card, but health care providers are not nearly as quick to respond to data breaches, and the law only requires reporting of stolen records when the data breach affects 500 records or more.[40]

Imagine that you receive a bill for $15,000 from your health insurance company for a medical treatment that you did not receive. You unsuccessfully try to explain that you never received that treatment, but your insurance carrier does not care. They send the bill to a collection agency, which now posts a negative comment on your credit history marking you as delinquent. You then discover that a hacker stole your medical record from your doctor's office and used it for fraudulent medical treatments.

What Do You Think?

1. Do some research on the law. Under which law is your doctor's office responsible for keeping your records private?
2. What can you do if you receive a bill that you know is fraudulent?

Potential/Emerging Perpetrators

Man in the Middle

In man-in-the-middle (MiTM) scams, criminals intercept e-mails between two businesses or a private person and a business, and direct the purchasing party to send the payment for the product to a new bank account. The victims don't realize that they are making the payment to the criminal—the man in the middle—rather than to the company they purchased the product from. In Washington State, such MiTM fraudsters stole a total of $1.65 million from three companies in Bellevue, Tukwila, and Seattle who were purchasing products from Chinese-based companies. The fraudsters impersonated the Chinese companies using spoofed e-mails.[41]

Private citizens may be victimized by MiTM scams if the fraudsters can access their computers and bank accounts or other information. If the fraudsters install a Trojan horse on the victim's computer, they can even make it appear as if everything is okay with the bank account when in reality the bank account has been wiped out. The victims checking their bank account on the screen will see their money in their account, and even the printed PDF statement will show the money. Only when the victims go to the bank and try to take out money will they realize that the account is empty. How is that possible? The MiTM intercepts the communication between the customer and the website the customer is visiting. When customers go to the Citibank website to check their accounts, the MiTM can see what the customers enter as their user name and password, and later use it to steal money from the customer.[42]

Swatting

The FBI currently has 56 field offices in the United States, and all of them have a Special Weapons and Tactics Team (SWAT). Each SWAT team has up to 42 members who are trained specifically to intervene in crisis situations, such as hostage taking, hijacking, fugitive pursuit, car assaults, and high-risk arrests. SWAT teams have specially trained officers, including snipers, assaulters, breachers, medics, fast-rope specialists, and Tactical Air Operations Officers. Whether a SWAT team is deployed depends on the following factors:

1. Likelihood of violence
2. Risk of harm to the public
3. Risk of harm to law enforcement officers
4. Case requirements[43]

SWAT teams are only used in very dangerous situations, and having a SWAT team show up at your door while you are watching a football game can quickly turn into a life or death situation. A new prank called *swatting* is not only draining law enforcement resources, it's also creating very dangerous situations for citizens. In January of 2014 at 4:30 p.m., the Atlanta police received a 911 call telling the dispatcher that a man, woman, and child had been shot, and a second child was being held hostage at a house in an affluent suburb of Atlanta called Johns Creek. The police reacted quickly by sending a SWAT team to the place of the alleged crime. In fact, the police sent several cruisers and emergency vehicles to the house, surrounding the house and preparing to kill the criminal if necessary. When the police entered the house, they found a nanny with two small children—no shooter in sight. A little later the mother arrived, finding her home surrounded by police. The father, who was traveling on a business trip, saw his house surrounded by police on TV and heard that his wife and children had been shot. None of that was true; it was a prank by a 16-year old who was into online gaming. Among these online gamers, swatting is a popular prank. One week later, the Atlanta police department received another call for the same house. This time, they only sent two police cars to check and make sure everything was OK. The second prank was a copycat of the first because the first attack had achieved a lot of attention on the news. The copycat was a serial swatter with more than 40 incidents. It took police $100,000 to find the two pranksters.[44]

Several public personalities and celebrities have also fallen victim to the swatting prank. For instance, Katherine Clark, a second-term congresswoman, was targeted, apparently as a response to a proposed bill, the Cybercrime Enforcement Training Assistance Act, which would allocate $20 million a year for the training of law enforcement officers to more effectively combat cybercrime. She told reporters that for the victims of swatting, the incident is quite traumatic:

> I'd heard all about swatting and have talked to the victims. But you get a different perspective when you're the mom standing in the doorway, with your family in the house behind you, looking at a full police response with long guns drawn on your front lawn. It gave me an idea of how frightening and dangerous this could be. And it made me more determined than ever to do something about it.[45]

It is only a question of time until someone dies because of a swatting prank.

Among the celebrities that were swatted are rapper Lil Williams, singers Justin Timberlake, Selena Gomez, Rihanna, Chris Brown, and Justin Bieber, and the Jenners. The Los Angeles Police Department announced that they would not issue press releases about swatting incidents any longer in an attempt to reduce publicity as much as possible, since publicity is one of the main motivators for the pranksters. [46]

Crime Inc.

Bjorn Daniel Sundin and Shaileshkumar P. Jain, along with others, owned and operated Innovative Marketing, Inc. (IM), a company that sold antivirus and related software to customers in 60 countries. The headquarters was based in Belize with another location in Kiev, Ukraine. IM quickly grew in response to the great demand by customers who contacted IM because their computer had shown a message indicating a malware infection. Between 2006 and 2008, IM made hundreds of millions of dollars in profits and continually grew its organization and number of employees. In 2008, the Federal Trade Commission began investigating IM after having received more than 1,000 complaints from customers. To their surprise, IM's computers were not password protected. The investigation showed that the customers of IM were in fact their victims, as IM itself had infected the computers with a malware. The malware showed a fake warning message about a virus infection and then prompted the victims to click on a link to IM to buy virus removal software for $30 to $70. The computers never had a virus, and the sole purpose of the company was the development and use of "scareware" as a means of defrauding individuals and companies.[47] In 2008, the FBI indicted Sundin and Jain on 24 counts of wire fraud, conspiracy to commit computer fraud, and computer fraud. They are on the FBI's Most Wanted list. They continue to be fugitives, hiding in countries that do not pursue cybercriminals.[48]

The Organizational Structure of Crime Inc.

The organizational structure of Crime Inc. mirrors that of legitimate businesses. Crime Inc. has a chief executive officer (CEO), who has connections to other influential criminals, makes important decisions about goals and targets, assembles the right team, and takes care of monetary decisions. Contrary to the CEO of a legitimate business, the identity of the Crime Inc. CEO is not known to most people in the company. Secrecy is important for the CEO and Crime Inc. because if someone gets arrested, they cannot snitch. Crime Inc. also has a leadership team that works on expanding profits, developing ideas for new products, and ensuring secrecy. The chief financial officer uses commercial business tools and networks with companies who will assist Crime Inc. with regard to money laundering and other tasks necessary to turn online payments into legitimate money. The chief marketing officer advertises to other criminal groups. Crime Inc. also has a research and development team that works on developing new malware and tools to spread the malware. Their ideas are then turned into products by engineers, hackers, and coders. New malware must, of course, also be tested for quality assurance. Thus, the quality assurance team checks whether the malware really does what it is supposed to do and suggests improvements to the malware. Crime Inc. also has affiliates who help promote the business and use spam, phishing, and other means to drive customers to Crime Inc. In the case of IM, the affiliates helped spread the malware to victims who would then call Innovative Marketing to buy the malware removal product. On the lowest level, Crime Inc. needs mules to launder the money into legitimate bank accounts. These mules are often unsuspecting individuals looking for a job and some quick money. They are asked to open two bank accounts: one for their salary and one for the illegitimate money. They are also the most likely to get caught by police because they use their true identities to open accounts. Banks become suspicious quickly if new accounts move large amounts of money in and out on a regular basis. The mules typically don't have any information about the true identity of the leadership of Crime Inc. The shortage of mules is the greatest obstacle for Crime Inc. because without these mules, the company cannot turn their stolen money into legitimate money by wiring the money into a legitimate bank account.[49]

Summary

An important part of the future of cybercrime and cybersecurity rests with the rapid growth of IoT devices and their potential as tools for cyberattacks and targets of cyberattacks. Criminals, and especially terrorists, may increasingly use advanced technologies such as GPS jammers and spoofers to manipulate cars, aircraft, and ships. To date, companies concentrate on developing new technologies and disregard the vulnerabilities of such technologies. Cybersecurity is still an afterthought rather than a main component during development. The reason is very straightforward: There is much money to be made with new technologies, and cybersecurity measures are expensive and time consuming. As long as profit trumps all, our cyberworld will continue to be a dangerous place.

Key Terms

Discussion Questions

1. Discuss the dangers of swatting for the victims, police, and the general public.
2. Discuss strategies to make your online behavior more secure.
3. What are social media cyberattacks, and how are they related to the Arab Spring?
4. Provide some examples of how data and information are manipulated. Discuss the dangers of censorship.
5. Discuss the similarities between legitimate businesses and Crime Inc.

Internet Resources

United States Computer Emergency Readiness Team (US-CERT)
https://www.us-cert.gov/sites/default/files/publications/money_mules.pdf

Google Terms of Service
https://www.google.com/policies/terms/

RSA Krypotsystem
https://www.rsaconference.com

Further Reading

Kelly, S., Truong, M., Shahbaz, A., & Earp, M. (2016). *Silencing the messenger: Communication apps under pressure*. Retrieved from https://freedomhouse.org/report/freedom-net/freedom-net-2016

Newcomb, D. (2017, April 14). *Connected car data is the new oil*. Retrieved from http://www.pcmag.com/news/353085/connected-car-data-is-the-new-oil

Digital Resources

Want a better grade?

Get the tools you need to sharpen your study skills. Access practice quizzes and eFlashcards, at **study.sagepub.com/kremling**.

• Appendix •

Cybersecurity-Related Organizations

Advanced Research Projects Agency (ARPA): An agency of the U.S. Department of Defense, ARPA underwrote development for the precursor of the Internet, known as ARPANET.

http://searchnetworking.techtarget.com/definition/ARPA

Advanced Research Projects Agency Network (ARPANET): A pioneering network for sharing digital resources among geographically separated computers.

http://www.darpa.mil/about-us/timeline/arpanet

Central Intelligence Agency (CIA): The CIA is an independent agency responsible for providing national security intelligence to senior U.S. policy makers.

https://www.cia.gov/about-cia/todays-cia

Computer Emergency Response Team (CERT): Strives for a safer, stronger Internet for all Americans by responding to major incidents, analyzing threats, and exchanging critical cybersecurity information with trusted partners around the world.

https://www.us-cert.gov

Computer Science Network (CSNET): A network system developed in 1981 which provided Internet services, including electronic mail and connections to ARPANET.

https://www.nsf.gov/about/history/nsf0050/pdf/internet.pdf

Democratic National Committee (DNC): The DNC was created during the Democratic National Convention of 1848. Since then, it's been responsible for governing the Democratic Party and is the oldest continuing party committee in the United States.

https://www.democrats.org/organization/the-democratic-national-committee

Department of Defense (DoD): The mission of the Department of Defense is to provide the military forces needed to deter war and to protect the security of our country. The department's headquarters are at the Pentagon.

http://www.defense.gov/About-DoD

Department of Homeland Security (DHS): The DHS was formed in the wake of the terrorist attacks of September 11, 2001, as part of a determined national effort to safeguard the United States against terrorism.

https://www.dhs.gov/homeland-security-enterprise

European Organization for Nuclear Research (CERN): The name CERN is derived from the acronym for the French Conseil Européen pour la Recherche Nucléaire, or European Council for Nuclear Research, a provisional body founded in 1952 with the mandate of establishing a world-class fundamental physics research organization in Europe.

http://home.cern/about

Federal Bureau of Investigation (FBI): The mission of the FBI—as a national security and intelligence organization—is to protect and defend the United States against terrorist and foreign intelligence threats, to uphold and enforce the criminal laws of the United States, and to provide leadership and criminal justice services to federal, state, municipal, and international agencies and partners.

https://www.fbi.gov

Massachusetts Institute of Technology (MIT): MIT is a private research university in Cambridge, Massachusetts.

http://web.mit.edu/

Military Network (MILNET): MILNET, along with the DARPANET (Defense Advanced Research Project Agency Network), was formed in 1983 as the successor to the ARPANET and was used for nonclassified U.S. military communications. It is also often perceived as being an early element of the Internet.

http://www.technology-training.co.uk/milnet.php

National Institute of Standards and Technology (NIST): NIST was founded in 1901 and is now part of the U.S. Department of Commerce. NIST is one of the nation's oldest physical science laboratories. Congress established the agency to remove a major challenge to U.S. industrial competitiveness at the time—a second-rate measurement infrastructure that lagged behind the capabilities of the United Kingdom, Germany, and other economic rivals.

https://www.nist.gov/about-nist

National Research Council (NRC): The National Academies of Sciences, Engineering, and Medicine are private, nonprofit institutions that provide expert advice on some of the most pressing challenges facing the nation and the world. Our work helps shape sound policies, inform public opinion, and advance the pursuit of science, engineering, and medicine.

http://www.nationalacademies.org/about/whoweare/index.html

National Science Foundation (NSF): The NSF is an independent federal agency created by Congress in 1950 "to promote the progress of science; to advance the national health, prosperity, and welfare; to secure the national defense . . ."

http://www.nsf.gov/about/

National Security Agency (NSA): The NSA leads the U.S. government in cryptology that encompasses both Signals Intelligence and Information Assurance (IA) products and services, and enables Computer Network Operations (CNO) in order to gain a decision advantage for the Nation and our allies under all circumstances.

https://www.nsa.gov/about/mission-strategy/

North American Aerospace Defense Command (NORAD): NORAD conducts aerospace warning, aerospace control, and maritime warning in the defense of North America.

http://www.norad.mil/

Office of Infrastructure Protection: Responsible for reducing risk to and vulnerability of critical infrastructure and key resources.

https://www.dhs.gov/office-infrastructure-protection

Strategic Air Command (SAC): U.S. military command that served as the bombardment arm of the U.S. Air Force and as a major part of the nuclear deterrent against the Soviet Union between 1946 and 1992.

https://www.britannica.com/topic/Strategic-Air-Command-United-States-Air-Force

Syrian Electronic Army (SEA): The SEA is a group of computer hackers targeting government opposition groups through cyberattacks.

https://opennet.net/emergence-open-and-organized-pro-government-cyber-attacks-middle-east-case-syrian-electronic-army

Union of Soviet Socialist Republics (USSR): A former federation of communist republics that occupied the northern half of Asia and the eastern part of Europe. Capital: Moscow.

http://www.oxforddictionaries.com/us/definition/american_english/soviet-union

World Wide Web Consortium (W3C): The W3C is an international community where Member organizations, a full-time staff, and the public work together to develop Web standards. Led by Web inventor Tim Berners-Lee and CEO Jeffrey Jaffe, W3C's mission is to lead the Web to its full potential. Contact W3C for more information.

https://www.w3.org/Consortium/

• Glossary •

Advanced Persistent Threats: Cyberattacks executed by sophisticated and well resourced adversaries targeting specific information in high-profile companies and governments, usually in a long-term campaign involving different steps.

Antivirus Software: Programs that recognize malware and prevent it from entering the computer by checking programs and comparing them to known malware.

Biometrics: The measurement and statistical analysis of people's physical and behavioral characteristics.

Bitcoins: A digital currency used by Internet users for anonymous online transactions.

Black Hats: The "bad guy" hackers, who intercept online communications, steal information and data, plant malware in computers, or engage in consumer scams.

Blockchain: Stores bitcoin transaction information so the identities of those involved in transactions are not identifiable.

Botnets: A collection of infected machines worldwide that receive commands from their botmaster and perform some illegal actions such as Distributed Denial-of-Service (DDoS) attacks, credential stealing, click fraud, spam sending, bank account and credit card theft, and downloading other malwares.

Brute-Force Attack: A brute-force attack is a trial-and-error method used to obtain information such as a user password or personal identification number (PIN). In a brute-force attack, automated software is used to generate a large number of consecutive guesses as to the value of the desired data. Brute-force attacks may be used by criminals to crack encrypted data, or by security analysts to test an organization's network security (https://www.techopedia.com/definition/18091/brute-force attack).

CBRNE Weapons: Chemical, biological, radiological, nuclear, and explosive weapons.

Child Pornography: The sexualized depictions of children produced, distributed, accessed, or stored via various Internet-facilitated paths such as webcams, bulletin boards, e-mail, websites, and peer-to-peer networks.

Consumer Crimes: Deceptive practices that result in financial or other losses for consumers in the course of seemingly legitimate business transactions.

Critical Infrastructure: The nation's critical infrastructure provides the essential services that underpin American society and serve as the backbone of our nation's economy, security, and health. Overall, there are 16 critical infrastructure sectors that compose the assets, systems, and networks, whether physical or virtual, so vital to the United States that their incapacitation or destruction would have a debilitating effect on security, national economic security, national public health or safety, or any combination thereof (https://www.dhs.gov/what-critical-infrastructure#).

Cryptocurrency: Currency that exists only in the digital arena; one way that purchases on the deep web can be made anonymously.

Cyberbullying: Intentional, aggressive behavior toward another person that is performed through electronic means (i.e., computers, cell phones, personal digital assistants).

Cyberespionage: Cyberspying is the act of engaging in an attack or series of attacks that let an unauthorized user or users view classified material. https://www.villanovau.com/resources/iss/cyber-espionage/#.WRfXasm1sdU

Cyberharassment: Threatening e-mails, instant messages, or social media posts.

Cyberincident: An incident, or an attempt to cause an incident, that, if successful, would: (1) jeopardize the security, integrity, confidentiality, or availability of an information system or network or any information stored on, processed on, or transiting such a system; (2) violate laws or procedures relating to system security, acceptable use policies, or acts of terrorism against such a system or network; or (3) deny access to or degrade, disrupt, or destruct such a system or network or defeat an operation or technical control of such a system or network.

Cyberintelligence: The collection and analysis of information that produces timely reporting with context and relevance to a supported decision maker.

Cybersabotage: Cyberattacks relating to industrial secrets that have commercial value to competitors.

Cybersecurity: Protection against unauthorized use of computers, computer systems, and/or electronic data.

Cyberspace: The interdependent network of information technology infrastructures, and includes the Internet, telecommunications networks, computer systems, and embedded processors and controllers in critical industries. Cyberspace refers to the virtual environment in which people communicate and interact with others. Cyberspace consists of four different layers: (1) physical layer, (2) logic layer, (3) information layer, and (4) personal layer.

Cyberstalking: Typically includes unwanted and repetitive behaviors that are perceived as intrusive, frightening, threatening, or harassing via e-mail, social media, or other electronic means.

Cyberterrorism: An intentional act, committed via computer or communication system, and motivated by political, religious, or ideological objectives against information, data, or computer systems/programs, intended to cause severe harm, death, or destruction to civilians.

Cyberthreat: Unauthorized access to a control system device and/or network using a data communications pathway.

Cyberwarfare: The actions by a nation-state or international organization to attack and attempt to damage another nation's computers or information networks through, for example, computer viruses or denial-of-service attacks.

Dark Web/Darknet: A part of the deep web with intentionally hidden information that requires a specialized browser to access.

Dash: A form of digital currency that claims to be more secure than bitcoins.

Deep Web: Information on the Internet that is not accessible by surface search engines.

Denial-of-Service Attack: In a denial-of-service attack, an attacker attempts to prevent legitimate users from accessing information or services (https://www.us-cert.gov/ncas/tips/ST04-015).

Denigration: The posting of harassing messages about the victim aiming to cause harm to the victim.

Differential Association: Nine-point theory proposed by Edwin Sutherland that asserts that criminal behavior is learned via intimate personal groups.

Digital Millennium Copyright Act: The DMCA updated U.S. copyright law to meet the demands of the digital age and to conform U.S. law to the requirements of the World Intellectual Property Organization and treaties that the U.S. signed in 1996.

Distributed Denial-of-Service (DDoS) Attack: A cyberattack in which a legitimate user of a computer or network connection is prevented from accessing information or services.

Domain Name System: A system for naming computers and network services that is organized into a hierarchy of domains. DNS naming is used in TCP/IP networks, such as the Internet, to locate computers and services through user-friendly names. When a user enters a DNS name in an application, DNS services can resolve the name to other information associated with the name, such as an IP address.

DomainKeys Identified Mail: A system for authenticating e-mail that works with modern Message Transfer Agent systems. The digital signature used in DKIM provides an additional way to tell whether an e-mail is forged. Spammers often forge headers or other aspects of an e-mail to make the message look like it comes from a legitimate source. DKIM uses domain information to authenticate the e-mail's origin.

Electronic Frontier Foundation: An advocacy group that works to protect the rights to free speech online, including the freedom to exchange ideas and opinions without the fear of prosecution. It also works to protect the right to anonymity on the Internet, especially on the dark web.

Exclusionary Rule: A legal interpretation of the Fourth Amendment stating that any evidence seized during an illegal search is not admissible in federal court.

Firewall: A software program or piece of hardware that helps screen out hackers, viruses, and worms that try to reach your computer over the Internet.

Fusion Center: A collaborative effort of two or more agencies that provide resources, expertise, and information to the center with the goal of maximizing their ability to detect, prevent, investigate, and respond to criminal and terrorist activity.

Gaming: The running of specialized applications known as electronic games or video games on game consoles like Xbox and PlayStation or on personal computers.

Gray Hats: Hackers who engage in both black- and white-hat hacking; hackers for hire.

Griefer: Those who make use of online games as a way to target children and sometimes even adults while they are taking part in online gaming.

Guardianship: Something or someone surrounding a potential victim that has a protective effect. Can be either a human presence, like a law enforcement officer, group of people, family at home, etc., or a nonhuman presence, like a well-lit street or security camera.

Hacker Subculture: Like-minded individuals who enjoy computer programming, information technology, hacking, and the like.

Hackernomics: The social science concerned chiefly with the description and analysis of hacker motivations, economics, and business risk.

Hacktivist: Politically motivated hackers who target large corporations.

Hidden Wiki: A way to search the darknet. It acts as a search engine for illicit goods, products, and services.

Homeland Security Presidential Directives: A series of directives that record and communicate presidential decisions about the Homeland Security policies of the United States.

Honeynet: Multiple honeypots that, combined, set up a fake network identical to the actual infrastructure network system.

Honeypot: A mechanism that tracks and monitors hackers to gather information on possible attack tactics prior to an attack.

Honeytokens: Digital data created specifically to monitor the behavior of potential attackers.

Hyperlink: A reference or navigation element in a hypertext document that offers direct access to another section of the same document or to another hypertext document that is on or part of a (different) domain.

Hypertext: A hyperlink that is embedded in words.

Identity Theft: All types of crime in which someone wrongfully obtains and uses another person's personal data in some way that involves fraud or deception, typically for economic gain.

Impersonation: When a person who knowingly and without consent credibly impersonates another actual person through or on an Internet website or by other electronic means, as specified, for purposes of harming, intimidating, threatening, or defrauding another person.

Information Sharing: The timely production of unclassified reports of cyberthreats to the U.S. homeland that identify a specific targeted entity.

Insider Threats: Harmful acts that trusted insiders might carry out; for example, something that causes harm to the organization, or an unauthorized act that benefits the individual.

Insider Trading: To buy and sell stock for illegal profits in breach of fiduciary duty or other relationship of trust and confidence.

Internet of Things: The connection between the Internet and everyday products, allowing for the transfer of data.

Internet Protocol Suite: TCP/IP is the commonly used nickname for the set of network protocols composing the Internet protocol suite. Many texts use the term *Internet* to describe both the protocol suite and the globalwide-area network. In this book, TCP/IP refers specifically to the Internet protocol suite; "Internet" refers to the wide-area network and the bodies that govern it.

Internet Service Provider: A company that provides customers with Internet access. Data may be transmitted using several technologies, including dial-up, DSL, cable modem, wireless or dedicated high-speed interconnects.

Internet: The hardware and software infrastructure that connects computers around the globe.

Intranet: A network operating like the World Wide Web but having access restricted to a limited group of authorized users (as employees of a company).

Key Assets: An aspect of critical infrastructure that, if it were attacked, would result in some damage but would not completely upset the company's ability to function.

Linux Redhat: Provider of open source, enterprising information technology solutions. Can modernize infrastructure, boost efficiency through standardization and virtualization, and prepare your datacenter for an open hybrid cloud IT architecture.

Logic Bomb: Small programs or sections of a program triggered by some event such as a certain date or time, a certain percentage of disk space filled, the removal of a file, and so on.

Lone-Wolf Terrorist: An individual acting on his or her own, for a specific political cause, but without affiliation with a specific terror network.

Mail-Order Brides: Women who publish in a catalog with intent to marry. This is done by a woman to marry someone from another country, usually a financially developed country.

Malware: Malware, short for *malicious software*, refers to a type of computer program designed to infect a legitimate user's computer and inflict harm on it in multiple ways.

Man in the Middle: A type of wireless attack in which a malicious party intercepts a message—to gather information, alter the message, attach a virus, steal the payment, etc.—and then sends the message on to the intended recipient with no indication that it had been intercepted.

Mitigate: The first step in the risk management process. Involves heightened inspections, improved surveillance, public health/agriculture testing, immunizations, and law enforcement operations to deter/disrupt illegal activity and apprehend perpetrators.

Moonlight Maze: Attacks in which Russia infiltrated military, governmental, educational, and other computer systems in the United States, United Kingdom, Canada, Brazil, and Germany. These attacks were significant, as they were some of the first to illustrate how vulnerable our technology is to malicious infiltration.

Network-Based Intrusions: When a computer system is accessed without permission.

Office of Infrastructure Protection: Federal office which leads and coordinates national programs and policies on critical infrastructure security and resilience and has established strong partnerships across government and the private sector.

Online Exclusion: When victims are rejected from their peer group and left out of technological communications.

Operation Onymous: The takedown of multiple darknet drug marketplaces by several collaborating countries.

Personal Computer: A small, relatively inexpensive computer designed for an individual user.

Phishing: The use of e-mail to solicit information from unsuspecting users or lure them into visiting fraudulent websites to download software that contains a virus, worm, or other malware.

Phone Spoofing: Soliciting information via the telephone.

Prepare: The second step in the risk management process. Involves efforts to identify threats, determine vulnerabilities, and identify required resources. Continuing process.

Presidential Policy Directive 21: This directive advances a national policy to strengthen and maintain secure, functioning, and resilient critical infrastructure. This directive supersedes Homeland Security Presidential Directive 7 and identifies the 16 sectors of critical infrastructure.

Private Sector: Made up of for-profit businesses that are not under government control.

Ransomware: A type of malware that severely restricts access to the computer, device, or file until a ransom is paid by the user.

Recover: The fourth step in the risk management process. Involves helping people and the community return to normal, if possible. This can include development, coordination, and execution of service and site restoration.

Red Team: A firm comprised of "white hat" hackers.

Respond: The third step in the risk management process. Involves implementing policies for federal, state, local, and private-sector support. Address long-term, short-term, and direct effects of an incident. Includes immediate actions to preserve life, property, and the environment.

Risk Management: Assessing the vulnerability of cybertargets; identifying what is possible versus what is probable. The four steps in the risk management process are: mitigation/prevention, preparedness, response, and recovery.

Ross Ulbricht: The creator of the Silk Road.

Routine Activity Theory: Posits that when the following factors occur at the same time in the same space, crime is increasingly likely to occur—a motivated offender, a suitable target, and a lack of capable guardianship.

Satoshi Nakamoto: The pseudonym for the individual who created bitcoins.

Silk Road: A darknet drug marketplace.

Simple Mail Transfer Protocol: Protocol that enables users to send and receive messages.

Snuff films: Films where a person or an animal is tortured and killed, or appears to be killed.

Social Engineering: Infecting a computer by fooling someone into giving out personal information.

Spam: E-mail spam, also known as junk e-mail, is unsolicited bulk messages sent through e-mail (http://searchsecurity.techtarget.com/definition/spam).

Spoofing: A fraudulent or malicious practice in which communication is sent from an unknown source disguised as a source known to the receiver. It's the most prevalent in communication mechanisms that lack a high level of security.

Spyware: Spyware is a type of malware that is installed on a computer without the knowledge of the owner in order to collect the owner's private information (http://www.pctools.com/security-news/what-is-spyware/).

Supervisory Control and Data Acquisition Systems (SCADA): Industrial computer system used to monitor and control electronic critical infrastructures.

Surface Web: Content on the World Wide Web that is available to the general public and for indexing by a search engine. It links to the pages on the surface Web and is displayed on search engine results pages. Descriptive text on the pages as well as metatags hidden within the web pages identify the page's contents for the various search engines.

Swatting: Falsely reporting a situation that requires SWAT team presence; a prank.

The Onion Router: Free software and an open network that helps you defend against traffic analysis, a form of network surveillance that threatens personal freedom and privacy, confidential business activities and relationships, and state security.

Trafficking: The recruitment and transportation of people using force, coercion, deception, or the abuse of vulnerability for the purpose of sexual exploitation, labor exploitation, slavery, or harvesting organs.

Transparent Citizen: The state in which a person, by operating online, blurs the line between public and private information and allows criminals to evade arrest and prosecution.

Trojan Horse: A program that poses as a legitimate program but performs unknown or unwanted functions.

Uniform Resource Locator: The address of a website or file.

Violence: The World Health Organization defines violence as "The intentional use of physical force or power, threatened or actual, against another person or against a group or community that results in or has a high likelihood of resulting in injury, death, psychological harm, maldevelopment, or deprivation."

Virus: A code that will duplicate itself into a host program when it is activated.

Vishing: Soliciting information via the telephone.

Vulnerability: A weakness in a product that could allow an attacker to compromise the integrity, availability, or confidentiality of that product.

White Hats: The "ethical" hackers, who use their abilities for legal purposes by researching vulnerabilities in software products and disclosing them to the companies who developed the software.

Wireless Attack: Deliberate attack against wireless networks or information systems.

World Wide Web: The interconnected documents and variety of resources that can be accessed via the Internet.

Worm: A self-replicating virus that does not alter files but resides in active memory and duplicates itself.

• Notes •

Chapter 1

1. File, T., & Ryan, C. (2014). *Computer and Internet use in the United States: 2013*. American Community Survey Reports. Washington, DC: U.S. Census Bureau. Retrieved from https://www.census.gov/history/pdf/2013computeruse.pdf
2. Katz, O., & Shaul, J. (2017, February). *The Internet of attacking things*. Presentation at RSA Conference, San Francisco, CA.
3. The White House, Office of the Press Secretary. (2015, February 13). *Remarks by the president at the Cybersecurity and Consumer Protection Summit*. Retrieved from https://obamawhitehouse.archives.gov/the-press-office/2015/02/13/remarks-president-cybersecurity-and-consumer-protection-summit
4. Timberg, C. (2015). *Net of insecurity: A flaw in the design*. Retrieved from http://www.washingtonpost.com/sf/business/2015/05/30/net-of-insecurity-part-1/
5. The White House, *Remarks by the president*.
6. The White House, *Remarks by the president*.
7. 2016 Data Breach Investigations Report. (2016). Retrieved from http://www.verizonenterprise.com/verizon-insights-lab/dbir/2016/
8. Fiegerman, S. (2016). *Yahoo says 500 million accounts stolen*. Retrieved from http://money.cnn.com/2016/09/22/technology/yahoo-data-breach/
9. Timberg, *Net of insecurity*.
10. Defense Advanced Research Projects Agency. (2017). *About DARPA*. Retrieved from http://www.darpa.mil/about-us/about-darpa
11. Licklider, J. C. R., & Clark, W. (1962). *On-line man-computer communication*. Cambridge, MA: Bolt Beranek & Newman. Retrieved from http://cis.msjc.edu/courses/internet_authoring/CSIS103/resources/ON-LINE%20MAN-COMPUTER%20COMMUNICATION.pdf
12. Kleinrock, L. (1961). Information flow in large communication nets. *RLE Quarterly Progress Report*.
13. Leiner, B. M., Cerf, V. G., Clark, D. D., Kahn, R. E., Kleinrock, L., Lynch, D. C., . . . Wolff, S. (2012). *Brief history of the internet*. Retrieved from https://www.internetsociety.org/internet/what-internet/history-internet/brief-history-internet
14. J. C. R. Licklider and the Universal Network. (n.d.). Retrieved from http://www.livingInternet.com/i/ii_licklider.htm
15. Leiner et al., *Brief history of the internet*.
16. European Organization for Nuclear Research. (2015). *Where the web was born*. Retrieved from http://home.cern/about/topics/birth-web/where-web-was-born
17. Leiner et al., *Brief history of the internet*.
18. Leiner et al., *Brief history of the internet*.
19. Toward a national research network. (1988). National Research Network Review Committee. Washington, DC: National Academy Press. Retrieved from https://www.nap.edu/read/10334/chapter/1#ix
20. National Research Council. (1994). *Realizing the information future: The internet and beyond*. Washington, DC: National Academies Press. doi:https://doi.org/10.17226/4755
21. Leiner et al., *Brief history of the internet*.
22. Sydell, L. (2009). *Napster: The file sharing service that started it all?* Retrieved from http://www.npr.org/2009/12/21/121690908/napster-the-file-sharing-service-that-started-it-all

23. Microsoft. (2015). *Definition of a security vulnerability*. Retrieved from https://msdn.microsoft.com/en-us/library/cc751383.aspx

24. Timberg, *Net of insecurity*.

25. The White House. (2008). *National Security Presidential Directive 54/Homeland Security Presidential Directive 23*. Cybersecurity Policy. DOCID: 4123697.

26. Clark, D. (2010). *Characterizing cyberspace: Past, present, and future*. Retrieved from https://projects.csail.mit.edu/ecir/wiki/images/7/77/Clark_Characterizing_cyberspace_1-2r.pdf

27. Internet. (n.d.). *New World Encyclopedia*. Retrieved from http://www.newworldencyclopedia.org/entry/Internet

28. World Wide Web. (n.d.). *New World Encyclopedia*. Retrieved from http://www.newworldencyclopedia.org/entry/World_Wide_Web

29. Hyperlink. (n.d.). *New World Encyclopedia*. Retrieved from http://www.newworldencyclopedia.org/entry/Hyperlink

30. Oracle. (1995). *The Java tutorials. What is a URL?* Retrieved from https://docs.oracle.com/javase/tutorial/networking/urls/definition.html

31. Universal City Studios, Inc. v. Corley, 273 F. 3d 429

32. Federal Bureau of Investigation. (2017). *Careers in the FBI's cyber crimes division*. Retrieved from http://www.fbiagentedu.org/careers/cyber-crimes/

33. Cyber Security Degrees. (2017). *Cyber security degrees in policing and law enforcement*. Retrieved from http://cybersecuritydegrees.org/police-and-law-enforcement-careers/#context/api/listings/prefilter

34. INFOSEC Institute. (2017). *Computer crime investigators*. Retrieved from https://www.infosecinstitute.com/careers/computer-crime-investigators

35. U.S. Department of Homeland Security. (2017). *Join DHS cybersecurity*. Retrieved from https://www.dhs.gov/homeland-security-careers/dhs-cybersecurity

36. U.S. Department of Justice. (2017). *Cybercrime*. Retrieved from https://www.justice.gov/criminal-ccips

37. U.S. Secret Service. (2017). *The investigative mission*. Retrieved from https://www.secretservice.gov/investigation/

Chapter 2

1. Singer, P. W., & Friedman, A. (2014). *Cybersecurity and cyberwar: What everyone needs to know*. New York, NY: Oxford University Press.

2. The weakest link. (2002, October 24). Retrieved from http://www.economist.com/node/1389553

3. Elliott, J. (2016). *How to explain cyber security to the board using a simple metaphor: FIRE*. RSA Conference Presentation. Retrieved from https://www.rsaconference.com/videos/webcast-how-to-explain-cybersecurity-to-the-board-using-a-simple-metaphor-fire

4. Computer Security Act of 1987, H.R. 145. (1987).

5. United States Computer Emergency Readiness Team. (n.d.). Retrieved from https://www.us-cert.gov/

6. Timeline: The U.S. government and cybersecurity. (2003, May 16). *Washington Post*. Retrieved from http://www.washingtonpost.com/wp-dyn/articles/A50606-2002Jun26.html

7. Timeline, *Washington Post*.

8. Badham, J. (Director). (1983). *WarGames* [Motion picture]. Beverly Hills, CA: Metro-Goldwyn-Mayer.

9. Weimann, G. (2006). *Terror on the internet*. Washington, DC: U.S. Institute of Peace Press.

10. Verton, D. (2003). *Black ice: The invisible threat of cyberterrorism*. Emeryville, CA: McGraw-Hill.

11. Agresti, E. (2013). *A look at cyber security in 2013*. Retrieved from https://www.gcsec.org/blog/look-cyber-security-2013.-elena-agresti-gcsec

12. Homeland Security Act of 2002.

13. Craigen, D., Diakun-Thibault, N., & Purse, R. (2014, October). Defining cybersecurity. *Technology Innovation Management Review*, 13–21. Retrieved from https://timreview.ca/sites/default/files/article_PDF/Craigen_et_al_TIMReview_October2014.pdf

14. Craigen et al., Defining cybersecurity.

15. Department of Homeland Security. (n.d.). Retrieved from https://www.dhs.gov/topic/cybersecurity

16. Craigen et al., Defining cybersecurity, p. 15.

17. Greene, T. C. (2013). *Chapter one: Kevin Mitnick's story*. Retrieved from http://www.theregister.co.uk/2003/01/13/chapter_one_kevin_mitnicks_story/

18. Greene, *Chapter One*.

19. Kevin Mitnick Case: 1999—No bail, no computer, hacker pleads guilty. http://law.jrank.org/pages/3791/Kevin-Mitnick-Case-1999.html

20. U.S. Department of Homeland Security. (2016). Fact sheet: Executive Order (EO) 13636 Improving Critical Infrastructure Cybersecurity and Presidential Policy Directive (PPD)-21 Critical Infrastructure Security and Resilience. Retrieved from https://www.dhs.gov/publication/eo-13636-ppd-21-fact-sheet

21. U.S. Department of Homeland Security. (2016). *National Cybersecurity and Communications Integration Center*. https://www.dhs.gov/national-cybersecurity-and-communications-integration-center

22. FusionX. (2015). Retrieved from http://fusionx.com/

23. Dorman, C. (2016). *The first cyber espionage attacks: How operation Moonlight Maze made history*. Retrieved from https://medium.com/@chris_doman/the-first-sophistiated-cyber-attacks-how-operation-moonlight-maze-made-history-2adb12cc43f7#.z1nonm713

24. CERT-UK. (2015). *Common cyber attacks: Reducing the impact*. Retrieved from https://www.gov.uk/government/uploads/system/uploads/attachment_data/file/400106/Common_Cyber_Attacks-Reducing_The_Impact.pdf

25. Abram, M., & Weiss, J. (2008, July 23). *Malicious control system cyber security attack case study—Maroochy Water Services, Australia*. Retrieved from http://csrc.nist.gov/groups/SMA/fisma/ics/documents/Maroochy-Water-Services-Case-Study_briefing.pdf

26. Crawford, M. (2006, February 16). Utility hack led to security overhaul. *Computer World*. Retrieved from http://www.computerworld.com/article/2561484/security0/utility-hack-led-to-security-overhaul.html

27. Morgan, B. (2013). *Wireless security attacks and defenses*. Retrieved from http://www.windowsecurity.com

28. Gregg, M. (2016). *Six ways you could become a victim of the Man-In-The-Middle (MiTM) attacks this holiday season*. Retrieved from http://www.huffingtonpost.com/michael-gregg/six-ways-you-could-become_b_8545674.html

29. Greenberg, A. (2015). *Hackers remotely kill a Jeep on the highway—with me in it*. Retrieved from https://www.wired.com/2015/07/hackers-remotely-kill-jeep-highway/

30. Greenberg, *Hackers*.

31. Spiegel interview with world-class hacker Kevin Mitnick. (2005, May 28). Retrieved from http://www.spiegel.de/international/spiegel/spiegel-interview-with-world-class-hacker-kevin-mitnick-the-americans-are-the-most-gullible-a-358787.html

32. Farina, R. (2017). *Securing what you don't own or control: The current state of WiFi security*. Presentation at the RSA Conference, San Francisco, CA.

33. Farina, *Securing*.

34. National Institute of Standards and Technology Act, 15 U.S.C. 271 (2010).

Chapter 3

1. Dallaway, E. (2017). Top ten data breaches. *InfoSecurity, 14*(1), 24–25.

2. Strickland, J. (n.d.). *10 worst computer viruses of all time*. Retrieved from http://computer.howstuffworks.com/worst-computer-viruses4.htm

3. U.S. Office of the Director of National Intelligence. (2017). *Assessing Russian activities and intentions in recent US elections*. Retrieved from https://www.intelligence.senate.gov/sites/default/files/documents/ICA_2017_01.pdf

4. Federal Bureau of Investigation. (2016). *Grizzly Steppe—Russian malicious cyber activity*. Retrieved from https://www.us-cert.gov/sites/default/files/publications/JAR_16-20296A_GRIZZLY%20STEPPE-2016-1229.pdf

5. Seddon, M. (2016). *Reports of treason and CIA spies shed light on Russian hacking*. Retrieved from https://www.ft.com/content/1b203b00-e7d7-11e6-967b-c88452263daf

6. Thompson, H. H. (2017). *Introduction: Security industry and trends: Trends, building blocks for a solid security plan basics*. Presentation at RSA Conference, San Francisco, CA.

7. Top 7 network attacks in 2016. (2016, June 13). Retrieved from http://www.calyptix.com/top-threats/top-7-network-attack-types-2016/

8. Paganini, P. (2013). *Hardware attacks, backdoors, and electronic component qualification*. Retrieved from http://resources.infosecinstitute.com/hardware-attacks-backdoors-and-electronic-component-qualification/

9. Prout, B. (2016). *How to protect your network from cyberattacks*. Retrieved from https://www.sophos.com/en-us/security-news-trends/security-trends/how-to-protect-your-network-from-cyber-attacks.aspx

10. Top 7 network attacks in 2016. (2016, June 13). Retrieved from http://www.calyptix.com/top-threats/top-7-network-attack-types-2016/

11. Vijayan, J. (2013). *Encryption still best way to protect data—despite NSA*. Retrieved from http://www.computerworld.com/article/2484714/security0/encryption-still-best-way-to-protect-data----despite-nsa.html

12. Computer viruses and other malware: What you need to know. (2016). Retrieved from http://help.uis.cam.ac.uk/user-accounts-security/security/malware

13. Peng, S., Yu, S., & Yang, A. (2014). Smartphone malware and its propagation modeling: A survey. *IEEE Communications Survey and Tutorial, 16*(2), 925–941.

14. Peng et al., Smartphone malware and its propagation modeling: A survey.

15. Spafford, E. H. (1994). Computer viruses as artificial life. *Journal of Artificial Life, 1*(3), 249–265.

16. Perez, E., Sciutto, J., & Raju, M. (2016). *Feds probing Clinton campaign hacking*. Retrieved from http://edition.cnn.com/2016/07/29/politics/democratic-congressional-campaign-committee-hacked/

17. Search the DNC E-mail database. (n.d.). Retrieved from https://wikileaks.org/dnc-emails/

18. Zeleny, J., Lee, M. J., & Bradner, E. (2016). *Dems open convention without Wasserman Schultz*. Retrieved from http://edition.cnn.com/2016/07/22/politics/dnc-wikileaks-emails/

19. Perez et al., *Feds probing Clinton campaign hacking*.

20. What is a computer virus? (n.d.). Retrieved from https://www.microsoft.com/en-us/safety/pc-security/virus-whatis.aspx

21. Smith, B. (2017, February 14). Keynote at RSA Conference, San Francisco, CA.

22. Cohen, F. (1987). Computer viruses—Theory and experiments. *Computers & Security, 6*(1), 22–35.

23. Cohen, Computer viruses—Theory and experiments.

24. Cohen, Computer viruses—Theory and experiments.

25. Gupta, R. (2011). *First computer virus and first antivirus?* Retrieved from http://techsalsa.com/first-computer-virus-and-first-antivirus/

26. Spafford, Computer viruses as artificial life.

27. Galea, D. (2015). *The ILoveYou Bug 15 years later: How has malware changed*. Retrieved from https://www.opswat.com/blog/iloveyou-bug-15-years-later-how-has-malware-changed

28. Chen, P., Desmet, L., & Huygens, C. (2014). *A study of advanced persistent threats*. Retrieved from https://lirias.kuleuven.be/bitstream/123456789/461050/1/2014-apt-study.pdf
29. Walker, D. (2014). *Advanced attack group Deep Panda uses PowerShell to breach think tanks*. Retrieved from http://www.scmagazine.com/advanced-attack-group-deep-panda-uses-powershell-to-breach-think-tanks/article/359723/
30. Wagstaff, J. (2015). *Hunt for Deep Panda intensifies in trenches of U.S.-China cyberwar*. Retrieved from http://www.reuters.com/article/us-cybersecurity-usa-deep-panda-idUSKBN0P102320150621
31. Common threats to be aware of. (n.d.). Retrieved from http://www.getcybersafe.gc.ca/cnt/rsks/cmmn-thrts-en.aspx
32. Magee, C. S. (2013). Awaiting the cyber 9/11. *Joint Force Quarterly, 70,* 76–82.
33. Common threats to be aware of. (n.d.). Retrieved from http://www.getcybersafe.gc.ca/cnt/rsks/cmmn-thrts-en.aspx
34. Wang, P., Gonzalez, M. C., Memezes, R., & Barabasi, A. L. (2013). Understanding the spread of malicious mobile-phone programs and their damage potential. *International Journal of Information Security, 12,* 383–392.
35. Peng et al., Smartphone malware and its propagation modeling: A survey.
36. Elk Cloner. (n.d.). Retrieved from http://searchsecurity.techtarget.com/definition/Elk-Cloner
37. Leyden, J. (2006). *PC virus celebrates 20th birthday*. Retrieved from http://www.theregister.co.uk/2006/01/19/pc_virus_at_20/
38. Shoch, J. F., & Hupp, J. A. (1982). The "worm" programs—early experience with distributed computation. *Computing Practices, 25*(3), 172–180.
39. Worm. (n.d.). Retrieved from http://searchsecurity.techtarget.com/definition/worm
40. Balthrop, J., Forrest, S., Newman, M. E. J., & Williamson M. M. (2004). Technological networks and the spread of computer viruses. *Science, 304*(5670), 527–529.
41. Spafford, E. (1988). *The Internet worm program: An analysis*. Purdue Technical Report CSD-TR-823. Retrieved from http://spaf.cerias.purdue.edu/tech-reps/823.pdf/
42. Phillips, J. (n.d.). *Harmful effects of a computer worm*. Retrieved from http://techin.oureverydaylife.com/harmful-effects-computer-worms-2531.html
43. Wang et al., Understanding the spread of malicious mobile-phone programs and their damage potential.
44. Peng et al., Smartphone malware and its propagation modeling: A survey.
45. Martin, A. (2016). *List the risks of a computer worm*. Retrieved from http://techin.oureverydaylife.com/list-risks-computer-worm-2040.html
46. ABC News. (2016). *Slammer computer worm slows down*. Retrieved from http://abcnews.go.com/Technology/story?id=97758&page=1
47. Common threats to be aware of. (n.d.). Retrieved from http://www.getcybersafe.gc.ca/cnt/rsks/cmmn-thrts-en.aspx
48. What is a Trojan virus? Definition. (n.d.). Retrieved from https://usa.kaspersky.com/internet-security-center/threats/trojans#.V5NoB2PVMaM
49. Peng et al., Smartphone malware and its propagation modeling: A survey.
50. Common threats to be aware of. (n.d.). Retrieved from http://www.getcybersafe.gc.ca/cnt/rsks/cmmn-thrts-en.aspx
51. Crapanzano, J. (2003). *Deconstructing SubSeven, the Trojan horse of choice*. Retrieved from https://www.sans.org/reading-room/whitepapers/malicious/deconstructing-subseven-trojan-horse-choice-953
52. Landesman, M. (2016). *What is a Keylogger Trojan?* Retrieved from http://antivirus.about.com/od/whatisavirus/a/keylogger.htm
53. Russell, J. (2011). *Japanese government hit by Chinese Trojan horse attack*. Retrieved from https://thenextweb.com/asia/2011/10/25/japanese-government-hit-by-chinese-trojan-horse-attack/#.tnw_FXvRO1fQ

54. US government firewall virus removal guide. (2013). Retrieved from http://www.malwareremovalguides.info/us-government-firewall-virus-removal-guide/
55. Ransomware—Definition, prevention, and removal. (n.d.). Retrieved from http://usa.kaspersky.com/internet-security-center/definitions/ransomware#.V6L0UWPVMaM
56. US government firewall virus removal guide. (2013). Retrieved from http://www.malwareremovalguides.info/us-government-firewall-virus-removal-guide/
57. Ransomware—Definition, prevention, and removal. (n.d.). Retrieved from http://usa.kaspersky.com/internet-security-center/definitions/ransomware#.V6L0UWPVMaM
58. Antivirus software. (n.d.). Retrieved from http://searchsecurity.techtarget.com/definition/antivirus-software
59. Antivirus software. (n.d.). Retrieved from http://searchsecurity.techtarget.com/definition/antivirus-software
60. Castelli, J. (2001). *Choosing your anti-virus software*. Retrieved from https://www.sans.org/reading-room/whitepapers/commerical/choosing-anti-virus-software-784
61. Lu, J., Xiao, Y., Li, S., Liang, W., & Chen, P. (2012). Cyber security and cyber issues in smart grids. *IEEE Communications Survey and Tutorials, 14*(4), 981–997.
62. More, R. M. (2014). A study of cyber security practices with respect to the use of firewall and IDPS in educational institutions in Pune area. *International Journal of Research, 1*(7), 251–255.
63. Lu et al., Cyber security and cyber issues in smart grids.
64. Thompson, H. H. (2017). *Introduction: Security industry and trends: Trends, building blocks for a solid security plan basics*. Presentation at RSA Conference, San Francisco, CA.
65. Computer viruses and other malware: What you need to know. (2016). Retrieved from http://help.uis.cam.ac.uk/user-accounts-security/security/malware
66. Wee Sile, A. (2016). *Overeager "Pokémon Go" fans are an opportunity for cybercriminals, cybersecurity expert says*. Retrieved from http://www.cnbc.com/2016/07/14/overeager-pokemon-go-fans-are-an-opportunity-for-cybercriminals-cybersecurity-expert-says.html
67. Vijayan, J. (2013). *Encryption still best way to protect data—despite NSA*. Retrieved from http://www.computerworld.com/article/2484714/security0/encryption-still-best-way-to-protect-data----despite-nsa.html
68. Chia, T. (2012). *Confidentiality, integrity, availability: The three components of the CIA triad*. Retrieved from http://security.blogoverflow.com/2012/08/confidentiality-integrity-availability-the-three-components-of-the-cia-triad/
69. McDowell, M. (2009). *Security tip. Understanding denial-of-service attacks*. Retrieved from https://www.us-cert.gov/ncas/tips/ST04-015
70. DigiCert. (2017). *Check our numbers: The math behind estimations to break a 2048-bit certificate*. Retrieved from https://www.digicert.com/TimeTravel/math.htm
71. Ciampa, M. (2009). *Security awareness: Applying practical security in your world* (3rd ed.). Boston, MA: Cengage.
72. Biometrics. (n.d.). Retrieved from http://searchsecurity.techtarget.com/definition/biometrics
73. Bo, C., Zhang, L., Jung, T., Han, J., Li, X-Y., & Wang, Y. (2014). *Continuous user identification via touch and movement biometrics*. In 2014 IEEE International Conference on Performance Computing and Communications, pp. 1–8, IEEE.

Chapter 4

1. Bradbury, D. (2017). Killing me softly with his hack. *InfoSecurity, 14*(1), 33–35.
2. Armerding, T. (2015). *Cybercrime: Much more organized*. Retrieved from http://www.csoonline.com/article/2938529/cyber-attacks-espionage/cybercrime-much-more-organized.html
3. Federal Trade Commission. (n.d.). *Identity theft*. Retrieved from https://www.consumer.ftc.gov/features/feature-0014-identity-theft

4. Federal Trade Commission, *Identity theft.*
5. Federal Trade Commission, *Identity theft.*
6. Federal Trade Commission, *Identity theft.*
7. Federal Trade Commission, *Identity theft.*
8. Anti-Phishing Working Group. (n.d.). *Origins of the word* phishing. Retrieved from http://www.antiphishing.org/resources/apwg-reports/phishing-origin
9. Identity Theft Resource Center. (n.d.). *Identity theft facts and statistics.* Retrieved from http://www.idtheftcenter.org/facts.shtml (April 2004)
10. Elledge, A. (2004). *Phishing: An analysis of a growing problem.* Retrieved from https://www.sans.org/reading-room/whitepapers/threats/phishing-analysis-growing-problem-1417
11. Federal Trade Commission. (2016). *Consumer Sentinel Network Databook January—December 2015.* Retrieved from https://www.ftc.gov/system/files/documents/reports/consumer-sentinel-network-data-book-january-december-2015/160229csn-2015databook.pdf
12. Internal Revenue Service. (2017). *Report phishing and online scams.* Retrieved from https://www.irs.gov/uac/report-phishing
13. Better Business Bureau. (2016). *The Nigerian prince: Old scam, new twist.* Retrieved from https://www.bbb.org/new-york-city/get-consumer-help/articles/the-nigerian-prince-old-scam-new-twist/
14. Urrico, R. (2016). *5 countermeasures to phishing attacks.* Retrieved from http://www.cutimes.com/2016/08/26/5-countermeasures-to-phishing-attacks?page=6&slreturn=1486870848
15. Yu, S. (2011). E-mail spam and the CAN SPAM Act: A qualitative analysis. *International Journal of Cyber Criminology, 5*(1), 715–735.
16. Carter, M. (2008, July 22). *Spammer sentenced to 47 months in prison.* Retrieved from http://www.seattletimes.com/seattle-news/spammer-sentenced-to-47-months-in-prison/
17. Yu, E-mail spam and the CAN SPAM Act.
18. Yu, E-mail spam and the CAN SPAM Act.
19. Soltani, S., Seno, S. A. H., Nezhadkamali, M., & Budirato, R. (2014). A survey on real world botnets and detection mechanisms. *International Journal of Information and Network Security,* 3(2), 116–127.
20. Soltani et al., A survey on real world botnets.
21. George, T. (2014). *The internet's big threat: Drive-by-attacks.* Retrieved from http://www.securityweek.com/internets-big-threat-drive-attacks
22. Dell SecureWorks Counter Threat Unit Threat Intelligence. (2016). *Banking botnets: The battle continues.* Retrieved from https://www.secureworks.com/research/banking-botnets-the-battle-continues
23. Northcutt, S. (n.d.). *Logic bombs, Trojan horses, and trap doors.* Retrieved from http://www.sans.edu/research/security-laboratory/article/log-bmb-trp-door
25. Northcutt, *Logic bombs.*
25. Lewis, N. (n.d.). *Understanding logic bomb attacks: Examples and countermeasures.* Retrieved from http://searchsecurity.techtarget.com/tip/Understanding-logic-bomb-attacks-Examples-and-countermeasures
26. Shield Security Research Center. (2013). *Massive cyber attacks launched against South Korea on March 20.* Retrieved from http://www.shield.ne.jp/ssrc/topics/SSRC-ER-13-014-en.html
27. Kovacs, E. (2016). *Hybrid Trojan "GozNym" targets North American banks.* Retrieved from http://www.securityweek.com/hybrid-trojan-goznym-targets-north-american-banks
28. Dombrowski, S. C., LeMasney, J. W., Ahia, C. E., & Dickson, S. A. (2004). Protecting children from online sexual predators: Technological, psychoeducational, and legal considerations. *Professional Psychology: Research and Practice, 35*(1), 65–73.
29. Seto, M. (2011). *Internet-facilitated sexual offending.* Office of Justice Programs. Retrieved from https://www.smart.gov/SOMAPI/sec1/ch4_internet.html
30. Powell, M., Cassematis, P., Benson, M., Smallbone, S., & Wortley, R. (2015). Police officers' perceptions of their reactions to viewing internet child exploitation material.

Journal of Police and Criminal Psychology, 30, 103–111.

31. United States Sentencing Commission. (2012). *2012 report to the Congress: Federal child pornography offenses.* Retrieved from http://www.ussc.gov/research/congressional-reports/2012-report-congress-federal-child-pornography-offenses

32. United States Sentencing Commission. (2012). *2012 report to the Congress: Federal child pornography offenses.* (Chapter 5). Retrieved from http://www.ussc.gov/sites/default/files/pdf/news/congressional-testimony-and-reports/sex-offense-topics/201212-federal-child-pornography-offenses/Chapter_05.pdf

33. Babchishin, K. N., Hanson, R. K., & VanZyulen, H. (2014). Online child pornography offenders are different: A meta-analysis of the characteristics of online and offline sex offenders against children. *Archives of Sexual Behavior.*

34. Briggs, P., Simon, W. T., & Simonsen, S. (2011). An exploratory study of internet-initiated sexual offenses and the chat room sex offender: Has the internet enabled a new typology of sex offender? *Sexual Abuse: A Journal of Research and Treatment, 23,* 72–91.

35. Sexual offender tactics and grooming. (n.d.). Retrieved from http://laurelhouse.org.au/?page_id=36

36. Aliens, C. (2016). *Yahoo helped the FBI catch a pedophile in France and identified a CP network online.* Retrieved from https://www.deepdotweb.com/2016/12/18/yahoo-helped-fbi-catch-pedophile-france-identified-cp-network-online/

37. Jennings, D. (2013). *Plano victim hopes her story helps others understand the impact of child pornography.* Retrieved from https://www.dallasnews.com/news/crime/2013/07/20/plano-victim-hopes-her-story-helps-others-understand-the-impact-of-child-pornography

38. Steel, C. M. S. (2015). Web-based child pornography. The global impact of deterrence efforts and its consumption on mobile platforms. *Child Abuse and Neglect,* 44, 150–158.

39. Virtual Global Taskforce. (2012). *'Dreamboard' members sentenced to life in prison for exploiting children.* Retrieved from http://virtualglobaltaskforce.com/2012/dreamboard-member-sentenced-to-life-in-prison-for-exploiting-children/.

40. Rigby, M. (2010). *Child porn investigations may snare the innocent.* Retrieved from https://www.prisonlegalnews.org/news/2010/nov/15/child-porn-investigations-may-snare-the-innocent/

41. Tate, T., & Jeory, T. (2014). *Police did nothing to track down victim of child porn snuff film.* Retrieved from http://www.express.co.uk/news/uk/475207/Police-did-nothing-to-track-down-victim-of-child-porn-snuff-film

42. Burke, J., Gentleman, A., & Willan, P. (2000, September 30). *British link to 'snuff' videos.* Retrieved from https://www.theguardian.com/uk/2000/oct/01/ameliagentleman.philipwillan

43. Anderson, L. (2012). *Snuff: Murder and torture on the internet, and the people who watch it.* Retrieved from http://www.theverge.com/2012/6/13/3076557/snuff-murder-torture-internet-people-who-watch-it

44. Powell et al., Police officers' perceptions.

45. United Nations Office of Drugs and Crime. (n.d.). *Human trafficking.* Retrieved from https://www.unodc.org/unodc/en/human-trafficking/what-is-human-trafficking.html

46. United Nations Office of Drugs and Crime. (n.d.). *Human trafficking.* Retrieved from https://www.unodc.org/unodc/en/human-trafficking/what-is-human-trafficking.html

47. Dixon, H. B., Jr. (2013). *Human trafficking and the Internet* (*and other technologies, too).* Retrieved from http://www.americanbar.org/publications/judges_journal/2013/winter/human_trafficking_and_internet_and_other_technologies_too.html

48. Butler, C. N. (2014). Kids for sale: Does America recognize its own sexually exploited minors as victims of human trafficking? *Seton Hall Law Review, 44*(3), 1–39.

49. Hughes, D. (2000). The internet and sex industries: Partners in global sexual exploitation. *Technology and Society Magazine, IEEE, 19*(1), 35–42.

50. Crimes Against Children Research Center. (n.d.). The role of technology in child sex trafficking. Retrieved from http://www.unh.edu/ccrc/projects/technology_in_child_sex_traffic.html

51. National Human Trafficking Hotline. (n.d.). *Hotline statistics*. Retrieved from https://humantraffickinghotline.org/states

52. U.S. Department of Homeland Security. (n.d.). *Overview*. Retrieved from https://www.ice.gov/predator

53. U.S. Legal. (n.d.). *Mail order bride law and legal definition*. Retrieved from http://definitions.uslegal.com/m/mail-order-bride/

54. Sarker, S., Chakraborty, S., Tansuhaj, P. S., Mulder, M., & Dogerlioglu-Demir, K. (2013). The "mail order bride" (MOB) phenomenon in the cyberworld: An interpretive investigation. *ACM Transactions on Management Information Systems, 4*(3), 1–43.

55. Sarker et al., p. 18.

56. Sarker et al., p. 18.

57. Filippone, M. (2014). *You can always find a bride in Russia: An investigation of the mail order bride industry*. Retrieved from http://spectrum.library.concordia.ca/978692/1/CompletedMA.pdf

58. Sims, S. (2009). A comparison of laws in the Philippines, the U.S.A., Taiwan, and Belarus to regulate the mail-order bride industry. *Akron Law Review, 42*(2), 606–638.

59. Dixon, *Human trafficking and the Internet*.

60. U.S. Government Accountability Office. (2008). *International Marriage Broker Regulation Act of 2005*. Retrieved from http://www.gao.gov/products/GAO-08-862

61. Marcum, C. D., Higgins, G. E., Freiburger, T. L., & Ricketts, M. L. (2011). Battle of the sexes: An examination of male and female cyber bullying. *International Journal of Cyber Criminology, 6*(1), 904–911.

62. Ballard, M. E., & Welch, K. M. (2015). Virtual warfare: Cyberbullying and cyber-victimization in MMOG play. *Games and Culture*, 1–26.

63. Kowalski, R. M., & Limber, S. P. (2013). Psychological, physical, and academic correlates of cyberbullying and traditional bullying. *Journal of Adolescent Health, 53*(1), S13–S20.

64. Ballard & Welch, Virtual warfare.

65. Marcum et al., Battle of the sexes.

66. Dressling, H., Bailer, J., Anders, A., Wagner, H., & Gallas, C. (2014). Cyberstalking in a large sample of social network users: Prevalence, characteristics, and impact upon victims. *Cyberpsychology, Behavior, and Social Networking, 17*(2), 61–67.

67. Dressling et al., Cyberstalking.

68. Hazelwood, K., & Koon-Magnin, S. (2013). Cyberstalking and cyberharassment legislation in the United States. *International Journal of Cyber Criminology*, 17(2), 155–168.

69. Long, C. (2006, May). Sugar and spice? *NEA Today, 24*, 30–33.

70. Burst, J. (2012). *10 most common cyberbullying tactics*. Retrieved from http://bullyproofclassroom.com/10-most-common-cyber-bullying-tactics

71. Chibbaro, J. (2007). *School counselors and the cyberbully: Interventions and implications*. Retrieved from http://asca.dev.networkats.com/asca/media/asca/home/chibbarovol11no1.pdf

72. Burst, *10 most common cyberbullying tactics*.

73. Burst, *10 most common cyberbullying tactics*.

74. PureSight. (n.d.). *Hope Witsell*. Retrieved from http://www.puresight.com/Real-Life-Stories/hope-witsell.html

75. Siegle, D. (2010). Cyberbullying and sexting: Technology abuses in the 21st century. *Technology, 32*(2), 14–65.

76. Ballard & Welch, Virtual warfare.

77. Yang, S. C. (2012). Paths to bullying in online gaming: The effects of gender, preference for playing violent games, hostility, and

aggressive behavior on bullying. *Journal of Educational Computing Research, 47*, 235–249.

78. ACEgruben. (2012, October 16). *Amanda Todd story official documentary* [Video file]. Retrieved from https://www.youtube.com/watch?v=EKFr3TNMJ4k
79. Gaming. (n.d.). Retrieved from http://whatis.techtarget.com/definition/gaming
80. Ballard & Welch, Virtual warfare.
81. Yang, Paths to bullying in online gaming.
82. Ballard & Welch, Virtual warfare.
83. The rise of bullying in online games. (2015). Retrieved from https://nobullying.com/the-rise-of-bullying-in-online-games/
84. Megan Meier Foundation. (n.d.). *Bullying, cyberbullying, and suicide statistics*. Retrieved from http://www.meganmeierfoundation.org/statistics.html
85. Hinduja, S., & Patchin, J. W. (2010). Cyberbullying and suicide. *Archives of Suicide Research, 14*(3), 206–221.

Chapter 5

1. Mylrea, M. (2009, November 15). Brazil's next battlefield: Cyberspace. *Foreign Policy Journal*. Retrieved from http://www.foreignpolicyjournal.com/2009/11/15/brazils-next-battlefield-cyberspace/
2. Federal Bureau of Investigation. (2015). *2014 Internet Crime Report*. Retrieved from https://www.fbi.gov/news/news_blog/2014-ic3-annual-report
3. U.S. Department of Homeland Security. (n.d.). *Cyber threat source descriptions*. Retrieved from https://ics-cert.us-cert.gov/content/cyber-threat-source-descriptions
4. Greitzer, F., Moore, A., Capelli, D., Andrews, D., Carroll, L., & Hull, T. (2007). Combating the insider cyber threat. *The IEEE Computer Society*, 61–64.
5. Greitzer et al., Combating the insider cyber threat.
6. Greitzer et al., Combating the insider cyber threat.
7. Miller, R., & Maxim, M. (2015). *I have to trust someone . . . don't I? Dealing with insider threats to cybersecurity* [White paper]. Retrieved from http://www.ca.com/content/dam/ca/us/files/white-paper/dealing-with-insider-threats-to-cyber-security.pdf
8. Giandomenico, N., & de Groot, J. (2016). *Insider vs. outsider data security threats: What's the greater risk?* Retrieved from https://digitalguardian.com/blog/insider-outsider-data-security-threats
9. Smith, H. (2016). *Corporate espionage case underscores seriousness of insider threats*. Retrieved from https://www.nuix.com/blog/corporate-espionage-case-underscores-seriousness-insider-threats
10. Yang, Jianxiang. (2015). *Sinovel claims court win over AMSC*. Retrieved from http://www.windpowermonthly.com/article/1350760/sinovel-claims-court-win-amsc/
11. Shaw, S. (2013). *AMSC/Sinovel industrial espionage thriller takes a procedural detour, threatening U.S. criminal prosecution*. Retrieved from http://www.lexology.com/library/detail.aspx?g=c06d91c6-1d63-4fb0-a1a7-d803bf90ef60
12. Herhalt, J. (2011). *Cyber crime—a growing challenge for governments*. Retrieved from https://www.kpmg.com/Global/en/IssuesAndInsights/ArticlesPublications/Documents/cyber-crime.pdf
13. Minsky, A. (2015). *'Anonymous' claims responsibility for cyber attack that shut down government websites*. Retrieved from http://globalnews.ca/news/2060036/government-of-canada-servers-suffer-cyber-attack/
14. Waqas. (2016). *Anonymous target North Carolina government sites against anti-LGBT law*. Retrieved from https://www.hackread.com/anonymous-ddos-north-carolina-anti-lgbt-law/
15. Anonymous, MIT, DoJ, embroiled in aftermath of Aaron Swartz' death. (2013, January 15). Retrieved from http://www.infosecurity-magazine.com/news/anonymous-mit-doj-embroiled-in-aftermath-of-aaron/
16. Denning, D. (2001, Autumn). Cyberterrorism. *Global Dialogue*.

17. Marloff, S. (2016, April 22). Cyber attacks stymie abortion fundraiser. *Austin Chronicle*.
18. Williams, K. B. (2015, November 14). *4 tips from Edward Snowden to keep your private data private*. Retrieved from http://thehill.com/policy/cybersecurity/260089-4-tips-from-edward-snowden-to-keep-your-private-data-private
19. BBC News. (2015). *Syrian president Bashar al-Assad: Facing down rebellion*. Retrieved from http://www.bbc.com/news/10338256.
20. Clayton, M. (2013, February 27). Exclusive: Cyberattack leaves natural gas pipelines vulnerable to sabotage. *Christian Science Monitor*.
21. Goldstein, M., & Stevenson, A. (2015, August 11). Nine charged in insider trading case tied to hackers. *New York Times*. Retrieved from https://www.nytimes.com/2015/08/12/business/dealbook/insider-trading-sec-hacking-case.html?_r=0
22. Government Accountability Office. (2005). Critical infrastructure protection: Department of Homeland Security faces challenges in fulfilling *cybersecurity responsibilities* [GAO-05-434]. Retrieved from http://www.gao.gov/new.items/d05434.pdf
23. Andrews, N. (2016, February 24). Islamic State hackers aim at Facebook's Zuckerberg, Twitter's Dorsey. *Wall Street Journal*. Retrieved from https://www.wsj.com/articles/islamic-state-hackers-take-aim-at-facebooks-zuckerberg-twitters-dorsey-1456362911
24. Mid-market mayhem: Cybercriminals wreak havoc beyond big enterprises. (2015). Retrieved from http://faculty.washington.edu/blabob/bob/Docs/2015%20Cybercriminals%20Wreak%20Havoc%20Beyond%20Big%20Enterprises.pdf
25. Bradbury, D. (2017). Killing me softly with his hack. *InfoSecurity, 14*(1), 33–35.
26. Mazari, A. A., Anjarini, A. H., Habib, S. H., & Nyakwende, E. (2016). Cyber terrorism taxonomies: Definition, targets, patterns, and mitigation strategies. *International Journal of Cyber Warfare and Terrorism, 6*(1), 1–12.
27. Mazari et al., Cyber terrorism taxonomies.
28. U.S. Army Training and Doctrine Command, Deputy Chief of Staff for Intelligence, Assistant Deputy Chief of Staff for Intelligence—Threats. (2006). *Critical infrastructure: Threats and terrorism* [DCSINT Handbook No. 1.02]. Retrieved from https://fas.org/irp/threat/terrorism/sup2.pdf
29. Ponemon Institute. (2015). *2015 cost of cyber crime study: United States*. Retrieved from http://www.ponemon.org/blog/2015-cost-of-cyber-crime-united-states
30. Peterson, A. (2015, September 23). OPM says 5.6 million fingerprints stolen in cyberattack, five times as many as previously thought. *Washington Post*. Retrieved from https://www.washingtonpost.com/news/the-switch/wp/2015/09/23/opm-now-says-more-than-five-million-fingerprints-compromised-in-breaches/?utm_term=.ba6d6275c003
31. Reuters. (2016, December 29). *Bangladesh cyber heist: Suspicion on IT technicians*. Retrieved from http://timesofindia.indiatimes.com/world/south-asia/bangladesh-cyber-heist-suspicion-on-it-technicians/articleshow/56235865.cms
32. Hacker. (n.d.). In *Oxford English Dictionary* online. Retrieved from http://www.oed.com/viewdictionaryentry/Entry/83045?prin
33. Hacker. (n.d.). *The Jargon File*. Retrieved from http://www.catb.org/jargon/html/H/hacker.html
34. Yagoda, B. (2014, March 6). A short history of "hack." *New Yorker*. Retrieved from http://www.newyorker.com/tech/elements/a-short-history-of-hack
35. Yagoda, A short history of "hack."
36. Hacker. (n.d.). *The Jargon File*. Retrieved from http://www.catb.org/jargon/html/H/hacker.html
37. Jordan, T., & Taylor, P. (1998). The sociology of hackers. *Sociological Review, 46*(4), 757–780.
38. Mahmood, M. A., Siponen, M., Straub, M., Rao, H. R., & Raghu, T. S. (2010). Moving toward black hat research in information systems security: An editorial introduction to the special issue. *Management Information Systems Quarterly, 34*(3), 431–433.
39. Ashford, W. (2015). *BlackHat 2015—industrial hacking: The untold story*. Retrieved from http://

www.computerweekly.com/news/4500251365/BlackHat-2015-Industrial-hacking-the-untold-story

40. Ashford, W. (2014). *Industrial control systems: What are the security challenges?* Retrieved from http://www.computerweekly.com/news/2240232680/Industrial-control-systems-What-are-the-security-challenges

41. Social-Engineer, Inc. (n.d.). *The social engineering framework*. Retrieved from http://www.social-engineer.org/framework/general-discussion/social-engineering-defined/

42. Rafia, S. (2016). *FBI paid gray hat hackers, not Israel-based Cellebrite, one-time fee to hack iPhone*. Retrieved from https://www.mitnicksecurity.com/S=0/site/news_item/fbi-paid-grey-hat-hackers-not-israel-based-cellebrite-one-time-fee-to-hack

43. Reidenberg, J. R. (2015). The transparent citizen. *Loyola University of Chicago Law Journal, 47*, 437–463.

44. Spidalieri, F. (2015). *State of the states on cybersecurity*. Retrieved from http://pellcenter.org/eight-states-lead-the-rest-in-cybersecurity/

45. Kharpal, A. (2016). *Apple vs FBI: All you need to know*. Retrieved from http://www.cnbc.com/2016/03/29/apple-vs-fbi-all-you-need-to-know.html

46. Nakashima, E. (2016, April 12). FBI paid professional hackers one-time fee to crack San Bernardino iPhone. *Washington Post*. Retrieved from https://www.washingtonpost.com/world/national-security/fbi-paid-professional-hackers-one-time-fee-to-crack-san-bernardino-iphone/2016/04/12/5397814a-00de-11e6-9d36-33d198ea26c5_story.html

47. Henna_M_. (2008, July 3). Hated it! [TripAdvisor review]. Retrieved from https://www.tripadvisor.com/ShowUserReviews-g1380108-d592779-r26102743-Uluwatu_Temple-Pecatu_Nusa_Dua_Peninsula_Bali.html

48. Thompson, H. (2017). *Introduction: Security industry and trends: Trends, building blocks for a solid security plan basics*. Presentation at RSA Conference, San Francisco, CA.

49. CyLab, Carnegie Mellon University. (n.d.). *The reCAPTCHA project*. Retrieved from https://www.cylab.cmu.edu/partners/success-stories/recaptcha.html

50. Thompson, H., *Introduction: Security industry and trends*.

51. Thompson, H., *Introduction: Security industry and trends*.

52. Koller, M. S. (2015). *California amends its breach notification statute*. Retrieved from https://www.dataprivacymonitor.com/data-breach-notification-laws/california-amends-its-breach-notification-statute/

Chapter 6

1. RAND Corporation. (n.d.). *Cyberwarfare*. Retrieved from http://www.rand.org/topics/cyber-warfare.html

2. Makovsky, D. (2012). The silent strike. How Israel bombed a Syrian nuclear installation and kept it secret. *New Yorker*. Retrieved from http://www.newyorker.com/magazine/2012/09/17/the-silent-strike

3. Weinberger, S. (2007). *How Israel spoofed Syria's air defense system*. Retrieved from https://www.wired.com/2007/10/how-israel-spoo/

4. Nye, J. S., Jr. (2010). *Cyber power*. Retrieved from http://www.dtic.mil/dtic/tr/fulltext/u2/a522626.pdf

5. U.S. Department of Defense. (2011). *U.S. Department of Defense strategy for operating in cyberspace*. Retrieved from http://csrc.nist.gov/groups/SMA/ispab/documents/DOD-Strategy-for-Operating-in-Cyberspace.pdf

6. Kshetri, N. (2014). *Cybersecurity and international relations: The U.S. engagement with Russia and China*. Retrieved from http://web.isanet.org/Web/Conferences/FLACSO-ISA%20BuenosAires%202014/Archive/6f9b6b91-0f33-4956-89fc-f9a9cde89caf.pdf

7. Noman, H. (n.d.). *The emergence of open and organized pro-government cyberattacks in the Middle East: The case of the Syrian Electronic Army*. Retrieved from https://opennet.net/emergence-

open-and-organized-pro-government-cyber-attacks-middle-east-case-syrian-electronic-army

8. Al-Rawi, A. K. (2014). Cyber warriors in the Middle East: The case of the Syrian Electronic Army. *Public Relations Review, 40,* 420–428.
9. Al-Rawi, Cyber warriors in the Middle East.
10. Lindsey, J. R. (2014/15). The impact of China on cybersecurity: Fiction and friction. *International Security, 39*(3), 7–47.
11. Rubenstein, D. (2014). *Nation state cyberespionage and its impacts*. Retrieved from http://www.cse.wustl.edu/~jain/cse571-14/ftp/cyber_espionage/
12. Walters, R. (2016, January 14). Russian hackers shut down Ukraine's power grid. *Newsweek*. Retrieved from http://www.newsweek.com/russian-hackers-shut-ukraine-power-grid-415751
13. Walters, Russian hackers.
14. Geers, K., Kindlund, D., Moran, N., & Rachwald, R. (2014). *World War C: Understanding nation-state motives behind today's advanced cyberattacks*. Retrieved from https://www.fireeye.com/content/dam/fireeye-www/global/en/current-threats/pdfs/fireeye-wwc-report.pdf
15. Haggard, S., & Lindsey, J. R. (2015). North Korea and the Sony hack: Exporting instability through cyberspace. *Asia Pacific Issues from the East-West Center, 117,* 1–8.
16. Kovarik, B. (2011). *Revolutions in communication: Media history from Gutenberg to the digital age*. New York, NY: Continuum.
17. History Channel. (2015). *Code breaking*. Retrieved from http://www.history.co.uk/topics/history-of-ww2/code-breaking
18. Davison, J. (2015). *Russian spies in Canada: New lessons from the Gouzenko defection*. Retrieved from http://www.cbc.ca/news/canada/russian-spies-intelligence-canada-gouzenko-1.3269032
19. *2016 Data Breach Investigations Report*. (2016). Retrieved from http://www.verizonenterprise.com/verizon-insights-lab/dbir/2016/
20. Sang-Hun, C., & Markoff, J. (2009, July 8). Cyberattacks jam government and commercial web sites in U.S. and South Korea. *New York Times*. Retrieved from http://www.nytimes.com/2009/07/09/technology/09cyber.html?_r=0
21. Christie, M., Schwartz, R., Margolin, J., & Ross, B. (2016). *Christmas party may have triggered San Bernardino terror attack: Police*. Retrieved from http://abcnews.go.com/US/christmas-party-triggered-san-bernardino-terror-attack-police/story?id=43884973
22. Roberts, J. J. (2016). *Twitter shut down 235,000 terrorist accounts this year*. Retrieved from http://fortune.com/2016/08/18/twitter-terrorists/
23. Vermes, K. (2016). *Facebook and Twitter continue their shutdown of pages linked to Hamas*. Retrieved from http://www.techtimes.com/articles/153482/20160425/facebook-twitter-shutting-down-hamas-accounts.htm
24. Trujillo, M. (2015). *FCC says it can't shut down ISIS websites*. Retrieved from http://thehill.com/policy/technology/260438-fcc-says-it-cant-shutdown-online-terrorist-activity
25. Economic Espionage Act, 18 U.S.C. § 1843 (1996).
26. Office of the National Counterintelligence Executive. (2011). *Foreign spies stealing US economic secrets in cyberspace. Report to the Congress on foreign economic collection and economic espionage, 2009–2011*. Retrieved from https://www.ncsc.gov/publications/reports/fecie_all/Foreign_Economic_Collection_2011.pdf
27. Office of the National Counterintelligence Executive, *Foreign spies*.
28. Gady, F.-S. (2016). *Top U.S. spy chief: China still successful in cyber espionage against U.S.* Retrieved from http://thediplomat.com/2016/02/top-us-spy-chief-china-still-successful-in-cyber-espionage-against-us/
29. Office of the National Counterintelligence Executive, *Foreign spies*.
30. Economic Espionage Act, 18 U.S.C. § 1843 (1996).

31. Economic Espionage Act, 18 U.S.C. § 1843 (1996).

32. Economic Espionage Act, 18 U.S.C. § 1843 (1996).

33. Landau, S. (2013). *Making sense from Snowden: What's significant in the NSA surveillance revelations*. Retrieved from http://www.cs.siue.edu/~wwhite/IS376/ReadingAssignments/0930_MakingSenseFromSnowden.pdf

34. Office of the National Counterintelligence Executive. *Foreign spies*.

35. U.S. Const. amend. IV.

36. Intelligence and National Security Alliance. (2013). *Operational levels of cyber intelligence*. Retrieved from http://csrc.nist.gov/cyberframework/framework_comments/20131213_charles_alsup_insa_part3.pdf

37. Menn, J. (2015). *Russian researchers expose breakthrough U.S. spying program*. Retrieved from http://www.reuters.com/article/us-usa-cyberspying-idUSKBN0LK1QV20150216

38. Rid, T. (2013). *Cyberwar and peace*. Retrieved from http://www.saintjoehigh.com/ourpages/auto/2014/3/14/40536284/13-1112%20Cyberwar%20and%20Peace.pdf

39. U.S. Legal. (n.d.). *Sabotage law and legal definitions*. Retrieved from http://definitions.uslegal.com/s/sabotage/

40. Sanger, D. E. (2013, May 6). U.S. blames China's military directly for cyberattacks. *New York Times*. Retrieved from http://www.nytimes.com/2013/05/07/world/asia/us-accuses-chinas-military-in-cyberattacks.html

41. *2016 Data Breach Investigations Report*. (2016). Retrieved from http://www.verizonenterprise.com/verizon-insights-lab/dbir/2016/

42. Overill, R. E. (2007). Denial-of-service attacks: Threats and methodologies. *Journal of Financial Crime, 6*(4), 351–354.

43. Anderson, E. A., Irvine, C. E., & Schell, R. R. (2004). Subversion as a threat in information warfare. *Journal of Information Warfare, 3*(2), 51–64.

44. Musthaler, L. (2015, October 16). *Rutgers University gets an F for its failure to prevent DDoS attacks*. Retrieved from https://www.corero.com/blog/676-rutgers-university-gets-an-f-for-its-failure-to-prevent-repeated-ddos-attacks.html

Chapter 7

1. Rabasa, A., Blackwill, R., Chalk, P., Cragin, K., Fair, C. C., Jackson, B. A., . . . Tellis, A. J. (2009). *The lessons of Mumbai*. Retrieved from http://www.rand.org/content/dam/rand/pubs/occasional_papers/2009/RAND_OP249.pdf

2. Collin, B. (1997). The future of cyberterrorism. *Crime and Justice International*, pp. 15–18.

3. Conway, M. (2002). What is cyberterrorism? *Current History, 101*(659), 436–442.

4. National Institute of Justice. (2017). *Terrorism*. Retrieved from https://www.nij.gov/topics/crime/terrorism/Pages/welcome.aspx

5. 22 U.S. Code § 2656f.

6. Terrorism [definition]. (n.d.). Retrieved from http://www.militaryfactory.com/dictionary/military-terms-defined.asp?term_id=5407

7. Human Rights Voices. (n.d.). *UN 101: There is no UN definition of terrorism*. Retrieved from http://www.eyeontheun.org/facts.asp?1=1&p=61

8. Denning, D. (2000). *Cyberterrorism* [Testimony before the Special Oversight Committee on Armed Services, U.S. House of Representatives]. Retrieved from https://pdfs.semanticscholar.org/7fdd/ae586b6d2167919abba17eb90e5219b7835b.pdf

9. Gordon, S., & Ford, R. (2002). Cyberterrorism? *Computers and Security, 21*(7), 636–647.

10. Pollitt, M. (2004). *Cyberterrorism—fact or fancy?* Retrieved from https://www.scribd.com/document/21173253/Mark-M-Pollitt-Cyber-Terrorism-Fact-or-Fancy

11. Weimann, G. (2006). *Terror on the Internet*. Washington, DC: U.S. Institute of Peace Press.

12. Krasavin, S. (2002). *What is cyberterrorism?* Retrieved from www.crime-research.org/library/Cyber-terrorism.htm
13. Sullivan, B. (2007). *Cyberterror and ID theft converge in London.* Retrieved from www.redtape.msnbc.com/2007/07/cyber-terror-an.html
14. Kouri, J. (2008, August 25). *Brazilian man charged in cyber-terrorism case.* www.renewamerica.com/columns/kouri/080825
15. Gilbert, D. (2014, April 10). *Iran: The world's worst cyber-terrorists—for now.* Retrieved from http://www.ibtimes.co.uk/iran-worlds-worst-cyber-terrorists-now-1444223
16. Ahmad, R., Yunos, Z., Sahib, S., & Yusoff, M. (2012). Perception on cyber terrorism: A focus group discussion approach. *Journal of Information Security, 3*(3), 231–237.
17. Parker, A. (2009). Cyberterrorism: The emerging worldwide threat. In D. Canter (Ed.), *The face of terrorism* (pp. 245–255). Oxford, England: Wiley-Blackwell.
18. Parker, Cyberterrorism.
19. Jackman, M. (2002). Violence in social life. *Annual Review of Sociology, 28*, 387–415.
20. Singer, P. (2012). *The cyber terror bogeyman.* Retrieved from https://www.brookings.edu/articles/the-cyber-terror-bogeyman/
21. National Research Council. (1991). *Computers at risk: Safe computing in the information age.* Retrieved from http://www.nap.edu/catalog.php?record_id=1581
22. Weimann, *Terror on the Internet.*
23. Verton, D. (2003). *Black ice: The invisible threat of cyberterrorism.* Emeryville, CA: McGraw-Hill.
24. Council on Foreign Relations. (2004). *Cyberterrorism.* Retrieved from http://www.cfr.org/search/?Ntt=cyberterrorism&submit.x=0&submit.y=0
25. BBC Monitoring. (2015). *Is Islamic State shaping Boko Haram media?* Retrieved from www.bbc.com/news/world-africa-31522469
26. Nathaniel, S. (2016). *Chibok girls: Timeline of events after 2-years of bondage.* Retrieved from https://www.naij.com/834605-timeline-200-girls-kidnapped-boko-haram.html
27. Barkoukis, L. (2015). *Why you should care about ISIS.* Retrieved from http://townhall.com/tipsheet/leahbarkoukis/2015/03/13/why-you-should-care-about-isis-n1969994#ifrndnloc
28. Laub, K., & Al-Soud, H. (2015). *ISIS recruitment methods exposed after Jordanian woman flees secret compound.* Retrieved from http://www.cbc.ca/news/world/isis-recruitment-1.3362668
29. Opelka, M. (2015). *Where are pro-ISIS tweets coming from? Read the top 10 list—and prepare to be shocked by No. 4 and No. 10.* Retrieved from http://www.theblaze.com/news/2015/03/22/where-are-pro-islamic-state-tweets-coming-from-read-the-top-10-list-and-prepare-to-be-shocked-by-no-4-and-no-10/
30. Weimann, *Terror on the Internet.*
31. National Association of Regulatory Utility Commissioners. (2005). *Technical assistance briefs: Issue paper on critical infrastructure protection.* Retrieved from https://pubs.naruc.org/pub/536D823B-2354-D714-514E-C323D556C672
32. Cacas, M. (2013). *Helping the grid to bounce back.* http://www.afcea.org/content/?q=node/11116/
33. Barron, J. (2003). The Blackout of 2003: The overview; Power surge blacks out Northeast, hitting cities in 8 states and Canada; Midday shutdowns disrupt millions. *New York Times.* Retrieved from http://www.nytimes.com/2003/08/15/nyregion/blackout-2003-overview-power-surge-blacks-northeast-hitting-cities-8-states.html
34. Breen, G. (2008). Examining existing counterterrorism tactics and applying social network theory to fight cyberterrorism: An interpersonal communication perspective. *Journal of Applied Security Research, 3*(2), 191–204.
35. Collins, P. A., & Baggett, R. K. (2009). *Homeland security and critical infrastructure protection.* Westport, CT: Praeger Security International.
36. Collins & Baggett, *Homeland security and critical infrastructure protection.*
37. U.S. Department of Homeland Security (n.d.). *Critical infrastructure sectors.* https://www.dhs.gov/critical-infrastructure-sectors

38. Collins & Baggett, *Homeland security and critical infrastructure protection.*

39. U.S. Department of Homeland Security. (n.d.). *Homeland Security Presidential Directives.* https://www.dhs.gov/presidential-directives

40. Collins & Baggett, *Homeland security and critical infrastructure protection.*

41. Roberts, C. (2016). *Critical infrastructure vulnerabilities of railways.* Presentation at Wiggins Memorial Symposium, Buies Creek, NC.

Chapter 8

1. Paganini, P. (2014). *Operation Onymous, the joint attack against dark markets in Tor.* Retrieved from http://securityaffairs.co/wordpress/29952/cyber-crime/operation-onymous-vs-dark-markets.html

2. Thompson, K. (2015). *Beyond Google: Everything you need to know about the hidden internet.* Retrieved from http://www.businessinsider.com/difference-between-dark-web-and-deep-web-2015-11

3. Most of the web is invisible to Google. Here's what it contains. (2015). Retrieved from http://www.popsci.com/dark-web-revealed

4. Thompson, *Beyond Google.*

5. Thompson, *Beyond Google.*

6. Cooper, E., & Chikada, A. (2015). *The deep web, the darknet, and Bitcoin.* Retrieved from https://www.markmonitor.com/download/webinar/2015/MarkMonitor-Webinar-150715-DeepWebDarknetBitcoin.pdf

7. Freenet. (n.d.). Retrieved from https://freenetproject.org/

8. The Invisible Internet Project. (n.d.). Retrieved from https://geti2p.net/en/

9. Yeung, P. (2014). *A tour of the best, entirely legal hangouts on the deep web.* Retrieved from https://motherboard.vice.com/en_us/article/the-legal-side-of-the-deep-web-is-wonderfully-bizarre

10. Tor. (n.d.). Retrieved from https://www.torproject.org/

11. Yeung, *A tour of the best, entirely legal hangouts on the deep web.*

12. Karimi, F. (2014). *Ebola patients buying survivors' blood from black market, WHO warns.* Retrieved from http://www.cnn.com/2014/09/18/health/ebola-blood-black-market/index.html

13. Historic Silk Road. (n.d.). Retrieved from http://www.china.org.cn/english/MATERIAL/139504.htm

14. Federal Bureau of Investigation. (2015). *Ross Ulbricht, aka Dread Pirate Roberts, sentenced in Manhattan Federal Court to life in prison.* Retrieved from https://www.fbi.gov/contact-us/field-offices/newyork/news/press-releases/ross-ulbricht-aka-dread-pirate-roberts-sentenced-in-manhattan-federal-court-to-life-in-prison

15. Van Hout, M. C., & Bingham, T. (2014). Responsible vendors, intelligent consumers: Silk Road, the online revolution in drug trading. *International Journal of Drug Policy, 25*(2), 183–189.

16. Van Hout & Bingham, Responsible vendors.

17. Federal Bureau of Investigation, *Ross Ulbricht, aka Dread Pirate Roberts, sentenced in Manhattan Federal Court to life in prison.*

18. Federal Bureau of Investigation, *Ross Ulbricht, aka Dread Pirate Roberts, sentenced in Manhattan Federal Court to life in prison.*

19. Nielsen, M. (2013, December 6). *How the Bitcoin protocol actually works.* Retrieved from http://www.michaelnielsen.org/ddi/how-the-bitcoin-protocol-actually-works/

20. Jessop, N. (2015). *A brief history of bitcoin—and where it's going next.* Retrieved from https://thenextweb.com/insider/2015/03/29/a-brief-history-of-bitcoin-and-where-its-going-next/#.tnw_kYlRvTvB

21. Coinbase. (2016). *Instant exchange.* Retrieved from https://support.coinbase.com/customer/portal/articles/2021569-what-is-instant-exchange-

22. Duffield, E., & Diaz, D. (n.d.). *Dash: A privacy-centric crypto-currency.* Retrieved from https://www.dash.org/wp-content/uploads/2015/04/Dash-WhitepaperV1.pdf

23. What is Dash? (n.d.). Retrieved from https://www.dash.org
24. Paganini, *Operation Onymous, the joint attack against dark markets in Tor.*
25. Vinton, K. (2014). *So far Feds have only confirmed seizing 27 "Dark Market" sites in Operation Onymous.* Retrieved from http://www.forbes.com/sites/katevinton/2014/11/07/operation-onymous-dark-markets/#3d1b4d672d82
26. Vinton, *So far Feds have only confirmed seizing 27 "Dark Market" sites in Operation Onymous.*
27. Cimpanu, C. (2017). *Anonymous hacks and takes down 10,613 dark web portals.* Retrieved from https://www.bleepingcomputer.com/news/security/anonymous-hacks-and-takes-down-10-613-dark-web-portals/
28. Cimpanu, *Anonymous hacks and takes down 10,613 dark web portals.*
29. Vigilante. (n.d.). In *Merriam-Webster's online dictionary* (11th ed.). Retrieved from https://www.merriam-webster.com/dictionary/vigilante
30. Henderson, L. (2012). *Darknet: A beginner's guide to staying anonymous online.* North Charleston, SC: CreateSpace.
31. Palmer, A. (2012). *Deep web: Drugs, guns, assassins, jet planes all for sale on vast anonymous network.* Retrieved from http://www.mirror.co.uk/news/uk-news/deep-web-drugs-guns-assassins-1337131
32. Chin, H. (2012). Weapons of mass destruction (WMD) on the dark web. In H. Chin (Ed.), *Dark web: Exploring and data mining the dark side of the web* (pp. 341–353). New York, NY: Springer.
33. Ward, O. (2016). *Investigating Daesh on the dark web.* Retrieved from https://www.thestar.com/news/world/2016/06/19/investigating-daesh-on-the-dark-web.html
34. Ward, *Investigating Daesh on the dark web.*
35. U.S. Const. amend. I.
36. Clear-and-present danger. (n.d.). Retrieved from http://legal-dictionary.thefreedictionary.com/Clear-and-present+danger+test
37. Paganini, P. (2012). *The good and the bad of the deep web.* Retrieved from http://securityaffairs.co/wordpress/8719/deep-web/the-good-and-the-bad-of-the-deep-web.html
38. U.S. Const. amend. IV.
39. Exclusionary Rule. (n.d.). Retrieved from http://legal-dictionary.thefreedictionary.com/Exclusionary+Rule
40. Badertscher, D. (2009). *Law enforcement case study: Search and seizure in cyberspace.* Retrieved from http://www.criminallawlibraryblog.com/2009/03/law_enforcement_case_study_sea.html

Chapter 9

1. Cohen, L., & Felson, M. (1979). Social change and crime rate trends: A routine activities approach. *American Sociological Review, 44,* 588–608.
2. Cohen & Felson, Social change and crime rate trends.
3. Grabosky, P. (2001). Virtual criminology: Old wine in new bottles? *Social and Legal Studies, 10*(2), 243–249.
4. Leukfeldt, E. R., & Yar, M. (2016). Applying routine activity theory to cybercrime: A theoretical and empirical analysis. *Deviant Behavior, 37*(3), 263–280.
5. Sutherland, E. (1947). *Principles of criminology* (4th ed.). Philadelphia, PA: Lippincott.
6. Subculture. (n.d.). In *Merriam-Webster's online dictionary* (11th ed.). Retrieved from https://www.merriam-webster.com/dictionary/subculture
7. Cohen, A. K. (1955). *Delinquent boys: The culture of the gang.* New York, NY: Free Press.
8. Cyber crime/hacker terminology. (n.d.). Retrieved from https://evestigate.com/cyber-crime-hacker-terms-to-know/
9. DEFCON official site. http://www.defcon.org
10. The Hacker's Manifesto. http://www.mithral.com/~beberg/manifesto.html
11. National Security Agency. (2016). *Mission and strategy.* Retrieved from https://www.nsa.gov/about/mission-strategy/

12. National Security Agency, *Mission and strategy*.
13. Department of Homeland Security. (2016). *Our mission*. Retrieved from https://www.dhs.gov/our-mission
14. Department of Homeland Security. (2016). *Safeguard and secure cyberspace*. Retrieved from https://www.dhs.gov/safeguard-and-secure-cyberspace
15. Department of Homeland Security, *Safeguard and secure cyberspace*.
16. Federal Bureau of Investigation. (n.d.). *What we investigate: Cybercrimes*. Retrieved from https://www.fbi.gov/investigate/cyber
17. Federal Bureau of Investigation. (2016). *Countering the cyber threat*. Retrieved from https://www.fbi.gov/news/stories/new-us-cyber-security-policy-codifies-agency-role
18. Keating, G. (2006). Catastrophic terrorism: Local response to a national threat. In R. Howard, J. Forest, & J. Moore (Eds.), *Homeland security and terrorism* (pp. 259–265). New York, NY: McGraw Hill.
19. Freilich, J., Chermak, S., & Simone, J. (2009). Studying American state police agencies about terrorism threats, terrorism sources and terrorism definitions. *Terrorism and Political Violence, 21*(3), 450–475.
20. Matusitz, J., & Breen, G. (2011). A solution-based examination of local, state and national government groups combating terrorism and cyberterrorism. *Journal of Human Behavior in the Social Environment, 21*(2), 109–129.
21. Ortiz, C., Hendricks, N., & Sugie, N. (2007). Policing terrorism: The response of local police agencies to Homeland Security concerns. *Criminal Justice Studies, 20*(2), 91–109.
22. Kelling, G., & Moore, M. (1988). *The evolving strategy of policing*. Retrieved from https://ncjrs.gov/pdffiles1/nij/114213.pdf
23. Henry, V. E. (2002). *The COMPSTAT Paradigm*. Flushing, NY: Looseleaf Law Publications.
24. Carter, D., & Carter, J. (2009). Intelligence-led policing: Conceptual and functional considerations for public policy. *Criminal Justice Policy Review, 2009*(20), 310–325.
25. Oliver, W. M. (2007). *Homeland security for policing*. Upper Saddle River, NJ: Prentice Hall.
26. Stewart, D., & Morris, R. (2009). A new era of policing? An examination of Texas police chiefs' perceptions of Homeland Security. *Criminal Justice Policy Review, 2009*(20), 290–309.
27. Stewart & Morris, A new era of policing?
28. Keating, Catastrophic terrorism, p. 265.
29. Breen, G. (2008). Examining existing counter-terrorism tactics and applying social network theory to fight cyberterrorism: An interpersonal communication perspective. *Journal of Applied Security Research, 3*(2), 191–204.
30. Carter & Carter, Intelligence-led policing, pp. 321–322.
31. Hua, J., & Bapna, S. (2012). How can we deter cyber terrorism? *Information Security Journal: A Global Perspective, 21*(4), 102–114.
32. Trim, P. (2003). Public and private sector cooperation in counteracting cyberterrorism. *International Journal of Intelligence and CounterIntelligence, 16*(4), 594–608.
33. Cyberterrorism Defense Initiative. (2013). *Website overview*. Retrieved from http://www.cyberterrorismcenter.org
34. Hua & Bapna, How can we deter cyber terrorism?
35. Hua & Bapna, How can we deter cyber terrorism?
36. Hua & Bapna, How can we deter cyber terrorism? p. 109
37. Hua & Bapna, How can we deter cyber terrorism?
38. Red Hat. (n.d.). Linux platforms. Retrieved from https://www.redhat.com/en/technologies/linux-platforms
39. Richey, D. (2010). *Public and private security: Bridging the gap*. Retrieved from http://www.securitymagazine.com/articles/80710-public-and-private-security-bridging-the-gap-1
40. Germano, J. H. (2014). *Cybersecurity partnerships: A new era of public-private collaboration*. Retrieved from http://www.lawand

security.org/wp-content/uploads/2016/08/Cybersecurity.Partnerships-1.pdf

41. Richey, D. (2010). *Public and private security: Bridging the gap*. Retrieved from http://www.securitymagazine.com/articles/80710-public-and-private-security-bridging-the-gap-1
42. National Commission on Terrorist Attacks Upon the United States. (2004). *The 9/11 Commission Report: Final report of the National Commission on Terrorist Attacks Upon the United States*. Washington, DC: Author.
43. McKenna, C. (2009). *The cyber fusion center, existing law, InfraGard tools for fighting cyber-crime*. Retrieved from http://www.govtech.com/templates/gov_print_article?id=99358524
44. U.S. Department of Homeland Security. (n.d.). *State and major urban area fusion centers*. Retrieved from https://www.dhs.gov/state-and-major-urban-area-fusion-centers
45. Newbill, R. R., III. (2008). *Intelligence sharing, fusion centers, and homeland security* [Graduate research paper]. Air Force Institute of Technology. Ohio: Wright-Patterson Air Force Base.
46. U.S. Department of Homeland Security. (n.d.). *State and major urban area fusion centers*.
47. McKenna, *The cyber fusion center*.
48. 10 tips for making sure your firewall is really secure. (n.d.). Retrieved from http://www.itsecurity.com/whitepaper/firewall-secure-10-tips/
49. 10 tips for making sure your firewall is really secure.
50. Hildick-Smith, A. (2005). *Security for critical infrastructure SCADA systems*. Retrieved from http://www.sans.org/reading-room/whitepapers/warfare/security-critical-infrastructure-scada-systems-1644
51. Improving SCADA system security. (n.d.). Retrieved from http://resources.infosecinstitute.com/improving-scada-system-security/
52. Pouget, F., Dacier, M., & Debar, H. (2003). Honeypot, honeynet, honeytoken: Terminological issues [White paper]. Institut Eurecom Report RR-03-081, France.
53. Rosenberg, M., & Bilstrup, U. (2013, August). *A pilot study of using honeypots as cyber intelligence sources*. European Intelligence and Security Informatics Conference, Uppsala, Sweden.
54. Honeynet Project. (2006). *Know your enemy: Honeynets*. Retrieved May 19, 2014, from http://old.honeynet.org/papers/honeynet
55. Honeynet Project, *Know your enemy: Honeynets*.
56. Honeynet Project, *Know your enemy: Honeynets*.
57. Rosenberg & Bilstrup, *A pilot study of using honeypots as cyber intelligence sources*.
58. Germano, *Cybersecurity partnerships*.
59. The Honeynet Project official website. http://www.honeynet.org/
60. U.S. Const. amend. IV.

Chapter 10

1. Thielman, S., & Johnston, C. (2016). *Major cyber attack disrupts internet service across Europe and US*. Retrieved from https://www.theguardian.com/technology/2016/oct/21/ddos-attack-dyn-internet-denial-service
2. Woolf, N. (2016). *DDoS attack that disrupted internet was largest of its kind in history, experts say*. Retrieved from https://www.theguardian.com/technology/2016/oct/26/ddos-attack-dyn-mirai-botnet
3. U.S. House of Representatives, Committee on Energy & Commerce. (2016). *Understanding the role of connected devices in recent cyberattacks* [Hearing]. Retrieved from http://docs.house.gov/meetings/IF/IF17/20161116/105418/HHRG-114-IF17-20161116-SD005-U2.pdf
4. LeTellier, V. (2016). *The argument for holistic cybersecurity*. Retrieved from http://www.securitymagazine.com/blogs/14-security-blog/post/87239-the-argument-for-holistic-cybersecurity
5. LeTellier, *The argument for holistic cybersecurity*.

6. LeTellier, *The argument for holistic cybersecurity*.
7. Office of the President. (2008). *The Comprehensive National Cybersecurity Initiative*. Retrieved from http://nsarchive.gwu.edu/NSAEBB/NSAEBB424/docs/Cyber-034.pdf
8. Callimachi, R. (2014). Obama calls Islamic State's killing of Peter Kassig "pure evil." *New York Times*. Retrieved from https://www.nytimes.com/2014/11/17/world/middleeast/peter-kassig-isis-video-execution.html
9. Marion, N. (2010). The Council of Europe's Cyber Crime Treaty: An exercise in symbolic legislation. *International Journal of Cyber Criminology*, *4*(1&2), 699–712.
10. Marion, The Council of Europe's Cyber Crime Treaty.
11. California hospital pays $17,000 to hackers in "ransomware" attack. (2016). Retrieved from http://sanfrancisco.cbslocal.com/2016/02/18/california-hospital-ransomware-attack-hackers/
12. Cybersecurity Workforce Assessment Act, H.R. 2952 (2014).
13. National Cybersecurity and Critical Infrastructure Protection Infrastructure Protection Act of 2014, H.R. 3696 (2014).
14. Clarke, R. (2015). *The cyberwars in the Middle East: What corporations and governments need to do about it*. Keynote at RSA Conference, Abu Dhabi. Retrieved from https://www.rsaconference.com/videos/the-cyberwars-in-the-middle-east-what-corporations-and-governments-need-to-do-about-it
15. Wilson, D. (2014). *Bank of England turns to "ethical hackers" to fix financial sector security*. Retrieved from http://www.techradar.com/news/internet/web/bank-of-england-turns-to-ethical-hackers-to-fix-financial-sector-security-1244589
16. Raul, A. C. (2016, February). *Touring the world of cybersecurity law*. Presentation at RSA Conference, San Francisco, CA.
17. Kushner, D. (2013). *The real story of Stuxnet*. Retrieved from http://spectrum.ieee.org/telecom/security/the-real-story-of-stuxnet
18. Goldman, F. (2012). *Major banks hit with biggest cyberattacks in history*. Retrieved from http://money.cnn.com/2012/09/27/technology/bank-cyberattacks/
19. Clarke, *The cyberwars in the Middle East*.
20. Clarke, *The cyberwars in the Middle East*.
21. Cieply, M., & Barnes, B. (2014). Sony cyberattack, first a nuisance, swiftly grew into a firestorm. *New York Times*. Retrieved from https://www.nytimes.com/2014/12/31/business/media/sony-attack-first-a-nuisance-swiftly-grew-into-a-firestorm-.html?_r=0
22. 2015 Paris terror attacks fast facts. (2016). Retrieved from http://www.cnn.com/2015/12/08/europe/2015-paris-terror-attacks-fast-facts/
23. Bruer, W. (2015). *FBI chief worries ISIS could use cyberattacks against the United States*. Retrieved from http://www.cnn.com/2015/05/20/politics/isis-cyberattack-fbi-director/
24. ISIS propagandist ShamiWitness: Man charged in India. (2015). Retrieved from https://www.channel4.com/news/isis-shami-witness-medhi-masroor-biswas-charged
25. Callimachi, Obama calls Islamic State's killing of Peter Kassig "pure evil."
26. Hall, J. (2014). *U.S. hostage Peter Kassig was killed by gunshot before being beheaded, analysis shows, suggesting that he may have resisted ISIS captors*. Retrieved from http://www.dailymail.co.uk/news/article-2874226/US-hostage-Peter-Kassig-killed-gunshot-beheaded-analysis-shows-suggesting-resisted-ISIS-captors.html
27. ISIS propagandist ShamiWitness: Man charged in India.
28. Ghosa, A. (2015). *Worried about my son's condition, not virtual charges: IS suspect's father*. Retrieved from http://indianexpress.com/article/india/india-news-india/kolkata-worried-about-my-sons-condition-not-virtual-charges-islamic-state-suspects-father-2802433/
29. Marion, The Council of Europe's Cyber Crime Treaty.
30. Marion, The Council of Europe's Cyber Crime Treaty.

31. U.S. v. Warshak, 631 F.3d 266 (2010).

32. Perry, C. (2011). U.S. v. Warshak: Will Fourth Amendment protection be delivered to your inbox? *North Carolina Journal of Law and Technology, 12*(2), 345–368.

33. Perry, U.S. v. Warshak: Will Fourth Amendment protection be delivered to your inbox?

34. Email Privacy Act, H.R. 699 (2015).

35. Turkey announces plans "for gas" and cyber security in face of Gezi protests. (2013, June 20). Retrieved from https://www.rt.com/news/turkey-gas-cybersecurity-protests-013/

36. Miller, G., & Entous, A. (2016). U.S. intelligence officials say Russian hacks "prioritized" Democrats. *Washington Post*, Retrieved from https://www.washingtonpost.com/world/national-security/us-intelligence-officials-say-russian-hacks-prioritized-democrats/2016/12/12/0fbea4da-c09b-11e6-b527-949c5893595e_story.html?utm_term=.12b0bb13fca5

37. Raul, *Touring the world of cybersecurity law.*

38. Marion, The Council of Europe's Cyber Crime Treaty.

39. Paganini, P. (2016). *The EU passed the NIS directive, its first ever cyber security rules*. Retrieved from http://securityaffairs.co/wordpress/49133/laws-and-regulations/nis-directive.html

40. Paganini, *The EU passed the NIS directive.*

41. Sutliff, U., & Richardson, T. (2016). *Cybersecurity guide for state and local law enforcement.* Retrieved from https://cchs.gwu.edu/sites/cchs.gwu.edu/files/downloads/NCAPCybersecurityGuide-2016.pdf

42. Marion, The Council of Europe's Cyber Crime Treaty.

43. Shinder, D. (2011). *What makes cybercrime laws so difficult to enforce*? Retrieved from http://www.techrepublic.com/blog/it-security/what-makes-cybercrime-laws-so-difficult-to-enforce/

44. Marion, The Council of Europe's Cyber Crime Treaty.

45. Marion, The Council of Europe's Cyber Crime Treaty.

46. Marion, The Council of Europe's Cyber Crime Treaty.

47. Shinder, *What makes cybercrime laws so difficult to enforce?*

48. Shinder, *What makes cybercrime laws so difficult to enforce?*

49. Marion, The Council of Europe's Cyber Crime Treaty.

50. Sutliff & Richardson, *Cybersecurity guide for state and local law enforcement.*

51. Division for Ocean Affairs and the Law of the Sea. (2012). *The United Nations Convention on the Law of the Sea (A historical perspective).* Retrieved from http://www.un.org/depts/los/convention_agreements/convention_historical_perspective.htm

Chapter 11

1. Dvorak, P. (2016). At a D.C. pizzeria, the dangers of fake news just got all too real. *Washington Post.* Retrieved from https://www.washingtonpost.com/local/at-a-dc-pizzeria-the-dangers-of-fake-news-just-got-all-too-real/2016/12/05/b8ae43b8-baf4-11e6-94ac-3d324840106c_story.html?utm_term=.600c8419edd9

2. Sneed, A. (2015). *Moore's law keeps going, defying expectations.* Retrieved from https://www.scientificamerican.com/article/moore-s-law-keeps-going-defying-expectations/

3. Wallace, G. (2013). *Target credit card hack: What you need to know.* Retrieved from http://money.cnn.com/2013/12/22/news/companies/target-credit-card-hack/

4. Groden, C. (2015). *Here's who's been hacked in the past two years.* Retrieved from http://fortune.com/2015/10/02/heres-whos-been-hacked-in-the-past-two-years/

5. Orwell, G. (1949). *Nineteen eighty-four.* London, England: Secker & Warburg.

6. Kubota, Y. (2009). *Google reshoots Japan views after privacy concerns.* Retrieved from http://www.reuters.com/article/us-google-japan-idUSTRE54C22R20090513

7. Hearn, K. (2007). *Terrorist use of Google Earth raises security concerns.* Retrieved from

http://news.nationalgeographic.com/news/2007/03/070312-google-censor.html

8. Kimery, A. L. (2008). *Mumbai terrorists' use of Google Earth re-ignites concerns*. Retrieved from http://www.hstoday.us/columns/the-kimery-report/blog/mumbai-terrorists-use-of-google-earth-re-ignites-concerns/642770639e0a4ae59d34a79be3a628fa.html

9. Harding, T. (2007). *Terrorists 'use Google maps to hit UK troops.'* Retrieved from http://www.telegraph.co.uk/news/worldnews/1539401/Terrorists-use-Google-maps-to-hit-UK-troops.html

10. Orwell, Nineteen eighty-four.

11. California releases 450 'violent and dangerous' criminals after computer glitch sets them free. (2011). Retrieved from http://www.dailymail.co.uk/news/article-1391454/Computer-glitch-led-450-highly-dangerous-inmates-released-California-prisons.html

12. World Anti-Doping Agency. (2016). *Medical data 'may be doctored.'* Retrieved from http://www.sportinglife.com/other-sports/news/article/678/10606902/wada-says-hackers-may-have-doctored-leaked-tue-data

13. Committee to Protect Journalists. (2015). *10 most censored countries*. Retrieved from https://cpj.org/reports/2012/05/10-most-censored-countries.php

14. Committee to Protect Journalists, *10 most censored countries*.

15. Reuters. (2016, December 4). *The EU is warning American tech giants to crack down on hate speech*. Retrieved from http://fortune.com/2016/12/05/eu-google-microsoft-facebook-twitter/

16. Reuters. (2016, December 3). *Will Rand Paul fight fake news with a filibuster?* Retrieved from http://www.thedailybell.com/news-analysis/will-rand-paul-fight-fake-news-with-a-filibuster/

17. Spoofing. (n.d.). *Techopedia*. Retrieved from https://www.techopedia.com/definition/5398/spoofing

18. Email Spoofing. (n.d.). *TechTarget*. Retrieved from http://searchsecurity.techtarget.com/definition/email-spoofing

19. Email spoofing, *TechTarget*.

20. Internal Revenue Service. (2016). *Scam e-mail sends malicious software to recipients' computers*. Retrieved from https://www.irs.gov/uac/scam-e-mail-sends-malicious-software-to-recipients-computers

21. Hope, B. (2015). As 'spoof" trading persists, regulators clamp down. *Wall Street Journal*. Retrieved from http://www.wsj.com/articles/how-spoofing-traders-dupe-markets-1424662202

22. Hope, As 'spoof" trading persists, regulators clamp down.

23. Bray, C. (2016, March 23). Judge orders extradition to U.S. in 'flash crash' case. *New York Times*. Retrieved from https://www.nytimes.com/2016/03/24/business/dealbook/judge-orders-extradition-to-us-in-flash-crash-case.html?_r=0

24. Bray, Judge orders extradition to U.S. in 'flash crash' case.

25. Porche, I. R., III. (2016). *Emerging cyber threats and implications* [Testimony presented before the House Homeland Security Committee, Subcommittee on Cybersecurity, Infrastructure Protection]. Retrieved from https://www.rand.org/content/dam/rand/pubs/testimonies/CT400/CT453/RAND_CT453.pdf

26. van der Meulen, R. (2015). Gartner says 6.4 billion connected "things" will be in use in 2016, up 30 percent from 2015 [Press release]. Retrieved from http://www.gartner.com/newsroom/id/3165317

27. Porche, *Emerging cyber threats and implications*.

28. Porche, *Emerging cyber threats and implications*.

29. What is a real-time location system? (n.d.). Retrieved from http://searchmobilecomputing.techtarget.com/definition/real-time-location-system-RTLS

30. National Coordination Office for Space-Based Positioning, Navigation, and Timing. (n.d.). *Information about GPS jamming*. Retrieved from http://www.gps.gov/spectrum/jamming/

31. Hendrix, S. (2016). Traffic-weary homeowners and Waze are at war, again. Guess who's

winning? *Washington Post.* Retrieved from https://www.washingtonpost.com/local/traffic-weary-homeowners-and-waze-are-at-war-again-guess-whos-winning/2016/06/05/c466df46-299d-11e6-b989-4e5479715b54_story.html?utm_term=.7f42cc11eafe

32. Petrovsky, O. (2016). *Spoofing GPS for the budget conscious.* Retrieved from https://community.hpe.com/t5/Security-Research/Spoofing-GPS-for-the-budget-conscious/ba-p/6838676#.WGTGzGM9Ybo
33. Donahue, B. (2013). *Researchers hack GPS, $80M yacht veers off course.* Retrieved from https://threatpost.com/researchers-hack-gps-80m-yacht-veers-off-course/101533/
34. Donahue, *Researchers hack GPS, $80M yacht veers off course.*
35. Green, P. S. (2015). *America's air traffic control system is finally going digital.* Retrieved from http://www.foxbusiness.com/features/2015/09/28/america-s-air-traffic-control-system-is-finally-going-digital.html
36. Farberov, S., & Evans, S. J. (2015). *Revealed: Security expert who 'hacked the commercial flight and made it fly sideways' bragged that he also hacked the International Space Station.* Retrieved from http://www.dailymail.co.uk/news/article-3090288/Security-expert-admitted-FBI-took-control-commercial-flight-bragged-hacker-convention-2012-playing-International-Space-Station-getting-yelled-NASA.html
37. Life Science Staff. (2012). *Insurgents destroyed US helicopters found in online photos.* Retrieved from http://www.livescience.com/19114-military-social-media-geotags.html
38. Scheck, J. (2010). Stalkers exploit cellphone GPS. *Wall Street Journal.* Retrieved from http://www.wsj.com/articles/SB10001424052748703467304575383522318244234
39. Scheck, Stalkers exploit cellphone GPS.
40. Humer, C., & Finkle, J. (2014). *Your medical record is worth more to hackers than your credit card.* Retrieved from http://www.reuters.com/article/us-cybersecurity-hospitals-idUSKCN0HJ21I20140924
41. Dietrich-Williams, A. (2013). *'Man-in-the-e-mail' fraud could victimize area businesses.* Retrieved from https://archives.fbi.gov/archives/seattle/press-releases/2013/man-in-the-e-mail-fraud-could-victimize-area-businesses
42. Gregg, M. (2015). *Six ways you could become a victim of man-in-the-middle (MiTM) attacks this holiday season.* Retrieved from http://www.huffingtonpost.com/michael-gregg/six-ways-you-could-become_b_8545674.html
43. Federal Bureau of Investigation. (n.d.). *FBI tactical operations.* Retrieved from http://www.fbiagentedu.org/careers/tactical-operations/
44. Tynan, D. (2016). *The terror of swatting: How the law is tracking down high tech prank callers.* Retrieved from https://www.theguardian.com/technology/2016/apr/15/swatting-law-teens-anonymous-prank-call-police
45. Tynan, The terror of swatting.
46. Sterling, S. (2015). *Swatted? 6 celebrities who were victims of 911 hoax.* Retrieved from http://radio.com/2015/03/11/swatting-hoax-celebrities/
47. Federal Bureau of Investigation. (2010). *U.S. indicts Ohio man and two foreign residents in alleged Ukraine-based "scareware" fraud scheme that caused $100 million in losses to internet victims worldwide.* Retrieved from https://archives.fbi.gov/archives/chicago/press-releases/2010/cg052710-1.htm
48. Federal Bureau of Investigation. (2016). *Most wanted.* Retrieved from https://www.fbi.gov/wanted/cyber/shaileshkumar-p.-jain
49. Goodman, J. (2016). *Future crimes: Inside the digital underground and the battle for our connected world.* New York, NY: Anchor.

• Index •

• About the Authors •

Janine Kremling, PhD, is an associate professor in the Criminal Justice Department at California State University, San Bernardino, California. She received her PhD from the University of South Florida. Dr. Kremling has been studying cybercrime since 2014 and is currently focusing on the organizational aspects of cybercrime, also referred to as Crime Inc. She resides in Fontana, California.

Amanda M. Sharp Parker, PhD, is an assistant professor of homeland security and coordinator of the homeland security program at Campbell University in Buies Creek, North Carolina. She obtained her PhD in criminology from the University of South Florida. Dr. Parker has been studying cyberthreats and transnational terrorism threats since 2005. She has presented nationally and internationally (England, Spain, Poland, Northern Ireland, and Wales) on many aspects of cybercrime and cybersecurity, including cyberterrorism. She resides in Dunn, North Carolina, with her daughter Tatiana (8) and her son Jax (6).